BUILD YOUR OWN PENTIUM II PC

OTHER BOOKS BY AUBREY PILRIM

Build Your Own Pentium Pro Processor PC
Build Your Own Pentium Processor PC, 2/e
Build Your Own Multimedia PC, 2/e
Build Your Own 486/DC PC
Upgrade and Repair Your PC

ADVANCED PC REPAIR TITLES

Stephen Bigelow	*Troubleshooting and Repairing Computer Monitors, 2/e*
Stephen Bigelow	*Troubleshooting and Repairing Computer Printers, 2/e*
Stephen Bigelow	*Troubleshooting and Repairing PC Drives and Memory Systems, 2/e*

Build Your Own Pentium II PC

Aubrey Pilgrim

McGraw-Hill, Inc.

New York • San Francisco • Washington, D.C.
Auckland • Bogotá • Caracas • Lisbon • London
Madrid • Mexico City • Milan • Montreal • New Delhi
San Juan • Singapore • Sydney • Tokyo • Toronto

Library of Congress Cataloging-in-Publication Data

Pilgrim, Aubrey.
Build your own Pentium II PC / Aubrey Pilgrim.
p. cm.
Includes index.
ISBN 0-07-050239-0
1. Pentium (Microprocessor) 2. Microcomputers — Design and construction. I. Title.
QA76.8.P46P52 1998 98-9670
621.39'16—dc21 CIP

McGraw-Hill

A Division of The ***McGraw-Hill*** *Companies*

3 4 5 6 7 8 9 0 DOC/DOC 9 0 3 2 1 0 9

ISBN 0-07-050239-0

The sponsoring editor for this book was Scott Grillo, the editing supervisor was Bernard Onken, and the production supervisor was Tina Cameron. It was set in Vendome ICG by McGraw-Hill's Professional Book Group composition unit, Hightstown, N.J.

Printed and bound by R. R. Donnelley & Sons Company.

This book is printed on recycled, acid-free paper containing a minimum of 50% recycled, de-inked fiber.

CONTENTS

	Introduction	XIII
Chapter 1	What's Inside	1
	Tools Needed	2
	Major Computer Components	3
	Minimum System Requirements	4
	How Computers Work	18
	Moore's Law	26
Chapter 2	The Motherboard	27
	Motherboard Sources	28
	Motherboard Specifications	34
	The ATX Motherboard and Power Supply	40
	Motherboard Variations	42
	Jumpers	44
	DRAM Bus Frequency	44
	ROM BIOS	45
	Some Basic Stuff about Motherboards	47
	Architecture	56
	Deciding What to Buy	61
	Replacing a Motherboard	61
Chapter 3	The CPU	63
	PR Hype	64
	How a CPU is Made	77
	What's in a Number?	77
	Basic Characteristics of CPUs	78
	CPU Sockets	83
	Resources	87
Chapter 4	Memory	91
	Memory Slots	92
	Types of Memory Modules	94

How Much Memory Do You Need? 96
Basics 96
A Brief Explanation of Memory 99
Things to Consider Before You Buy Memory 105
SRAM 107
Cache Memory 108
CMOS 109
Why the 640-Kb Limit? 110
Conventional Memory 111
Extended Memory 111
Buying Chips 112
Installing the Chips 112

Chapter 5 Floppy Drives and Disks 115

1.44-Mb Floppy 116
2.88-Mb Floppy Drive 117
The Iomega 100-Mb Zip Drive 118
The LS120 118
The 200-Mb Floppy Drive 122
How Floppy Drives Operate 125
Differences among Floppy Disks 131
Disk Format Structure 134
Formatting 138
Cost of Disks 140

Chapter 6 Choosing a Hard Disk 141

What Should You Buy? 142
Removable Disk Drives 145
Data Compression 151
Floppy and Hard-Drive Similarities 152
How They Can Make Smaller Drives 160
Cables and Connectors 162
Installation and Configuration 162
Sources 170

Chapter 7 Backup and Disaster Prevention 171

Write-Protect Your Software 172
.BAK Files 173
Unerase Software 173
Delete Protection 174

	Jumbled FAT	174
	Reason for Smaller Logical Hard Disks	175
	Partition Magic and Partition-It	175
	Head Crash	176
	Preventing Hard Disk Failures	180
	A Few Reasons Why People Don't Back Up and Why They Should	181
	Theft and Burglary	182
	Archival	182
	Data Transfer	182
	Types of Backup	183
	Uninterruptible Power Supplies	188
Chapter 8	CD-ROM	191
	CD-ROM Drives	192
	CD-ROM Titles	194
	How CD-ROM Works	197
	CD-ROM Differences	202
	CD-ROM Recorders (CD-R)	206
	Kodak Photo CD	211
	Digital Videodisc (DVD)	212
	Installing CD-ROM Drives	213
Chapter 9	Monitors and Adapters	217
	Flat-Panel LCD Monitors	219
	USB Monitors	220
	AGP Adapters	221
	3D Adapters	221
	Video Memory	223
	Adapter Memory Chips	223
	MPEG Boards	225
	Using a TV as a Monitor	226
	Monitor Basics	227
	Adapter Basics	232
	Choosing a Monitor	235
	Installation	241
	Glossary of Monitor Terms from Princeton Graphics	242
	Other Resources	246
Chapter 10	Input Devices	247

	Keyboards	248
	Mouse Systems	255
	Touch Screens and Light Pens	258
	Joysticks	259
	Digitizers and Graphics Tablets	259
	Pressure-Sensitive Graphics Tablets	259
	Scanners	260
	Voice Recognition Input	267
	Computers and Devices for the Handicapped	270
Chapter 11	Communications	275
	Telephones	276
	Modems	277
	Installing a Modem	282
	Bulletin Boards	287
	Viruses	288
	Virus Hoaxes	289
	Online Services	289
	Banking by Modem	290
	Facsimile Machines	290
	Telephone Outlets for Extensions	294
	Combination Devices and Voice Mail	295
	Telecommuting	296
	Remote-Control Software	297
	Telephony	298
	National Telephone Directories	300
	ISDN	301
	Cable Modems	301
	Sources	302
Chapter 12	Upgrading an Older PC	303
	Why You Should Do It Yourself	304
	What If It Is Too Old to Upgrade	304
	Upgrading to a New Hard Disk	305
	Buying a Used Computer	308
	Buying a Barebones System	309
	Upgrading to a New Computer	310
	Minor Upgrades	311
	Memory Upgrade	312
	Upgrading the CPU	313

	Replacing the Motherboard	314
	Pentium II Motherboard with a 300-MHz MMX CPU	315
	Back to Reality	317
	Steps to Replace a Motherboard	318
	There Is No End to Upgrade Possibilities	324
Chapter 13	Assembling Your Computer	327
	Needed Components and Tools	328
	Static Electricity Warning	328
	Assembly Steps	329
	Software Installation and Formatting	346
	Install in the Case	353
	Congratulations	353
Chapter 14	The Internet	355
	Voice and Video on the Internet	357
	Modems and Access Numbers	358
	Free ISP	359
	Services	360
	House-Wiring Intranet	363
	E-Mail	364
	J-Mail and Spamming	365
	Connections	366
	Distance Learning	367
	Internet Magazines	369
	Your Own Web Page	370
	Web Hosting	371
	Sex on the Web	371
	The Future	372
	Emoticons and Acronyms	372
Chapter 15	Printers	373
	Printer Life Expectancy	374
	Inkjets	375
	Multifunction Laser Machines	380
	Wide-Format Printers	380
	Laser Printers	381
	Color Laser Printers	386
	Plotters	387

	Dot-Matrix Printers	388
	Installing a Printer or Plotter	392
	Printer Sharing	392
	Green Printers	395
	Progress	395
Chapter 16	Essential Software	397
	Off-the-Shelf and Ready-to-Use Software	398
	List Price vs. Discount Price	398
	Surplus Software	399
	Software Upgrades	399
	CD-ROM Discs and Multimedia	401
	Shareware and Public-Domain Software	402
	Try Before You Buy	402
	Software Catalogs	402
	Essential Software Needed	403
	Computer-Aided Design	414
	Miscellaneous Software Programs	415
	Software Training	419
	LapLink for Windows	420
	Summary	420
Chapter 17	How Your Computer Can Help You	421
	Resumé	423
	Home Office	424
	Other Tools of the Trade	429
	Networks	432
	Desktop Publishing	435
	Presentations	436
	Digital Cameras	440
	For the Kids	442
	Summary	442
Chapter 18	Computer Sound of Music	443
	What Sound Board Should You Buy?	444
	Speakers	445
	Microphones	446
	Music	447
	Internet Telephone and Video	448

	Teleconferencing	449
	Sound, Microphones, and Speakers	450
	Digital Sampling	450
	Installing a Sound Board	453
	Musical Instrument Digital Interface (MIDI)	455
	Synthesizers	457
	Piano Keyboards	460
	Music Software and Hardware	461
	Catalogs	461
	Trade Shows	462
Chapter 19	Component Sources	463
	Computer Shows and Swap Meets	464
	Magazines and Mail-Order	466
	Sources of Knowledge	471
	Public-Domain and Shareware Software	479
	Computer Books	480
Chapter 20	Troubleshooting and Repairing Your PC	481
	Computer Basics	483
	Electrostatic Voltage	484
	Document the Problem, Write It Down	484
	Instruments and Tools	485
	Solving Common Problems	487
	Beep Error Codes	493
	Diagnostic and Utility Software	496
	Spares	502
	DOS Error Messages	503
	Glitches	504
	Power Supply	505
	Intermittent Problems	506
	User Groups	510
	Glossary	511
	Index	529

INTRODUCTION

Why You Need A Computer

We are in the midst of the computer age. Today, computers are as necessary as indoor plumbing, not only in business, but in the home as well. If you are a student or have a child who is a student, then by all means you need a computer. A recent issue of *Information Week* estimated that there are 108.2 million PCs in this country. There are about 270 million men, women and children. We are approaching the point where almost every home has a PC. What will your neighbors think if you don't have a PC?

One very big reason to have a computer is the Internet. In just a few years, it has brought about enormous changes in the way we communicate, our entertainment, gathering information, and the way we do business. There are very few businesses that do not have a Web site. For most companies, to access their Web site, just type www.companyname.com.

Buying Instead of Building

You might complain that you don't have the money for a new computer. That is not a good excuse. Computers are very inexpensive today. Even if you have to skip going to the opera a few times or to an NFL football game every weekend, save the money and build yourself a computer. You owe it to yourself and family to have a good computer. If you are in business, it is an essential tool.

You might feel a bit apprehensive about building your own. That is understandable, considering what they can do. Actually, though, a computer is very easy to assemble. If you still feel that you don't want to put one together yourself, there are several good computers available now for under $1000. Cyrix Corporation is expected to introduce one for less than $500. Of course, these low-price computers will not be as fast and as powerful as some of the high-cost ones, but they might be able to do all that you need to do.

Even if you do take the easy way out and buy a preassembled unit, you still need this book. It can help you decide what peripherals you need and help you understand how a computer works.

Upgrade and Save a Bundle

You might lust for a powerful Pentium II or AMD K6, Cyrix 6x86MX, or one of the new Centaur C6 machines. You might not have the money at this time to buy all the components. No problem. There is a very inexpensive way to get your hands on one. Just upgrade an older system, such as a 486 or a Pentium. It can be easily and inexpensively upgraded. In this computer age, a three-year-old 486 or Pentium is as ancient as a dinosaur. With a few new components, though, it can be as good as brand-new.

If you don't have an older computer, you might consider buying a used one. You can get some fantastic deals on some of them. You can then use this book to upgrade any of the older 486 or Pentium systems. Chapter 12 can show you how to do it.

The B-B Gene

If at all possible, go ahead and build the biggest and fastest computer you can afford. I postulated in one of my earlier books that there is no doubt a gene in some people that causes them to insist on having the biggest and best. If and when this gene is proven, I suggested that it be named the "B-B gene", for biggest and best. I am a bit ashamed to admit it, but I am one of those afflicted with this gene. Unfortunately, I don't have the money necessary to satisfy all of my desires for the biggest and best. That is one reason I build my own systems.

Don't Be a Pioneer

There is one other gene that resides in a lot of people, and that one causes them to want to be the first with any new toy or device that is ever invented. Unfortunately, many new computer devices and software often have a few bugs when first introduced. If at all possible, resist the urge to buy the first release of a product. It is best to wait until it has proven that it will work as promised. Most of the components discussed in this book have been around long enough to have been proven.

Someone once said that pioneers often end up with arrows in their backs. Buying a new product that doesn't work can cause almost as much pain as an arrow.

You Can Do It

With this book as a guide, you can build a computer that will be very fast and powerful. It can be faster and more powerful than many of the multimillion dollar mainframes were just a few years ago. And it won't cost you a million dollars; you can do it for just a few hundred dollars. This is truly a fantastic age that we are living in!

Ease of Assembly

You can build this powerful computer without having any advanced knowledge about electronics or computer science. Nor do you need to have an IQ that is above average or be a member of Mensa. Some of the most popular books on the market are those written for "dummies." I know that you are not a dummy, but even a dummy can build a computer. This book shows you how easy it is to assemble all the parts. There are lots of photos and clear instructions in the book.

The beauty of assembling your own computer is that you can include only those items that you want. One of the greatest benefits of building your own is that you will have a sense of accomplishment that is priceless. You will know what is inside your computer. It will help take away a bit of the mystery.

Computers are made up of discrete components. They all plug together somewhat like a toy Erector set. You can plug in dozens of different components. The components are all made to standards and are interchangeable, so you can shop around to find the best buy and not have to worry about whether it will work or not. This is one of the fantastic features that makes computers so versatile and functional. For almost any purpose for which you might need a computer, there are components available that will allow you to build it.

How Much Can You Save?

You will probably save some money in building your own, but the number-one reason to do it is to gain the experience. Since all my books have the subtitle "Save a Bundle," I am often asked how much one can save. The answer depends on a lot of factors, such as how well you shop, whether you want brand names, and the type and kind of items you want to include.

Where you shop can make a big difference. Some stores have a lot of salespeople, are in a high-rent district, carry a lot of stock, and have a very high overhead. In order to make ends meet, their prices are probably higher than a small shop in a low-rent district that has a low overhead.

Brand names make a big difference. Some people must have the very latest clothing style. They pay outrageous prices for a suit or dress just because it has a famous designer label. I buy clothes to hide my nakedness. Designer brand labels don't do anything for me. Similarly, some people are convinced that brand-name computer components are superior to the no-name brands. Like the clothes that hide my nakedness, though, in most cases, the no-name components will be all that you need to do the job.

Another reason to build your own is that you might not be able to afford all that you want at this time. You can build a basic system, then add to it as you can afford to. For instance, you might want a couple of 4.3-Gb hard drives, but you might only be able to afford one at this time, or you might have to settle for a 2.5-Gb drive. You can always add a larger one later. Another bit of good news: if you wait a little while, the price of hard disk drives and most other components will go down.

Again, one of the best ways to save is to upgrade an older computer, as outlined in Chapter 12. I know that you are anxious to get started, but if you are fairly new to computers, I hope that you will read about the various components in the first few chapters, so that you will know what components to buy. Chapter 13 has the photos and instructions for assembling the computer after you have bought your components.

Brief Summary of Chapters

Here is a brief overview of the contents of this book:

- Chapter 1, "What's Inside"—A brief description of each component needed in a computer.

- Chapter 2, "The Motherboard"—The motherboard is the most important board in the system. They are basically all the same. However, some vendors differentiate their products in certain ways. There is a major difference between the Pentium II motherboard and the AMD K6 and Cyrix 6x86MX motherboards in the way that the CPUs are installed. Intel designed a new slot for the Pentium II CPU instead of the usual Zero Insertion Force (ZIF) sockets. You can easily upgrade a system by replacing the motherboard.
- Chapter 3, "The CPU"—You have a choice of several CPUs. This chapter gives the facts about them.
- Chapter 4, "Memory"—This chapter is all about memory. There are several types. You must use whatever the motherboard was designed to use.
- Chapter 5, "Floppy Drives and Disks"—How floppy drives operate. How disks are organized and formatted into tracks, sectors, and cylinders. Disk differences are also discussed.
- Chapter 6, "Choosing a Hard Disk"—How hard drives operate and how they are formatted. IDE and SCSI hard disk differences.
- Chapter 7, "Backup and Disaster Prevention"—Why backup is critical. Some methods of backup and recovery.
- Chapter 8, "CD-ROM"—How CD-ROMs, recordable CD-ROMS, and DVD operate.
- Chapter 9, "Monitors and Adapters"—How monitors operate. The need for adapters, and how they operate.
- Chapter 10, "Input Devices"—There are several input devices, such as keyboards, mice, scanners, and digital cameras. This chapter describes how these devices operate.
- Chapter 11, "Communications"—How modems and fax machines work.
- Chapter 12, "Upgrading an Older PC"—You can save a lot of money by simply upgrading an older system. This chapter shows you how.
- Chapter 13, "Assembling Your Computer"—Photos and instructions for the assembly process.
- Chapter 14, "The Internet"—In the last few years, the Internet has brought about enormous changes. It has changed the way we do business, play, learn, and acquire information, and has affected just about all aspects of our lives.

- Chapter 15, "Printers"—The different types of printers (dot matrix, inkjet and laser), and how they operate.
- Chapter 16, "Essential Software"—Just some of the software you will need includes an operating system, word processor, database, spreadsheet, and utilities. There are thousands of other miscellaneous programs that might be needed for specific applications.
- Chapter 17, "How Your Computer Can Help You"—Some home office and small business applications, as well as a discussion of laptops and handhelds.
- Chapter 18, "Computer Sound of Music"—How music is digitized. Using your computer to make sounds and music.
- Chapter 19, "Component Sources"—There are several places where you can buy the components you need. In the larger cities, there are usually several large computer discount stores. There might also be several small stores who will have most of the components needed, as well as swap meets and trade shows. Sources for Internet and mail-order shopping are included in this chapter.
- Chapter 20, "Troubleshooting and Repairing Your PC"—You will need to know how computers operate in order to diagnose and fix any problems. This chapter offers basic troubleshooting tips to help you find and fix any problems.

A glossary with definitions of computer terms is also included in the back of the book.

Aubrey Pilgrim

CHAPTER 1

What's Inside

This chapter briefly describes the basic components you'll find inside a computer. Each component is discussed in detail in later chapters. This chapter also lists the few tools needed to assemble your new computer, whether it is a Pentium II, AMD K6, Cyrix 6x86MX, or IDT Centaur C6. (They are all basically the same.)

At the end of the chapter is a brief explanation of how computers work. If you are fairly new to computers, this can help you. If you are an old pro, you might want to skip that section.

Tools Needed

You will only need a few tools to assemble your computer. You will need some small screwdrivers. You should have a couple of different-sized flatblade screwdrivers and Phillips screwdrivers. Most computer systems use Phillips-type screws, although some use a Phillips-type head with a slot so that you can use either a Phillips or flatblade screwdriver. Some systems use Phillips screws that also have hexagonal heads. You can use a $^1/_4$-inch nut driver on these screws, which makes them very easy to install or remove. Magnetized screwdrivers will help you to get the screws started. (**Caution!** Be very careful not to let a magnetized screwdriver or any magnet near your floppy disks. A magnet can erase or partially destroy the data on the disks.)

Long-nose pliers are absolutely essential for installing the small jumper blocks that are used to configure the motherboard. Most motherboards can now be used with dozens of different CPUs, but they have to have small jumpers installed to configure them. It is almost impossible to move the jumper blocks with your fingers. If you don't have a pair of long-nose pliers, you can use a pair of tweezers.

The long-nose pliers are also very handy for retrieving dropped screws. The flat portion of the long-nose blades is also excellent for straightening the pins on integrated-circuit (IC) chips or pins on connectors. A pair of standard pliers might be helpful, although not absolutely necessary.

A flashlight or a good bench light is essential for troubleshooting and exploring your computer. A good magnifying glass can also come in handy for reading the types and part numbers on some of the chips.

Major Computer Components

Before you start building a computer, you should know what the inside of one looks like. If you have never looked inside, it might seem a bit formidable. You will see several cables, plug-in boards, disk drives, and electronic components. Figure 1-1 gives you an idea of what a typical computer looks like inside.

Figure 1-1
Inside a computer.

If you have an older computer, just pull the cover off and look inside. Most computers look pretty much the same, whether it is an old 286 or a powerful Pentium II. There will be a large motherboard with several slots that will have other boards plugged into them. You will see several cables and connections to the motherboard and to the plug-in boards. Some of the cables connect the power supply to the motherboard and to the disk drives. Other cables connect the floppy disk drive, the hard disk drive, and the CD-ROM drive to upright pins on the motherboard or into a board that is plugged into a slot on the motherboard.

Minimum System Requirements

Here is a list of the major components that will be needed for a minimum system. Later you may also want to add several other components such as one or two more hard drives, a network card, and several other goodies. But it is best to start out with a minimum system.

Case and power supply
Motherboard with CPU and fan
Floppy drives
Hard drives
Keyboard
Mouse
Monitor and adapter board
Modem/fax board
CD-ROM drive
Sound card and speakers
Case and power supply

Case

The power supply usually comes with the case. Almost any case will do if you are building an AMD K6, IDT C6, Intel Pentium MMX, or a Cyrix 6x86MX. If you are building the Pentium II, however, make sure that you get a special case that will accommodate the motherboard with the CPU installed. The Pentium II CPU is mounted on a daughter card that plugs into a slot on the motherboard. Before the advent of the Pentium II, the fan was mounted inside the power supply. Some of the systems now mount the fan outside the power supply. The fan is also reversed. The old system had the fan draw air from the front of the computer, pull it over the components, then exhaust it out the back of the case through a grill. The newerPentium II systems have the fan draw air in from the rear of the power-supply grill, and blow it over the components and out the front grill of the case. Even though the CPU assembly has its own cooling fan, the assembly sits directly under the power-supply fan and is first to receive fresh air.

The standard case is 6$^3/_4$ inches wide. In order to accommodate the Pentium II CPU assembly, some of the cases are 8$^5/_8$ inches wide. It is possible to mount the Pentium II in a standard case, but I do not recommend it. Semiconductors and transistors should last for several lifetimes, since there is nothing inside them to wear out, but they are very susceptible to heat. Heat is their enemy. Make sure they get as much cooling as possible.

The desktop-type case is still quite popular. Most desktop cases are limited to three or four bays for mounting disk drives. If you want to install two hard disk drives, a 1.44-Mb floppy drive, and a CD-ROM drive, you will need a case with at least four bays. At least two of the bays, those for the floppy disk and CD-ROM, should be accessible from the front.

The tower cases are about the same as the desktop cases, but they stand on one side. There are usually six screws on the back that holds the cover in place. On most tower cases, the front bezel has a groove that accepts the front part of the cover so that no screws are needed in the front.

Tower cases are very popular and handy. A tower case can sit on the floor and not use up any of your desktop space. The larger ones have space for up to eight drive bays, providing room for up to four hard drives, a floppy, a tape backup, a couple of CD-ROM drives, and other components.

Tower cases are a bit more expensive than the standard or "baby-size" cases. There are three sizes of tower cases: a mini tower, a medium size, and a large standard size. The smaller sizes do not have as many bays for mounting drives. Most of the cases include a power supply with the cost. Make sure that any power supply is at least 200 watts; 300 watts is even better. When you buy a new case, it will come with several small bags of screws, stand-offs, cables, and other necessary mounting hardware.

A case may cost from $40 to $100.

Power Supply

If you have a desktop case, the power supply will be located in the right rear corner of the chassis. If you have a tower case, the power supply will be located in the upper rear corner of the case. It will have a metal cover around it. The power supply usually has four screws on the back panel that holds it in place.

When your computer is running, the only noise you hear, except for the disk drives, is the cooling fan in the power supply. The cooling fan sucks air in from the front of the computer and forces it out through the grill in the back of the power supply. All holes in the computer and blank slots in the back panel should be covered so that the air is drawn only from the front grill of the computer, over the components. Make sure that nothing in the front or back of the computer impedes the air flow.

The newer ATX-type power supplies have a fan that is just the opposite of older systems. It pulls air in from the grill in the back of the computer and forces it over the components and out the front grill.

Transforming the Voltage

Computer systems use direct current (dc). The original systems used voltages of 12 V dc and 5 V dc. The CPUs used 5 volts. As more transistors were enclosed in the CPUs, more current was used, and the hotter the CPU became. Heat sinks and fans were used to keep the CPUs from burning up. The newer CPUs use a lower voltage, such as 3 volts, 2.5 volts, or 2.2 volts. By lowering the voltage, the current is lowered, and they don't run quite as hot. With millions of transistors, however, they still need heat sinks and a special fan to keep them from burning up.

The voltage that is provided by the wall socket is usually 110 volts alternating current (ac). The computer's power supply uses rectifiers and transformers to convert the ac voltage to the proper dc voltages. Motherboards have special circuits built in for providing the precise voltage and regulating it.

The ac voltage that comes from the wall plug is alternating at 60 cycles per second, or 60 Hz. (*Hz* stands for *Hertz*. Rudolph Heinrich Hertz, 1857—1894, was a German physicist who was the first to produce artificial radio waves. In order to honor him, a standards committee decreed that the frequency of cycles should be called Hertz. Many old-timers still call it cycles per second.) To transform 110 volts at 60 Hz would require a large transformer, but a fairly small transformer can be used if the frequency is very high. Rectifiers can be used to transform the 60-Hz ac voltage to a 120-Hz chopped dc voltage. An oscillator circuit takes this 120-Hz chopped voltage and changes the frequency to as high as 50,000 Hz or more. The higher the frequency of the voltage, the smaller the transformer can be. This high frequency is still 110 volts, which is much too high for our components, so the 110 volts is input to a small transformer, which reduces it to the required 12 volts, 5 volts, and lesser voltages. Since the voltage that comes from the transformer is still ac, it must be rectified and converted to dc.

The 110 volts in the power supply is the only voltage in your computer that might harm you. That is one reason for the cover over it. Another reason for the cover is to reduce any stray radiation that might emanate from the high-frequency conversion process.

The early IBMs and most clones had a switch on the side of the power supply for turning on the computer. This switch turned the current on and off. It was a bit inconvenient to reach around near the back of the computer, so many of the newer systems have a switch on the front panel. There is usually a four-wire electrical cord that goes from the power supply to the switch. Often, when you buy a new case, this switch is not connected to the power cord. The switch will have four terminals for the power connection. The four power cords connect to the switch terminals with slip-on connectors. Two of the four wires in the power cord bring 110 volts from the wall socket to the switch; the other two return the switched voltage back to the power supply. Be careful when connecting the power to the switch. If it is not connected properly, it could cause a direct short across the power line. If you short the line out this way, you will see a lot of sparks, smoke, and maybe even a fire. You should get some documentation as to how the wires should be connected. The power supply might have a diagram showing how the switch should be connected.

The newer ATX system has a "soft" power-sense system built into most of the new motherboards so the power can be turned on from the keyboard.

Power Strip

Since you will have your computer, a monitor, a printer, and perhaps three or four more units plugged into the wall outlet, you should buy a power strip that has four or five outlets. Power strips usually have a circuit breaker in case of power overload. Some have surge protection that can help protect your computer and the delicate electronics in it. Some strips may cost as little as $5, while others may cost $25 or more.

Power Distribution Panel

Even more convenient than a power strip is a power panel that is about an inch high and about the size of a desktop computer case. Your computer or monitor can sit on top of it. I use a power panel that is about 15 inches square and has six individual lighted switches: one for the master input power, one for the computer, one for a monitor, one for printer, and two for auxiliary devices. I can use the switches on the front of the panel to turn any of the devices on or off. It is very convenient and rather inexpensive, at about $15.

Surge Protection

When large, heavy-duty electric motors and other electrical equipment are turned on, they sometimes send very high-voltage surges through the nearby power lines. If you are in an area where there are large, heavy-duty electric motors, these surges could severely damage your system, causing glitches and data corruption. A good surge protector causes the spikes to be shunted to ground. Electrical storms can also cause surges in the power lines and telephone lines.

Some of the more expensive power-distribution panels include surge protection. Some also have sockets with surge protection for connecting a telephone line for a modem. There are different levels of quality surge protectors. Some are very inexpensive, but may not offer much protection. Many of the UPS companies listed in the next section also sell good-quality surge protectors.

The Need for an Uninterruptible Power Supply

If you are working on data that is critical, and you live in an area where there are a lot of electrical storms, power outages, or brownouts, you should install an uninterruptible power supply (UPS). When you are working on a file, it is loaded into Random Access Memory (RAM). This memory is volatile, that is, if the power is interrupted, even for a brief fraction of a second, the RAM loses all of its contents. The data that is being worked on will disappear and be gone forever. A UPS can take over when the power is interrupted, keeping the computer running until it can be safely shut down.

Basically, a UPS is a battery that is kept charged by the voltage from the wall socket. If there is an interruption of power, the electronic circuits immediately switch so that the computer is supplied by the battery. Depending on the UPS model and the amount of wattage you are drawing from it, it might be able to keep your system going for 10 to 15 minutes or more. This should give you plenty of time to close all your work and save it to disk.

If you live in an area where there are electrical storms, you should also have a good lightning rod installed. If a severe electrical storm comes up, even with a good lightning rod, you should turn off your computer and unplug it. Just one bolt can zap your system and fry it to a crisp.

Figure 1-2 shows an uninterruptible power supply from American Power Conversion. It is one of the better ones available. I live in the Los Angeles area, where we seldom have lightning or thunderstorms, but we do have electrical problems once in a while. With my computer plugged into this unit, I never have to worry about losing data due to loss of power.

Several companies manufacture UPS systems. Here are just a few:

American Power Conversion
888-289-APCC, extension 8129
www.apcc.com

Best Power Technology
800-356-5794
http://bestpower.com

Deltec
800-854-2658
www.deltecpower.com

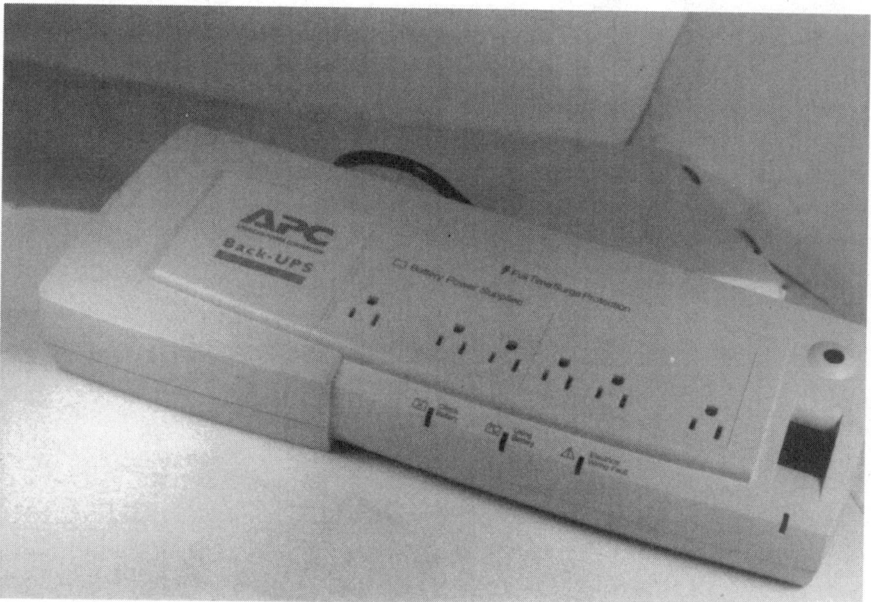

Figure 1-2
An Uninterruptible Power Supply

Exide Electronics
800-554-3448
www.exide.com/p-ups.htm

MGE UPS Systems
800-523-0142
www.mgeups.com

Tripp Lite
312-755-5400
http://tripplite.com

Visit their Web sites or call these companies for brochures and information.

Some of the UPS systems, such as the one from American Power Conversion, have several outlets so that you do not need a power strip. Each of the companies listed here has several models to choose from. Basically, the different models are designed for the amount of power or wattage they have to supply. The expense of a UPS will be more than offset if it saves you even once from a disaster.

Motherboard

The large motherboard sits on the floor of the chassis or on the back of an upright tower case. There are usually eight slots on the motherboard for various types of plug-in boards. Some of the boards that you might attach to the motherboard are an adapter board for your monitor, a modem/fax board, a sound board, and a Network Interface Card (NIC).

There are usually four or five Industry Standard Architecture (ISA) slots, and three or four Peripheral Component Interconnect (PCI) slots. If you look at one of the ISA slots on motherboard, you might notice that it is divided. The longer portion of the slot was the original, standard 62-contact slot for 8-bit boards. When the 286 was developed, an additional 36-contact slot was added to the original for 16-bit boards. As you have probably deduced, an 8-bit plug-in board, even one designed for the antique XT, can be used in your new computer.

The type of CPU you use will be a determining factor in what motherboard you buy. There are several motherboard manufacturers. Each one tries to differentiate its product from the others. Basically, they are all the same, but there will be some slight differences. Chapter 2 discusses motherboards in more detail.

CPU

The cost of a motherboard depends largely on the brand name and CPU manufacturer. The cost will vary considerably depending on the operating frequency of the CPU: the higher the frequency, the higher the cost.

At one time, Intel was the only manufacturer of the x86-type CPUs. Now, however, Cyrix, AMD, and IDT have x86 CPU clones on the market. The Cyrix, AMD, and IDT CPUs are equivalent to the Intel chips, but usually sell for about 25% less. This added competition will force the CPU prices down even more. When the CPU prices go down, the motherboard prices usually go down. Chapter 3 discusses CPUs in more detail.

Memory

When a computer runs a program, the program is temporarily loaded into memory (RAM) and processed there. When the processing is completed, it is then loaded back on the hard disk, printed out, or sent to wherever you want it to go.

At one time, we got by with as little as 64 Kb of RAM. It is now difficult to run most programs with less than 16 Mb of RAM, and 32 Mb or 64 Mb is better. You can start out with 16 Mb and add more later. You cannot have too much money or memory.

On the older systems, the memory chips were usually located in the left front quadrant of the motherboard. They used chips with dual in-line pins (DIP). Chips to make 640 Kb used about a fourth of the entire motherboard's real estate. Most systems today use either single in-line memory module (SIMM) or dual in-line memory module (DIMM) memory. These are small boards that have miniature chips on them. The board has an edge connector that plugs into special sockets on the motherboard. SIMM and DIMM technologies allow 128 Mb or more of memory to be installed in an area smaller than that required for 640 Kb using DIP chips.

There are many different types of memory. Chapter 4 goes into detail about them.

Floppy Disk Drives

At one time, an IBM 360-Kb floppy drive cost over $400. Today, it is completely obsolete. You might still have some data on 360-Kb and 1.2-Mb floppies. If you insist on keeping these floppies, I recommend that you buy a $5^1/_4$- inch 1.2-Mb and $3^1/_2$-inch 1.44-Mb combination drive. The 1.2-Mb drive will read and write to both the 360-Kb and 1.2-Mb floppies. You might even have some old $3^1/_2$-inch 720-Kb floppies with data on them. The 1.44-Mb drive will read and write to these as well.

See Chapter 5 for more details on floppy drives.

Hard Disk Drives

Most of the older systems used MFM, RLL, or ESDI hard drives. They were physically large, clunky, and slow. They were also very limited in storage capacity. One of my early hard disk drives was 40 Mb. It was 3 inches high, 6 inches wide, and 8 inches long. I paid almost $1000 for it when $1000 was worth about $3000 today. Since DOS 2.0 could only handle 32 Mb, I had to buy special software in order to use the full 40 Mb. A couple of years ago, I bought a 1-gigabyte (Gb) drive for $740. It is an inch high, 4 inches wide, and 6 inches long. Today, I can buy a 4.3-Gb drive for about $200.

There are several hard disk manufacturers with hundreds of different models, sizes, and types of hard disks. The older hard drives needed a controller board that plugged into one of the slots on the motherboard. Often, the controllers were made by companies other than the ones who manufactured the hard drives. The controllers often cost almost as much as the hard drives.

Today, the integrated disk electronics (IDE) drives have all of the controller electronics on the drive itself. They still need an interface to the system, however. The older systems used a low-cost interface that plugged into one of the slots. This interface is now built in on most motherboards as upright pins that accept the hard drive's cable. In fact, most motherboards now have two sets of pins and can handle up to four IDE hard drives, or a combination of hard drives and CD-ROM drives.

The Small Computer System Interface (SCSI, pronounced *scuzzy*) drive also has all of its controller functions built in. It needs a separate interface card, but an SCSI card can handle up to seven different devices.

It would be a good idea to install both an IDE hard drive and an SCSI hard drive. One advantage of this type of system is that you can use the two drives to back up each other. It is possible that one of the drives might crash or fail, but it is not very likely that both will fail.

For your new computer, I recommend that you install at least a 2.5-Gb drive, larger if you can afford it. Some of the manufacturers are no longer manufacturing hard disk drives with a capacity less than 1 Gb.

See Chapter 6 for more details on hard drives.

Backup

It is very important that you keep copies or backups of all of your software programs and important data. You never know when your hard disk might crash or have a failure.

There are thousands of ways that you can lose some very important data. You should always have a current backup. There are many methods for backing up, some using hardware and some requiring special software programs. See Chapter 7 for more details.

CD-ROM Drives

Your computer is not complete without a CD-ROM. Most software now comes on CD-ROM. You cannot load Windows 95 or Windows 98 into your system without a CD-ROM. CD-ROMs are discussed in more detail in Chapter 8.

Monitor

You can choose from a large variety of monitors. You can buy a fairly good color monitor for about $250, while a large-screen, very high-resolution monitor will cost much more. The type of monitor you buy should match whatever you are using your computer for. If you are doing a lot of high-end graphics or computer aided design (CAD), then you need a large screen with high resolution.

You will need a plug-in adapter board to drive the monitor. (Some motherboards have a built-in adapter). For standard VGA color, you should be able to buy one for about $40. For very high-resolution color, it might cost up to $500. See Chapter 9 for more details on monitors and adapters.

Keyboard and Mouse

The keyboard cable is plugged into a connector that is mounted on the back of the motherboard and is accessible on the back panel. The keyboard is a very important part of the computer. It is the main device for communicating with the computer. There are many keyboard manufacturers. Most of them have slight differences in the placement and feel of the keys, and special adjuncts such as trackballs, calculators, and keypads.

To run Windows and other graphical user interface (GUI) programs, it is essential to have a mouse, trackball, or other pointing device. Chapter 10 discusses keyboards and other input devices in some detail.

Modem, Fax, and Communications

You can use your computer to communicate with millions of other computers, with online services and a host of other services. You can download software from bulletin boards. You can send low-cost fax transmissions to millions of other fax sites.

You will definitely need some communications hardware and software if you want to get the most from your computer. Communication hardware and software are discussed in Chapter 11.

Cost of Components

All PCs use the same basic components, except for the motherboard and the CPU. Since the common components are all interchangeable, you can shop around for the best buys. Look at the ads in computer magazines such as *Computer Shopper, PC Magazine, PC World,* and *PC Computing* for an idea of what is available. These ads will also give you an idea of the cost of the various components and options. You can order the components through the mail, or if you live near a large city, go to a swap meet or to a local store.

It is almost impossible to put a real cost on components. The prices change daily, usually downward. A few approximate costs are listed here for comparison purposes. There are hundreds of different manufacturers and many, many options, so the prices will vary. To get a better idea of the cost, look through computer magazines. Of course, brand names and the type of component will be factors.

TABLE 1.1
Component Prices

Component	Price
Power supply and case	\$35—\$150
Motherboard, no CPU	\$75—\$300
CPU (Intel, Cyrix, or AMD)	\$200—\$1000
Monitor	\$200—\$1200

Component	Price
Monitor adapter	\$40—\$400
Memory, 16—32 Mb	\$75—\$150
Floppy drive 1.4 Mb	\$25—\$50
Hard drive 1—4 Gb	\$150—\$300
CD-ROM drive	\$50—\$200
Keyboard	\$20—\$150
Mouse	\$10—\$100
Modem	\$50—\$150
Total	**\$930—\$4150**

As you can see, there can be quite a large variation in the cost. The cost will depend on several available options, and whether the components have well-known brand names. There is also a large variation in cost from dealer to dealer. Some of the high-volume dealers charge less than the smaller ones, so it will pay to shop around a bit and compare prices. These figures are only rough approximations. The market is so volatile that the prices can change overnight. If you are buying through the mail, you might even call or check the advertised prices before ordering. Often, the advertisements have to be made up one or two months before the magazine is published, so the prices could have changed considerably.

Upgrading an Older System

You can save a lot of money by upgrading an older system. In most cases, you can use most of your older components. See Chapter 12 for more details.

System Assembly

After you have read all the chapters about the components and purchased the components, it is time to assemble them. Chapter 13 goes into detail on the system assembly.

The Internet

In just a few short years, the Internet has become one of the most important devices that we have today. It is a communications device, an information device for all sorts of things, a device for fun and entertainment, a business device, a device for learning, and a host of other things. If for no other reason, you should have a computer for the Internet. The Internet is discussed in Chapter 14.

Peripheral Components

Besides the components inside your computer case, you will need some peripheral components. One peripheral component, the monitor, has already been listed because it is absolutely necessary. There are several common components that are not absolutely necessary for a system. If you don't need a lot of goodies at this time, you can buy the minimum components and add to your system later.

It would be almost impossible to get by without a printer. An external fax machine is essential for most businesses. A scanner is also necessary for most businesses and can be great for home use. You can get by without a sound board and a couple of good speakers, but you would be missing out on an excellent reason to have a computer.

You will have lots of options when it comes to buying your printer. There are several manufacturers and hundreds of different types and models. There are dot matrix, laser, and ink jet printers, among others. Some types are better for a particular application than others, so which one you choose depends on what you want to do with your computer and how much you want to spend. Chapter 15 discusses the various types of printers.

Software

You will need software for your computer. Before you even turn it on, you will need operating software, such as Win95, Win 98, or UNIX. There are billions of dollars worth of off-the-shelf software that you can use. If some of the commercial programs seem a bit expensive, there are inexpensive public-domain and shareware programs that can do just about everything the commercial programs do. See Chapter 16 for more about software.

Some Applications

Once you have a big powerful computer, there are several applications for it. It is ideal for large businesses or for small office/home office (SOHO) applications. Some of the applications are listed in Chapter 17.

The computer is a fantastic tool for creating music or for just listening to it. Sound is also necessary for several computer applications. Sound is discussed in detail in Chapter 18.

Sources

You will need to know where to buy all of the components that you will need to upgrade or repair your PC. If you live near a large city, there are probably local stores that sell the parts. The local vendors and computer stores will be happy to help you. They might charge a bit more than a mail-order house, but if anything goes wrong, they are usually very quick to help you or make it right.

There are also frequent computer swaps in most large cities. A computer swap is just a gathering of local vendors at a fairground, a stadium, or some other area. Vendors usually set up booths and tables and present their wares. You can usually find all that you need at these meets. You can go from booth to booth and compare the components and prices. The prices are usually very competitive, and you might even be able to haggle a bit with the vendors.

The other good source for components is through the mail. Just look at the ads in any of the computer magazines. At one time, mail order could be a bit risky, but it is very safe today.

If a price seems too good to be true, then the vendor has probably cut a few corners somewhere. There are some very good bargains out there, but you should be careful. Your best protection is to be fairly knowledgeable about the computer business. Computer magazines, and books like the one you are holding, are some of the better sources for this knowledge.

Another excellent source of knowledge and help is a local computer user group. If you live near a large city, you will probably be able to find several groups. Most of the people in these groups are very friendly and anxious to help you with any problem.

If you are fairly new to computing, be sure to read the chapters on floppy disk drives, hard disk drives, monitors, keyboards, and the other major components before you buy your parts. There are billions of dollars worth of products available. Many of them are very similar in functionality and quality. What you buy should depend primarily on what you want your computer to do, and how much you can afford to spend. If you are knowledgeable and shop wisely, you can save a bundle. Chapter 19 discusses the many sources and lists several magazines.

Troubleshooting

Computers are just dumb machines. In most cases, there is only one way to do something right, but there might be thousands and thousands of ways that it can be done wrong. There is no way that a book could cover all the possible things that can go wrong, but there are a few things that can be done to find and fix most of the common problems. Chapter 20 goes into detail about troubleshooting.

How Computers Work

This section is very basic. If you are an old pro, you might want to skip ahead. If you are a beginner, this section should answer a lot of your questions as to how a computer works.

A computer is made up of circuits and boards that have resistors, capacitors, inductors, transistors, motors, and many other components. These components perform a useful function when electricity passes through them. The circuits are designed so that the paths of the electric currents are divided, controlled, and shunted to do the work that needs to be done. The transistors and other components force the electrons to go to memory, or to a disk drive, or to the printer, or wherever the software and hardware directs it to go.

Computers are possible only because of our ability to control voltages. Small voltages, usually direct-current (dc) voltages, are controlled by turning them on or off. When the voltage is on, it can represent a 1; when it is off, it is a 0. With these two digits, we can digitize a world of things, such as drawings, photographs, movies, sound, speech, music, and virtual reality. Once these objects are digitized, we can compress them, add to them, delete portions, or manipulate them in hundreds of ways. It can sometimes even be difficult to determine reality from virtual reality, as when Forrest Gump had a conversation with LBJ, who has been dead for many years. Since that movie, several others have used this technique. Many commercials have also been made using dead guys—maybe because they don't have to pay them any fees and residuals.

Computers and Electricity

Computers are possible because of electricity. Under the control of software and hardware, small electric on/off signal voltages are formed when you type from the keyboard. The absence or presence of magnetic bits on a hard or floppy disk can be detected and represented as on or off voltages. The small pits and lands on a CD-ROM disk can also be detected and represented as on or off voltages. The data sent or received over a telephone line from a fax or modem are just bits of on and off voltages. These on and off voltages are used to turn transistors on or off.

Electricity is the lifeblood of a computer. Under the control of the software and hardware, small voltage signals are sent to different areas of the computer to accomplish the various tasks.

Electricity is something that you cannot see, but you can see the effects of it. And, of course, you can feel it. If it is a fairly high voltage, it can knock you on your fanny or even kill you.

An electric charge is formed when there is an imbalance or an excess amount of electrons at one pole. The excess electrons will flow through whatever path they can find to get to the other pole, much like water flowing downhill to find its level.

All matter is made up of atoms. Atoms are made up of a nucleus that contains a given number of protons and neutrons and several electrons in orbits around the nucleus. The number of protons, neutrons, and electrons in the atom depends on what the substance is. Ordinarily, the number of electrons in orbit around a nucleus balances the protons and neutrons in the nucleus. Electrons can be displaced from the orbits of some substances, however. When this happens, there is an imbalance. Just as water will seek its own level, an atom that is imbalanced will try to regain its balance.

An Italian, Count Alessandro Volta (1745—1827), developed the first battery. Batteries have improved considerably since then, but they still use the same basic principle. Electric generators have also developed since then. Batteries and generators are used to create an imbalance of electrons.

Batteries and other electric sources have two electrodes, a positive, and a negative, or *ground*. The negative pole has an excess of electrons. If a path with no resistance is provided between the electrodes, the excess electrons will rush through the path at almost the speed of light to get to the positive pole.

Most electric or electronic paths have varying amounts of resistance so that work or heat is created when the electrons pass through them. For instance, if a flashlight is turned on, electrons pass through the bulb, which has a resistive filament. The heat generated by the electrons passing through the bulb causes the filament to glow red-hot and create light. If the light is left on for a period of time, the excess electrons from the negative pole of the battery will pass through the bulb to the positive pole of the battery. Electrons will continue to flow until the amount of electrons at the negative and positive poles are equal. At this time, there will be a perfect balance and the battery will be dead. If you place a motor in the path between the electrodes, the flow of electrons through the coils of wire around the rotor creates a magnetic force that causes the rotor to spin.

Soon after the battery was developed, Georg Simon Ohm (1789—1854), discovered that there was a direct relationship between the amount of voltage, the resistance of the path, and the number of electrons passing through the path. Resistance (R) is equal to the voltage (E) divided by the current (I). This is known as *Ohm's Law.* Using Ohm's Law, if you know any two of these values, you can determine the other one. Electrons moving through a circuit can be called *current* or *amperes.* The ampere is a very large number of electrons that passes a given point in a given amount of time. It was named for French mathematician Andre Marie Ampere (1775—1836).

When presented with two or more resistive paths, electricity obeys Ohm's Law exactly. Using Ohm's Law, circuits can be designed in thousands of ways to make electricity work for us by controlling and directing it to where we want it to go. Voltage can be controlled with switches, transistors, resistors, capacitors, inductive coils, transformers, and various other electronic components.

Transistors and Computers

The first and foremost reason that we have computers today is because we have transistors. The transistor effect was discovered by three scientists working in the Bell Labs in the late 1940s. The scientists, William Shockley, John Bardeen, and Walter Brattain were awarded a Nobel prize in 1956. (I believe that the discovery and development of the transistor should rank right up there in importance alongside the discovery of the wheel and fire.)

A very basic computer, the Electronic Numerical Integrator and Computer (ENIAC), was developed in the early 1940s. There were no transistors in those days, so ENIAC used thousands of vacuum tubes and cost millions of dollars. It took several large rooms to house one of these computers. It was used during World War II to calculate cannon trajectories.

It took 30 to 40 hours for each trajectory to be calculated by hand, but the new computer could do it in 30 seconds. Nevertheless, it could perform fewer functions than a present-day two-dollar calculator. Computers now can do the same trajectory calculations in about 30 nanoseconds (billionths of a second).

Technology made a quantum leap forward when the transistor was invented. So how do we get those transistors to work for us? Software instructs the computer to turn the transistors on and off to perform the various tasks. Although most software is something that is written, when it is typed into the computer from a keyboard, each time a key is depressed, it generates electrical pulses that turn the transistors on and off. When the software is loaded in from a disk, the magnetic flux of the disk is converted to electrical pulses that are identical to those created by the keyboard. The result of all software applications, no matter how they are input to the computer, is to cause the generation of on and off voltages that control the transistors. Ordinarily, the more complex the software and the more transistors available, the more work that a computer can accomplish.

The transistor can act as a switch. It has three basic elements: the collector, the base, and the emitter. Suppose the collector of a transistor is connected to the positive pole of a 6-volt battery and the emitter is connected to the negative pole. No voltage or electrons will pass through the transistor. If we connect a small voltage, as little as a millionth of a volt, on the base of the transistor, it can act like a switch and allow a large number of electrons to flow through the transistor and anything that is connected between its collector and the battery. So, a very small voltage on the base of a transistor can cause it to switch a much larger voltage on or off.

The transistor can also act as an amplifier. If the small voltage signal on the base of the transistor goes up gradually, then goes down, the transistor can cause a large voltage to go up and down in an exact replica of the input signal. When a radio or TV station broadcasts its signal, it throws a high voltage out into the air. By the time it gets to your radio or TV, it might only be a millionth of a volt. Using transistors, this voltage can be amplified in an exact replica of the original voltage signal so that it is strong enough to power a loudspeaker or to drive a 25,000-volt electron gun in a TV set. The picture tube or cathode ray tube (CRT) of a TV or computer monitor is similar to a vacuum tube. Figure 1-3 is a diagram of an old-fashioned vacuum tube circuit and a transistor circuit. The transistor circuit can be thousands of times smaller and use only a fraction of the energy needed for the vacuum tube. The radio

Figure 1-3
A Vacuum tube and transistor circuits.

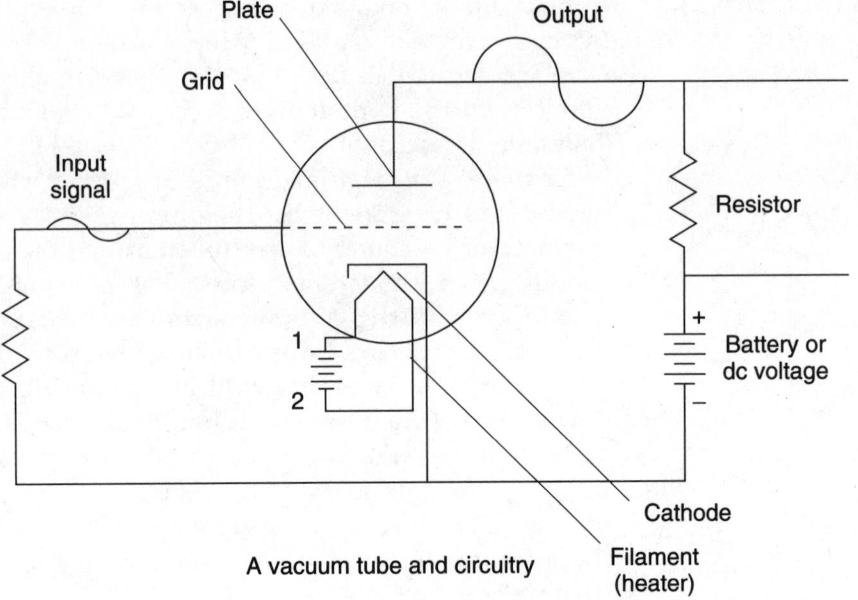

A vacuum tube and circuitry

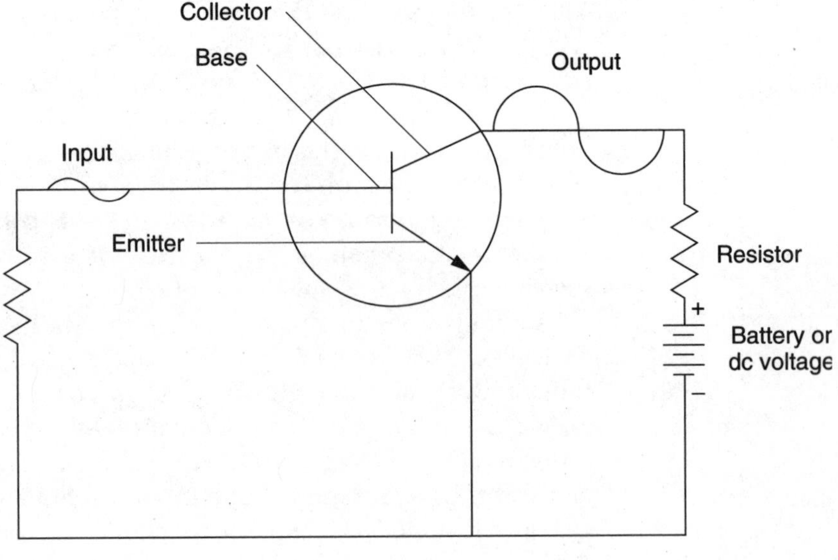

A transistor and circuitry

and TV voltages vary up and down and are called *analog voltages*. Figure 1-4 is a diagram of square waves and analog sine waves.

Computers use thousands of transistors. The main chip, or brains, of a computer is the central processing unit (CPU). The 486 CPU has 1.2 million transistors, the Pentium CPU has 3.1 million, and the Pentium Pro CPU has 5.5 million. In addition to the CPU, there are several other chips and components on the motherboard with many more thousands of transistors.

The transistors in the CPU, those on the motherboard, and those on the various plug-in boards and peripherals all respond to signals or voltages that are fed to them from input sources such as the keyboard, floppy disk drive, hard disk drive, modem, and scanner. The voltages used by computers are digital voltages that have two states, off and on.

Suppose you have two switches or two transistors. You can therefore have four different states:

1. #1 off and #2 off
2. #1 on and #2 off
3. #1 off and #2 on
4. #1 on and #2 on

If you have four transistors, you can have 16 different states. If you double the amount of transistors to eight, which would be two to the power of eight (2^8), you can have 256 different states. If you double the number again to 16 (2^{16}), you can have 65,536 different states. The different number of states goes up by the power of 2 with each additional

Figure 1-4
Square waves and analog sine waves.

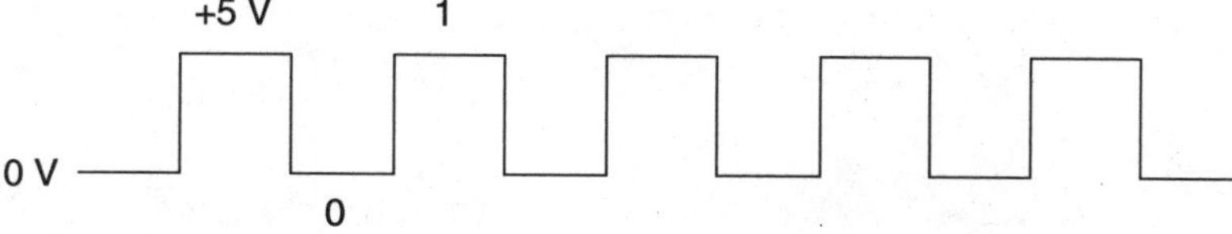

Square waves representing 0s and 1s

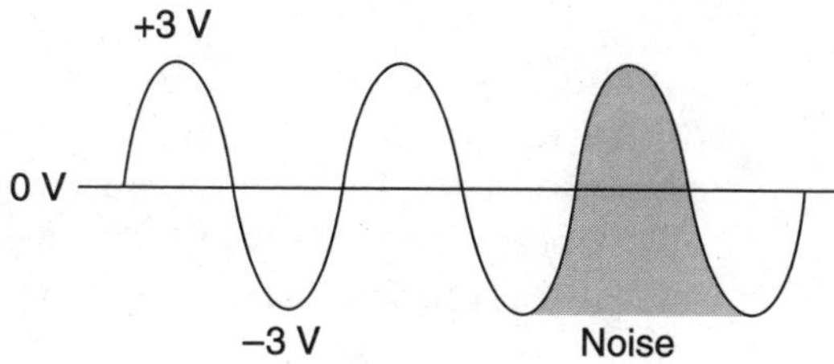

Analog voltage

transistor or switch. With 32 transistors, 4,294,967,296 different signals can be produced.

Computers work with ones and zeros, or *bits*. (The term *bit* is a contraction of *binary digit*). It takes eight bits to make one byte. It takes eight bits or one byte to represent one letter of the alphabet or a single number.

For certain digital states, we can assign a number or a letter of the alphabet. In the decimal system, we assign values to wherever the numeral happens to be. For instance, in the number 321, the 3 is in the hundred place, the 2 is in the ten place, and the 1 is in the 1 place. In the digital system, each place also has a value, but it works a bit differently than the decimal system. The right column is 1, the next is 2, the next is 4, then 8, then 16, 32, 64, 128, 256, etc. Note that each new column toward the left doubles. Here is what the output of four different switches or transistors would look like:

0000 = 0 = all off
0001 = 1 (the 1 place)
0010 = 2 (the 2 place)
0011 = 3 (the 2 place + 1)
0100 = 4 (the 4 place)
0101 = 5 (the 4 place + 1)
0110 = 6 (the 4 place + 2)
0111 = 7 (the 4 place + 2 +1)
1000 = 8 (the 8 place)
1001 = 9 (the 8 place + 1)
1010 = 10 (the 8 place + 2)
1011 = 11 (the 8 place + 2 + 1)
1100 = 12 (the 8 place + 4)
1101 = 13 (the 8 place + 4 + 1)
1110 = 14 (the 8 place + 4 + 2)
1111 = 15 (the 8 place + 4 + 2 + 1)

The ASCII Code

When the teletype was developed, its inventors used the digital system to devise a code so that messages could be sent over telephone wires. This was called the *American Standard Code for Information Interchange* or *ASCII* (pronounced "asskee"). The original code was 128 different characters: all of the characters found on a typewriter keyboard, including punctuation and spaces.

Typing the letter A on a teletype keyboard would cause a voltage to be turned on and off, producing 100001 (equivalent to decimal 65) to be sent over the teletype wire. If a teletype machine in another city was connected to this teletype, the letter A would be typed out. If a B was typed, the signal 100020 (decimal 66) would be produced. (The fourth place to the left is 16, 2^4, the fifth is 32, 2^5, and the sixth is 64, 2^6.)

This 128-character code worked very well for several years. Later, the ASCII code was extended by an additional 128 characters and symbols for a total of 256, or 2^8. The extended ASCII code includes smiling faces, playing-card symbols, Greek letters, and several other symbols. If you would like to see what some of these symbols look like, at the DOS prompt, use the command TYPE to type out any command that has an .EXE or .COM extension. For instance at the DOS prompt, type TYPE COMMAND.COM.

If you type an A on a computer keyboard, like the teletype, it causes a digital voltage to be created equivalent to 1000001, or 65 decimal. This causes certain transistors inside the computer to be turned on or off, and the A character would be displayed, stored, printed, or whatever the software told it to do.

Inputs

The computer keyboard creates digital voltages for each key that is typed, but there are other ways to input data to a computer. Floppy and hard disks have a magnetic coating very similar to that on the tape in a tape recorder. A small voltage is created when the data is read by the drive head. This voltage is then amplified and routed to wherever the software tells it to go.

Input can also come from such things as a mouse, a modem, a scanner, or a network. They all produce a digital voltage that is used by the software and hardware to accomplish a task.

If an electronic circuit is designed properly, it should last several lifetimes. There is nothing in a semiconductor or transistor to wear out. Occasionally, however, too many electrons find their way through a weakened component and cause it to heat up and burn out, or for some reason, the electrons may be shunted through a path or component where they shouldn't go. This can cause an intermittent, partial, or complete failure.

System Clock

The computer has a real-time clock and calendar that keeps track of the date and the time. It also has a system clock that is much more precise than the real-time clock. Everything that a computer does is precisely timed. The timing is controlled by crystal oscillators. The computer carries out each instruction in a certain number of clock cycles. On the early XT system, the clock operated at 4.77 million Hertz (MHz), or cycles, per second. Even so, it often took several clock cycles, moving eight bits at a time, to perform a single instruction. The Pentium II can operate as fast as 266 MHz and process several instructions per cycle.

Moore's Law

A few years ago, Gordon Moore, then chairman of Intel Corporation, studied the microprocessor industry and noticed a very definite trend. He observed that the 286 had 125,000 transistors, more than three times the 29,000 in the XT. Very soon the 386 was introduced with 275,000 transistors, which more than doubled the 286, then the 486 with 1.2 million, followed by the Pentium with 3.1 million, and then the Pentium Pro with 5.5 million. The new Pentium II will have over 10 million transistors. The trend is that every 18 months or so the number of transistors and computing power more than doubles. This trend has become so predictable that it is now known as *Moore's Law.* Intel said at one time they would eventually have microprocessors with 100 million transistors. According to Moore's Law, it will only take another three or four generations to reach that level, which should occur sometime within the next five or six years.

So go ahead and build your computer to the very latest specifications, and enjoy the power and speed it can deliver. However, you should know that within a very short time, your wonderful machine will be obsolete again. But not to worry; with this book, you can deal with obsolescence by upgrading it.

CHAPTER 2

The Motherboard

The motherboard is the largest and most important board in your system. It has the central processing unit (CPU) and all of the chips, electronics, and slots for plug-in boards that makes computing possible. If you have an old system, you can upgrade it to a Pentium II-class machine by replacing the motherboard. It is one of the easiest upgrades that you can make. It can give you most of the benefits of a new system at a fairly reasonable cost. Figure 2-1 shows a socket-7 motherboard that can accept the AMD K 6, Cyrix 6x86MX, or IDT C6 CPUs.

If you are building a system from scratch, the motherboard will be high on your list of components to buy. If you are upgrading an older system, the motherboard will also be one of the most important components on your shopping list. I have to tell you up front that a lot of this chapter is about basic stuff. You might not be interested in the basics—you might just want to get started. If so, the following section is a short list of manufacturers of motherboards. If you have access to the Internet, by all means visit the sites listed in this chapter. The computer industry changes so quickly that many things become obsolete overnight. The Web sites are usually up-to-date and can show you what is available.

Motherboard Sources

There are several motherboard vendors, each trying to differentiate its product from the others, so you will have several choices. Which system you should choose depends on what you want to use your computer for and how much money you want to spend. I hate to quote prices, but at this time, in early 1998, a Pentium II motherboard is selling for about $200 to $300. It will probably be less by the time you read this. Of course, if you want a 300-MHz Pentium II CPU, it will cost an additional $1200 to $1400. A 266 MHz at this time costs about $700 to $900, a 233 MHz about $500 to $700.

If you don't have that kind of money, you can buy a universal motherboard with a Zero Insertion Force (ZIF) socket number 7. You can buy one of these motherboards for about $150 at this time. You can then buy a 233-MHz AMD K6 or Cyrix 6x86MX for about $300. This would give you a motherboard and CPU for a total of $450 or less. An equivalent Intel 233-MHz Pentium II CPU and motherboard would cost from $700 to $900. The AMD and Cyrix systems will do just about everything that the 233-MHz Pentium II will do. By the time you read this, AMD and Cyrix will have 266-MHz CPUs available.

Figure 2-1
A socket 7 type motherboard. Beneath the fan is a Cyrix 6x86Mx CPU.

There are hundreds of other Pentium-class motherboard available. Most of them are now universal with a socket 7 and lots of jumpers. They can be configured to accept almost any Pentium-type CPU. You will see the term *socket 7* mentioned several times throughout this chapter. Several different sockets have been designed for the Intel CPUs. Table 3-4 in the next chapter lists the various sockets that have been used on motherboards.

If you don't have a lot of money, there are lots of Pentium, AMD K5, and Cyrix 5x86 CPUs and motherboards still available. Since they are now obsolete, the vendors are practically giving them away. One of these motherboards and CPUs might be all you need at the moment. You could put one of these together now, then upgrade to a new motherboard and CPU later. Intel Pentium MMX CPUs can still be used with motherboards that have socket 7. They are available in frequencies from 150 MHz up to 200 MHz, and they do almost everything that the Pentium II will do.

Since there are several Pentium motherboard manufacturers, the competition will keep the prices fairly reasonable. I do a lot of my buying and shopping by mail order. I look through computer magazines to compare prices and products. Some computer magazines, such as *Computer Shopper*, have a section near the back where they list the products advertised for that month. The items are categorized and grouped by product type, and the page number for each ad is listed so you can easily find what you are looking for. This is a great help, considering that *Computer Shopper* might have over 1000 tabloid-sized pages.

If you live near a large city, there will probably be several computer dealers in your city. The local dealers might be a bit more expensive than mail order, but you can usually get better results if there is a problem. You can also see the product before you buy it. Again, if you live in a large city, there will probably be computer swap meets every so often, where local dealers will meet at a large auditorium or fairground and set up booths to sell their wares. It is very competitive, and dealers usually offer very good prices and discounts. You can go from booth to booth and compare prices and products. You might even be able to haggle a little bit.

I often go to swap meets even if I don't need anything. There is usually a large crowd and lots of excitement in the air. It's almost like a circus.

If you have access to a computer and the Internet, here are some Web sites related to motherboards:

A-Trend Technology
www.a-trend.com
800-866-0188

Elitegroup
www.ecsusa
888-327-2288

FIC
www.fica.com
800-878-4726

Intel Corporation
www.intel.com
408-765-8080

JM Computers
www.jmcomputers.com
800-331-2128

LPC Technology
www.lpc-tech.com
909-598-2710

M Technology
www.mtiusa.com
800-420-3636

Micronics Corporation
www.micronics.com
800-577-0977

QDI
www.qdigrp.com
510-668-4933

Redington USA
www.redingtonusa.com
978-988-7500

Tyan Computer
www.tyan.com
408-956-8000

These sites have lots of information that I can't possibly include in this book. Besides that, the products are changed and updated frequently. The Web sites can easily reflect these changes.

If you are building a Pentium II, you will need a special motherboard with the Intel slot 1. Intel and most other manufacturers now offer these motherboards. All of these companies also have motherboards with the CPU socket 7 that is necessary for the Pentium MMX, AMD K6, Cyrix 6x86MX, and IDT C6.

Accelerated Graphics Port (AGP)

Many of the Pentium II motherboard now have an extra slot for the Accelerated Graphics Port (AGP). The PCI bus is limited to 33 MHz and can be a bottleneck for extensive graphics work. The newer AGP port operates at 66 MHz, twice the maximum speed of the PCI bus. As you might imagine, being able to run graphics at twice the speed possible with PCI will be a fantastic advantage for those who do a lot of graphic design.

Several companies are manufacturing AGP plug-ins, including these:

Number Nine Revolution 3D AGP
Number Nine Corporation
617-674-0009
www.nine.com

ASUSTek 3DexPlorer V3000
ASUSTek
408-474-0567
www.asus.com

ATI Xpert@Play
ATI Technologies
905-882-2600
www.atitech.com

It is expected that some companies will build or integrate the AGP system onto the motherboard so that you will not need the slot and plug-in board. The AGP system uses the Intel 440LX core-logic chipset. This chipset was developed by Intel for the Pentium II and is proprietary. Because of this, there are no AMD or Cyrix systems currently available. However, both AMD and Cyrix are working on a clone system, so that eventually there will be motherboards with socket 7 and AGP available.

The *Windows Magazine* test lab tested several PCI graphics boards against the AGP system. According to their tests, AGP didn't offer any significant performance over the high-end PCI boards, so you can get by with the socket-7 motherboards. (For more about graphics and graphic adapters, see Chapter 9.)

Here are the specifications for an A-Trend Company motherboard:

ATC-6120 Intel.

Pentium II

440LX PCIset Motherboard

Manual

Here is what *PC Magazine* has to say about the LX motherboard:

Processor Pentium II MMX processor 233MHz to 300MHz
Chipset Intel 440LX PCIset Feature
Switching Voltage Regulator built-in
ACPI Power Management, Soft-OFF Control
LDCM Support(LM78)
Option CPU overheat auto detected and warning
Auto detected CPU voltage mode
Bus Architecture AGP, 32-bit PCI BUS and 16-bit ISA BUS
  System Memory:
  Three 168-pin DIMM sockets for 3.3V SDRAM and EDO DRAM
  Capacity 8 MB to 384 MB
On Board Dual Channel USB
IrDA TX/RX header
Dual Bus Master IDE ports
Floppy port (720KB/1.44MB/2.88MB)
Two Serial ports (16550 Fast UART compatible)
Parallel port (EPP/ECP) support
PS/2 keyboard connector
PS/2 mouse connector
Expansion Slots:
  Four 32-bit PCI slots (Concurrent PCI 2.1)
  Three 16-bit ISA slots
BIOS AWARD FlashFlash EEPROM

DMI, Green, and Plug-and-Play functions
Dimension Four layers PCB
ATX Form Factor, 30.5cm × 21cm; 12.0″ × 8.26″

A-Trend Technology Corp.
46600 Fremont Blvd.
Fremont, CA 94538
Phone (510) 226-6290/(800) 866-0188
Fax (510) 226-6296
www.a-trend.com
For sales, please send to sales@a-trend.com.

Intel Motherboards

Intel sold $20 billion worth of chips in 1997, but that is not enough. They have also gone into the business of making motherboards. They design and build motherboards for their Pentium, Pentium Pro, and Pentium II systems. Some of Intel's biggest buyers also make motherboards. Many of them are not too happy with the Intel competition.

Intel NLX

For some unknown reason, a few designers like to make low-profile computers. A few companies did it with the 386 and 486 systems. It was very difficult to add any plug-in boards or to just work on the systems. Thankfully, they were never very popular, and most manufacturers stopped making them. Because they were such a failure before, you would think that the manufacturers would have learned. But one of the biggest companies, Intel, has designed a low-profile NLX motherboard. The NLX motherboard looks much like a plug-in board. In fact, it *is* a plug-in board that plugs into a back plane. Since there is no room on the motherboard for plug-in slots, the back plane provides slots for plug-in boards. I would bet a whole lot of money that the NLX form factor will be no more popular than the earlier low-profile systems. It would be very difficult to upgrade an NLX system. I would not recommend it. Even to someone I didn't like very much.

You can see photographs of the NLX system and other Intel motherboards and chips on the Intel Web site at www.intel.com.

Motherboard Specifications

Each motherboard manufacturer has specifications and information about all of its products. Some of them even have online manuals for anyone who might not have gotten one or has lost it. They will also have technical support if you run into problems. I have listed the specifications (specs) for two motherboards in this section, as examples of what you may find. One set of specs is for the Pentium II-type motherboard, and the other is for a socket-7-type motherboard. Most motherboard companies, of course, make a large variety of motherboards.

The Micronics Tigercat

Here are the specifications from the Micronics Web site (www.micronics.com/products/tigercat.html) for their Tigercat Pentium II motherboard:

> The Tigercat is a single state-of-the-art Intel Pentium II solution with processors running at speeds of 233 up to 333MHz. Based on the Intel 440LX AGPset, Tigercat provides LM78 Microprocessor System Hardware Monitor support and Ultra DMA133 IDE hard drive protocol (up to 33MBytes/sec transfer rate) support. Tigercat's flexibility is augmented by its support for the ISA, PCI, and AGP (Accelerated Graphics Port) bus. The AGP bus slot has greater bandwidth capacity, which provides a higher data transfer rate than the PCI bus. Other features include SDRAM (Synchronous Dynamic RAM) memory and Wake-On-Lan, which provides a way to access a local-area or wide-area network to turn on desktop PCs remotely. Manufacturing options include 16-bit Yamaha sound with wavetable synthesis.

Specifications:

Processors:

- Single Intel Slot 1
- Intel Pentium II chip 233/266/300/333MHz
- Integrated VRM

System Management:

- Microprocessor System Hardware Monitor
- CPU temperature sensor
- CPU Fan Speed Monitoring 3-pin header
- Chassis Intrusion 2-pin header
- Chassis Fan Speed Monitoring 3-pin header
- Intel LANDesk Client Manager software (Ver. 3.0)

Wake On LAN ready (3-pin header)

Expansion:

Four 32-bit PCI slots
Two 16-bit ISA slots
One is a shared PCI/ISA slot
One AGP

CPU Clock Select:

Support for 66MHz CPU bus speed configurations

Chipset:

Intel 440LX AGPset
Intel PIIX 4
SMC FDC37C68x Ultra I/O chip

Memory:

Four 3.3V unbuffered 64/72-bits 68-pin DIMM sockets
Maximum memory 512 MB for SDRAM
Maximum memory 1GB for EDO
Supports EDO and SDRAM memory
ECC supported via chipset

PCI (Local Bus) IDE:

Ultra DMA/33 IDE
Two 40-pin IDE connectors (Primary and Secondary IDE)
Auto detection of add-in IDE board
Supports ATAPI devices
Multiple sector transfer support

Floppy:

Supports 360K to 2.88MB formats
LS-120
Auto detection of add-in floppy controllers

Sound (Manufacturing Option):

Yamaha OPL3 and OPL4
Sound Blaster_Compatible 16-bit Stereo
Line-in, Line-out, Mic, and Game/MIDI ports
4-pin CD-ROM audio header (ATAPI & SB)
4-pin modem audio header (ATAPI)
4-pin Line-in header (ATAPI)
Built-in Wavetable (Yamaha OPL4ML)
Sound drivers (1)OS, Win 95/NT, OS/2

Communication Ports:

Two 9-pin 16550 compatible serial ports
One 25-pin parallel port (ECP, EPP)
IrDA compliant IR header
Two USB ports

Keyboard and Mouse:

PS/2 style keyboard & mouse connectors

BIOS:

Phoenix 4.06 BIOS on 2MB Flash
PCI auto configuration
"Plug and Play" ready
APM1.2
Auto detection of memory size
Auto detection and display of EDO, ECC, and SDRAM memory
Auto configuration of DE hard disk types
SoftPowerDown
Multiboot II
DMI/SMI/ACPI
WakeonLAN

Form factor:

ATX footprint (12″ × 9.6″)
Four Layer Board
20-pin ATX power connector
Stack mouse/keyboard connectors
Stack 3-output audio/game port connectors
Stack serials/parallel connectors

The Tigercat is extensively tested for compatibility under various operating systems, including:

OS/2 Warp
ODT
NOVELL
Windows 95 & NT
SCO UNIX
MS-DOS versions 5.0, 6.2
PC-DOS

The Tyan S1571S Titan Turbo AT-2

Here are the specifications from the Tyan Web site (www.tyan.com) for their S1571S motherboard with the socket 7, suitable for Pentium MMX, AMD, and Cyrix CPUs:

S1571S Titan Turbo AT-2 Pentium 75-233 MHz System Board

Intel Pentium, Pentium
MMX, AMD K6 and Cyrix
120+, 150+ & 166+

New Switching Power Supply for complete CPU Support!

5 PCI and 4 ISA Slots

Ultra DMA133 drive support & PI0 modes 1

The S1571S is a quality, high performance mainboard designed for Intel Pentium microprocessors. This mainboard utilizes the Intel 430TX chipset and can support CPU speeds of 75MHz through 233MHz. The S1571S will also support the CyrixMlI6x86 CPUs, AMD K6, and the Intel multimedia Pentium with MMX processor, both the P550 and P54CTB Overdrive versions.

The S1571S's PCI Local Bus provides high performance capabilities that are ideal for a wide range of demanding applications such as: CAD, CAM, CAE, networking, multiuser environments, database management, desktop publishing, image processing and 3D animation. This integrated system board achieves high reliability with numerous features and yet is small enough to be supported in an NATH form factor.

Some of the features included are: on-board dual channel PCI PIO, DMA IDE and Ultra DMA33, on-board floppy controller, on-board high speed I/O, and on-board 512k burst SRAM.

Flexibility and expandibility have been designed into the S1571S. With I/O and drive controller support built on-board, the five PCI and four ISA (one ISA and one PCI as a shared slot) slots are free for numerous add-on expansion cards.

Specifications:

Processor

Pentium/Pentium MMX/AMD K6

Supports 75MHz through 233MHz

Cyrix/SGSIIBM 6x86 P120+, P150+, P166+

M2/K6 266MHz Support builtin #7 ZIF Socket/ Wide Voltage Range

Chipset:

Intel 430TX

Main Memory:

8-256MB

Six 72-pin SIMM Sockets

Two 168-pin DIMM Sockets

Fast Page Mode or EDO DRAM Support

EDO DIMM and SDRAM Support

Cache Memory:

On-board 512K Burst Cache

Expansion Slots:

Five 32-bit PCI Bus Mastering Slots

Four 16-bit ISA Slots

One Shared PCI/ISA Slot - 8 usable

On-board PCI Bus Mastering IDE:
Two PCI Bus-Master enhanced IDE Ports
4 HDD + EIDE CD-ROM Support (4 IDE Devices Total)
Ultra DMA/33 Support
Bus-Mastering DMA Modes 1 & 2
PIO Modes 3 & 4
On-board I/O with IR:
Two Floppy Drives
Two serial ports (16550 UART's)
One ECP/EPP parallel port
One IR (InfraRed) I/O interface port
Two USB rev 1.2 port support
Flash BIOS:
Award standard, AMI BIOS Available
Green PC Compatible
Microsoft Plug and Play Readv
DM1
Physical Dimensions:
Intel Baby AT (11″ × 8.8″) Reduced Form Factor
Warranty:
2 Years

Intel Pentium II Motherboards

Intel not only manufactures the CPU, it also designs and manufactures motherboards for the CPU. Here is some information from the Intel Web site (www.intel.com) about Pentium II motherboards:

Pentium II processor-based Motherboards
Easy to Integrate

Intel's boxed motherboards and boxed processors provide a comprehensive set of building blocks to integrators and OEMs assembling systems based on the Pentium II processor.

By ordering just two boxes from an Intel Authorized Distributor—the PD440FX motherboard and boxed Pentium II processor—an integrator needs to supply only tools and a suitable chassis and power supply complying with ATX specification 2.01. A processor installation video designed for the boxed motherboard is included on a CD-ROM in the box, along with the processor retention mechanism.

The DB440FX is a low profile motherboard designed for the Pentium II processor. There are several custom configurations available to direct OEM customers.

Time to market with a proven design

The PD440FX and DB440FX motherboards offer time to market for the Pentium II processor using a proven design. Both boards are based on the second generation of products built around the Pentium Pro processor, including the Intel 82440FX PCIset . The chip set optimizes system performance for 32-bit application software in 32-bit operating system environments.

Performance and Features

Motherboards manufactured by Intel for the Pentium II processor offer a high level of flexibility for today's multimedia applications and tomorrow's uses. The Pentium II processor combines the design/Pentium II performance of the Pentium Pro processor with the multimedia enhancement capabilities of MMX technology. The motherboard products also provide a high level of integration, including such advanced features as dual Universal Serial Bus (USB) connectors.

A lower total cost of ownership

Manageability was designed into the PD440FX and DB440FX motherboards from the beginning. The Desktop Management Interface (DMI) compliant BIOS and on-board hardware management ASIC provide constant monitoring of voltage and temperature to ensure high up-time and allow for preventative maintenance. The boxed PD440FX motherboard also ships with Intel's LANDesk Client Manager application to enable remote monitoring and configuration of the system.

Available in the most popular form factors

Intel-manufactured motherboards for the Pentium II processor are available in form factors adopted by the industry's largest companies. The PD440FX board complies with ATX specification 2.01. And future motherboards for the Pentium II processor will use the emerging NLX low profile form factor. Both layouts were designed with the latest processor technology in mind for ease of integration and maintenance.

Dual Pentium II Motherboards

Some manufacturers have designed motherboards with dual slot 1s. The M Technology model Stallion AT-M668, for example, is designed for dual Pentium II CPUs. M Technology has several other motherboards. Check their Web site at www.mtiusa.com or call 408-441-8818 for more information.

You could build a dual Pentium II system with 300-MHz CPUs for less than $10,000 that could perform as well as a $50,000 minicomputer. I have not seen any dual socket-7 motherboards. Dual socket-7 motherboards would allow you to build a very powerful machine for much less than the cost of building dual Pentium IIs. I have been told that a few companies are making dual socket-7 motherboards, so there might be several by the time you read this. One problem is that it takes a special chipset for a dual processor. At present, only Intel has designed one for the Pentium Pro and the Pentium II.

The ATX Motherboard and Power Supply

Most of the cooling in a computer is from a small fan in the power supply. Originally, the power supply drew air in from the front grill and pulled it over the components. The newer ATX power supply draws air in from the back and blows it over the components. The power supply has a socket that can only be connected to a motherboard with an ATX socket.

Figure 2-2 shows the power connectors from the power supply. If you buy a motherboard for a Pentium-class machine, be sure to check the power supply connector. Some of them still use the original connector, but most of the later models use the ATX socket. Figure 2-3 shows a motherboard with both connectors. All of the Pentium II motherboards will use the ATX socket.

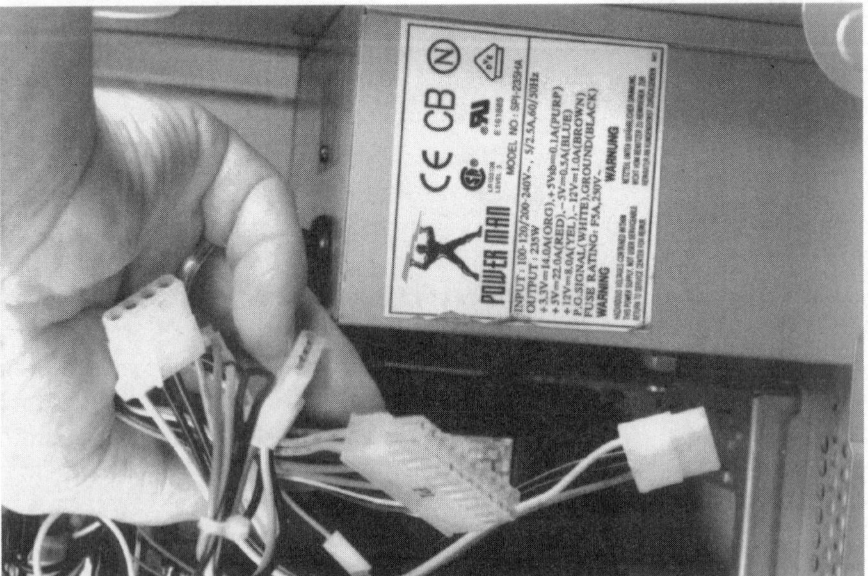

Figure 2-2
An ATX power supply.

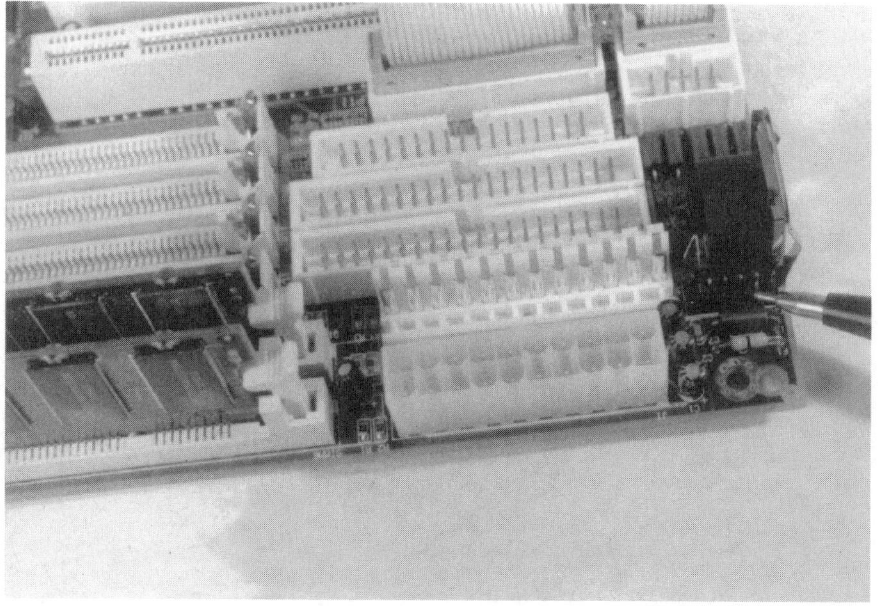

Figure 2-3
A socket-7 motherboard with both ATX and standard power connections.

The original power supply had two connectors with six wires each for the inline motherboard socket. The power connectors plugged side by side into the motherboard socket. If you were not careful, it was possible to plug them in backwards or improperly. This could be disastrous and ruin the motherboard. When properly plugged in, the four black ground wires should be in the center of the socket. Figure 2-4 shows the connector plugged in so that the four black wires are in the center. The ATX power supply has a connector that can only be plugged in properly to the motherboard socket.

If your new motherboard has an ATX socket, you can buy an ATX power supply for about $30 to $40, but it would be better to buy a new case with the power supply already mounted for $60 to $70. The original system's power supply had an output of −5 V, +5 V, −12 V, and +12 V. The new ATX system has added 3.3 V for the newer CPUs.

In the older systems, an on/off switch was provided either on the front panel or on the side of the case. This switched the incoming 110 V to the power supply. The 110 V goes directly to the power supply on ATX systems. These *Soft Power* power-supply systems provide Power_On and 5V_Standby signals. Power_On is a signal that Windows 95 and NT can use to power the system on or off. An option allows the keyboard to use these signals to power up or down. The low current, 5V_Standby signal is present at all times, even when the main system is powered down.

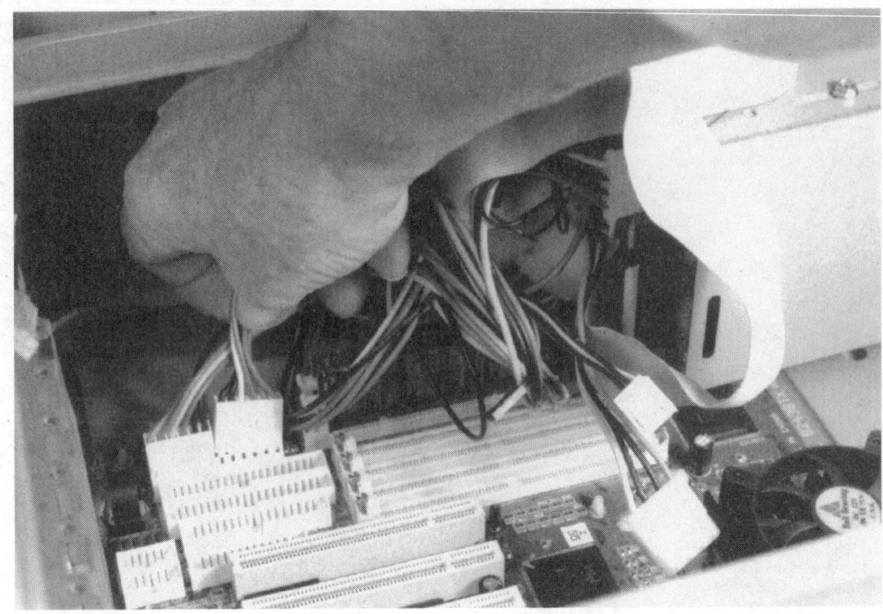

Figure 2-4
A motherboard power connection with a standard connector. Note that the four black wires are in the center when connected properly.

Motherboard Variations

Some motherboard manufacturers are building in several goodies such as sound, video, Universal Serial Bus, and SCSI. This integration saves precious slots and even a bit of money over plug-in boards. Unfortunately, many of the motherboard manufacturers do not adhere to any standards. Some of these motherboards still use the old-style power supply connectors. Some of them cover all bases and install both the ATX and the old-style connectors side by side.

Another variation is that some of the motherboards have a PS/2-type keyboard and mouse connector. That means that you cannot use your standard keyboard and mouse. Several cable companies provide adapters that will let you use the old keyboard and mouse. The adapters cost about $5 each, which isn't bad, but it might cost more in the time it takes to find a vendor and order the parts. This can be especially frustrating if you have ordered a motherboard through the mail, hoping to be able to use it right away, but then find that you either have to buy a new mouse and keyboard or some adapters. Figure 2-5 shows some adapters.

One reason for using the PS/2 connector for the mouse is that it saves having to use one of your two COM ports. The PS/2 keyboard and mouse connectors may be side by side or stacked one on the other. The mouse or keyboard can be plugged into either connector. Figure 2-6 shows the rear of my Pentium II motherboard. The two round connectors are the PS/2 type. While it saves having to use the COM ports, a PS/2 mouse still uses one of the precious IRQs.

Most Pentium II motherboards now have Universal Serial Bus (USB) connectors. This bus is faster and simpler to configure than SCSI, and will handle up to 127 devices. It will be the new standard, but at this time there are not many components available that can use it.

Local computer stores will have many of the adapters and cables that you need, but it is often easier to order by mail rather than go to a store and look for things like these. Here are a few companies that can send you adapters for the PS/2 connectors and the USB cables and connectors:

- ASP, 800-445-6190
- Belkin, 310-898-1100
- Cables to Go, 800-826-7904
- Monster Cable, 415-871-6000
- Primax Cables to Go, 800-826-4000
- QVS, 313-641-6700

Figure 2-5
Keyboard and mouse cable adapters from PS/2 to standard.

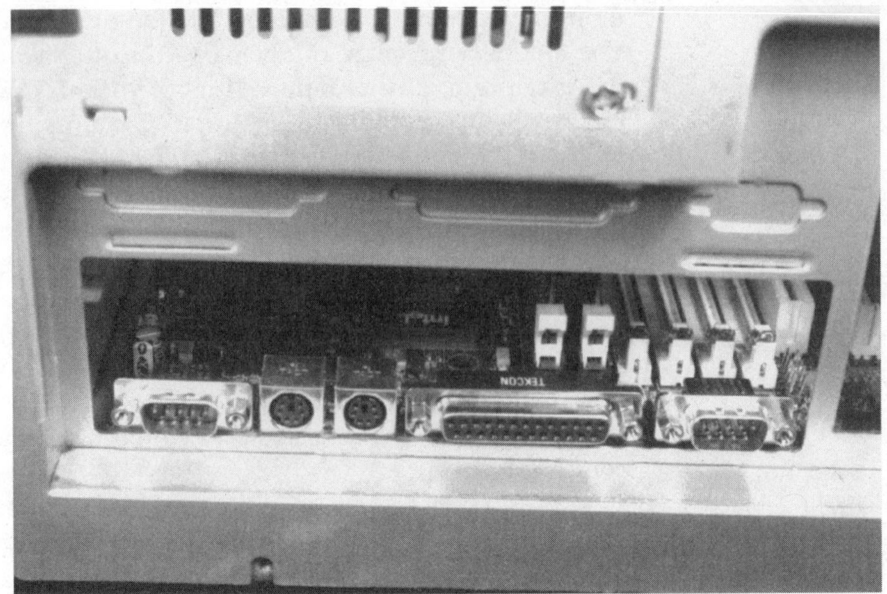

Figure 2-6
The rear of my Pentium II. The two round connectors are PS/2 connectors for the keyboard and mouse. Either connector can be used for keyboard or mouse.

Jumpers

At one time there weren't many CPUs, and there were very few differences in their frequencies. Each CPU had a separate motherboard. Some early motherboards actually came with the CPU soldered in place. Now, however, there are dozens and dozens of different CPUs, different frequencies, different voltages, and several other options. Rather than design a motherboard for each type of CPU, most motherboards are designed to accept many different CPUs.

To configure the motherboard to accept a certain CPU type, jumpers and switches are used. A *jumper* is a small shorting bar that connects upright pins on the motherboard. If the CPU requires a certain voltage, it can be selected by the jumper system. The frequency can also be selected by jumpers. There are dozens of ways to configure a motherboard by use of jumpers. In the photograph in Fig. 2-7, the pen points to some jumpers.

DRAM Bus Frequency

When a program is run, it is loaded into the system memory, usually Dynamic Random Access Memory (DRAM). In order to process the program, the CPU does a lot of communicating with the DRAM. It does this over a special bus. The bus frequency is usually a fraction of the internal frequency of the CPU. For instance, a 133-MHz Pentium will communicate over a 66-MHz bus, which is just half the frequency of the CPU. A 180-MHz Pentium CPU communicates at one-third of the frequency, or 60 MHz. Even the 333-MHz Pentium II will only be able to communicate with its DRAM at 66 MHz.

One advantage of the Cyrix 6x86MX is that it has the fastest memory bus available at this time, which can run at 75 MHz. It is expected that Intel will introduce a 100 MHz memory bus very soon. For more on memory bus frequencies, see Table 3-2 in the next chapter.

ROM BIOS

Before the plug-and-play era, when you installed a hard drive, you had to tell the system configuration setup what type it was. You had to input the number of heads, sectors, cylinders, and other information. This information had to be exact, or the hard disk would not operate. The

Figure 2-7 The pen points to some configuration jumpers.

manufacturers now put all this information in the circuitry of the hard drive. The BIOS in most newer systems can automatically detect this information and configure the system, but you might still want to input it yourself.

The configuration system also needs to be informed as to what kind of floppy drives you have. If you want to reset the time or date, you do it with the CMOS system setup. You should get some sort of documentation with your system or with a new motherboard that tells you what options you have when configuring your system through the BIOS.

You won't have to worry about Read-Only Memory (ROM). ROM is memory that cannot ordinarily be altered or changed. ROM comes with the motherboard. The principal use of ROM in PCs today is for the Basic Input/Output System (BIOS). The BIOS chip is second in importance only to the CPU. Every time you turn your computer on, the BIOS does a power-on self-test (POST). The BIOS checks all of the major components to make sure that they are operating properly. It also facilitates the transfer of data among peripherals. Many BIOS chips also have diagnostics and utilities built in. BIOS sounds a bit like BOSS, and that is its principal job.

The BIOS performs its important functions under the control of *firmware* programs. These programs are similar to software programs, except that the ROM is actually made up of hundreds of transistors that are programmed to perform certain functions.

Until recently, ROM BIOS programs were usually burned into electrically programmable read-only memory (EPROMs) chips. Special devices were used to input a software program into the ROM chip. As the program voltages passed through the chip, the transistors turned on and off to match the input program. When a normal transistor has voltage applied to it, it will turn on or off as long as the voltage is present. EPROM transistors are different from ordinary transistors. When the EPROM transistors are turned on or off, they remain in that condition.

Fairly large programs and text can be stored on a ROM chip. The ROM BIOS for an early XT (for *Extended Technology*) could be programmed onto a 64-Kb ROM chip. The ROM BIOS for newer systems need 512 Kb or more. All of the text in a large book can be stored in less than 512 Kb.

Companies that manufacture BIOS chips are constantly improving and adding new functionality to BIOS. Most motherboards now come with the BIOS in a *flash memory* chip. The flash memory chips can be upgraded by software from a floppy disk or even downloaded by modem through the telephone line. Many motherboard companies have flash updates available on their Web sites.

Some Basic Stuff about Motherboards

In early 1985, I spent $2500 for a 286 motherboard. This was in the days when each dollar was worth about three times what it is today. I still have it. If I tried, I couldn't even give it away; people would probably laugh. Figure 2-8 shows my old 286 alongside a modern socket-7 motherboard.

The 286 motherboard was bigger than my XT motherboard, so I had to buy a bigger case. However, I was able to use almost all of the components from my old XT. The old XT ran at a piddling 4.77 MHz. The new 286 ran at a "blazing" 6 MHz. The new Pentium II runs at 300 MHz. Today, a 300 MHz motherboard and CPU costs about one-third as much as my early 286. I cannot say it often enough, these are fantastic times we are living in.

Many Different Motherboard Options

Besides the CPU, the motherboard has several other chips, five to eight slot connectors for plug-in boards, sockets or slots for memory chips, and upright pins for printer, mouse, and disk-interface cable connections. The early AT (for *Advanced Technology*), or 286, from IBM was the "standard" size, about one-third larger than the "baby" AT size of almost all motherboards today. My old 286 motherboard has over 150 separate

Figure 2-8
My old 286 motherboard on the left, and a much smaller, modern, socket-7 motherboard on the right.

chips on it. Soon after the 286 came out, a few companies started integrating several chips into a single package. Most of the motherboards now have just a few separate chips. With fewer chips, there is less chance of having solder problems, less chance of stray capacitance, less distance between the components, and much greater reliability. It also costs much less to manufacture a board with fewer chips.

Even with 150 separate chips on the old 286 motherboard, I still had to buy a separate board for the mouse and printer, a separate controller board for the floppy drives, and one for the hard drives. Motherboards now have sets of upright pins for most of those functions. All that is needed are cables from components such as the disk drives, mouse, printer, and CD-ROM.

The set of pins for the floppy drives can control two floppy disk drives. They can be any two drives, such as 360 Kb, 1.2 Mb, 720 Kb, 1.44 Mb, or 2.88 Mb. The parallel-port connector is for the printer or other parallel device. It has Enhanced Parallel Port (EPP) and Expanded Capability Port (ECP). The parallel port has eight lines and transmits one bit of data at a time on each line. Ordinarily, a parallel port only transmits data out, but these newer ports can be used for output or input. The EPP and ECP ports can transfer data at up to 1 Mb/second. The ports can be used not only for printers, but for tape backup drives, external hard disks, CD-ROMs, small LANs, and several other new products.

The serial COM1 and COM2 ports have the 16550 Universal Asynchronous Receiver Transmitter (UART). This UART is much faster than the earlier 16450 chips. Remember that each single on or off, or zero and one, are single bits. It takes eight of these single bits to make one byte. Computers handle data in 8-bit bytes, or one word. Mice, modems, and several other peripherals, however, are serial devices; they handle data one bit at a time. For output, the serial ports change the standard 8-bit bytes into single bits for transmission. When receiving data, it changes the single bits back into 8-bit bytes. In addition to the COM ports, many of the newer motherboards now have a built-in SCSI port, a USB, sound chips, an AGP, an Ultra DMA/33 IDE, and more.

Expansion Slots

The motherboard usually lies on the floor of the chassis of a desktop case or on the right side of a tower case. Most motherboards have eight slots or connectors for plug-in boards. Almost all motherboards now have three or four Peripheral Component Interconnect (PCI) slots. In Fig. 2-8, the four white slots are for PCI devices. A few years ago, all the slots were the Industry Standard Architecture (ISA) slots.

There are still several ISA-type boards in use. These are for items that don't need the higher speed of the PCI, such as modems, sound cards, and SCSI interface cards.

We never seem to have enough slots. There are so many different boards to use in them. Because of this problem, some special motherboards have up to 12 slots. Of course, with this many slots, it has to be the large, standard-size board. This board would also require a special case to accommodate extra slots for rear panel connections.

Since many companies are designing motherboards with more built-in functions, there is less need for the expansion slots, especially the ISA slots.

Expansion Bus

The slot connectors have two rows of contacts that mate with both sides of the edge connector of the plug-in boards. Each contact in each slot is connected to the same contact on all of the other slots. This is called a *bus*. Since all slots have the same bus connections, a plug-in board may be inserted into any one of the slots.

A bus is more or less a generic term. It may be etched circuits on a board, some wires, or anything that provides a signal path. There are several different types of buses, including the input/output (I/O) bus, a memory bus, ISA bus, the PCI bus, and the PC-Card bus (formerly known as the Personal Computer Memory Card International Association, or PCMCIA, bus.)

Buses are also differentiated by their width or number of lines. The XT had an 8-bit bus, and the 286 had a 16-bit bus for accessing memory and for I/O. The 386 and 486 each had a 32-bit memory bus, but the ISA boards still operated their I/O bus at 16 bits and were limited to a speed of 8 MHz to 10 MHz. Any board or peripheral that wanted to communicate with the CPU had to do so over the 16 bit I/O bus at a fairly low speed.

To help overcome this problem, faster systems such as the PCI were designed. The PCI helps to overcome part of this bottleneck. Boards and components manufactured to the PCI specifications can operate at higher speeds. None of the ISA boards will fit in the PCI slots, however, so the manufacturers compromise and put both systems on the motherboards. Billions of dollars' worth of hardware is still available for the older ISA-type systems. Many businesses and individuals still have large investments in the ISA hardware.

In the early days, the bus to the RAM operated at the same speed or frequency as the CPU. The early XT operated at 4.77 MHz, and the first 286 increased that to 6 MHz. However, as the frequency of the CPUs were doubled, then tripled, the RAM bus just couldn't match the CPU. The Pentium II can run as fast as 300 MHz internally, but it cannot communicate with the RAM at this speed.

One other thing that contributes to the higher speed of today's computers is that they have moved up from the original 8-bit memory bus to a bus that is 64 bits wide. That is like moving from a one-lane country road to an eight-lane super freeway.

The CPU

Computers are named according to the CPU that is mounted on the motherboard. The 286 had an 80286 CPU, the 386 an 80386 CPU, the 486 an 80486 CPU. Intel tried, but could not, copyright the CPU numbers. So what should have been the 586 was called the Pentium, which they could copyright. (The name *Pentium* is derived from the Greek *pente*, meaning five.) Cyrix and AMD continued with the number scheme. Cyrix issued a 5x86 and AMD issued a K5. Cyrix now has a 6x86MX and AMD has a K6 that is equivalent to the Intel Pentium II. CPUs are so important that the next chapter will devoted to them.

Within the latest CPU designations, there are several variations. Variations of the Pentium CPU include the Pentium MMX, the Pentium Pro, and the Pentium II. The Pentium II is the MMX version of the Pentium Pro.

Motherboard Memory

A Pentium II, or clone equivalent, motherboard should have slots, or *provisions,* for the installation of at least 128 Mb of RAM onboard. Most motherboards will have four 72-contact slots for SIMMs and up to four 168-contact slots for DIMMs. Before you order memory, make sure that you get the right type for your motherboard. Get the right speed, the right memory size, and the right physical size. For more about memory, see Chapter 4.

Cache SRAM

When processing data, quite often, the same data is used over and over again. Having to traverse the bus to retrieve the data can slow the system down considerably. Most CPUs now have a small L1 cache built into the chip. The Pentium II has a large L2 cache in the same enclosure. The AMD and Cyrix have L2 caches on their motherboards.

Other Motherboard Chips

Besides the CPU and memory chips, there are several other chips and systems on the motherboard.

Keyboard BIOS

The keyboard is a small computer in itself and has its own special BIOS chip on the motherboard. It is usually a long 40-pin chip located near the keyboard connector. The chip marked Amikey is the keyboard BIOS in Fig. 2-9.

You might not see this chip on some of the newer motherboards because many of them now integrate it into a VLSI chip. A scan code or

Figure 2-9
The keyboard BIOS chip marked Amikey.

signal is sent to the BIOS when a key is pressed, and another signal is sent when the key is released. When two keys are pressed, it can detect which one was pressed first. It can also detect when a key is held down longer than normal and will start beeping at you. The last 20 keystrokes are stored in the keyboard memory and are continually flushed out and replaced by new keystrokes.

CMOS Battery

Every time you booted up an old PC and XT, you had to input the date and time. It is helpful if the time and date is correct because every time a file is created, it includes the time and date. This makes it very easy to determine which of two files is the later one. Several companies made fortunes selling plug-in boards with a battery-operated clock. When the 286 was introduced, it had a battery-operated clock built onto the motherboard. The early systems used batteries that lasted about two or three years.

The batteries supply power for a Complimentary Metal Oxide Semiconductor (CMOS) transistor circuit. Besides keeping the date and time when the power was turned off, these low-power transistors kept the system configuration. They also kept a record of the types and kinds of floppies, hard drives, monitors, and keyboards, that were used in the system. In some cases, they remembered what files or programs you were working on when the computer was turned off.

If your system does not keep accurate time, the battery might need to be replaced. The early IBM 286 ATs used a battery that cost over $30. Many of the clone builders designed a system that used low-cost alkaline batteries. Most systems used a tubular lithium battery that was soldered to the motherboard. This made it very difficult to replace. Modern systems use batteries that are easily replaced.

The batteries may last three years or more. One factor in the battery life is how often you use your computer. While the computer is on, it draws its power from the wall socket. When it is off, the CMOS transistors must be kept alive by the lithium battery. If a system consistently loses time, it could be that the battery needs to be replaced. If the battery goes completely dead, it will lose all of the CMOS configuration data. In the old days, if you lost your CMOS configuration data, it could be disastrous. Today, with plug-and-play, it is not much of a big deal.

If you replace the battery, make sure that you install the new one the same way. Make a diagram showing the + and – ends before you remove the battery. It is very easy to forget how a battery or other chip was installed. Some of the batteries on the newer motherboards might be in a square chip like device that can be plugged into a socket. Many of the new motherboards use a round lithium battery such as that shown in Fig. 2-1 just below the CPU fan. They are inexpensive and very easy to replace.

Timing

A computer depends on precise timing. Several of the chips on a motherboard control the frequency and timing circuits. The timing is so critical that there are usually one or more crystals on the motherboard that oscillate at a precise frequency to control the timing circuits. The crystals are usually in a small, oblong, shiny can. In Fig. 2-9, the pen points to a crystal oscillator can.

Internal Frequency vs. External Frequency

Strange things happen when a circuit operates at high frequencies. In a low-frequency circuit, the effect of stray capacitance and inductance can usually be ignored. In high-frequency circuits, it becomes a very big factor, and the higher the frequency, the more of a problem it becomes. It might be such a problem that a circuit will not operate at all. It is very difficult and costly to devise high-frequency circuits. The distance between the components might also be problem in high-frequency circuits. Even if the distance is only a half-inch or so between components, at a high frequency, a large portion of the signal can be lost.

The distance between transistors inside the CPU is very small. The capacitive and inductive effects are also small, so the frequency inside the CPU can be much faster than that in the external circuits.

DMA

The direct memory access (DMA) system allows some processing to take place without having to bother the CPU. For instance, the disk drives can exchange data directly with the RAM without having to go through the CPU. Many of the newer motherboards are designed with an Ultra DMA/33 IDE hard drive protocol. This allows the hard drive to transfer data at up to 33 Mb/second.

IRQ

The interrupt request (IRQ) system is a very important part of the computer. It can cause the system to interrupt whatever it is doing and take care of the request. Without the interrupts, nothing would get done. Even if the computer is doing nothing, it must be interrupted and told to perform a task.

There are 16 IRQs, numbered from 0 to 15. Each I/O device on the bus is given a unique IRQ number. Software can also perform interrupt requests. There is a priority system, and some interrupts take precedence over others. Sixteen IRQs might seem like a large number, but it isn't nearly enough. Several of the interrupts are reserved or used by the system so that they are not available. It would have been wonderful if the Pentium had provided about twice as many, but no such luck.

If you want to see how your system is using IRQs, in Windows 95, double-click My Computer, then Control Panel, System, then click the Device Manager tab, highlight Computer, and click the Properties button. The Control Panel will not only let you look at your IRQs, it will tell you about most of the other important elements in your computer. Here is how the 16 IRQs might be used:

TABLE 2-1 IRQ Assignments

IRQ	Address	Description	Detected
0	OCO8:0103	Timer Click	Yes
1	OCO8:0113	Keyboard	Yes
2	OA7D:OO57	Second 8259A	Yes
3	E939:1FAD	COM2: COM4	COM2
4	OA7D:0087	COM1: COM3	COM1
5	OA7D:OO9F	LPT2:	No
6	OA7D:OOB7	Floppy Disk	Yes
7	OO7O:O6F4	LPT1:	Yes
8	OA7D:OO52	Real-Time Clock	Yes
9	FOOO:EED3	Redirected IRQ2	Yes
13	FOOO:EEDC	Math Coprocessor	Yes
14	OA7D:O117	Fixed Disk	Yes

As you can see, out of the 16 IRQs, 10, 11, 12, and 15 are not shown. Windows shows those that are in use, but does not show those that are available. IRQ 5 is for LPT2, but since I don't have a second printer attached, it could be used for other devices such as a mouse, sound board, or network card.

UARTs and Serial Ports

Mice, modems, UPSs, game controllers, sound controllers, fax boards, some printers, plotters, and many other devices communicate with the computer through a serial port. They operate with serial data. The data must be furnished over a single line with one bit following another. The computer operates with parallel data. It takes eight bits to make a byte, so for eight bits, it will have eight lines; for 16 bits, 16 lines. Obviously, this data cannot be sent out over a modem or any other serial device. The serial ports receive these 8-bit bytes, then convert them to single bits so that they can be transmitted over the telephone lines or wherever. When receiving data from an outside source, it must be converted back to 8-bit form. The conversion is done with a special Universal Asynchronous Receiver Transmitter (UART) chip.

Ordinarily, only two serial ports can be used, and each requires a dedicated IRQ. COM1 uses IRQ4, COM2 uses IRQ3. You might have four or more different serial devices that you would like to attach to your computer. It is possible to add two more virtual ports, COM3 and COM4, but they must share the COM1 and COM2 IRQ lines; COM3 uses IRQ4 and COM4 uses IRQ3. Some devices are rather selfish and don't like to share. You need special software in order to use COM3 and COM4.

The COM ports also have specific addresses in memory. COM1 uses 3F8h, COM2 uses 2F8h, COM3 uses 3E8h, and COM4 uses 2E8h. Life would be a whole lot simpler if only we had four or more dedicated IRQ lines for the COM ports. Of course, you would also need two more UART chips for the additional ports.

Many of the problems encountered in adding or upgrading a system are due to the serial ports and IRQs. If a device's IRQ or memory address conflicts with another one, neither device will work. (Refer to Table 2-1 to see how IRQs are assigned.) Several programs can help you determine which ports are being used. One of the better ones is a low-cost shareware program called Port Finder. It is available from James McDaniel of mcTRONic Systems at 713-462-7687.

Architecture

The architecture of the computer refers to the overall design and the components it uses. The architecture is also concerned with the type of bus that is used. The bus is the internal pathways over which data is sent from one part of the computer to another. The 8-bit systems use 8-bit parallel paths, 16 use 16, 32 use 32, and 64 use 64. The flow of data over a bus is often compared to the flow of traffic on a highway. If there are only two lanes, the flow of traffic may be limited. Adding more lanes can vastly improve the flow of traffic.

ISA

ISA was once known as the IBM-compatible standard. However, IBM more or less abandoned the standard when they introduced their Micro Channel Architecture (MCA) in 1987. By then, there were far more IBM-compatible clone PCs in existence than PCs manufactured by IBM. Since IBM was now directing most of its efforts toward the MCA, the clone makers took over the standard.

An ISA computer can be anything from the oldest and slowest XT up to the newest and fastest Pentium. The old XT used an 8-bit. When the 286 was being developed by IBM, it became apparent that an 8-bus bit was too slow and was clearly inadequate, so they devised a 16-bit slot connector by adding a second 36-contact connector in front of the original 62-contact connector. This was a brilliant innovation. In Chapter 5, Fig. 5-7 shows an 8-bit ISA board on the bottom and a 16-bit ISA board on the top.

Compatibility

About $5 billion worth of 8-bit hardware was in existence when IBM introduced their 16-bit 286. With the 16-bit connector, however, either an 8-bit or 16-bit board could be used in a 16-bit system. The industry loved it because it did not make their present investment in plug-in boards obsolete.

This downward compatibility still exists, even with the fastest and most powerful Pentium II. There is a price to pay for compatibility, however. The CPU operates over a special memory bus to communicate with RAM at the CPU's rated frequency. The 386 and 486 are 32-bit systems;

the Pentium is 64 bits. The 386 and 486 ISA systems communicate with the system RAM over a 32-bit bus back and forth to memory, but the system can only communicate with its plug-in boards and peripherals over a 16-bit bus. Even though the 486 may operate at 66 MHz, to be able to run all previous software and hardware, the ISA I/O bus is limited to a speed of about 8 MHz and an I/O bus width of 16 parallel lines.

The Intel PCI Bus

The Intel PCI bus has become the standard on all new motherboards. In the past, it was sometimes very frustrating when adding a plug-in board. Often, you had to set several dip switches or jumpers so that it did not conflict with the assigned IRQs, serial and parallel ports, and DMA channels of other plug-in boards. Almost all boards and peripherals are now made to the plug-and-play specification. While the old ISA bus for I/O operates at about 8 MHz, the PCI bus can operate at 33 MHz or more.

PC-Card Bus

Many personal and desktop computers now have a PC-Card slot. PC-Card was formerly known as PCMCIA (Personal Computer Memory Card International Association). The PCMCIA specification was originally developed for adding memory to laptop and notebook computers, using credit-card-size memory cards. You might wonder why anyone would want a desktop computer with a PC-Card slot. The answer is because there are now many devices and components besides memory that can be plugged into this slot. Dozens more new devices and components are being developed every day. For example, Adaptec has a SlimSCSI adapter that can be used with several SCSI devices.

A PC-Card slot can be more useful than an extra slot on the motherboard. In order to change a board on the motherboard, you have to shut everything down, remove the cover, and then install the new board. On a PC-Card slot, if you want to use a modem, you just plug it in. You don't even have to shut off the power. After you have finished with the modem or fax, you can plug in an Ethernet card, a hard disk, a sound card, an SCSI interface, or any of the other PC-Card devices that are available. A PC-Card slot can add a vast amount of utility and expansion capabilities to a computer.

Built-in Goodies

It is amazing how soon you can fill up all of the available slots on the motherboard. One way to get around having to use plug-in boards is to have many of the functions built in on the motherboard. At one time, there were very few built-in functions. Most motherboards now have several built-in functions and utilities. One of the arguments against built-in functions is that the functions might become obsolete or defective. If necessary, however, the onboard functions can usually be disabled and replaced with a plug-in board. Here are some of the things that may be built in:

- IDE Interface—Many motherboards now have the IDE interface for hard disks and a floppy disk controller built in on the motherboard. They have rows of pins protruding from the motherboard that accept the ribbon cables from the drives.
- SCSI Interface—Many Macintosh models have built-in SCSI interfaces. That is one of the reasons for their popularity. The PC industry has been lax in not following suit. SCSI is something that is essential, not only for multimedia, but for many PC applications. A few motherboard manufacturers are now including a built-in SCSI interface.
- Universal Serial Bus—The USB is being integrated on most newer high-end motherboards.

Advantages of Built-In Utilities

It can be great to have so many utilities built into the motherboard. All computers need these utilities. This integration reduces, or eliminates in some cases, the need for cables. Cables can be the source for many problems. Integration also reduces problems by reducing the number of solder joints and components. The more solder joints and components there are, the more chance for errors and failures.

Disadvantages of Built-Ins

The disadvantages of built-ins are that if one of the utilities fail, the entire motherboard might have to be replaced. The motherboard is usually the most expensive component in the system. If the utilities are on a plug-in board, and it fails, it is fairly inexpensive to replace the single board. Most systems today that have built-in utilities also have jumpers or switches that allow you to disable the utilities, in case of failure, so that a board can be installed.

The biggest disadvantage of these proprietary systems is that technology does not stand still. The clone machines can be upgraded in thousands of ways with thousands of different components. If you have one of the proprietary systems, however, you might not be able to do much to upgrade other than adding a few things such as more memory or larger disk drives.

USB Peripherals

Here is some information about the USB from the Intel Web site:

> **What it is**
>
> USB will allow users to connect up to 127 different peripherals all at once, using a single standard connector type. There will be no more guesswork about which serial or parallel port to choose, and nontechnical PC users will be able to say good-bye to DIP switches, jumpers, IRQ settings, DMA channels, and I/O addresses. USB features hot insertion and removal, so users will be able to attach and detach peripherals anytime, without powering down their system. It will have a 12Mb/s data rate.
>
> In fact, USB hardware solutions from Intel are so flexible, they will make it easy to connect with the fast-growing world of new and existing digital peripherals, computer telephony integration (CTI) applications and popular multiuser games. In addition, USB enjoys widespread support from the industry's leading suppliers of PCs, peripherals, and software. Intel supports USB with PCI chipsets and the industry's first single-chip USB peripheral USB Controller. For those developing and marketing products for PCs, it's time to make your own connection with USB now.
>
> USB is an open and royalty-free specification with broad industry support, developed by Compaq, Digital Equipment, IBM, Intel, Microsoft, NEC, and Northern Telecom.
>
> The USB Implementers Forum consists of more than 250 semiconductor, computer, peripheral and software companies, providing marketing and technical support to help accelerate USB product development.
>
> For those people who have bought machines that do not have the USB built-in port, USB Host Adapter PCI boards will be available from several manufacturers.

Several peripherals are being developed for the USB. The USB can handle up to 127 different devices, so things like a monitor, keyboard, mouse, scanner, and printer can all be attached to it. Instead of having several cables that connect to the motherboard, the USB will be the only one necessary.

Of course, the peripherals must be manufactured to the USB specifications. You will still need adapter and plug-in boards, but they will also have to be designed and manufactured to the USB specifications. Windows 98 will be needed to run most of the USB devices.

Printer Port

There are very few computers that are not tied to a printer of some sort. There are still a few printers that use the serial port, but most printers today use one of the two parallel ports, LPT1 or LPT2. Usually, the motherboard will come with cables for the printer and COM ports. The short printer and COM-port cables have connectors that plug into the upright pins on the motherboard. The other end of the cables are usually attached to a bracket with a connector for external connections.

Game Ports

Many of the multifunction boards sold today have a game port for the joysticks used with many popular games. With the increased interest and popularity of multimedia, the game port has become almost mandatory. The game port connector may also be a set of upright pins on the motherboard. A short cable with a connector may be attached to the motherboard pins. The other end of the short connector may be attached to a bracket and connector for external connection.

Monitor Adapter

Every computer needs a board or adapter to drive the monitor. Some motherboards have had built-in monitor adapters for some time. They are great for many applications. The main problem is that the developers keep making the adapters faster, with better resolution, true color, and more and more complexity. If your adapter is built in, then you are stuck with whatever resolution or functions that it provides. Most of the motherboards with built-in functions have jumpers or switches that allow you to disable those functions so that a board can be plugged in to take over from the built-in functions.

Benchmarks

Benchmarks are tests designed to give a standard measure of performance that can be used to predict how well and how fast a computer will run actual applications. Many factors affect the outcome of a benchmark test, including the computer's CPU, architecture, design, and system software. There are several different benchmarks. Some are designed to test only a specific portion of a system.

Deciding What to Buy

One of the first things that you will have to decide is which motherboard you want. Or, if you are like me, you will have to decide which one you want at a price you can afford.

I subscribe to several computer magazines. Most of them have articles and reviews of software and hardware, and, of course, lots of ads from stores that sell by mail. The ads give me a fairly good idea of the prices so that I know what I can afford. Mail-order might be one of the better ways to purchase your parts, especially if you don't live near a large city.

Usually, the larger cities have lots of computer stores. The San Francisco Bay area and the Los Angeles area have hundreds. There are also computer swap meets every weekend. If I need something, I go to one of the swap meets and compare the prices at the various booths. I often take a pad along, write the prices down, then go back, and make the best deal that I can. Sometimes, you can haggle with the vendors for a better price, especially if it is near closing time.

Replacing a Motherboard

It is very easy to pull out a motherboard and install a Pentium. Basically, it is the same whether it is an XT, 286, 386, 486, or Pentium. Step-by-step instructions and photographs for doing this are in Chapter 11. Some of the Cyrix 5x86 and AMD 586 motherboards are very reasonable. This would be one of the more cost-effective upgrades.

A new Pentium motherboard will give you all of the advantages of a new Pentium, but will be much less expensive than buying a completely new system. The Pentium allows graphics and CAD programs to run much faster. It also allows full-screen motion pictures to run. At one time, the price of the Pentium CPU chip was $750 each for 1000-lot orders. The motherboard with CPU sold for $1100 to $2000. Today, you can buy a Pentium-class motherboard with an AMD 586 or Cyrix 5x86 for less than $100—less than what a pair of modern tennis shoes costs. No one should be without a Pentium.

CHAPTER 3

The CPU

There are several highly integrated chips on the motherboard, but the most important one is the Central Processing Unit (CPU). It is the brains of the computer. It is so important that the whole computer system is named for the CPU that is installed on the motherboard.

This chapter reviews the CPUs that you will want to look at for building your new machine. There are three major CPU manufacturers that you are probably familiar with: Intel, American Micro Devices (AMD), and Cyrix. Cyrix is now a part of National Semiconductor, which should give them a bit more clout. A fourth company, the IDT Corporation, has recently entered the CPU market with the WinChip C6. Each of these companies' CPUs have some advantages. Of course, Intel is the original, and foremost, CPU maker in the world. Last year, it sold over $20 billion worth of chips. In order to compete, the clone makers have had to offer CPUs that were compatible with the Intel, as fast and powerful, and less expensive.

Within the latest CPU designations, there are several variations. There are variations of the Pentium CPUs, the Pentium MMX, the Pentium Pro, and the Pentium II. The Pentium II is the MMX version of the Pentium Pro. The cloners also have several CPU variations, such as the Cyrix 5x86, the 6x86, and 6x86MX, and the AMD 586 and K6. The Cyrix 5x86 and AMD 586 are equivalent to the Intel Pentium. The Cyrix 6x86 is equivalent to the Pentium Pro. The Cyrix 6x86MX and the AMD K6 are equivalent to the Intel Pentium II.

Eventually, MMX technology will be a valuable and excellent feature. At the present time, except for games, there isn't too much software available to take advantage of it.

PR Hype

Intel, AMD, and Cyrix all have Web sites with all the latest information about their products. I am sure that you are aware that you must consider the source of the information there. In some cases, the truth might be stretched a bit and the facts colored somewhat. With this in mind, the Web sites are still an excellent information resource.

The following articles are taken from the Web sites as noted. Please note also that the sites are constantly updated, so some of the information will have changed by the time you read this.

Intel Pentium II

The following is an article from Intel about the Pentium II:

Intel's highest performance processor combines the power of the Pentium Pro processor with the capabilities of MMX technology. At 266MHz, the Pentium II processor delivers a 1.6x to over 2x performance boost compared to the 200 MHz Pentium processor on industry standard processor benchmarks and over twice the performance on multimedia benchmarks. It takes advantage of the same high-performance Dual Independent Bus architecture used in the Pentium Pro processor for high bandwidth and performance.

Single Edge Contact (S.E.C.) cartridge packaging technology delivers high performance processing and bus technology to mainstream systems. It is optimized for 32-bit applications running on advanced operating systems. 32 KByte (16K/16K) nonblocking level one cache. 512 KByte unified, nonblocking level two cache. Enables systems which are scalable up to two processors and 64 GByte of physical memory.

Data integrity and reliability features include system bus ECC, Fault Analysis, Recovery, and Functional Redundancy Checking.

Highlights

The Pentium II processor integrates the best attributes of Intel's processors, the Dynamic Execution performance of the Pentium processor plus the capabilities of MMX technology, bringing a new level of performance to PC buyers. The Pentium II processor is easily scalable to two microprocessors in a multiprocessor system. The Pentium II processor extends the power of the Pentium Pro processor with performance headroom for business media, communication, and Internet capabilities. Software designed for Intel's MMX technology will unleash full-screen, full-motion video, enhanced color, realistic graphics and other multimedia enhancements. Systems based on Pentium II processors also include the latest features to simplify system management and lower the total cost of ownership for large and small business environments.

Product Description

The Intel Pentium II processor family includes 233, 266 MHz versions for desktops, workstations, and servers, and a 300 MHz version especially for workstations. All are binary compatible with previous generation Intel Architecture processors. Pentium II processors provide the best performance available for applications running on advanced operating systems such as Windows 95, Windows NT, and UNIX.

The Pentium II processor core has 7.5 M transistors and is based on Intel's enhanced 0.35 micron CMOS process. The processor core is provided in Single Edge Contact cartridge package enabling ease of design and a flexible motherboard architecture.

The Pentium II processor family's significant performance improvement over previous Intel Architecture processors is based on the seamless combination of Pentium Pro processor technology and Intel's MMX media enhancement technology.

The result is higher software performance plus headroom for applications that take advantage of Intel's MMX technology.

Pentium Pro Processor's Dynamic Execution Technology

Multiple branch prediction: predicts the flow of the program through several branches, accelerating the flow of work to the processor.

Dataflow analysis: creates an optimized reordered schedule of instructions by analyzing data dependencies between instructions.

Speculative execution: carries out instructions speculatively, based on this optimized schedule, keeping the processor's Superscalar execution units busy and boosting overall performance.

Intel's MMX Media Enhancement Technology

Intel's MMX technology includes new instructions and data types that allow applications to achieve a new level of performance. Intel's MMX technology is designed as a set of basic, general purpose integer instructions that can be easily applied to the needs of a wide diversity of multimedia and communications applications. The highlights of the technology are:

- Single Instruction, Multiple Data (SIMD) technique
- 57 new instructions
- Eight 64-bit wide MMX technology registers
- Four new data types

Other Features

High-performance Dual Independent Bus architecture (system bus cache bus) for high bandwidth, performance, and scalability with future system technologies.

The system bus supports multiple outstanding transactions to increase bandwidth availability. It also provides "glueless" support for up to two processors. This enables low-cost, 2-way symmetric multiprocessing, providing a significant performance boost for multitasking operating systems and multithreaded applications.

A 512KByte unified nonblocking level two cache, which improves performance by reducing the average memory access time and providing fast access to recently used instructions and data. The performance is enhanced through a dedicated 64-bit cache bus. The level two cache scales with the processor core frequency. With the core at 266 MHz, the cache bus runs at 133 MHz, twice the speed of a Pentium processor's cache access. Level two cache data bus ECC is planned for a future version of the Pentium II processor family. Also incorporates separate 16K instruction and 16K data level one caches, each twice the size of the Pentium Pro processor's caches.

A pipelined Floating-Point Unit (FPU) for supporting the 32-bit and 64-bit formats specified in IEEE standard 754, as well as an 80-bit format. It is capable of sustaining over 300 Million Floating Point Instructions Per Second (MFLOPS) at 300 MHz.

Parity-protected address/request and response system bus signals with a retry mechanism for high data integrity and reliability.

Error Correction Code (ECC) allowing for correction of single bit data errors and detection of 2-bit errors on the system bus.

The Pentium II processor also includes several features used for testing and performance monitoring. These features include:

Built-in Self Test (BIST), providing single stuck-at fault coverage of the microcode and large logic arrays, as well as testing of the instruction cache, data cache, Translation Lookaside Buffers (TLBs) and ROMs. IEEE 1149.1 Standard Test Access Port and Boundary Scan mechanism, allowing testing of the Pentium II processor and system connections through a standard interface.

Internal performance counters for performance monitoring and event counting.

Figure 3-1 shows an Intel Pentium II CPU. For more Intel literature, call 800-548-4722 or visit their Web site at www.intel.com.

AMD-K6 MMX Enhanced Processor

The following is from the Advanced Micro Devices (AMD) Web site at www.amd.com. AMD can also be reached at 408-732-2400.

Experience the Performance...

Introducing the sixth-generation AMD-K6™ MMX™ Enhanced Processor. A technological breakthrough designed to advance personal computing to higher levels of performance and affordability.

Leading-Edge Performance

When it comes to performance, the AMD-K6 MMX enhanced processor puts you on a fast track, delivering leading-edge, sixth-generation performance on both the Microsoft Windows NT and Windows 95 operating systems competitive with the Pentium II processor.

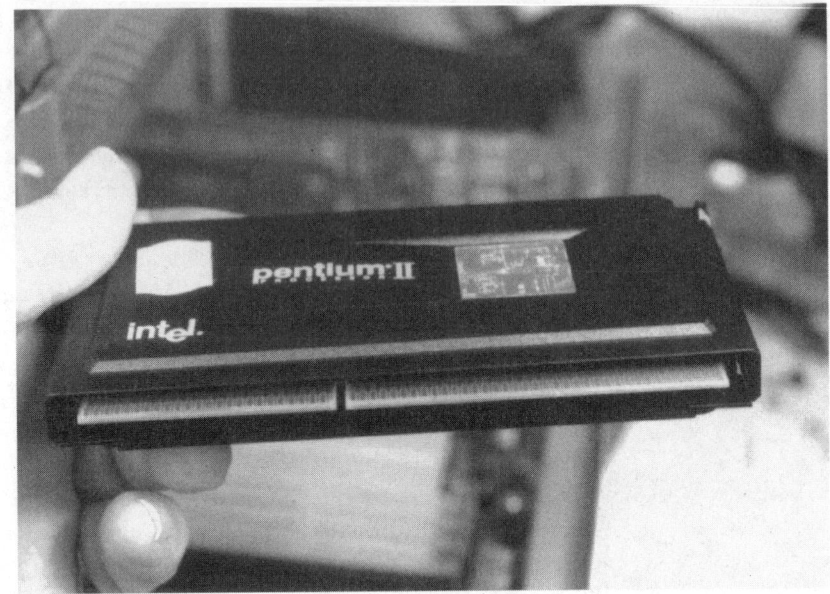

Figure 3-1
An Intel Pentium II CPU mounted on a single edge board.

Easy to Use

AMD designed the AMD-K6 processor to fit the low-cost, high-volume Socket 7 infrastructure. The result: fast time to market and an easier upgrade path to future members of the high-performance AMD-K6 family.

More Advanced

The AMD-K6 processor is the most advanced Windows-compatible processor available. The AMD-K6 is based on AMD's six-issue RISC86. superscalar microarchitecture—a state-of-the-art design that's superior to Pentium II. The AMD-K6 also executes high-performance, industry-standard MMX™ instructions to accelerate emerging multimedia applications.

Affordable

The AMD-K6 processor makes sixth-generation personal computing more affordable for the majority of PC users. With the AMD-K6, you get leading-edge Windows performance at mainstream prices.

Leading-Edge Performance

The superior engine for running Windows—The AMD-K6 MMX™ enhanced processor is the best Windows-compatible processor available for mainstream computing. In the existing 16-bit software environment, as well as complex 32-bit operating systems and applications, the AMD-K6 is competitive with the Pentium II processor. The fact that the AMD-K6 performs equally well running either 16-bit or 32-bit code makes it the superior engine for running both the Windows 95 and Windows NT™ operating systems. The AMD-K6 runs all Windows versions at top speed—without performance trade-offs. You get superior, "no-compromise" Windows performance. And you also get MMX™ capability, for a richer multimedia experience, enabling the latest multimedia software—from audio to video to 3D graphics—to run faster on your PC.

More Advanced

Superior, six-issue RISC86 microarchitecture...The key to the AMD-K6 processor's leading-edge performance is its advanced, six-issue RISC86 superscalar microarchitecture—superior in design to Pentium. II. The RISC86 microarchitecture's decoupled decode/execution superscalar design provides enhanced sixth-generation performance and full x86 binary software compatibility. AMD's innovative RISC86 microarchitecture implements the x86 instruction set by internally decoding x86 instructions into RISC86 operations that support the x86 instruction set while adhering to RISC performance principles. Rather than directly executing complex x86 instructions, the AMD-K6 executes the simpler, fixed-length RISC86 opcodes, while maintaining instruction coding efficiencies found in x86 software programs.

To ensure leading-edge performance, the AMD-K6 features the industry's largest level-one (L1) caches (32-Kbyte data cache and 32-Kbyte instruction cache with predecode data), a powerful floating-point unit, and high-performance, industry-standard MMX™ instructions.

State-of-the-art design techniques include multiple x86 instruction decode, single-clock internal RISC operations, out-of-order execution, data forwarding, speculative execution, and register renaming. In addition, the processor supports the industry's most advanced branch prediction logic by implementing an 8,192-entry branch history table, the industry's only branch target cache, and a return address stack, which combine to deliver a prediction rate better than 95 percent. The AMD-K6 processor also contains parallel decoders, a centralized operation scheduler, and seven execution units that enable superscalar operation of x86 instructions—all packed into a highly efficient six-stage pipeline.

The AMD-K6 processor is proof that a next-generation design can make an enormous difference to PC users who want topnotch performance—the kind of performance driven by the superior RISC86 microarchitecture.

Easy Upgrades

Socket 7 compatibility for easier upgrades and fast time to market.

AMD designed the AMD-K6 processor to be Socket 7 compatible for a very good reason: to deliver sixth-generation performance within the industry's most cost-effective, widely used PC infrastructure (motherboards, chipsets, and BIOS). By working within the Socket 7 environment, PC manufacturers and resellers can leverage high-volume, low-cost system designs and mature infrastructure.

The result: fast time to market, lower system costs, and an easy upgrade path to even more powerful AMD-K6 processors in the near future.

Low Cost

The most cost-effective sixth-generation processor solution.

The AMD-K6 processor is the industry's most affordable sixth-generation solution. While the processor's Socket 7 compatibility enhances cost savings at the system level, the AMD-K6 itself is highly affordable relative to other sixth-generation processors. This affordability is due in part to the processor's compact die size (162 mm2) and the use of space-saving C4 flip-chip interconnection technology. It all adds up to lower system costs and something that all PC users want—more affordable PC solutions.

"AMD is poised...to become the most significant alternate to Intel in 1997. At 8.8 million transistors, AMD's K6 is the most complex of the next-generation designs...With a compact, high-performance design, lots of fab capacity, strong sales and support, and multiple design teams, AMD should be in a strong position." (Michael Slater, *Microprocessor Report*)

AMD's Advanced Manufacturing and Process Technology

The 8.8-million-transistor AMD-K6 processor is manufactured in AMD's state-of-the-art Fab 25 using advanced 0.35-micron, five-layer-metal silicon process technology. The AMD-K6 also uses innovative C4 flip-chip technology, which enhances the performance, reliability, and affordability of state-of-the-art processors.

AMD continues to invest in submicron process technology and production capacity not only at Fab 25 but also at AMD's new Fab 30 facility under construction in Dresden, Germany. AMD's migration path to 0.25-micron process technology and beyond will enable even higher performance AMD-K6 solutions in the future. In short, AMD's road map will take you where you need to be—at the leading edge of PC performance.

Windows-compatible by design

AMD—the world's second largest supplier of Windows-compatible PC processors—has delivered more than 50 million Windows-compatible CPUs in the last five years. The AMD-K6 processor is fully compatible with the Windows 95, Windows NT, and Windows 3.x operating systems. Not to mention other leading OSs, including MS-DOS, Novell NetWare, OS/2 Warp, and Unix, as well as 60,000 other software packages and the latest multimedia applications.

The AMD-K6 MMXTM enhanced processor—The Smart Choice

When you choose the AMD-K6 processor, you're choosing a fast, more advanced, easy to use, and more affordable solution. The AMD-K6

MMXTM enhanced processor: It's the superior engine for Windows computing.

Jerry Sanders, CEO of AMD, has said that AMD will have a 266-Mhz CPU. In the first half of 1998, they expect to introduce the AMD-K6 3d MMx enhanced processor with clock speeds of 300 MHz, and soon after up to 350 MHz. In the second half of 1998, he promised that this CPU would run at 400 MHz. These CPUs will be socket-7 compatible. It has been rumored, however, that AMD is working on a slot-1 clone of the Intel Pentium II slot 1. The competition can only benefit us, the end users.

Figure 3-2 shows an AMD K6 in socket 7.

Cyrix 6x86MX Processor

The following is from Cyrix. Cyrix can be reached on the Web at www.idt.com, by telephone at 800-345-7015, or by fax at 408-492-8674.

Processor Brief

The 6x86MX processor is an MMX enhanced CPU offering the highest level of Windows 95 performance available for mainstream desktop systems. The 6x86MX processor is compatible with MMX technology to run the latest MMX games and multimedia software. With its enhanced memory management unit, a 64-KByte internal cache, and

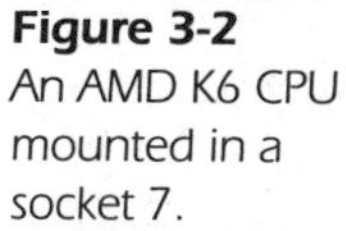

Figure 3-2
An AMD K6 CPU mounted in a socket 7.

other advanced architectural features, the 6x86MX processor achieves higher performance and offers better value than competitive processors.

Architectural Overview

The 6x86MX processor offers significant enhancements over the 6x86 processor. These enhancements enable the 6x86MX processor to achieve higher performance at any given clock speed.

The 6x86MX design quadruples the internal cache size to 64-KBytes, triples the TLB size, and increases the frequency scalability to 200 MHz and beyond, relative to the 6x86 processor. Additionally, it features 57 new MMX instructions that speed up the processing of certain computing-intensive loops found in multimedia and communication applications. The 6x86MX processor also contains a scratchpad RAM feature, supports performance monitoring and allows caching of both SMI code and SMI data. It delivers optimum 16-bit and 32-bit performance while running Windows 95, Windows NT, OS/2, DOS, UNIX, and other operating systems.

The 6x86MX processor features a superpipelined architecture that increases the number of pipeline stages to reduce timing constraints and increase frequency scalability. Advanced architectural techniques include register renaming, out-of-order completion, data dependency removal, branch prediction and speculative execution. These design innovations eliminate many data dependencies and resource conflicts to achieve higher performance when executing both 16-bit and 32-bit software.

6x86MX Processor Performance Benchmarks

The "PR" Means Performance

The high-performance you get with Cyrix processors doesn't come from megahertz alone—it comes from a superior architectural design. That's why the megahertz (MHz) speed doesn't tell the whole performance story.

Cyrix uses a performance rating (P-Rating) to categorize our processors. The P-Rating (e.g., PR233) gives you the performance class of a Cyrix processor compared to a Pentium processor. With the Cyrix P-Rating, you know you're getting the performance you want and the test results prove it. So check the Cyrix P-Rating. You can be sure you're getting the highest performance in the Cyrix processor class you choose.

TABLE 3-1 Architectural Comparison

Architectural Features	6x86MX	6x86	Pentium MMX	Pentium II
MMX Instruction Set	X		X	X
Superscalar	X	X	X	X
Superpipelined	X	X		X

Architectural Features	6x86MX	6x86	Pentium MMX	Pentium II
Register Renaming	X	X		X
Data Dependency Removal	X	X	X	
Multibranch Prediction	X	X		X
Speculative Execution	X	X		X
Out-of-Order Completion	X	X		X
80-Bit Floating Point	X	X		X
Primary Cache	64K	16K	16+16K	16+16K

The Cyrix 6x86MX is the same size as the AMD K6. Refer back to Fig. 2-1.

IDT WinChip C6 Processor

The following is from Integrated Device Technology, Inc. and Centaur Technology, Inc.

The IDT WinChip C6 is the first microprocessor from Centaur Technology Inc., a subsidiary of Integrated Device Technology, Inc. (IDT). Using a unique design approach, the IDT WinChip C6 delivers competitive performance, lower cost, and lower power dissipation than offerings from other x86 microprocessor suppliers. This combination of features is expected to shift the price/performance paradigm in the personal computer industry and will allow computer manufacturers to deliver higher value to the end customer. IDT WinChip C6 is targeted at the sub-$1,000 desktop and sub-$2,000 notebook product categories. The IDT WinChip C6 includes MMX compatible instructions and is offered in processor speeds of 180 MHz and 200 MHz, with faster speeds to come.

Architecture

The IDT WinChip C6 uses a unique design concept which goes back to the principles of RISC (Reduced Instruction Set Computing) architecture. This unique design approach focuses on optimizing the microprocessor for highly used simple instructions and improving the overall clock frequency. Memory performance is further improved by using large on-chip caches and sophisticated cache and translation look aside (TLB) algorithms to reduce bus utilization. In addition, the IDT WinChip C6 processor is highly optimized for small physical size, which results in lower manufacturing costs as well as lower power consumption.

Performance

The IDT WinChip C6 offers competitive performance to Pentium with MMX Technology, AMD-K6, and Cyrix 6x86MX microprocessors running Windows 95 business applications.

Suggested System

Holco Shuttle 565 Motherboard: (Socket 7)

Intel 430 TX Chipset

Award BIOS 4.5x

512 KB Level 1 Cache

32MB EDO DRAM 60 ns

Diamond 3D 2000 Graphics (S3 Virge) with 2 MB EDO DRAM driver

Western Digital Caviar 1.6 GB IDE hard disk

Power Dissipation

IDT WinChip C6 power dissipation is much lower than other Pentium-class processors with MMX Technology, making it suitable for mobile systems and the rapidly growing sub-$1,000 PC product category.

The WinChip C6 has a die size of only 88 square mm or about .4 inches square. The smaller die area means lower production cost, lower power consumption and less heat dissipation. It is important to note that the IDT WinChip C6 power dissipation advantage is achieved while operating at 3.3 or 3.52 volts where other microprocessors require dual voltage operation. Thus, the IDT WinChip C6 is expected to offer even lower power dissipation in the future with dual voltage support.

Compatibility

Centaur Technology has extensively tested the IDT WinChip C6 processor with x86 operating systems such as DOS, Windows 3.1, Windows 95, Windows NT, OS/2, Linux and a large number of software applications. In addition, many third-party motherboards, and chipsets from ALI, VIA, SIS, and Intel have been tested to ensure compatibility. BIOS support is also available from Award, AMI, and SystemSoft. IDT WinChip C6 third-party verification includes Microsoft Certified Compatibility with Windows 95 and XXCAL Platinum Certification.

The IDT WinChip C6 is a plug compatible processor to Pentium with MMX Technology and is offered in a 296-pin grid array, Socket 7 compliant ceramic package (CPGA). IDT WinChip C6 leverages the established and low cost Socket 7 motherboard infrastructure.

Manufacturing Capabilities

The IDT WinChip C6 processor is a 5.4 million transistor device manufactured using IDT's 0.35 micron, 4-layer metal CMOS technology.

At only 88 square millimeters in size, the IDT WinChip C6 processor is between 30 and 60 percent smaller than comparable Pentium-class processors with MMX Technology. The combination of small die size coupled with a simplified CMOS process allows IDT to manufacture the WinChip C6 very efficiently and at a low cost.

The WinChip C6 is manufactured at IDT's state-of-the-art facilities in Hillsboro, Oregon and San Jose, California. IDT will continue to drive its manufacturing and process technology with new microprocessor designs from Centaur Technology, delivering value to buyers of mainstream PC desktop and mobile computers.

Features and Benefits Summary

Superior Price/Performance versus Pentium, AMD-K6, and Cyrix 6x86MX processors.

Lowest Power Dissipation. Better than Pentium, AMD-K6 and Cyrix 6x86MX.

Compatible with the Socket 7 infrastructure: motherboards, chip sets, and BIOS.

Higher margin for resellers for a lower system price for end customer.

Allows added features such as more memory, larger hard disk, better graphics, faster modem, etc.

Simpler mobile system design (lower cost system).

Suitable for small form factor desktop and mobile systems.

Leverages established industry infrastructure.

Lower cost systems with competitive performance.

Single Edge Connector

The Pentium Pro CPU was mounted in a Pin Grid Array (PGA) that fit in socket 8. The Pentium II CPU is installed on a circuit board with etched contacts, as shown in Fig. 3-1. This board plugs into a special slot on the motherboard that Intel calls *slot 1*. The Pentium Pro has the L2 cache nearby in the same enclosure. The Pentium II has the L2 cache mounted on the circuit board on each side of the CPU. If you want to use a Pentium Pro on one of these motherboards, the CPU can be installed on a special riser board which plugs into slot 1.

When the Pentium II was first introduced, I called several Intel distributors and tried to buy a 266-MHz CPU. There were lots of 233-MHz units available, but no one had a 266-MHz unit. Every other week there is a large computer swap meet at the Los Angeles County Fairgrounds. There were over 300 booths at a recent meet. I tried all of the booths and found one that had just sold his last 266 MHz. There was another booth nearby that had one for sale at $860. I decided to look around a bit more, but no one else had the 266-MHz units. About 20 minutes later

I went back to the booth and the price had been raised from $860 to $870. I quickly bought it before they had a chance to raise the price even more. It was still a bargain, even at that price—the Intel distributors had quoted me a price of $1130.

MMX Technical Details

The Pentium was almost obsolete until Intel came up with the MMX addition. The following is a press release about MMX from Intel's Web site.

> The MMX processors are built on Intel's enhanced 0.35 micron CMOS process technology which allows it to deliver high performance with low power consumption. Packed with 4.5 million transistors, the Pentium processor with MMX technology includes several architectural enhancements, in addition to MMX instructions. They include a doubled onchip cache size to 32KB and more efficient branch prediction, which provide increased performance of 10 to 20 percent on standard CPU benchmarks. The addition of MMX technology-enabled software will provide even more performance and quality improvements, depending on the type of application and the extent to which the software developer incorporates the new instructions.
>
> On Intel's Media Benchmark the Pentium processor with MMX technology delivers more than 60 percent performance improvement when compared with an equivalent speed Pentium processor. This benchmark, which measures performance on media-rich applications, consists of audio, video, imaging, and 3D geometry components.
>
> SPEC CPU95 performance for the 200 MHz processor is 6.41 SPECint95 and 4.66 SPECfp95. Performance for the 166 MHz processor is 5.59 SPECint95 and 4.30 SPECfp95. The iCOMP© Index 2.0 ratings are 182 and 160, respectively.
>
> Both the desktop and mobile versions of the processor utilize dual voltage levels. The processors input and output pins operate at 3.3 volts for compatibility with today's components. The desktop processors inner core operates at 2.8 volts while the mobile processor operates at 2.45 volts. The lower core voltage enables desktop and mobile systems to operate within efficient thermal ranges. Maximum power dissipation for the desktop processor is 15.7 watts and thermal design power for the mobile version is 7.8 watts.
>
> Boxed processors for desktop systems are packaged with a fan heatsink, CD sampler with software developed for MMX technology, installation manual, certificate of authenticity, and Intel Inside© program label.

Pricing and availability of boxed processors can be obtained from authorized Intel distributors.

How a CPU Is Made

Designing and creating a CPU or an integrated circuit is a very complex procedure. A large, high-powered workstation and CAD software may be used for the early design. The transistors and circuit paths are actually drawn to scale. The design may then be printed out on a very large piece of paper. Once the design is checked for accuracy, it is reduced by several magnitudes, then photographed. The negative image is then transferred to a silicon die. Then, using acids and photoengraving procedures and methods, portions of the die are etched away. The photographic image has then become a CPU made up of transistors and circuits in the silicon die.

The CPUs are etched onto a thin slab of silicon about 6 to 8 inches in diameter. Several CPUS can be etched onto a single slab. The chips go through several stages of processing. At the end of the processing, the individual CPUs are cut and separated. They are then tested and selected.

There is a lot of money in manufacturing CPUs. Before you decide to go into the business, however, remember that this description is very simplified. The actual cost of setting up an advanced CPU manufacturing facility may be $2 billion or more.

What's in a Number?

At one time, there were only two types of CPUs and systems: the original IBM PC and later the XT. Soon after, IBM introduced the AT. Most people eventually called it 286 because it used the 80286 CPU. Then came the 386, and the 486. Several companies began to make clones of the 286, 386, and 486. This did not make Intel very happy. They went to court and sued the companies for using their designations, but found that they could not copyright the CPU numbers. The next logical CPU number should have been 586, but since Intel couldn't copyright it, they called it the *Pentium,* which is copyrighted.

This didn't bother the clone makers too much. AMD came out with a 586 and Cyrix with a 5x86. To match the Pentium Pro, Cyrix came out with a 6x86. Intel introduced the Pentium II with MMX technology;

Cyrix introduced their 6x86MX and AMD their K6. The clones are usually a few steps behind Intel, but are usually able to match anything that Intel produces—and at about 25 percent less cost.

Basic Characteristics of CPUs

The chart in Table 3-2 shows some of the characteristics of some CPUs.

Addressable Memory

Note in Table 3-2 that the 386, 486, and Pentium can address up to 4 Gb, or 4,000,000,000 bytes, of memory. The Pentium Pro can address 16 times more, at 64 Gb. At the present time, I don't know of any vendor who makes a motherboard that would accept even 1 Gb of memory. Most Pentium Pro motherboards are designed to accept up to 128 Mb of RAM. Eventually, motherboards that will accept several gigabytes of memory will be available.

A few years ago, Gordon Moore, then chairman of Intel Corporation, noticed a very definite CPU trend. The chart above basically shows what he observed. Note that the 286 had 125,000 transistors, more than three times the 29,000 in the XT. The 386 was introduced with 275,000 transistors, which more than doubled the 286, then the 486 with 1.2 million, then soon after the Pentium with 3.1 million, and then the Pentium Pro with 5.5 million. The next Pentium generation (P7) will have over 10 million transistors. The trend is that every 18 months or so, the number of transistors and computing power more than doubles. Another trend is that as the power goes up, the price goes down, which is great news for us consumers.

In Table 3-2, the CPU operating frequency listed is the introductory value. Intel was usually rather conservative in the operating frequency recommended. In every case, soon after introduction, the frequency was revised upward. Even the old 8088 was eventually boosted up to as high as 10 MHz. The 286 was introduced to run at 6 MHz, but very soon many were running it at 8 MHz, then as high as 12 MHz. Near the end of its reign, some 286s running as high as 25 MHz.

The 386 was introduced to operate as 16 MHz. Almost overnight, people were boosting it to 20 MHz. Eventually, it was revved up as high as 40 MHz. When the 486 was introduced, it operated at 25 MHz, so

TABLE 3-2
CPU Characteristics

CPU	Frequency	Volt	Bus	Address	Memory	Cache	Transistors	Date
8088	4.77	5V	8 bit	20 bit	1 Mb	no	29 K	06/79
286	6	5V	16 bit	24 bit	16 Mb	no	134 K	02/82
386	16	5V	32 bit	32 bit	4 Gb	no	275 K	10/85
486	25	5V	32 bit	32 bit	4 Gb	8 Kb	1.2 M	04/89
486DX2	66	5V	32 bit	32 bit	4 Gb	8 Kb	1.2 M	03/92
486DX4	99	5V	32 bit	32 bit	4 Gb	16 Kb	1.6 M	02/94
Pentium	60	5V	32 bit	32 bit	4 Gb	16 Kb	3.1 M	03/93
Pentium	75	3.3V	32 bit	32 bit	4 Gb	16 Kb	3.3 M	03/94
Pentium Pro	150	2.9V	32 bit	36 bit	64 Gb	16 Kb	5.5 M	09/95

some of the 386 CPUs actually ran faster than some of the new 486s. Because of the internal design and number of transistors, however, the 486 could still outperform a 386 that was running faster.

The first Pentium operated at 60 MHz, but before long it was revised so that it ran as high as 200 MHz. Currently, the Pentium II can run as fast as 300 MHz and will eventually run as high as 400 MHz. We have certainly come a long way since that first XT that ran at 4.77 MHz!

CPU Frequency and Motherboard Speed

When a software program is run, the program is copied from a hard disk or some other source and loaded into RAM. (Actually, Dynamic RAM, or DRAM, is most often used.) To process the data, the CPU runs back and forth to the DRAM, brings part of the data into the CPU, processes it, and sends it back to DRAM. After the processing is completed, the data is sent back to the hard disk, the printer, or wherever it is needed.

The speed at which the CPU operates internally and the external speed used on the motherboard to run back and forth to the DRAM might not be the same. The internal operating frequency may be 1, 1.5, 2, or 2.5 times more than the external motherboard speed, as shown in Table 3-3.

TABLE 3-3
Memory Bus Speed

CPU Type	Internal Frequency	Speed Factor	External Speed
Pentium 60	60 MHz	1×	60 MHz
Pentium 66	66 MHz	1×	66 MHz
Pentium 75	75 MHz	1.5×	50 MHz
Pentium 100	100 MHz	1.5×	66 MHz
Pentium 120	120 MHz	2×	60 MHz
Pentium 133	133 MHz	2×	66 MHz
Pentium 150	150 MHz	2.5×	60 MHz
Pentium 166	166 MHz	2.5×	66 MHz
Pentium 180	180 MHz	3×	60 MHz
Pentium 200	200 MHz	3×	66 MHz
Pentium II 300	300 MHz	4.5×	66 MHz

Memory Bus

Note that the 60-MHz system processes the data internally at 60 MHz and externally to RAM memory also at 60 MHz. The Pentium 90 MHz, 120 MHz, 150 MHz, and 180 MHz operate internally at those frequencies, but externally at 60 MHz. The Pentium 75 MHz operates internally at 75 MHz, but externally at 50 MHz. The Pentium 66 MHz, 100 MHz, 133 MHz, 166 MHz, 200 MHz, and 300 MHz operate internally at those frequencies, but externally at a fraction of that frequency, 66 MHz. Many motherboards have jumpers so that they can be configured for whatever the speed of the installed CPU.

One reason these systems don't operate faster going back and forth to RAM is that very high frequencies are difficult to control. The longer the distance and the length of the bus, the more problems. At very high frequencies, two circuit paths alongside one another will have a capacitance and an inductance. It is possible that the contents or signals on one circuit could be picked up by the adjacent circuit. It takes extremely careful and costly engineering to design high-frequency circuits.

Cyrix has systems that will operate externally at 75 MHz, which is faster than any of the Intel systems. By the time you read this, Intel will probably have systems that will operate externally between the CPU and the RAM at 100 MHz.

Remember that the memory bus is not the same as the bus for peripherals. Many of the peripherals, especially the ISA-type boards and components, might still operate at 8 or 10 MHz. Because of this limitation, several faster bus systems have been developed: Micro Channel Architecture (MCA) by IBM, Enhanced Industry Standard Architecture (EISA), Video Electronics Standards Association (VESA) Local Bus (VLB), and Peripheral Component Interconnect (PCI).

Only PCI has survived. All of the other systems are now obsolete. Newer, special systems have been developed that surpass the speed of PCI for certain applications. These include the Accelerated Graphics Port (AGP) for faster graphics and the Ultra DMA/33 for faster hard disk access. Despite the improved buses, however, few of them can feed data to the CPU fast enough to keep it busy.

Cache Systems

One solution to the high-frequency problem is to build a cache system as near to the CPU as possible. Often, when a program is being processed, the CPU uses blocks of the same data over and over. If a cache is set up nearby to hold this data, then the processing speed can be improved. Having the cache nearby is so important that, beginning with the 486, a small Local 1 (L1) cache of 8 Kb was built onto the same die as the CPU. Beginning with the 486DX4, the internal L1 cache was doubled to 16 Kb. All Pentiums have the 16-Kb L1 cache.

In addition to the L1 cache, all systems beginning with the 486 also have an L2 cache on the motherboard, as close to the CPU as possible. The L2 cache may be from 256 Kb up to 512 Kb or more. With the Pentium Pro, Intel put the L2 cache about as close as it could possibly be to the CPU. They installed it in the same package, very near the CPU.

The cache must be very fast, at least 15 nanoseconds (ns). The fastest standard DRAM is about 60 ns. For the faster systems, Static RAM (SRAM) is often used. The SRAM systems require six to seven times more transistors than DRAM. The Pentium Pro's 256 Kb cache uses 15.5 million transistors; for 512 Kb, it requires 31 million transistors.

Chip Sets

The CPU needs support for several functions, such as for Direct Memory Access (DMA), the interrupts, the timer, and the clock generator. In the early systems, these were all separate chips installed on the motherboard. Now, many of the support chips are integrated into a single set, such as the Triton for the Pentium and the Orion for the Pentium Pro. AMD has developed a chipset for their K6 called the 640 chipset.

CPU Competition

It is rather interesting to note some of the dates for the introduction of the new CPUs shown in Table 3-2. From the introduction of the 8088 in 1979 to the 286 in 1982 was three years. It was also about three years after this that the 386 was introduced in 1985, and a little over three years before the 486 was introduced in April of 1989. It was at about this time that Advance Micro Devices (AMD) and Cyrix Corporation introduced clones of some of the Intel CPUs. Up until this time, Intel had no competition. They were selling every CPU that they could make. There was little incentive to spend a lot of money to build new fabrication factories. Such a factory might cost $2 billion or more.

Ordinarily, Intel would develop a product, then leave it on the market as long as it was still selling well. They would milk it as long as possible, even though they might have had more powerful and better products on hand. No one can dispute the fact that this was good business. However, ever since Intel was presented with a little competition in 1991, one or more new products have been introduced every year. Quite often, new products are introduced even though the old ones are still selling well. As soon as a competitor shows any sign of taking a bit of the market, Intel immediately switches to the new product. Then, high-cost ad campaigns are instituted to try to convince everyone that the old product is no longer a good buy—even though, just a few months earlier, Intel was trying to convince everyone that this product was the best buy in the world.

We have no way of knowing whether competition has forced Intel to introduce new products, but in any case, the competition has been good for consumers. Besides having a greater choice of products, they are much less expensive. I paid $4450 for my first 486 motherboard, which operated at 25 MHz. A motherboard with a Pentium II 266 MHz costs less than $1100 today, less than one-fourth of what I paid for my old 486 CPU and motherboard.

CPU Sockets

Intel has designed several sockets for the motherboard. Most of the later sockets are the Zero Insertion Force (ZIF) type.

Some of the Pin Grid Array (PGA) sockets were designed for 238 pins up to 387 pins. The sockets are simply called sockets 1 through 8. Table 3-4 is a chart of the various sockets.

TABLE 3-4 Standard CPU Socket

Socket Number	Number of Pins	Voltage	CPUs
Socket 1	169	5V	486SX, 486DX, 486DX2, 486DX4 OverDrive
Socket 2	238	5V	486SX, 486DX, 486DX2, 486DX4 OverDrive, 486 to Pentium OverDrive
Socket 3	237	5 V/3.3V	486SX, 486DX, 486DX2, 486DX4 Over Drive, 486 to Pentium OverDrive
Socket 4	273	5V	Pentium 60/66, Pentium 60/66 Over Drive
Socket 5	320	3.3V	Pentium 75-133, Pentium 75+ OverDrive

TABLE 3-4 Standard CPU Socket (continued)

Socket Number	Number of Pins	Voltage	CPUs
Socket 6	Not used		
Socket 7	321	VRM	Pentium 75-200, Pentium 75+ OverDrive
Socket 8	387	VRM	Pentium Pro
SEC Socket 1		VRM	Pentium II

Socket Standardization

Most of the sockets have the socket number on them, but in some cases, it is very lightly molded onto the socket. For socket 7 and 8, *VRM* means Voltage Regulator Module. The VRM is a small circuit board that is plugged into a socket on the motherboard near the CPU. Pentium CPUs may operate at different voltages, anywhere from 3.3 V down to 2.5 or lower. The low voltage for the CPU must be well regulated, clean, and devoid of spikes.

The Pentium MMX, AMD K6, and Cyrix M2 all use the standard socket 7. These CPUs can be used on any of the motherboards with the standard socket 7. Intel has created a new socket, the single edge connector (SEC) for their Pentium II-type CPU. AMD and Cyrix are not too happy because this will create a separate proprietary standard. Some have accused Intel of acting like IBM when they created their proprietary MCA system. Intel is working on a new slot 2 connector for their next-generation CPU. The Pentium II will eventually be able to run at 400 MHz.

Why Lower Voltage

Heat is an enemy of transistors and other semiconductors. The more transistors, the higher the frequency, the more current is required, the more wattage used, and the more heat generated. Watts used is equal to the amount of current times the voltage. So the lower the voltage, the less wattage used, and the less heat to worry about. Another reason to use less voltage is that the etched lines between the transistors are becoming thinner and thinner, some as thin as 0.25 microns, or 25 millionths of an inch. That would be several times smaller than a human hair. The connecting lines are made thinner in order to crowd more transistors into the limited space, but it wouldn't take much for a voltage to break through the thin lines and short out. So the voltage is carefully regulated, and fans and heatsinks are used to dissipate the heat.

When you order a motherboard and CPU, you will probably have to order a fan and heatsink assembly. They might cost about $10 for socket-7 CPUs. For Pentium II, they might cost $25 to $30. Figure 3-4 shows a fan and heatsink assembly for a socket-7 CPU.

The early XT, 286, 386, and 486 did not need heatsinks or special cooling. Although they all used 5 volts, the fewer transistors and lower frequency did not generate enough heat to cause a problem. The later 486DX2 and 486DX4 did require extra heatsinks and fan cooling.

ZIF Sockets

Almost all motherboards now use ZIF sockets for the CPU. These sockets have a lever that, when raised, allows the chip to be easily removed and replaced. The ZIF socket has split contacts for the pins from the chip. A lever opens the socket contacts so that the chip just falls in. When the lever is closed, the contacts are forced together so that they make intimate connection with the pins, as shown in Fig. 3-5.

Figure 3-6 shows the back of a socket-7 CPU. The pins are very fragile and easily bent. Be very careful while inserting the CPU. Note in Fig. 3-6

Figure 3-4
A fan and heatsink assembly for socket-7 CPUs.

Figure 3-5
A ZIF socket.

Figure 3-6
The pin side of a socket-7 CPU. Pin 1 is located at the top left corner. Note that the corner has been cut at an angle.

that the top left corner has been cut on a slant. This indicates pin 1. (No matter whether it is the old-style socket or the ZIF, you must note carefully where pin one is located.) With the ZIF lever open, the CPU should just fall in if it is aligned properly.

In the early days, there was very little need to remove and replace a CPU. Today, however, there are so many different CPUs and so many options that the ZIF socket is a necessity.

Again, you should be aware that it might be more cost-effective and less expensive to buy a new motherboard and CPU rather than install a CPU upgrade. Some of the clone motherboards are very inexpensive. Be sure to check all of your options.

Resources

For more information on any of the CPUs discussed in this chapter, contact the following companies:

AMD Corporation
One AMD Place, P.O. Box 3453
Sunnyvale, CA 94088-9968
408-749-5703
http://www.amd.com

Cyrix Corporation
P.O. Box 853917
Richardson, TX 75086-3917
214-968-8388
http://www.cyrix.com

Intel Corporation
2200 Mission College Boulevard
Santa Clara, CA 95052
408-765-7525
http://www.intel.com

For the latest press releases from Intel, point your browser to www.intel.com/pressroom/archive/releases/DP050797.HTM

SPEC92

A group of organizations got together in January of 1992 and formed the Systems Performance Evaluation Cooperative (SPEC). They developed a suite of benchmark programs that effectively measures the performance of computing systems in actual application environments. The SPEC92 tests have become the industry standards. The tests for various applications are identified by including the acronym SPEC. For instance, SPECint92 is a very effective benchmark to measure integer application performance; SPECfp92 measures floating-point performance.

Other Benchmarks

An early benchmark was the Norton System Information (SI) that came with Norton's utilities. It provided a measure for a system's throughput, including processing speed and the speed of some peripherals. The Norton SI reference 1.0 is based on the original IBM XT, which had a CPU frequency of 4.77 MHz. Later systems are measured against this reference. My 486DX2-66 system, for example, measures 42.4, which means that it is over 42 times faster than the original XT. The 66-MHz frequency of the 486 is just a little over 13 times faster than the XT at 4.77 MHz, but newer technologies and more efficient operation of the CPU system yields over 42 times better performance.

There are several other benchmarks. Whetstones measures arithmetic operations. Dhrystones measures MIPS. WinBench executes on top of Windows and gives WinMark measures. Other benchmarks have been developed by organizations such as the Ziff-Davis Labs. They do a lot of testing for the system reviews that are reported in their magazines. Landmark Research at 800-683-6696 has developed the Landmark benchmark which, among other things, measures CPU operations. The Landmark Company has also the developed several diagnostic software tools, such as WinProbe and DOS for Windows.

iCOMP Index

The Intel COmparative Performance (iCOMP) index rating provides a simple relative measure of microprocessor performance. It is not a system benchmark, but a test intended to help nontechnical end users decide which Intel CPU best meets their needs. The iCOMP is based on both 16- and 32-bit CPU performance, processing integer, floating-point, graphics, and video performance. The higher the iCOMP index, the higher the relative performance.

History

One of the first CPUs was the 4004, introduced by Intel in 1971. It had 2,300 transistors, a fantastic amount at that time. It ran at a blazing 1 MHz. In contrast, the next-generation Pentium from Intel will have over 10 million transistors and operate at frequencies above 300 MHz. Comparing the early

4004 to some of the CPUs today is like comparing a World War I biplane to the Space Shuttle.

At one time, there were three major automobile makers in this country. I could look at almost any car, and tell you the manufacturer, year, and model. Now there seems to be hundreds of auto makers and thousands of models. It is nearly impossible for the average person to look at a car and tell the year or even the manufacturer.

It is getting to be about the same with the CPUs. For several years, Intel was the sole manufacturer of CPUs for the IBM-compatible machines. Now, there are several companies making CPUs. Though Intel still has well over 80 percent of the CPU market, it has to constantly be on its toes in order to retain this share. The competition has helped keep the prices down and has spurred companies to develop newer and better products.

At one time, the motherboard and CPU were sold as a single unit. In some cases, the CPU was actually soldered to the motherboard. But no more. Today, many of the motherboards are designed so that you may use a large number of different CPUs with them. A good upgrade strategy, then, might be to simply pull out the old CPU from the motherboard and replace it with a newer one. More about upgrading in Chapter 11.

CHAPTER 4

Memory

Memory is one of the most critical elements of the computer. Computing as we know it would not be possible without memory. I know that you want to get started, so here is a bit about the kind of memory you will be using. The latter part of this chapter goes into memory basics, how memory operates, and how it is arranged.

Memory Slots

Your motherboard will have several slots on it. It will probably have two or more slots for 72-contact Single In-line Memory Modules (SIMMs), and two or more 168-contact slots for Dual In-line Memory Modules (DIMMs). Refer back to Fig. 2-1. The six white slots at the top of the photograph are for 72-contact SIMMs. Below the SIMM slots are two long black slots for 168-contact DIMMs. Figure 4-1 shows a couple of 72-contact SIMMs in the upper photograph and a couple of 168-contact DIMMs in the lower photograph.

Figure 4-1 Memory modules. The upper photo shows two 72-contact SIMMs, the lower shows two 168-contact DIMMs.

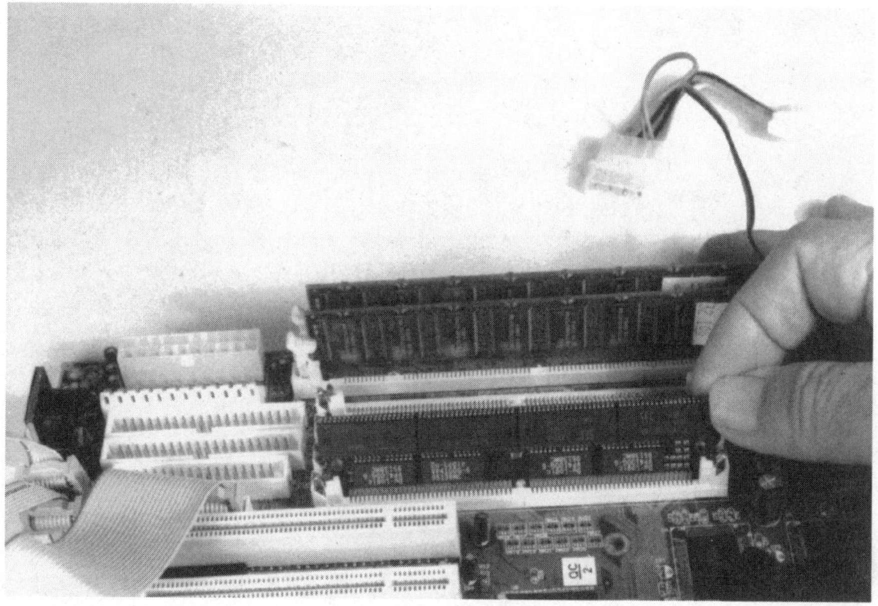

Figure 4-2 Installing SIMM memory modules.

SIMM and DIMM chips are usually mounted on a small board that is plugged into the special slots. SIMMs and DIMMs are very easy to install. They usually have cutouts so that they can only be installed properly. Figure 4-2 shows SIMMs being installed. They are laid in the slot on a slant, then pulled forward until the retaining latches lock them in. To remove a SIMM, just press on the latch assembly on both ends. DIMMs are pressed into the slot straight down. When seated properly, the two latches on each end can be closed.

Memory must be configured in banks. Most motherboards are designed for four banks: 0, 1, 2, and 3. Check the documentation that came with your motherboard. You must fill the lowest-numbered bank before filling other banks. You must also install the SIMMs in multiples of two. For instance, for 32 Mb, you would have to install two 16 Mb modules. The bank designations may be different on motherboards from different vendors. Some motherboards may designate bank 0 on one side of the socket assembly, while others may designate the other side.

SIMM modules must be installed in pairs for the system to operate. The modules can be of different speeds, but must be of the same size or capacity. If a slower speed is installed, the system will operate at the speed of the slowest module.

Types of Memory Modules

You should have received a manual or some documentation with your motherboard. It should tell you what type of memory you should use and how it should be installed. There are several types of memory, such as standard Dynamic Random Access Memory (DRAM), Fast Page Mode, Extended Data Out (EDO) DRAM, and Synchronous DRAM (SDRAM). Your motherboard documentation should tell you what you can use.

DRAM SIMMs

The primary memory used in PCs is DRAM chips. The older PCs reserved about one-fourth of the motherboard area for memory chips. The early boards used 64-Kb chips. It took nine chips to make 64 Kb, and that is all that some of the motherboards had. Later, 256-Kb chips were developed, and up to 640 Kb was installed on some motherboards. Today, we have 64-Mb SIMMs that allow us to install up to 256 Mb on a motherboard in less space than it took for the original 64 Kb.

If you refer back to Fig. 2-2, the six white slots are for SIMM chips. The SIMM sockets may be located anywhere on the different motherboards. There are two types of SIMM configurations and sockets, 30 contacts and 72 contacts. The 30-contact SIMMs are obsolete. The older systems required one set of chips for parity. The 72-contact SIMMs are usually designated as 1×36, which is 4 Mb, 2×36 for 8 Mb, 4×36 for 16 Mb, and 8×36 for 32 Mb. Most newer systems don't use parity, so they now use only eight chips. The designations would be 1×32 or *n*×32.

DIMMs

DIMMs are very high density, fast memory chips. They look very much like SIMMs, but they have two banks of chips soldered to a circuit board. Because they require less space for the same amount of memory, it is expected that DIMMs will eventually become the chip of choice. Most SIMMs now have 72 pins. DIMMs may have 72 pins or 168 pins. The motherboard has to be designed to accept DIMMs. Figure 4-1 shows two, 168 dual-contact DIMM modules. Each module is 32 Mb.

Fast Page Mode

Fast Page Mode DRAM is faster than standard DRAM. It works on the principle that once an address has been accessed, the following address will be accessed next. Fast Page Mode works well with a large cache.

Extended Data Out (EDO)

As CPUs keep getting faster and faster, it is increasingly difficult to develop DRAM chips that can keep up. A type of DRAM being manufactured by Micron Technology (208-368-4000) is called Extended Data Out (EDO). It operates about 10 percent faster than ordinary DRAM and is still fairly reasonable in cost. Conventional DRAM requires two wait states for accessing and refreshment times. Due to its architecture, EDO only needs one wait state. EDO also uses a wider bandwidth during the address select so that there are fewer cache misses. The motherboard must be designed to accept EDO DRAM.

Burst EDO (BEDO)

An advanced type of EDO memory is Burst EDO. Its design and architecture requires zero wait states to read or write. BEDO DRAM increases system efficiency by 13 percent or more.

Synchronous DRAM

Another type of memory is Synchronous DRAM (SDRAM). SDRAM should not be confused with SRAM. The DIMM chips shown in Fig. 4-1 are SDRAM assemblies rated at 10 ns. The fastest standard DRAM is 60 ns.

The SDRAM system couples the operation of memory very tightly to the processor clock. At this time, not all motherboards accept SDRAM. The Pentium II motherboard made by Intel accepts it, but my Micronics Pentium II cannot use it. I tried it, and my system will not boot up. Several companies are manufacturing SDRAM. It is very fast and comparatively inexpensive. Some people believe that it will eventually displace standard DRAM chips and be the choice for main memory.

How Much Memory Do You Need?

Here is the answer to the question of how much memory you need: All that you can afford. You could probably get by with as little as 8 Mb, but you would have to get used to twiddling your thumbs while running many programs. You might have a very fast CPU, but if you don't have enough memory, it will sit idle for much of the time.

You have several options as to how much memory and how it is installed and configured. Check your documentation or motherboard manual. For your new, fast machine, don't even think of buying anything less than 32 Mb; 64 Mb would be even better. For some high-end applications you might need 256 Mb. (My first computer had 64 Kb of memory. I was really happy when my next one had 256 Kb. It really makes me appreciate the advances that have been made in the last few years.)

Basics

The rest of this chapter deals with memory basics. If you are an old pro, you might want to skip it.

The PC uses two primary types of memory, ROM and RAM.

ROM

Read Only Memory (ROM) is memory that cannot be altered or changed. The principal use of ROM in PCs is for the Basic Input/Output System (BIOS). The BIOS contains routines that set up the computer when you first turn it on. It facilitates the transfer of data among peripherals.

ROM programs are usually burned into EPROM chips. The ROM BIOS for an early XT could be programmed onto a 128 Kb chip. The 486 ROM BIOS needed 512 Kb. It is possible to print out the programs stored in ROM. To give you some idea of how much 512 Kb is, the entire text in some of my earlier books was less than 512 Kb. The ROM BIOS on a Pentium II motherboard is stored in flash memory. It takes about 2 Mb.

RAM

When you open a file from a hard disk or a floppy, the files and data are read from the disk and placed in Random Access Memory (RAM).

When you load a program, be it word processing, spreadsheet, database, or whatever, you are working in the system RAM. If you are writing, programming, or creating another program, you are working in RAM.

Actually, you are working with dynamic RAM, DRAM. *Random access* means that you can find, address, change, or erase any single byte among several million bytes. You can also randomly access any particular byte on a floppy or hard disk. You cannot randomly access data on a magnetic tape system. The data on the tape is stored sequentially. In order to find a particular byte, you would have to run the tape forward or backward to the proper area.

Being able to randomly access memory allows you to read and write to it immediately. It is somewhat like an electronic blackboard. In RAM, you manipulate data, do calculations, enter more data, edit, search databases, or do any of the thousands of things that software programs allow. You can access and change the data in RAM very quickly. RAM is an essential element of the computer. If you are working on a large file, you need a lot of RAM. If you are using Windows and you don't have enough RAM, some portions of the file might be loaded onto a special area of the hard disk and used as a *swap file*.

RAM Volatility

An important difference between ROM and RAM is that RAM is volatile. That is, it disappears if the machine is rebooted or if you exit a program without saving it. If there is a power interruption to the computer, even for a brief instant, any data in RAM will be gone forever.

You should get in the habit of saving your files to disk frequently, especially if you live in an area where there are power failures due to storms or other reasons. Many modern software programs automatically save open files to disk at frequent intervals. If the file is saved to disk, a power failure will not affect it.

How RAM Is Addressed

Each byte of memory has a separate address. The cells in the memory bank are analogous to the "pigeonholes" for the room keys of a large hotel. They could be arranged in rows and columns so that the pigeonholes correspond to each room on each floor. If the hotel had 100 rooms, you could have ten rows across and ten down. It would be very simple to find any one of the 100 keys by counting across and then down to the particular room number.

Memory addressing is a bit more complicated than the hotel pigeonholes, but with just 20 address lines (actually 2^{20}, or 1,048,576 bytes), any individual byte out of one million bytes can be quickly accessed. One byte is also called a *word*, so the old 8-bit XT could only address one word at a time. The 16-bit 286 could address two words, 32-bit 386 and 486 systems could address four words, and the 64-bit Pentium can address eight words at a time.

The CPU and the RAM Bus

The CPU is the brains of the computer. Almost everything that happens in a computer must travel over a bus path and go through the CPU.

You will soon have a very fast and powerful Pentium. You will probably have several plug-in boards and peripheral components. The peripheral components communicate with the CPU over a 16-bit bus at about 8 MHz, but data that moves between the RAM and the CPU has its own special memory bus. Data moves back and forth on the bus between the RAM and CPU at some fraction of the CPU speed or frequency, usually at 60 MHz or 66 MHz at this time. Eventually, newer systems will operate between the CPU and RAM at 100 MHz. The amount of work that a computer accomplishes depends on how fast it can process data. There might be billions of bits in a software program. It takes a lot of shifting and adding and moving around to process the program. The faster the computer can handle these billions of iterations, the better.

One of the critical factors that determines the speed of a computer is the time that is spent shifting the data back and forth from the CPU and RAM. The width of the path or bus between the CPU and the RAM is a critical factor in the operating speed of the computer. The original PC had an 8-bit memory bus connected to the CPU. The bus was doubled to 16 bits for the 286 CPU. It was doubled again to 32 bits for the 386 and 486 CPUs. For the Pentium II, the bus width is 64 bit. Some designers have developed a 64-bit bus going in one direction to the CPU and another 64-bit bus returning from the CPU.

The bus has been likened to a highway. If there are only eight lanes, it can be compared to a single-lane highway and will be rather slow. Twice as many cars can get through on a two-lane highway, and four times as many if there are four lanes. If there are eight lanes, analogous to a 64-bit system, the traffic can really whiz along.

A Brief Explanation of Memory

Computers operate in a binary system of zeros and ones, or off and on. A transistor can be turned off or on to represent the zeros and ones. Two transistors can represent four different combinations:

1. Both off
2. Both on
3. #1 on, #2 off
4. #1 off, #2 on

A bank of four transistors can represent 16 different combinations. With eight transistors, you can have 256 different combinations. It takes eight transistors to make one byte. With them, you can represent each letter of the alphabet and each number and each symbol of the extended American Standard Code for Information Interchange (ASCII). With eight lines, plus a ground, the eight transistors can be turned on or off to represent any single one of the 256 characters of the ASCII code.

Programs that Stay in RAM

In the DOS era, besides the application programs that were loaded into the 640 Kb of RAM, there were certain DOS programs that stayed in RAM at all times. These were programs such as Command.com and the internal commands, such as COPY, CD, CLS, DATE, DEL, MD, PATH, TIME, TYPE, and others.

Under DOS these commands were always in RAM and were available immediately. The Config.sys file and any drivers that you might have for your system were also loaded into RAM. Several other programs, such as SideKick, were also loaded into RAM and stayed there. They were called *Terminate and Stay Resident* (*TSR*) programs. I have Norton Utilities. It is loaded into memory each time I boot up. Microsoft Office 97 is also loaded into memory.

If you are running Windows 95 and would like to see what programs are in memory, just press the Ctrl, Alt, and Del keys all at the same time and the list of programs in memory will come up. (Be careful that you only press Ctrl, Alt, Del once. If you press it twice, you will reboot the computer.) Quite often, when you install a program, it will tell you to make sure that no other programs are running at the same time. If you would like to delete any of the programs from memory, just use the mouse or arrow key to highlight the program and press the Enter key. Note, however, that you cannot delete Microsoft Explorer from RAM. If you do, it will shut the computer down.

TSRs contributed to the utility and functionality of the computer and made it easier to use. Unfortunately, they also took big bites out of our precious 640 Kb of RAM. There might have been less than 400 Kb left for running applications after loading all these programs. Many programs would not run if you had less than 600 Kb of free RAM.

Windows 95 has now solved most of those problems. It can load several programs in extended memory, above the 640 Kb limit. These programs can then be available at any time. Windows 95 also allows you to have several programs open at the same time. You can be working on one in the foreground and have another running in the background. Of course, this requires lots of memory.

Cost of Memory

I don't like to talk about cost because it changes so quickly. Here is what I wrote three years ago about the cost of RAM:

> Although the 386 and 486 can address 4 gigabytes of RAM, without special software, DOS will not let you access more than 640 Kb. (Incidentally, 4 gigabytes of DRAM, in 1-Mb SIMM packages, would require 4096 modules. You would need a fairly large board to install that much memory. It would also be rather expensive. At $35 per megabyte, 4096 modules would cost $143,360.)

You can buy memory today for about $2 per megabyte, so you could install 4 Gb for about $8000, down from $143,360. What a fantastic change in just a few years!

Another change is that 64-Mb DIMMs are quite common. With these chips, you would only need 62.5 modules to make 4 Gb. Eventually, you will be able to buy 256-Mb DIMMs.

Memory prices are still coming down. By the time you read this, the prices will be even lower. One reason for lower prices is that most newer systems use the 8-chip nonparity system. Most older systems used the 9-chip parity system. The extra chip added to the cost.

Virtual Memory

In its virtual memory mode, the 386, 486, or Pentium class CPU can address 64 terabytes, or 64 trillion bytes, or 64,000,000,000,000 bytes. Virtual memory is a method of using part of a hard disk as RAM. Many large programs will not run unless the entire program resides in RAM. With virtual memory, the program can be partially loaded in the available RAM and the rest of it in a virtual RAM section of the hard disk. Of course, having to access the disk for data can slow the processing down considerably, but it is one solution. The virtual disk system must be implemented by the operating system.

How Memory Is Arranged

Early PCs used dual in-line pin (DIP) chips with two rows of 8 pins, or 16 pins total. DIP chips used up a lot of motherboard real estate because it takes nine chips of whatever type memory is designated. For instance, for 64 Kb, it takes eight 64-Kb-×-1-bit chips plus one 64-Kb-×-1-bit chip for parity checking. For 256-Kb chips, it takes eight 256-Kb-×-1-bit chips, plus one 256-Kb-×-1-bit chip for parity checking. Even with high-capacity SIMMs, it still takes nine chips to make up the designated memory. For one megabyte, it takes eight 1024-Kb-×-1-bit plus one 1024-Kb-×-1-bit for parity. For a 4-Mb SIMM, it takes eight 4096-Kb-×1-bit plus one 4096-Kb-×-1-bit for parity. The same system is used even for the n×36 SIMM chips. Sometimes, instead of having nine individual chips, they might have three or more integrated into a single chip. So you might see some SIMMs with only three chips in the module.

I know this is a bit confusing, so here is a brief chart:

64 Kb = 64 Kb × 1 bit + 64 Kb × 1 bit for parity
256 Kb = 256 Kb × 1 bit + 256 Kb × 1 bit for parity
1 Mb = 1024 Kb × 1 bit + 1024 Kb × 1 bit for parity
4 Mb = 4096 Kb × 1 bit + 4096 Kb × 1 bit for parity

Figure 2-2 in Chapter 2 shows two different motherboards, a large, standard-sized 286 at the left and a Pentium at right. To illustrate how much space the DIP chips require, there are four rows of DIP chips in the top right corner of the 286. It takes 36 of the 128-Kb chips to make one megabyte. The four white SIMM 72-contact sockets in the left center of the Pentium motherboard can accept up to 128 Mb.

The DIP chips were rather difficult to install. It was very easy to install them backwards in the socket or to bend one of the pins so that it did not make contact. Over a period of time, some of the DIP chips could actually creep up out of the socket. A board of SIMM chips is very easy to install. It has a cutout on one end so that it can only be inserted one way. Just lay it slantwise in the socket, then push it to an upright position. There is a small hole in each end of the SIMM board. A projection on the socket fits in this hole when the SIMMs are inserted in the socket.

Springloaded clamps on each end lock the assembly in place. To remove the assembly, press on the clamps on each end.

Memory Problems

Although SIMM chips are very easy to install, it is still possible to have a module that is not seated properly. If this happens, the computer might not boot up. The screen might be completely blank with no error messages or any indication of the problem.

I had a whole lot of problems when I tried to replace my old Cyrix 100 MHz with the Tyan motherboard and the AMD 233-MHz CPU. I had four 8×2 chips, for a total of 32 Mb, on my old board. It seemed to work fine. The memory check was okay each time I booted up, but I had a blank screen when I tried to boot up with the new motherboard and CPU. I checked the SIMMs to make sure they were seated properly. Then I tried and tried again. Sometimes, the computer would boot up, but then it would tell me that it had a fatal error and would shut down.

I reinstalled everything back in my old Cyrix motherboard and it worked fine. I reinstalled everything in my new motherboard, and it booted up once in a while, but then dropped out. I checked the SIMMs again, but thought that maybe my monitor adapter was bad. I replaced it with a spare, but I still had a blank screen. I then removed two of the SIMMs, or one bank of memory, and everything worked fine. I replaced one of the SIMMs with one of the two that I had removed, and sure enough, I had a blank screen. Evidently, one of the contacts on the chip was bad or the chip itself had an intermittent defect. It took me half a day of frustration to find it.

Parity

The old DIP chips had two rows of 8 pins, or 16 pins total. It requires nine chips of whatever type memory designated. For the older systems that still use parity, even with the high-capacity SIMMs, it still takes nine chips to make up the designated memory. The nine chips are all on the one, small SIMM plug-in board. Macintosh systems do not use the parity checking chip, so they have only the 8-×-whatever-the-SIMM designation. Similarly, most of the new PCs no longer use parity system.

Memory must be configured in banks. Most motherboards are designed for four banks: 0, 1, 2, and 3. Check the documentation that came with your motherboard. You must fill the lowest numbered bank before filling other banks. Because memory is interleaved on most systems, you must install the SIMMs in multiples of two. You cannot intermix SIMMs of different values. For instance, for 16 Mb, you would have to install two 8-Mb modules. If you install a single module instead of the required two, the computer might not boot up. The screen might be completely blank. Interleaved memory is discussed in more detail later in this chapter.

Caution: It is possible to have a module that is not seated properly. If this happens, the computer might not boot up. The screen might be completely blank with no error messages or other indication of the problem. When I installed two 8-Mb SIMMs in my K6 motherboard, I installed one behind the other. When I tried the system on the benchtop, I got one long, continuous beep. I finally looked at the documentation and it showed that the SIMMs should be mounted as shown in their manual.

Flash Memory

A few years ago, Intel developed *flash memory*, which is similar to EPROM. AMD and several other companies now also manufacture it. Flash memory is often installed on small plug-in cards about the size of a credit card. The cards are ideal for use on laptop and notebook computers. When first introduced, the cards were quite limited in the amount of memory that could be stored, but cards are now available that can store several megabytes. They can be a good substitute for a hard disk on small notebook computers.

Flash memory is fairly slow compared to DRAM and SRAM, so it can't replace them. It can, however, be equivalent to hard disk memory. The hard disk is a mechanical device that eventually wears out or fails. Flash memory is strictly electronic and should last several lifetimes. A disadvantage of flash memory is that it is still rather expensive and limited in the amount of memory that can be installed on a card.

Most Pentium Pros now use flash memory for the BIOS chip. The BIOS can then be updated electronically by floppy disk or by a modem from a BBS or over the Internet.

You will probably want a laptop or notebook computer for the times when you are on the road. If you do buy one, it should have the PC-Card (originally called PCMCIA) connectors for flash memory. The Personal Computer Memory Card International Association

(PCMCIA) adopted a standard and connectors so that several products can be used with laptop and notebook computers. Most laptop and notebook computers now include the PC Card connectors so that flash memory and other peripherals can be installed.

Using flash memory and the PC-Card standard, companies have developed several other peripherals for laptop and notebook computers, such as high-speed modems and network adapters. A flash floppy has even been designed that can store from 2 Mb up to 100 Mb. Some desktop PCs are installing PC-Card sockets so they can take advantage of this technology. It makes it easy to download or transfer data back and forth to a laptop.

Video RAM

Video RAM (VRAM) chips are a bit different than DRAM chips. They are special memory chips that are used on the better (and more expensive) monitor adapter cards. They are especially optimized for graphics. VRAM chips are unusual in that they have double ports so that they can be accessed and refreshed at the same time.

A new memory standard, the Unified Memory Architecture (UMA), is now being used on many of the high-end graphics and video accelerator adapters.

Printer Memory

Your laser printer probably came with a minimum amount of memory, perhaps about 512 Kb. Most printers require memory that is installed on special proprietary boards. You might need to add more memory for better printing speed. Most lasers will perform much better if they have a minimum of 2 Mb.

Memory Chip Capacity

The size and speed of the chip is usually printed on the top of the chip. For instance, a 256-Kb chip at 150 ns might have the manufacturer's logo or name and some other data, but somewhere among all this would be "25615." The *15* indicates 150 ns (the zero is always left off). Similarly, a 1-Mb, 100-ns chip might have "102410." The chips are usually arranged in banks or rows of nine. Almost all ISA computers use an extra ninth chip for parity checking. This chip checks and verifies the integrity of the memory at all times. It is usually the same type of chip as the eight that are used to make up the bank. The Macintosh systems don't use this chip, and some experts say that it is a waste of memory to use it on the ISA systems.

The XT and early 286 motherboards had their RAM memory usually located in the front right corner of the motherboards. They all used the DIP type of chips. To make 640 Kb, most boards filled the first two banks, banks 0 and 1, with 256-Kb chips, which equals 512 Kb. The next two banks, 2 and 3, were then filled with 64-Kb chips to make 128 Kb, for a total 640 Kb. Many of the early 286 and 386 systems filled all four banks with 256-Kb DIP chips, for a total of 1 Mb. Although the 286 was capable of addressing 16 Mb with special software, for most ordinary uses, it was still limited to 640 Kb. Boards that had the extra 384 Kb could use it for a RAM disk, print spooling, or for other extended memory needs, with the proper software.

Until Windows 95, the 386, 486 and Pentium were limited to 640 Kb without special software that could take advantage of extended memory.

The Need for More Memory

One of the upgrades that you probably need is more memory. For some applications, you might need to buy several megabytes more. In the old days, we got by fine with just 64 Kb of memory. However, many of the new software programs, such as spreadsheets, databases, and accounting programs require a lot of memory.

If you bought a new motherboard through mail order, you might have received it with 0K memory. You probably know that 0K does not mean "OKAY," it means zero kilobytes of memory. The price of memory fluctuates quite a lot. Because of the fluctuating prices, some vendors will not advertise a firm price for memory. Besides, if they included the price of the memory, it might frighten you away. They usually invite you to call them for the latest price. The good news for consumers is that memory prices are dropping every day.

Things to Consider Before You Buy Memory

There are several factors to consider before buying memory, including type, size, and speed. You should buy the type that is best for your computer.

Dynamic RAM (DRAM)

DRAM is the most common type of memory used today. Each memory cell has a small etched transistor that is kept in its memory state, either on or off, by an electrical charge on a very small capacitor. Capacitors are similar to small rechargeable batteries. Units can be charged up with a voltage to represent ones, or left uncharged to represent zeros. Those that are charged up, however, immediately start to lose their charge, so they must be constantly "refreshed" with a new charge.

Steve Gibson, the developer of SpinRite, compared the memory cell capacitors to small buckets that had holes in the bottom. Those buckets, or cells, that represented ones were filled with water, but it immediately started leaking out through the hole in the bottom, so it had to be constantly refilled. You didn't have to worry about filling those buckets, or cells, that represent zeros.

A computer might spend 7 percent or more of its time just refreshing the DRAM chips. Also, each time a cell is accessed, that small voltage in the capacitor flows through a transistor to turn it on. This drains the charge from the capacitor, so it must be refreshed before it can be accessed again. In our bucket-of-water comparison, when the cell is accessed, the bucket is turned upside down and emptied. So if it represents a one, it must be refilled immediately. Of course, it takes a finite amount of time to fill a bucket or to place a charge on a capacitor. If the memory cell has a speed of 70 nanoseconds (ns), it might take 70 ns, plus the time it takes to recycle, which might be 105 ns or more, before that cell can again be accessed.

Refreshment and Wait States

The speed of the DRAM chips in your system should match your system CPU. You might be able to install slower chips, but your system would have to work with wait states. If the DRAM is too slow, a wait state will have to be inserted. A wait state causes the CPU and the rest of the system to sit and wait while the RAM is being accessed and then refreshed. Wait states deprive your system of one of its greatest benefits, speed. They are a terrible waste of time.

If the CPU is operating at a very high frequency, it might have to sit and wait one cycle, or one wait state, for the refresh cycle. The wait state might be only a millionth of a second or less. That might not seem like much time, but if the computer is doing several million operations per second, it can add up.

It takes a finite amount of time to charge up the DRAM. Some DRAM chips can be charged up much faster than others. For instance, the DRAM chips needed for an XT at 4.77 MHz might take as much as 200 ns to be refreshed. A 486 running at 25 MHz would need chips that could be refreshed in 70 ns or less time. Of course, the faster chips cost more.

The 486DX2-66 and DX4-100 could both use the same speed memory of about 60 ns. The CPU might be operating internally at 66 MHz or 100 MHz, but they both accessed the RAM at the 33 MHz rate. Pentium-class CPUs might operate internally as high as 200 MHz, but externally over the memory bus to RAM at a speed of 60 MHz to 66 MHz.

Interleaved Memory

Most of the newer, faster systems use interleaved memory to prevent having to insert wait states. The memory is always installed in multiples of two. You can install two banks of 512 Kb, 2 Mb, 4 Mb, 8 Mb, 16 Mb, 32 Mb, 64 Mb, or 128 Mb of memory.

Half of the memory is refreshed on one cycle, then the other half. If the CPU needs to access an address that is in the half already refreshed, it is available immediately. This can reduce the amount of waiting by about half.

SRAM

Static RAM (SRAM) is made up of actual transistors that can be turned on to represent ones or left off to represent zeros. They will stay in that condition until they receive a change signal. They do not need to be refreshed, but they revert back to zero when the computer is turned off or if power is interrupted. SRAM is very fast and can operate at speeds of 15 ns or less.

A DRAM memory cell needs only one transistor and a small capacitor. It takes a very small amount of space. Each SRAM cell, on the other hand, requires four to six transistors and other components, so SRAM is much more expensive than DRAM. In older systems, SRAM chips were assembled in DIP packages, so they were physically larger and require much more space than the DRAM chips. Because of the physical and electronic differences, SRAM and DRAM chips are not interchangeable. Newer motherboards have the SRAM integrated into a single VLSI chip.

Cache Memory

A cache system can speed up computer operations quite a lot. When running an application program, the CPU often loops in and out of certain areas and uses portions of the same memory over and over. A cache system is usually made up of very fast memory chips such as SRAM that can store the frequently used data so that it is quickly accessible to the CPU.

Data is moved back and forth between the CPU and RAM as electrical on and off voltages. The electrons move at almost the speed of light. Still, it takes a finite amount of time to move a large amount of data. It takes even more time to access the RAM, find the data that is needed, then move it back to the CPU. The computer can also be slowed down considerably if it has to search the entire memory each time it has to fetch some data. If this frequently used memory is stored in a cache, it can be accessed by the CPU very quickly.

A good cache can greatly increase the processing speed. The Pentium CPU has a built-in 16-Kb L1 cache in among its 3.1 million transistors. This cache helps considerably, but a good, fast, external L2 cache can speed things up even more. The speed and static characteristics of SRAM make it an excellent device for memory cache systems. The Pentium II CPU has a 16-Kb L1 cache, but it also has a 256-Kb, 512-Kb, or 1-Mb cache nearby in the same enclosure.

Hit Rate

A well-designed cache system might have a "hit rate" of over 90 percent. This means that each time the CPU needs a block of data, it will find it in the nearby, fast cache. A good cache system can increase the speed and performance considerably.

Level 1 and Level 2 Caches

A Level 1 (L1) cache is one that is built into the CPU. This makes the cache very close and fast. The 486 was the first CPU with an internal L1 cache. Intel built in an 8-Kb cache among the 1.2 million transistors in the CPU. It increased the L1 cache to 16 Kb in the 486DX4 and all of the Pentium CPUs.

The L1 cache allows the CPU to access memory that is often used without having to travel outside to the external RAM. Because of the short distance and the high-speed transistors, the L1 cache operates at the same internal speed as the CPU. Many CPUs operate externally two to three times slower than they do internally. The 486 and Pentium CPUs also use a Level 2 (L2), or external, cache made up of fast SRAM located on the motherboard. But again, it takes a finite amount of time for the data to move from the CPU over the bus at an external frequency to the SRAM cache. The Pentium Pro lessened this problem by building an L2 cache in the same enclosure as the CPU. The L2 cache is closely coupled to the CPU and communicates with it over a very short 64-bit interface or special bus at the internal CPU frequency. The L2 cache is either 256 Kb or 512 Kb.

A cache made up of SRAM transistors is very fast, but requires lots of transistors. It takes six transistors for each bit of SRAM, so a 256-Kb cache requires 15.5 million transistors, and 512 Kb requires 31 million. It only takes one transistor for each bit of DRAM, so 256 Kb would require 2.6 million transistors, and 512 Kb would need 5.2 million.

Write-Through and Write-Back

After data is processed, it is returned to RAM. The write-through systems simply send the data back to RAM. System operations are delayed while the data is being written back to RAM. The delay might be only microseconds, but if you are processing a lot of data, it can add up.

The write-back systems keep the data in the cache until there is a break in operations, then write the data to RAM.

CMOS

Complementary Metal-Oxide Semiconductors (CMOS) require very little power to keep them alive. They are actually SRAM transistors that store your system's setup. Several of the computer features that are configurable, such as the time, date, and type of disk drives, are stored in CMOS. You should write down all of the features stored in your CMOS setup. For instance, if you lose the data in your CMOS, and you don't know what type of hard drive is in the setup, you will not be able to access your data on the hard drive.

A lithium or rechargeable battery keeps the data alive when the computer is turned off. If your computer is not used for a long period of time, you might have to reset the time. If you have to reset the time quite often, you might need a new battery. The early IBM AT used batteries that only lasted a couple of years. The batteries were soldered onto the motherboard and very difficult to change. Most motherboards today have lithium batteries that last about 10 years.

Why the 640-Kb Limit?

When DOS was first introduced in 1981, one megabyte of memory was an enormous amount. It was believed that this amount would be more than satisfactory. After all, many of the CP/M machines were getting by fine with just 64 Kb of memory. So DOS was designed to operate with a maximum of one megabyte. Of this megabyte, 640 Kb would be used for running programs and applications. The other 384 Kb was reserved for purposes such as the BIOS, the video control, and other special hardware control. This 384 Kb is called the *upper memory area* and is divided up into blocks called *upper memory blocks,* or *UMBs.*

Sometimes when I tried to load and run a program, I got an error message saying "Not enough memory" or "Insufficient memory," even though I had 32 Mb of DRAM in my computer. I knew that the program I was trying to run was less than 500 Kb, so why shouldn't I be able to run it if I have 32 Mb? The reason is simple. The program I was trying to run was a DOS-type program that could not handle extended memory. It was limited to the 640 Kb of conventional memory. But if the program is only 500 Kb, why can't it run in the 640 Kb? The reason is when I booted up my computer, Command.com and several other internal DOS commands were loaded into that 640 Kb. In addition, any TSR programs were also loaded into the 640 Kb. Any drivers listed in my Config.sys and Autoexec.bat files for special devices such as a fax-modem or CD-ROMs were also loaded into the conventional memory. After all of this stuff was loaded, there might be less than 400 Kb left, so if the program is larger than 400 Kb, it will not run. Many programs and applications today are so large that they need 600 Kb or more of RAM.

DOS's internal commands and many TSRs are loaded in memory at all times. These commands can be invoked by just a few keystrokes from any directory. There are about 75 DOS commands. About 30 of them are internal commands such as COPY, DEL, MD, CD, and TYPE. (In many of the early versions of DOS, these were separate commands, but DOS now incorporates them all into Command.com.) They are always loaded and immediately available.

Tremendous improvements have been made in computer technology since the original PC. In spite of all of the improvements in the technology, however, you are still limited to the original 640 Kb unless you have programs such as Windows that can take advantage of any extra extended memory that you have. One reason for this limitation was to make sure that the computers remained compatible with, and could still run, the billions of dollars' worth of software that was already created. You might still occasionally hear someone complain about the 640-Kb barrier, but this backward compatibility is one of the foremost factors that made the computer what it is today.

The 640-Kb barrier is not really much of a problem today. Much of the reserved 384 Kb of upper memory space is never needed by the system. MS-DOS and several other programs such as DESQview can load the internal commands, drivers, and TSRs into the unused 384 Kb of upper memory. In most cases, you can have over 600 Kb left for running programs. In MS-DOS version 5.0 and later, the MEMMAKER command can search the 384 Kb of upper memory and find all of the unused cracks and crannies. After this, every time you boot your computer, it will automatically load most of the internal commands, drivers, and TSRs into these upper memory blocks (UMBs).

Windows 95, Windows NT, and IBM's OS/2 are not limited to the 640-Kb barrier. When running programs designed for Windows, these systems let you use all of the RAM that is available, if it is needed.

Conventional Memory

Conventional memory is the one megabyte of memory that includes the 640 Kb. DOS applications are loaded into this area and processed here. In early versions of DOS, several commands were also loaded into this area, which decreased the usable area available for user applications.

Extended Memory

Extended memory is memory that can be installed above one megabyte. The Pentium can address up to four gigabytes of extended memory. If it weren't for DOS's 640 Kb limitation, there would be a seamless continuation of memory. Windows 95, Windows NT, and OS/2 2.1 can also use extended memory to run two or more programs at the same time, or do multitasking.

Buying Chips

Buying chips that are faster than what your system can use only costs you extra money. However, it doesn't hurt to use faster chips, or even to intermix faster ones with slower ones.

If you plan to upgrade the memory in an older system, you might have trouble finding the older chips. The older systems used DIP chips. Make sure that you buy only the type that will fit in your system. For instance, the 64-Kb and 256-Kb DIP chips have 16 pins, while the 1-Mb chips have 18. Some memory boards have both 256-Kb and 1-Mb sockets interlaced so that you can use either size chip. SIMM chips are the type of chip used most often today. You cannot use a SIMM module unless your motherboard is designed for it.

Installing the Chips

CAUTION! Electrostatic Voltage

Before handling memory chips, or any electronic components, the first thing that you should do is to discharge any electrostatic charge that might have been built up on you. If you have ever walked across a carpet and got a shock when you touched a doorknob, then you know that you can build up static electricity. It is quite possible to build up 3000 to 5000 volts of static electricity in your body, so if you were to touch a fragile piece of electronics that normally operates at 5 to 12 volts, you could severely damage it.

To discharge this static electricity from your body, touch any metal that goes to ground. The metal case of the power supply in your computer is a good ground if it is still plugged into the wall socket. The power does not have to be on for it to connect to ground. You can also touch an unpainted metal part of any device or appliance that has three wires and is plugged into a socket, such as a lamp that is plugged into an outlet. Always discharge yourself before you touch any plug-in board or other equipment where there are exposed electronic semiconductors.

Memory chips and most other critical electronic components come in special packaging. Before unwrapping any component, discharge any static electric charge that you might have on you. This is especially important if you are working in an area where there is carpet.

You can mix chips of different speeds in the same bank, such as 60 ns and 70 ns, but you are limited to the 70 ns speed. You should not use a chip slower than the speed of your CPU. You cannot mix chips of different capacities. To install SIMM modules, just lay the module in the socket at an angle, press down lightly, and pull forward until it locks in. A SIMM module has a cutout on one end of the small board. It can only be plugged in one way. DIMM modules have cutouts that match protrusions in the socket so that they can only be plugged in one way.

CHAPTER 5

Floppy Drives and Disks

Floppy disks were all the storage we had in the early days. Some PCs had a single floppy drive. Almost all of the early drives used single-sided floppy disks that were from 140 Kb to 180 Kb. It was a great leap forward when IBM introduced a PC with two floppy drives that could handle double-sided floppy disks. The first double-sided floppy disks could be formatted to a whopping 160 Kb on each side, for a total of 320 Kb. Later, 360-Kb systems were introduced. Even if you were fortunate enough to have a PC with two floppy drives, doing any kind of computing involved an endless amount of disk swapping and took forever to get anything done.

My first computer had two single-sided 140-Kb drives. It was slow and required a lot of disk swapping. Floppy systems have come a long way since those early days; from 140-Kb systems to 320-Kb double-sided systems, then 360 Kb, 1.2 Mb, 1.44 Mb, 2.88 Mb, and now even 120 Mb and 200 Mb on a floppy disk.

Most software programs today are very user-friendly. The more user-friendly they are, the larger they are. Many of these programs require from 80 Mb up to 120 Mb or more to be installed and run. It would be impossible to run programs such as these with the older floppy disk systems.

Until just a few years ago, most software programs came on floppy disks. Those programs were fairly small; in a compressed form, most of them didn't require more than four or five 1.44-Mb floppies. Many software programs today are over 100 Mb. Even in a compressed format, this would take a large number of floppies. Most companies now use CD-ROMs to distribute their software. For the last couple of years, I have not had to buy any 1.44 Mb disks. I have just erased and reused the floppies sent out by America Online. I subscribe to lots of computer magazines, and for a while, almost every one of them had an AOL disk with it every month. Lately, however, they are sending out CD-ROMs. A blank CD-ROM can cost as little as 7 cents, and it can be stamped out much quicker than making a floppy copy. I might eventually have to buy some floppy disks, but I don't use them that often anymore.

I don't think that the CD-ROM will ever completely replace the floppy disk. Floppy disks can do many things that a CD-ROM can't, such as making archive copies of small programs, backing up small files from a hard disk, or moving a small program from one computer to another. The floppy system will be around for a long time.

1.44-Mb Floppy

The 1.44-Mb floppy drives are very inexpensive at this time. I recently bought one at a swap meet for $17. I didn't need it, but for that price, it was worth it to just have on hand for use as a spare. I have had several 1.44-Mb drives become defective. Just as Murphy's Law predicts, it always happens at the most inopportune time.

I have a $3^1/_2$-inch and a $5^1/_4$-inch combination drive installed in one of my computers, as shown in Fig. 5-1. I have a lot of old $5^1/_4$ floppy disks, but I can't remember the last time I used the $5^1/_4$-inch drive. It can read and write to the 1.2-Mb and 360-Kb formats, but both formats are as obsolete as the Model T Ford.

At one time, you had to buy a rather expensive controller card for a floppy drive. The controller interface is now built in on motherboards as a set of 34 upright pins. The motherboard will usually have some sort of label or marking. Unless the pins have a shell around them, the cable connector can be plugged in backwards on these pins. If you do so, it will immediately erase and destroy any data on a floppy disk that you try to run. When you plug in the cable, make sure that the different-colored stripe on one side of the cable goes to pin 1 on the motherboard.

2.88-Mb Floppy Drive

The $3^1/_2$-inch, Extended Density (ED), 2.8-Mb floppy drives have been available for some time. The 2.8-Mb disks have a barium ferrite media

Figure 5-1
A combination $5^1/_4$-inch and $3^1/_2$-inch floppy drive.

and use perpendicular recording to achieve the extended density. In standard recording, the particles are magnetized so that they lay horizontally in the media. In perpendicular recording, the particles are stood vertically on end for greater density.

ED drives require a controller that operates at 1 MHz. The other floppy controllers operate at 500 KHz. Several companies are now integrating the ED controller with the other floppy controllers. Most of the Pentium II motherboards and those with socket 7 now have built-in floppy controllers for 2.88-Mb and other floppy drives. ED drives are downward compatible; they can read and write to 720-Kb and 1.44-Mb disks. At the present time, ED drives and disks are still rather expensive. Not many people are using them. They don't offer that much more advantage over the 1.44-Mb drives. I would not recommend them; they are obsolete.

The Iomega 100-Mb Zip Drive

The Iomega Zip drive uses a 3½-inch disk that is similar to a floppy, but this disk can store 100 Mb. This system is much less expensive than the Bernoulli. At this time, Zip drives cost less than $150, and the disks cost less than $20. With a few disks, you would never have to worry about running out of hard-drive space. There are over 8 million Zip drives installed. However, the LS 120-Mb drive is less expensive and compatible with 1.44-Mb disks. The LS 120 and the 200-Mb Sony HiFd will make the Zip drive obsolete.

The LS120

A floppy drive system called the LS120, shown in Fig. 5-2, may hasten the demise of the 1.44-Mb floppy as we know it. The LS120 can read and write to the 1.44 Mb format and can also read and write to a special 120-Mb floppy disk. The 120-Mb floppies are specially formatted with laser technology. They use a standard head for reading and writing to the 1.44-Mb disk, and a different head for reading and writing to the 120-Mb disks. The drive can work off the IDE or SCSI interface, or as an external drive on your parallel printer port.

With the LS120, there might be no need to upgrade to a larger-capacity hard disk. With several 120-Mb floppies, you would never run out of

Figure 5-2
An LS120 drive. It is a 120-Mb floppy drive that also reads and writes to 3½-inch, 1.44-Mb floppy disks.

space. A disadvantage, of course, is that the file that you need will always be on the other floppy disk. At the present time, the special 120-Mb disks cost $12 to $20 each.

Compaq Computer Corporation was one of the original developers of the LS120 system. Several Compaq systems now have it as standard equipment. By the time you read this, several laptop computers will also come with the LS120. The following information about a drive based on the LS120 is from the O.R. Technology Web site at www.ortechnology.com:

> The a:drive from O.R. Technology was designed to replace the floppy disk drive. While its outward appearance is almost indistinguishable from that of its floppy technology counterpart, the a:drive achieves 120 MB of storage when used with LS-120 media. At the same time, the a:drive is downward compatible with current 3.5-inch floppy disk technology. It can read and write to both 720 KB and 1.44 MB diskettes, providing an upward migration path for millions of personal computer users and the billions of diskettes they own. As its name indicates, the a:drive can be used as a bootable drive in any system in which it is installed. From the start, O.R. Technology created the 1-inch high a:drive with this purpose in mind. Extensive development has optimized the device for internal

use as an integral system component. It was designed to be the ideal form, fit and function replacement for the floppy disk drive. The a:drive is an advanced technology product, yet so familiar you already know how to use it.

O.R. Technology has worked closely with Microsoft Corp. and Compaq Computer Corp. developing standards to enable the operating system, the computer system, and the a:drive to work together. Both Windows 95 and Windows NT operating systems have now been updated to recognize the a:drive as a bootable drive in both 120 MB and 1.44 MB mode. To accomplish this, changes were required to the system BIOS.

In addition, O.R. Technology has been active in the ATAPI standards committee developing the necessary protocol for devices that read and write. As a result the a:drive is ATAPI compatible and can be attached to the same internal IDE cable the hard disk drive uses. Unlike alternative technologies, the compact a:drive meets current industry standards established for floppy disk drive and floppy diskette form factors. It can be easily configured for use in standard notebook or desktop PC drive bays.

At the present time, the drives are selling for about $150. The preformatted special 120-Mb floppy disks are selling for $19.95. I am sure that they will be less by the time you read this.

O.R. Technology
42 West Campbell Avenue
Campbell, CA 95008
Phone: 408-866-3000
Fax: 408-866-3008
E-mail: mktg@ortechnology.com

Here is some information from the Imation Company at www.imation.com, which also markets the LS120:

No matter how you use your computer, one thing is certain: the number and size of the files you deal with is constantly increasing. Hard drives have had to grow to gigabyte size to make room for huge applications that eat up more and more hard drive space.

But the 3.5-inch diskette hasn't kept up. At 1.44 MB, it often can't even hold an entire business presentation. And you need hundreds of them to back up that gig drive. Not anymore!

Make Room—The Next-Generation Diskette Is Here

The SuperDisk drive and diskette are here: A single 3.5-inch diskette that holds 120 MB. That's 83 times the capacity of a conventional 1.44 MB disk! Here's how we do it!

A single SuperDisk diskette can hold even the largest business presentation. Or that huge Internet download. A single SuperDisk diskette can be used to backup the important data on your hard drive. You can probably think of a zillion things you could do with all that extra storage.

Make Room—Two Drives Instead of One

Unlike other high capacity removable storage options, the SuperDisk LS-120 drive is the only one that lets you read and write all your old disks in addition to SuperDisk 120 MB diskettes. That makes it literally two drives in one.

You can move up to the SuperDisk LS-120 drive right now. The SuperDisk LS-120 drive is available on selected Compaq Deskpro and Compaq Presario models. Or replace the disk drive on your current computer with an easy upgrade. See Drive Options for lots more information about how you can take advantage of SuperDisk technology today.

Make Room on Your Tray Table

This Fall (1997), NEC will release an NEC Versa notebook computer that comes with an internal SuperDisk LS-120 drive. Just think what SuperDisk technology means for mobile users. They'll have a single internal drive that reads high capacity 120 MB SuperDisk diskettes as well as all their old disks. No external drive needed to get high capacity storage!

And accessing high capacity storage on the plane will be easy because the SuperDisk LS-120 drive needs no external power supply. What's more, its low power consumption means the SuperDisk LS-120 drive won't affect battery time.

Make Room for Corporate Users—Without Hassles for You

Many corporate IT professionals say that they can't keep up with demands from their users for hard drive upgrades. The SuperDisk LS-120 drive provides the solution. Companies can extend the life of present systems by giving users an alternative to upgrading all those hard drives.

You can give users one disk drive that reads/writes their old diskettes and provides the extended storage they need. And the SuperDisk looks and feels like a conventional 3.5-inch diskette. There's nothing new to learn.

Your users will love the increased capacity without having to learn a new technology. And the SuperDisk LS-120 drive is five times faster than the disk drives they're used to.

Technical Specifications

Have a look at the technical specifications of the SuperDisk LS-120 drive and diskettes. You can review the specifications for the internal drive in the Compaq Deskpro 4000 or for the parallel port drive, the Imation SuperDisk Drive. But specs are only a part of the story where SuperDisk technology is concerned.

Make Room: There's Nothing Else Like SuperDisk

The real performance advantage of SuperDisk technology is the unique benefits it provides business and home users, mobile users and IT professionals.

1. The SuperDisk LS-120 drive is compatible with both the SuperDisk diskette and standard 3.5-inch diskettes. Users get the benefits of increased removable storage without adding a second drive.
2. SuperDisks diskettes look, feel, and work just like conventional diskettes so users will be more comfortable with it. For IT professionals, you can give your users the storage they want without any additional training.
3. The SuperDisk diskette holds as much data as 83 conventional 1.44 MB diskettes.
4. The SuperDisk diskette has a read/write latch just like a conventional diskette so it is write-protectable. Users can easily protect their work from being overwritten.
5. Mobile users will be able to get the benefits of 120 MB of removable storage without having to carry an extra drive or giving up their ability to read their old disks.

You can reach Imation at

Imation Enterprises Corporation
1 Imation Place
Oakdale, MN 55128-3414
www.imation.com

The 200-Mb Floppy Drive

The Sony Company and Fuji Film Company have developed a 200-Mb floppy drive that will be available by the time you read this. See Fig. 5-3.

Here is a press release about this product:

Sony and FujiFilm Jointly Develop 200 MB High-Capacity 3.5-Inch Floppy Disk System—Compatible with Current 3.5-inch Floppy Disks

Sony Corporation and Fuji Photo Film Co., Ltd. have jointly developed "HiFD,"(x1) a new 3.5-inch floppy disk system with a 200 Megabyte (both sides) storage capacity. This is the largest capacity floppy disk system.

Figure 5-3
The Sony HiFD 200-Mb, 3½-inch floppy drive. (Photo courtesy of Sony.)

In recent years, the rapid increase in the processing power of personal computers and the large increase in size of data handled have led to growing demand for a new high-capacity data recording system that is more efficient and has a fast data transfer rate. Because the current 3.5-inch floppy disk is a convenient, easy-to-use recording medium that has wide penetration around the world, the ability to continue using the data accumulated on this medium in the future is also required of such a system.

In order to meet these demands, Sony and Fujifilm have developed the new HiFD 3.5-inch floppy disk system by combining the technologies of both companies to achieve a next-generation high-capacity floppy disk system that features 200 MB storage capacity, 3.6 MB/sec transfer rate, and backward read- and write-compatibility with current 3.5-inch floppy disks.

Sony and Fujifilm plan to introduce this system in spring 1998. The two companies have already received support for the basic specifications of the system from Alps Electric Co., Ltd. and TEAC Corporation. In the future, Sony and Fujifilm will propose the specifications of the system to a wide range of PC and drive manufacturers.

Sony and Fujifilm have achieved this industry-pioneering task based on the magnetic recording technology that each company possesses. In 1980, Sony developed the 3.5-inch floppy disk system which is widely used in computers throughout the industry. In 1992, Fujifilm developed its Advanced super Thin-layer and high Output Metal Media technology

(ATOMM technology), which has contributed to the realization of many high-capacity magnetic recording systems. In addition, both companies have been steady suppliers of high-quality recording media products for many years.

HiFD: main characteristics

1. **High capacity of 200 MB.** A high-capacity floppy disk with a 200 MB recording capacity has been achieved through the use of a newly developed super-thin layer coating metal disk and a dual discrete gap head.(x2) This disk can easily handle large files such as digitized audio and video data. (Current 3.5-inch floppy disks (2HD) have recording capacity of 1.44 MB when formatted.)
2. **High data transfer rate and quick access** Through high linear recording density and high disk rotational speed of 3600 rpm, a maximum 3.6 MB/sec transfer rate is achieved. Also, through use of a dual discrete gap head, which is a flying-head type(x3) similar to those used in hard disk drives, and a high speed head actuator with VCM (voice coil motor), quick access speed is possible. (Current 3.5-inch floppy disks (2HD)have data transfer rates of approximately 0.06 MB/sec.)
3. **Read/write-compatibility with current 3.5-inch floppy disks** In order to achieve read-and write-compatibility with current 3.5-inch floppy disks, a "dual discrete gap head" has been used. In drives that use the HiFD system, data can be read from current 3.5 inch floppy disks (2DD/2HD),and data can also be written to such disks. This ensures the continued utility of current 3.5-inch floppy disks widely used.
4. **High reliability** Through development of a new structure in which head-loading is done softly, wear on the disk is reduced. Also, through the error correction scheme, high data reliability is ensured. Furthermore, the cartridge uses a new shutter that makes it difficult for dust to enter into the disk.

Specification outline

Recording capacity	200 MB (both sides) (formatted) 240 MB (both sides) (unformatted)
Disk diameter	86 mm
Shell dimensions	94 mm × 90 mm × 3.3 mm (3.5 inch type)
Track pitch	9 micrometers
Track density	2,822 tpi (111 tpmm)
Linear recording density	72–91 kbpi (2.83–3.58 kbmm)
Modulation/Demodulation method	PRML(x4) (16–17 code)
Transfer rate	Maximum 3.6 MB/sec

(x1) HiFD is an abbreviation of "High Capacity Floppy Disk."

(x2) Dual discrete gap head. The head used in the drive for this system features both a narrow gap for 200 MB high density recording and a wide gap for current 3.5-inch floppy disks.

(x3) Flying head. Because the head is flying slightly due to the rotation of the disk when reading or recording, the disk and the head do not come in contact. The result is a long life and high reliability because the erosion due to wear on both the head and the disk is reduced in comparison with a contact head.

(x4) PRML is an abbreviation of "Partial Response Most Likelihood."

How Floppy Drives Operate

Computers rely to a very large extent on magnetism. Magnetic lines of force can be produced when voltage is passed through a coil of wire that is wrapped around a piece of iron. The amount of magnetism produced varies enormously depending on such factors as the voltage level, the number of turns of wire, the properties of the iron core, the frequency of the voltage, and many, many other factors.

Conversely, voltage can be produced when a coil of wire is passed through a magnetic field. So voltage can be used to make magnetism, or magnetism to make voltage.

The floppy drive spins a disk much like a record player. The floppy disk is made from a type of plastic material called *polyethylene terephthalate*. This is coated with a magnetic material made primarily of iron oxide. It is similar to the tape that is used in cassette tape recorders. The drive uses a head, which is basically a piece of iron with a coil of wire around it. The iron core for the head is shaped somewhat like a C. When voltage is passed through the coil of wire, a magnetic field is produced between the ends of the C. The space between the ends of the C, called the *gap,* may be very small. The head records (writes) and plays back (reads) the disk much like the record/playback head in a cassette tape recorder.

There is a considerable difference in the methods of recording on a tape recorder and digital recording. When audio is recorded, the sound waves cause a diaphragm to vibrate in a microphone. Attached to the diaphragm is a magnet that moves in and out of a coil of wire because of the sound vibrations. The movement of the magnet in the coil of wire generates a voltage that goes up and down to exactly match the up and down vibration of the sound. This sine-wave analog voltage is then amplified and fed to the tape-record head. The record head responds with a voltage, or current output, that is a replica of the original sound. The varying current from the head magnetizes the tape with an exact replica of the original sound. When the tape is played back, as the magnetized image on the tape passes by the head, it causes a voltage to be produced that is a replica of the original sound. Of course, the voltage produced by the magnetism on the tape is very small, so it must be amplified. Placing a small voltage on the base of a transistor can cause it to turn on and amplify, or create a much larger replica of the small original voltage.

The voltages in the tape recorder are *alternating current,* that is, they vary up and down. Most of the voltage used in computers is *direct current,* usually 3 to 5 volts dc. Transistors, which act like a switch, can be used to turn the direct current on and off. When the current is on, it can represent a one, when it is off it can represent a zero. A transistor can be switched on and off millions of times per second.

When the head on a disk drive writes or records on the iron oxide surface, a pulse of electricity causes the head to magnetize that portion of track beneath the head. A spot on the track that is magnetized can represent a one; if the next spot of the same track is not magnetized, it can represent a zero. When the tracks are read, the head detects whether each portion of the track is magnetized or not. If the spot is magnetized, it creates a small voltage signal to represent a one, or a zero if it is not magnetized.

Computers operate with a very precise clock rate based on internal crystal oscillators. If a voltage remains high for a certain length of time, it can represent two or more ones. If it is off for a certain length of time, it can represent two or more zeros.

Floppy disks are divided into several concentric *tracks.* Each track is then divided into *sectors.* This system allows the computer to find any particular item on the track. It is amazing to me that the head can find any one byte on a floppy disk that may have over a million bytes. It is even more amazing that the same system can find any one byte on a hard disk that may have over two billion bytes, or two gigabytes.

On a 1.2-Mb floppy disk, 80 tracks are laid down at the rate of 96 tracks per inch. So each track occupies $^1/_{96}$ of an inch, making it about 0.0104 inches wide. The record current that passes through the heads may vary considerably. A stronger current may even magnetize adjacent tracks. To prevent this, the actual recording part of the head is only about a third as wide as the track width. There are two erase heads on each side and behind the record head that extend to the full width of the track. As the record head lays down the square waves that represent ones and zeros, the erase heads trim any signal that may have exceeded the normal width of the track. These side-erase heads form guard bands between each track. (More about tracks and disk formats later in this chapter.)

The Virtual Drive

DOS reserves the letters *A* and *B* for floppy drives. If you have only one drive, you can call it both A and B. For instance, if you said, "copy A: to B:" the drive would copy whatever was in the drive, then prompt you to insert a disk in drive B:. Of course, you could have said "copy A: to A:" and got the same results.

High-Density Drives and Disks

By just looking at a 360-Kb drive and a 1.2-Mb drive, you wouldn't be able to tell which was which. The main differences between the two are magnetic and electrical. The 1.2-Mb drive has an *oersted* (*Oe*) of 600; the 360 Kb has an Oe of 300. The higher Oe means that the material requires a higher head current for magnetization. In order to store 1.2 Mb on the floppy, 80 tracks on each side of the disk are laid down. Each of these tracks is divided into 15 sectors, and 512 bytes can be stored in each sector. These 80 tracks are just half as wide as the 40 tracks of a 360-Kb disk. The 1.2-Mb drives switch to a lower head current when writing to the 360-Kb format.

The $3^1/_2$-inch 1.44-Mb and 720-Kb drives also look very much alike. The main difference is that the 1.44-Mb drive usually has a small microswitch that checks for the square hole in the right rear corner of 1.44-Mb disks. The 1.44-Mb drives will read and write to the 720-Kb format as well as the high density. The 720-Kb drive is as obsolete as the 360 Kb.

The All-Media or Combination Floppy Drive

The 1.2-Mb drive system is also obsolete. However, you might have several 1.2-Mb disks with small programs on them. I have about 500. I might never use them, but I just hate to throw them away. If you have several 1.2-Mb disks, you might consider buying a combination drive.

Most older systems never had enough bays. Many of the desktop cases only provided three or four bays to mount drives. You might not have had space to mount two floppies, two hard drives, a tape backup drive, and a CD-ROM.

The CMS Enhancements Company (714-222-6316) noted this problem. They created their All-Media floppy drive by combining a 1.2-Mb and 1.44-Mb floppy drive into a single unit. The 5¼-inch part of the drive can handle 360-Kb and 1.2-Mb floppies; the 3½-inch part handles 720-Kb and 1.44-Mb floppies. The combination drive requires only a single drive bay. The two drives are never both used at the same time, so there is no problem. They can even share most of the drive electronics. Teac, Canon, and several other companies also manufacture the combo drives. However, they are practically obsolete now, so you might have trouble finding one.

Disk Drive Motors

Disk drives have two motors. One motor drives the spindle that rotates the disk. Then a *stepping motor*, or *actuator*, moves the heads back and forth to the various tracks.

Spindle Motor

If you have an older computer, then no doubt you have a 5¼-inch, 360-Kb floppy drive, or maybe two such drives. If they are very old, they might be full height, or about 3½ inches high. If they are original IBM drives, then they probably have a plastic or rubber "O" ring for a drive belt from the motor to the disk spindle. The "O" ring deteriorates and stretches with time. The speed of the disk is very critical. When the "O" ring stretches, the speed slows down and the spindle might not even turn at all.

I replaced an IBM 5¼-inch, 360-Kb floppy drive in 1985 because it kept giving me errors in reading floppies. At that time, it cost $425 for a new IBM drive. (A 5¼-inch drive today costs about $25.) I didn't realize it at the time, but I could have just replaced the "O" ring.

Most of the newer drives use direct drive motors. Modern floppy drives use a direct drive, where the spindle is just an extension of the motor shaft. The motors are regulated so that the speed is usually fairly constant. The speed of the old 360-Kb floppy drive is 300 RPMs. The 1.2-Mb drive rotates at 360 RPMs, even when reading and writing to a 360-Kb disk. All of the 3½-inch floppy drives rotate at 300 RPMs.

Head Actuator Motor

The head actuator motor is electronically linked to the File Allocation Table. If a request is received to read data from a particular track, say track 20, the actuator motor moves the head, or rather heads to that track.

Floppy drives have two heads, one on top and one on the bottom. They are connected together and move as a single unit. Several large companies manufacture floppy drives, such as Sony, Toshiba, Fuji, Teac, and others. Each company's prices are within a few dollars of the others. Most of them are fairly close in quality, but there might be minor differences. On some of the older drives, a fairly large actuator stepping motor is used to position the heads. It is very quiet and works smoothly as it moves the heads from track to track. It has a steel band around the motor shaft that moves the heads in and out. The steel band is attached to the shaft of the stepper motor and to the heads, moving the heads in discrete steps across the disk. It can find and stop on any track.

The actuator stepping motors on combo drives are small cylindrical motors with a worm screw. The motors groan and grunt as they move the heads from track to track. Other than being a bit noisy, they have worked perfectly. The heads are mounted on the worm screw and as the motor turns, the heads move in and out to access the various tracks. If the software tells the motor to go to track 15, it knows exactly how far to move the heads.

If the worm screw becomes worn, or the steel band on the 1.2-Mb drive that is attached to the actuator motor shaft becomes loose or out of adjustment, a drive might not be able to find the proper tracks. If the hub of the disk you are trying to read has become worn or is not centered exactly on the cone spindle, the heads might not be able to find a track that was previously written, or one that was written on another drive. If your heads are out of alignment, you can write and read on your own machine, since you are using the same misalignment to write and read, but another drive might have trouble reading the disk recorded.

Floppy Controllers

A floppy drive must have a controller to tell it when to turn on, and to go to a certain track and sector. In the early days, the controller was a large board full of chips. Later, some manufacturers integrated the floppy disk controller (FDC) onto the same board as the hard disk controller (HDC). These large, full-length boards were rather expensive, at about $250.

Now, the FDCs are usually built into a single VLSI chip and integrated with a hard disk controller or IDE interface. The FDC and the IDE hard disk interface are often built in on the motherboard. These motherboards usually have a set of upright pins for the flat-ribbon cable connectors. There will usually be pins for the floppy drives, IDE hard drives, and CD-ROMs; for a short printer cable to a back-panel connector; for COM1 and COM2; and for short cables to back-panel connectors for the mouse.

The older controller boards had an edge connector for the cable. Later, boards had two rows of pins for the connector. Be very careful when plugging in the cable connector. Look for pin 1 on the board, and make sure that the different-colored wire goes to that side. If the cable is plugged in backwards, the floppy disk will not work properly—when you try to boot up, the floppy drive will erase portions of the boot section of floppy disk. You will then no longer be able to boot up with the disk. I know that this happens because I have made this stupid mistake. Fortunately, I had a backup boot disk.

Drive-Select Jumpers

It is possible to have four different floppy drives connected to one controller. The floppies will have a set of pins with a jumper so that each drive can be set for a unique number. The pins will be labeled DS0, DS1, DS2, and DS3. Some manufacturers label them DS1, DS2, DS3, and DS4. The vast majority of systems use only two drives. These jumpers will also let you determine which drive is A: or B:. In most cases, you will use them as they come from the factory and never have to worry about these jumpers. Most drives are received with the second set of pins jumpered, which means they are set for drive A:. If you install a second floppy drive, it will also have the second set of pins jumpered just like the A: drive. Don't change it. Since the floppy cable has some twisted wires in it, the controller automatically recognizes it as drive B:. This can be confusing, and you might not get any documentation at all with your drive. Fortunately, they usually work fine as received from the factory.

The combination drives usually have small jumper pins near the miniature power-cable connector. The combos have two columns of pins, one for each drive. There are six pins in each column, and four pins in each column are jumpered. Again, you should never have to reset or bother with these pins. The two drives share a single controller cable connector. If you want to use the 5¼-inch drive as drive A:, then plug the end of the cable with the twisted wires into the cable connector. If you want the 3½-inch drive to be drive A:, then plug in the middle connector that has no twists. Again, fortunately, there is usually no need to move the jumpers.

Data Compression

Data compression can double your disk capacity. It can be used on floppy disks as well as hard disks. Compression can be the least expensive way to increase disk capacity.

Differences among Floppy Disks

The 5¼-inch, 360-Kb and the 3½-inch, 720-Kb disks are called *Double Sided Double Density* (*DS/DD*). The 5¼-inch, 1.2-Mb and the 3½-inch, 1.44-Mb are called *High Density* (*HD*). The 3½-inch double-density disks are usually marked DD; the high-density ones are usually marked HD. The 5¼-inch DS/DD and HD disks usually have no markings, however. They look exactly alike, except that the double-density disk usually has a reinforcing ring or collar around the large center hole, while the high-density disk does not have the ring. Figure 5-4 shows a 1.2-Mb floppy in the upper left, a 360-Kb floppy in the upper right, a 1.44-Mb floppy in lower left, and a 720-Kb floppy in the lower right. The 360-Kb disk shown in the upper right has a white collar or ring; most of the new disks have a black ring.

One of the major differences between the 720-Kb and 1.44-Mb floppies is that the 1.44-Mb one has two small, square holes at the rear of the plastic shell, while the 720-Kb floppy has only one. The 3½-inch drive has a small media-sensor microswitch that protrudes upwards. If it finds a hole on that side of the disk, it knows that it is a 1.44-Mb disk. If there is no hole, it is treated as a 720-Kb. When looking at the back side of the two disks, the square hole on the right rear of the shell has a small black slide that can be moved to cover the hole. Another small microswitch on the drive protrudes upward and checks this hole when the disk is inserted. If the hole is covered, the switch is pressed downward, allowing the disk to be written on. If the hole is open, the switch protects the disk so that it cannot be written on or erased. This is referred to as a *write-protect system.*

Figure 5-4
Different floppy disks: 5¼-inch, 1.2-Mb in upper left; 360-Kb in upper right; 3½" 1.44-Mb in lower left; 720-Kb lower right.

The 5¼-inch write-protect system is just the opposite of that used by the 3½-inch disks. They have a square notch that must be covered with opaque tape to prevent writing or unintentionally erasing the disk. (Incidentally, you must use opaque tape. The 5¼-inch system uses a light that shines through the square notch. If the detector in the system can see the light through the notch, then it can write on the disk. Some people have used clear plastic tape to cover the notch, with disastrous results.)

There might be a time when you would want to make a disk copy of a 720-Kb disk, and all you have are 1.44-Mb disks. Or for some reason, you might want to use a 1.44-Mb disk as a 720-Kb. You can cover the hole with any kind of tape and it will format as 720 Kb.

360 Kb and 1.2 Mb

Although the 360-Kb and 1.2-Mb disks look exactly alike except for the hub ring on the 360-Kb ones, there is a large difference in their magnetic media formulation. Several materials, such as cobalt or barium, can be added to the iron oxide to alter the magnetic properties. Cobalt is added to increase the oersted (Oe) of high-density floppy disks. Barium is used for the 2.88-Mb, extra-high-density (ED) disks. Oe is a measure of the resistance of a material to being magnetized. The lower the Oe, the easier it is to be magnetized. The 360-Kb floppy has an Oe of 300, the 1.2-Mb has 600 Oe. The 360-Kb disks are fairly easy to magnetize or write to, so they require a fairly low head current. The 1.2-Mb disk is more difficult to magnetize, so a much higher head current is required. The 1.2-Mb system can switch the current to match whatever type of disk you tell the system you are using.

If you place a 360-Kb floppy in a 1.2-Mb drive and just type *format*, it will try to format it as a 1.2-Mb. It will find several bad sectors, however, especially near the center, where the sectors are shorter. These sectors will be marked and locked out. The system might report that you have over a megabyte of space on a 360-Kb disk. This disk could be used in an emergency, for instance to move data from one machine to another, but I would not recommend that you use such a disk for any data that is important. The data is packed much closer together when it is recorded as 1.2 Mb. Since the 300 Oe of the 360-Kb disks are so easy to magnetize, it is possible that nearby data might be affected. The data might migrate and eventually deteriorate and become unusable.

720 Kb and 1.44 Mb

The 3½-inch disks have several benefits and characteristics that make them superior to the 5¼-inch disks. The 720-Kb disk can store twice as much data as a 360-Kb in a much smaller space. The 1.44 Mb can store four times as much as the 360 Kb in the same small space. The 3½ inch floppy disks have a hard, plastic, protective shell, so they are not easily damaged. They also have a spring-loaded shutter that automatically covers and protects the head opening when they are not in use.

The 3½-inch systems are much more accurate than the 5¼-inch systems in reading and writing. The 5¼-inch systems have a cone-shaped hub for the large center hole in the disks. If the disks are used for any length of time, it is possible for the hole to become stretched or enlarged. If the disk is not centered exactly on the hub, the heads will not be able to find and read the data. The 3½-inch floppies have a metal hub on the back side. This gives them much greater accuracy in reading and writing, even though the tracks are much closer together.

The 720-Kb disks may have an Oe of 600 to 700. The 1.44-Mb ones may have an Oe of 700 to 720. The Oe of the EHD 2.88-Mb disks may be about 750.

One-Way Insertion

It is possible to insert a 5¼-inch floppy upside-down, backwards, or sideways. When I first started using computers, I inserted a floppy that had the original software on it into a drive. I waited for a while, and nothing happened. Then I got an error message, "Not ready reading drive A. Abort, Retry, Fail?" I almost panicked. I thought for sure that I had destroyed the software. I finally discovered that I had inserted the floppy upside-down. I was still scared that I had damaged the disk. So I did what I should have done when I first got the program: I made a backup copy of the disk. I found that the software was still okay.

You can't actually damage a disk by inserting it upside-down, but you can't read it because the small hole that tells DOS where track 1 begins is on the wrong side when inserted upside-down. And, of course, you can't write to it or format it because of the small hole, and also because the write-protect notch is on the other side. The 3½-inch disks are designed so that they can only be inserted properly. They have arrows at the left top portion of the disks that indicate how they should be inserted into the drive. They have notches on the back that prevents them from being completely inserted upside-down.

The 360-Kb and 720-Kb disks are both obsolete.

Disk Format Structure

Floppy disks are divided into tracks, cylinders and sectors.

Tracks

A disk must be formatted before it can be used. This consists of laying out individual concentric tracks on each side of the disk. If it is a 360-Kb disk, each side is marked or configured with 40 tracks, numbered from 0 to 39. If it is a 1.2-Mb, 720-Kb, or 1.44-Mb disk, each side is configured with 80 tracks, numbered from 0 to 79.

The tracks have the same number on the top and bottom of the disk. The top is side 0 and the bottom is side 1. When the head is over track 1 on the top, it is also over track 1 on the bottom. The heads move as a single unit to the various tracks by a head actuator motor or positioner. When data is written to a track, as much as possible is written on the top track, then the head is electronically switched and it continues to write to the same track on the bottom side. It is much faster and easier to electronically switch between the heads than to move them to another track.

Cylinders

If you could strip away all of the other tracks on each side of track 1 on side 0 and track 1 on side 1, what you would have would be very flat, but it might look like a cylinder. So if a disk has 40 tracks, such as the 360-Kb, it has 40 cylinders; the 1.2-Mb and 1.44-Mb have 80 cylinders.

Sectors

Each of the tracks is divided into sectors. Each track of the 360-Kb disk is divided into nine sectors; each of the 1.2-Mb tracks is divided into 15 sectors; each of the 720-Kb tracks is divided into nine sectors; each of the 1.44-Mb tracks is divided into 18 sectors; and each of the 2.88-Mb tracks is divided into 36 sectors. Each sector can contain 512 bytes. Multiplying the number of sectors times the number of bytes per sector times the number of tracks times the two sides gives the amount of data that can be stored on a disk. For instance, the 1.2 Mb has 15 sectors times 512 bytes times 80 tracks times two sides:

$15 \times 512 \times 80 \times 2 = 1{,}228{,}800$ bytes

The system uses 14,898 bytes to mark the tracks and sectors during formatting, so there is actually 1,213,952 bytes available on a 1.2-Mb floppy. Figure 5-5 is a diagram showing how the tracks and sectors are laid out on a disk.

Clusters or Allocation Units

DOS allocates one or more sectors on a disk and calls it a *cluster* or *allocation unit*. On the 360-Kb and 720-Kb disks, a cluster or allocation unit is two sectors. On the 1.2-Mb and 1.44-Mb disks, each allocation unit is one sector. Only single files or parts of single files can be written into an allocation unit. If two different files were written into a single allocation unit, the data would become mixed and corrupted.

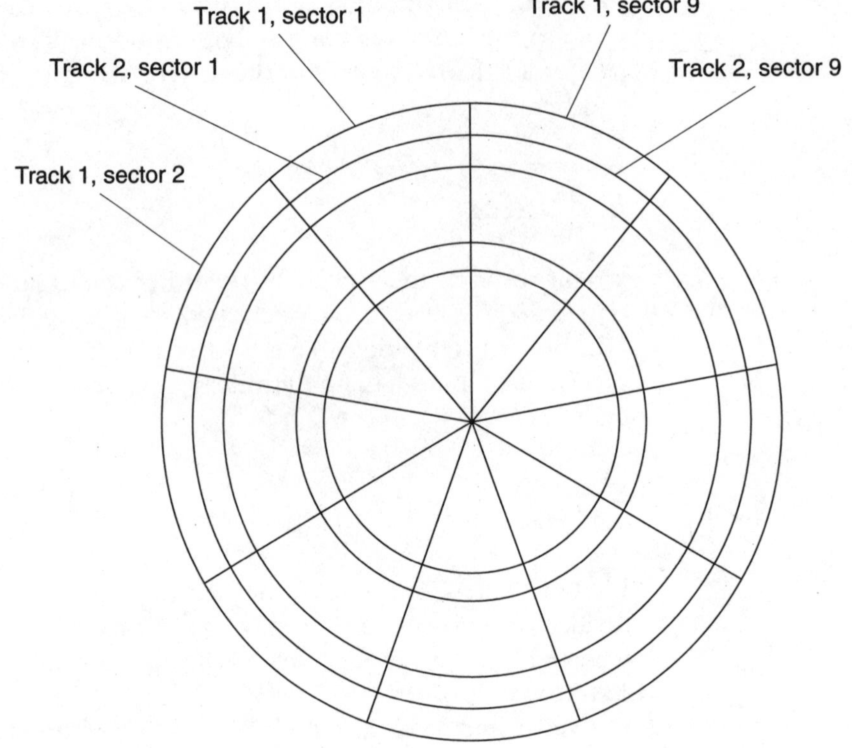

Figure 5-5
A diagram showing how the tracks and sectors are laid out on a disk.

File Allocation Table (FAT)

During formatting, a *File Allocation Table* (*FAT*) is created on the first track of the disk. This FAT acts like a table of contents for a book. Whenever a file is recorded on a disk, the file is broken up into allocation units. The head looks in the FAT to find empty units, then records the parts of the file in any empty units it can find. Part of the file may be recorded in sector 5 of track 10, part in sector 8 of track 15, and anyplace it can find empty sectors. It records the location of all the various parts of the file in the FAT. With this method, parts of a file can be erased, changed, or added to without changing the entire disk.

TPI

The 40 tracks of a 360-Kb disk are laid down at a rate of 48 tracks per inch (TPI), so each of the 40 tracks is $^1/_{48}$ of an inch wide. The 80 tracks of the 1.2-Mb disk are laid down at a rate of 96 TPI, so each track is $^1/_{96}$ of an inch. The 80 tracks of the $3^1/_2$-inch disks are laid down at a density of 135 per inch, or 0.0074 inches per track.

Read Accuracy

The $5^1/_4$-inch disks have a $1^1/_8$-inch center hole. The drives have a spindle with a conical hub that comes up through this hole when the drive latch is closed. This centers the disk so that the heads will be able to find each track. The plastic material that the disk is made from is subject to environmental changes and wear and tear. The conical spindle might not center each disk exactly, so head-to-track accuracy is difficult with more than 80 tracks. (If you have trouble reading a disk, it might be off center. It might help if you remove the disk and reinsert it.) Most 360-Kb disks use a reinforcement hub ring, but it probably doesn't help much. The 1.2-Mb floppies do not use a hub ring. Except for the hub ring, 360-Kb and 1.2-Mb disks look exactly the same.

If your drive consistently has trouble reading your disks, or especially reading disks recorded on another machine, the heads might be out of alignment. The steel band or worm screw from the actuator motor that moves the heads might have slipped or become worn, so the actuator or head positioner might not be able to move the heads to the proper track. It is possible to have the heads realigned, but it is time-consuming and expensive. Computer service time costs from $50 to $100 or more per hour. It would probably be much less expensive to scrap the drive and buy a new one.

The $3^1/_2$-inch disks have a metal hub on the back that is used to center the disks. The tracks of the $3^1/_2$-inch floppies are narrower and greater in density per inch, but because of the metal hub, the head-tracking accuracy is much better than that of the $5^1/_4$-inch systems.

Some Differences between Floppies and Hard Disks

Hard disks have very accurate and precise head-tracking systems. Some hard disks have a density up to 3000 or more tracks per inch, so much more data can be stored on a hard disk than on a floppy.

Floppy disks have a very smooth, lubricated surface. They rotate at a fairly slow 300 RPMs. Magnetic lines of force deteriorate very fast with distance, so the closer the heads, the better they can read and write. Floppy heads are in direct contact with the floppy disks. Hard disks rotate at speeds from 3600 up to 7200 RPMs. The heads and surface would be severely damaged if they came in contact at this speed, so heads "fly" over the surface of each disk, just a few millionths of an inch above it.

Comparison of Floppy Disks

Table 5-1 shows some of the differences in the various types of floppy disks. Notice that the maximum number of root directories is the same for the 720-Kb, 1.2-Mb, and 1.44-Mb. The 2.88-Mb has four times the capacity of the 720-Kb, yet allows only 16 more root entries. This means that you can enter 224 different files on a 1.2-Mb disk, but if you try to enter one more, it will not accept it, even though you might have hundreds of unused bytes. The reason is that DOS's FAT was designed for this limited number of files. There is an easy way around this problem. Just create subdirectories, like those created on a hard disk, by typing *MD* for *make directory*. If necessary, you can even make subdirectories of the subdirectories.

Formatting

Formatting with Windows 95 is much easier than with earlier DOS-based operating systems. Just point your mouse to the My Computer icon and click. All of your drives will be shown. Point to whichever one you want to format and click. It will be highlighted. Point to File and click, and you will be given several options, one of which is to format a disk.

For those who might still be using an older version of DOS, but have a 1.2-Mb disk for the A: drive, to format a 360-Kb disk with it, type FORMAT A: /4. To format a 1.2-Mb disk, you only have to type FORMAT A:. If you insert a 360-Kb disk, it will try to format it as 1.2-Mb, and will probably find several bad sectors.

To format a 720-Kb disk on a 1.44-Mb B: drive, type *FORMAT B: /f:720.* To format a 1.44-Mb disk, just type *FORMAT B:.*

The FORMAT command in newer versions of DOS and Windows can take a very long time before it starts. It searches the floppy disk, that you want to unformat the disk, just type *UNFORMAT.*

TABLE 5-1
Capacities of Various Disk Types

Disk Type	Tracks Per Side	Sectors/Track	Unformatted Capacity	System Use	Available to User	Maximum Directories
360 Kb	40	9	368640	6144	362496	112
1.2 Mb	80	15	1228800	14898	1213952	224
720 Kb	80	9	737280	12800	724480	224
1.44 Mb	80	18	1474560	16896	1457664	224
2.88 Mb	80	36	2949120	33792	2915328	240

In most cases, however, I don't want to unformat a disk—especially if it is one that has never been formatted before. You can speed up the formatting process by typing *FORMAT A:/U*. This performs an unconditional format. If the disk has been formatted before, you can type *FORMAT A:/Q*. This gives you a quick format by just erasing the first letter of the files in the File Allocation Table of the disk.

Cost of Disks

All floppy disks are now quite reasonable. The 1.44-Mb ones are so inexpensive that many companies send out demo disks, press releases, and junk mail on them. I usually erase them and reuse them. I feel it is my duty to recycle. One Internet company sent out several million copies of their sign-up software. I got so many copies of their software that I didn't have to buy any floppies for some time.

There are several discount mail-order floppy disk stores. Check the computer magazines for ads. Some companies are selling 1.44-Mb preformatted disks for as little as 20 cents apiece. These are real bargains. At one time, I paid as much as $2.50 each for 360-Kb floppy disks.

CHAPTER 6

Choosing a Hard Disk

This chapter covers some of the different types of hard drives and some hard-disk basics. Formatting of the hard drives is discussed in Chapter 12, after the system is assembled.

What Should You Buy?

You have a very large number of different types and capacities of hard disks to choose from. Of course, what you choose depends on what you need to do with your computer and how much you want to spend. I would recommend that you buy two drives; ideally, a large-capacity IDE and a similar SCSI. A similar SCSI drive will be a bit more expensive, however. In addition, if you don't already have an SCSI interface board, you will have to buy one. Except for some of the very high-end applications, there is very little if any difference in the SCSI and the IDE systems, so if you don't have a lot of money, you can do very well with two IDE drives.

The reason for having two drives is for backup purposes. You never know when disaster might strike. Disk drives are very reliable nowadays, but they are mechanical devices, and some of them do crash. You should always have your critical files backed up. You can easily and quickly copy and back up files to another hard disk. If you have two IDE drives, there is very little chance that both of them would crash at the same time. If you have an IDE and an SCSI, there is even less of a chance that both would crash at the same time.

Capacity

When you consider capacity, buy the biggest you can afford. You might have heard of Mr. C. Northcote Parkinson. After observing business organizations for some time, he formulated several laws. One law says, "Work expands to fill up available employee time." A parallel law that paraphrases Mr. Parkinson's immutable law might say, "Data expands to fill up available hard-disk space." Just a short time ago, 200 megabytes was a large disk. But that was before Microsoft and other companies began developing "bloatware" that required 200 Mb or more for a single program. Office 97 requires 191 Mb for a full installation. So don't even think of buying anything less than 2 Gb. A better minimum would be 4 Gb. New software programs have become more and more friendly and offer more and more options. Most of the basic application programs that you will need, such as spreadsheets, databases, CAD programs, and word processors, will each require 40 to 80 Mb of disk storage space.

Cost

Most of the major hard disk drives are fairly close in quality and price. My recommendation is to buy the highest-capacity drive that you can possibly afford. I recently bought a 3.5-Gb hard disk drive for $215, which is about 6 cents per megabyte. (You will be able to buy a similar drive for even less by the time your read this.) That is absolutely fantastic. A couple of years ago, I paid $750 for a 1.05-Gb hard drive. I would not have believed that it was possible for a precision piece of machinery like this to be sold for any less. As I write this, I am looking at an ad in *PC Magazine* (December 2, 1997) from the Bason Company (800-238-4453), advertising several hard drives. One is an IDE Maxtor 8700, 7-Gb drive for $359, or just a bit more than 5 cents per megabyte.

Similarly, the Seagate Company's Medalist Pro 9140 is 9.1 Gb. The estimated street price at this time is $495. That is 5.4 cents per megabyte. The prices are fantastically low. They will be even less by the time you read this.

IDE or ATA Drives

The most popular drives today are those with Integrated Drive Electronics (IDE). They are sometimes called ATA (for Advanced Technology Attachment) drives because they were first developed for use on the 286 AT. The drives are similar to SCSI drives in that all of their controller electronics are integrated on the drive. You do not need a controller card such as those required by the older MFM, RLL, and ESDI drives, but you do need an interface. The interface will be a set of upright pins on the motherboard.

IDE drives are a bit less expensive than SCSI. One major difference is that the IDE interface might cost nothing because it is usually built in on all new motherboards. The newer IDE drives are designed for the Ultra DMA/33 specification.

SCSI

At one time, SCSI drives were usually reserved for larger-capacity and faster drives. Now, however, IDE drives are equivalent in almost all respects. Most companies who manufacture IDE drives also make identical SCSI drive models. The built-in electronics on the two drives are very similar, except one has an SCSI adapter.

SCSI stands for Small Computer System Interface. It is called "small computer" because when it was first proposed, the big iron mainframes ruled the computer world. However, the desktop PCs were proliferating and there was a real need to be able to connect various peripherals to these PCs. It was a very ambitious undertaking. There wasn't even a standard among PCs at that time. Imagine the problems in trying to devise a standard that would work with several nonstandard machines. In addition, this standard would have to work with several different peripherals from different companies.

Devices that conform to the SCSI standard have most of their controller functions built into the device. The different devices may be two or more SCSI hard-disk drives, one or more CD-ROM drives, a scanner, a tape backup unit, or other products.

An SCSI board can be an interface for up to seven different intelligent devices to a computer. SCSI devices are called *logical units*. Each device is assigned a *logical unit number* (*LUN*). The devices have switches or jumpers that must be set to the proper LUN. If you have several SCSI devices attached to your system, you should keep a list of the LUNs used. This will make it easier to know what number to assign a new device. Ordinarily, your system will look for the C: drive or floppy (A:) drive to boot your computer. Usually, the system will assign drive letters first to any IDE drives that are present, then the SCSI. If you have only SCSI drives, and will be using one as a boot drive, you should assign it a lower LUN number than any other devices so that it will be loaded first.

IDE and SCSI drives have most of the disk controlling functions integrated onto the drive. This makes a lot of sense because the control electronics can be optimally matched to the drive. The equivalent SCSI and IDE hard drives made by most companies are physically the same size. They both use the same type of zone bit recording and rotational speed. The only difference in the two is the onboard electronics.

SCSI systems need a host adapter, or interface card, to drive them. SCSI interfaces are rather complex. Some of the older systems were very difficult to set up. The newer systems are the Plug-and-Play (PNP) variety and are very easy to install. Many of the newer motherboards now have the SCSI interface built in. There will be a set of pins or a connector for the SCSI cable.

Removable Disk Drives

Several companies manufacture removable disk drives of various models and types. There are some advantages and disadvantages in removable drives.

SyQuest Drives

SyQuest (800-245-2278, www.syquest.com) has several models of hard-disk drives with removable cartridges. Each cartridge is actually a single hard-disk platter. Their Syjet has 1.5-Gb cartridges. Their EZ230, as the name implies, uses 230-Mb cartridges.

I have one of their earlier models, an EZ135, which uses 135-Mb cartridges. Shown in Fig. 6-1, it is great for backup, to transfer large files from one machine to another, and just general storage. The cartridges sold for about $20. The EZ135 has now been discontinued.

SyQuest has different models of each unit so that they can be mounted internally, on SCSI, or externally through parallel ports.

Olympus MOS330E

Olympus (800-347-4027, www.olympus.com) markets its MOS330E with a 3.5-inch magneto-optical drive system. It uses 230-Mb cartridges. The cost

Figure 6-1
A SyQuest 135-Mb drive with removable disks. It plugs into the printer port so it can be moved easily to other computers. Newer SyQuest models are 270 Mb.

of the drive is about the same as the SyQuest, but the cartridges are very reasonable, at about $10 each.

Fujitsu DynaMO 230

The Fujitsu (800-626-4686, www.fcpa.com) DynaMO 230 is a 230-Mb magneto-optical drive. It is designed to be used in a PC Card Type II slot. (*PC Card* is the new name for the PCMCIA system.) This drive can be used with most laptops or any desktop that is equipped with a PC Card slot.

Iomega Jaz Drive

The Iomega Jaz Drive from the Iomega Company (800-697-8833, www.iomega.com) is a drive that originally used 1.07-Gb magneto-optical cartridges. They now have 2-Gb cartridges. It is an SCSI device. If you have a laptop with SCSI, it can be plugged in externally. Cartridges are less than $100 each. It is very fast and great for backing up data.

Iomega 100-Mb Zip Floppy Disk and Drive

The Iomega Zip drive uses a $3^1/_2$-inch disk that is similar to a floppy, but this disk can store 100 Mb. This system is fairly inexpensive.

Iomega 40-Mb clik! Disk and Drive

The following is an Iomega press release about their clik! drive.

> clik! technology is a clik! disk and a clik! drive. The clik! disk holds 40Mb of data and fits in the palm of your hand. The clik! drive, about the size of a mouse, works with just about every handheld digital device and desktop product on the market. clik! is the connection between your handheld devices and your PC. Here's what you can do with clik!:
>
> *Digital Camera*—clik! disks let you store up to 40 high-res (megapixel) images or hundreds of low-res images. A clik! disk becomes your digital "roll of film," releasing you from the PC to take pictures wherever you choose.

Handheld PC (HPC)—clik! disks let you bring more of your desktop to your palmtop. clik! disks let you store a number of color Microsoft PowerPoint presentations or graphic-heavy spreadsheets or hundreds of word documents, e-mails, and attachments.

Personal Digital Assistant (PDA)—On one clik! disk you can store thousands of addresses or hundreds of notes, faxes, and e-mails. clik! disks offer you unlimited, inexpensive (under $10 MSRP), removable storage.

Smart Phone—The clik! removable storage disk gives you the capacity to store up to 4 hours of voice messages or hundreds of e-mails.

Global Positioning System (GPS)—Store maps and e-mails on one clik! disk. And clik! disks offer you unlimited, inexpensive (under $10 MSRP), removable storage.

Personal Projector—clik! disks let you store approximately 25-color, ten-page, PowerPoint presentations with graphics. clik! disks offer you unlimited, inexpensive (under $10 MSRP), removable storage.

Avatar Shark 250

The Avatar Shark 250, from Avatar Peripherals (408-321-0110, www.goavatar.com), as its name implies, is a 250-Mb drive. Avatar advertises it as the world's smallest drive. The drive, shown in Fig. 6-2, is about 5 inches long and 3½ inches wide. It weighs less than a half-pound and the 250-Mb 2½-inch cartridge is about the size of a matchbook. It plugs into the parallel port. Unlike other parallel-port drives, the Shark gets all the power that it needs from the parallel port, and does not need a separate power supply. It is great for desktops as well as laptops.

Parallel Port Hard Drives

Many of the drives just listed are available as parallel port models. As such, they can be used with laptops, PS/2s, or any computer with a parallel port. These drives are great for backup, for removal and security, and for data transport. They come in several capacities from 100 Mb up to 1 Gb or more.

Since these drives plug into the computer's only parallel port, they usually provide a parallel-port connector for the printer. Most of them come with a small transformer power supply.

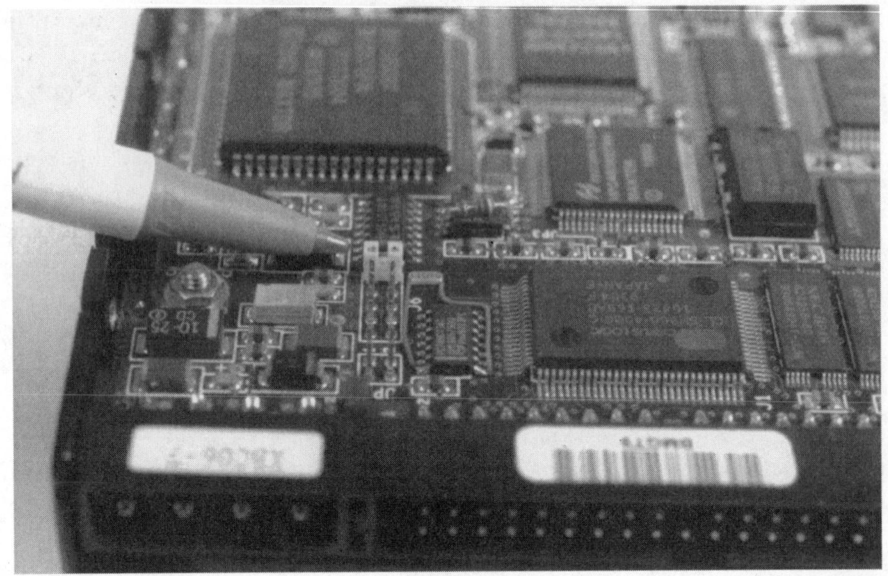

Figure 6-2 The small Avatar Shark 250-Mb drive and cartridge. The 250-Mb cartridge is about the size of a matchbook.

Magneto-Optical Drives

Magneto-optical (M-O) drives combine the magnetic and optical technologies. Magnetic disks, especially floppies, can be easily erased. Over a period of time, the data on a magnetic disk, hard or floppy, will gradually deteriorate. Some critical data must be renewed about every two years.

If a magnetic material has a high coercivity, or a high resistance to being magnetized, it will also resist being demagnetized. (Coercivity is measured by oersteds, Oe). The higher the Oe, however, the more current is needed to magnetize the area. A large amount of current can magnetize a large area of the disk. In order to pack more density, the magnetized area must be very small.

The Oe of a material decreases as it is heated. Most materials have a Curie temperature at which the Oe becomes zero. By heating the magnetic medium with a laser beam, a very small current can be used to write data to a disk. The heated spots cool very quickly and regain their high coercivity. The disks can be easily written over or changed by heating up the area again with the laser beam.

The most popular M-O drives at this time have a capacity of 128 Mb and 256 Mb. M-O disks have a minimum lifetime of more than ten years without degradation of data.

Recordable CD-ROMs

Several companies now offer drives that can record CD-ROM discs. When first introduced, the recordable drives cost up to $10,000. There are some that are available today for less than $3500. A blank CD-ROM disc can hold up to 600 Mb of data. This is a great way to back up or archive data and records that should never change. Blank CD-ROM discs cost just a few dollars each, so if you wanted to change some of the data, just change the data and record it onto another disc.

Unlike magnetic media that deteriorates or can be erased, data on a CD-ROM should last for many, many years.

WORMs

The Write-Once, Read-Many (WORM) type of drive is a laser system similar to the recordable CD-ROM. One difference is that it uses a larger disk and can store much more data. Another is that there are no standards for the system. Several companies manufacture proprietary systems that are incompatible with other systems. WORM systems are also much more expensive than CD-ROM systems.

Advantages of Removable Disk Drives

The following are some of the advantages of removable disks or cartridges.

Security There might be data on a hard disk that is accessible to other people. If the data is sensitive, such as company design secrets or personal employee data, the removable disks can be removed and locked up for security. After all, you wouldn't want anyone seeing just what salary the boss was getting, or what his golf score might be.

Unlimited Capacity With enough cartridges, you will never have to worry about running out of disk space. If you fill one cartridge, just pop in another and continue.

Fast Backup One reason people don't like to back up their data is that it is usually a lot of trouble and takes a lot of time, especially if you are using tape backup. It might take several hours to back up a large hard drive onto tape; it can take only seconds or minutes to back up the same data onto a removable drive. A big advantage of the removable cartridge backup is that the data can be randomly accessed; a tape backup can only be accessed sequentially. If you want a file that is in the middle of the tape, you must run through the tape to find it.

Moving Data to Another Computer If you have two or more computer systems with the same type of removable drives, you can easily transfer large amounts of data from one machine to another. It is possible to send the data on a cartridge through the mail to other locations that have the same type of system.

Multiple Users of One Software Copy Most people don't bother to read the license agreements that come with software—and who can blame them. The agreements are often several pages long, in small type, and filled with legal jargon. Essentially, most of them simply say you are granted the right to use one copy of the enclosed software on a single computer.

Suppose, however, that you have several computers in an office. Some people might be doing nothing but word processing on their computers most of the time. Others might be running only databases or spreadsheets. Occasionally, these users might need to use one of the other programs for a short time. If these users all have standard hard disks, then legally, you need a separate copy of all of the software used on the computers. Some software programs cost from $500 to $1000 or more. If you have several computers in an office, providing individual packages for each machine can be quite expensive.

If these computers had removable disks, then a copy of a software program could be installed on the cartridge and the cartridge could be used on the different machines.

Some Disadvantages of Removable Drives

There are disadvantages to removable drives, as well as advantages. The following are some of the disadvantages.

Limited Cartridge Capacity Many removable cartridges have a capacity of only 100 Mb to 250 Mb. At one time, that was a whole lot of storage space. Today, however, that might not be enough to store all of the data that you need to operate some large programs.

According to Murphy's Law, there will always be times when you need to access a file that is on another cartridge. If you only have one removable drive, it could be a problem. Since these are SCSI drives, though, you could solve that problem by installing up to seven removable drives.

Data compression can also be used with all of the removable disks as easily as on hard disks.

Cost of Cartridges Another disadvantage is that removable drives cost a bit more than a standard hard drive. A cartridge might cost from $25 to over $100. However, if you consider that, with enough cartridges, the capacity is unlimited, the cost might be quite reasonable.

M-O disks are about the least expensive of all the cartridges, but the initial cost of the drive itself might be a bit higher than other drives.

Need for Accessible Bays If you intend to buy an internal system with removable cartridges, you will need to access it from the front panel. If you have a system that has a limited number of bays that are accessible from the outside, this might be a problem. Some desktop cases only have four bays, two accessible bays for floppy disk and CD-ROM drives, and two internal bays for hard disks. If your system does not have enough bays, you might consider buying a larger case, perhaps a tower case. A case and power supply will cost from about $35 to over $100 for the large tower case with a 325-watt power supply. Many tower systems have from five to eight bays. It is very easy to transfer a system from one case to another.

The external drives with removable disks usually cost a bit more than the internally mounted drives. The extra cost is because of the need for the power supply and drive case.

Access Speed Still another disadvantage is that some of the removable drives are a bit slower than most standard hard drives. The M-O drives are especially slow because it takes time to heat the area with the laser. If you don't mind waiting a few milliseconds, however, it shouldn't be too much of a problem.

Data Compression

The capacity of all of the hard drives mentioned so far in this chapter can be doubled by using data compression with them. Windows 95 comes with a utility called DriveSpace that can compress data on hard drives and on floppies. Before Windows 95, MS-DOS, IBM PC DOS, and DR DOS all had a disk-compression utility. Stacker, from Stac Electronics, was one of the most popular stand-alone compression utilities. Microsoft and Stac Electronics are now partners. The DriveSpace utility is the result of that partnership.

Using data compression is certainly inexpensive and easier than installing a second, or larger, hard disk. As the cost of hard-disk drives are now very reasonable, however, you might sleep better at night if you install a larger hard disk rather than compress your data.

Floppy and Hard-Drive Similarities

A hard-disk drive is similar to a floppy-disk drive in some respects. Floppy drives have a single disk, while hard drives might have an assembly of one or more rigid disks. The hard disk's platters are coated with a magnetic plating, similar to that of floppy disks. Depending on the capacity, there might be several disks on a common spindle. A motor turns the floppy spindle at 300 RPMs; the hard-disk spindle can turn from 3600 RPMs to 10,000 RPMs.

There will be a read/write head on the top and one on the bottom of each platter or disk. On floppy-disk systems, the head actually comes in contact with the disk; on a hard-disk system, the head "flies" just a few millionths of an inch from the disk on a cushion of purified air. If the head were to contact the disk at the high speed that it turns, it would cause a "head crash." A crash can destroy the disk, the head, and all the data that might be on the disk.

Formatting

You cannot use a floppy disk or a hard disk until it has been formatted. Formatting divides the disk up into partitions—tracks and sectors—so that any information on the disk can be instantly found and accessed. Formatting hard disks is discussed in detail in Chapter 12.

Tracks and Sectors

Like the floppy disk, the hard disk is formatted into several individual concentric tracks. A 360-Kb floppy has 40 tracks on each side; a high-capacity hard disk might have 3000 or more tracks. Also like the floppy, each hard-disk track is divided into sectors, usually of 512 bytes. While the 360-Kb floppy system divides each track into nine sectors, however, a hard-disk system might divide each track into as many as 84 sectors.

Clusters and Allocation Units

A sector is only 512 bytes, but most files are much longer than that, so DOS lumps two or more sectors together and calls it a *cluster* or *allocation unit.* If an empty cluster is on track 5, the system will record as much of the file as it can there, then move to the next empty cluster, which could be on track 20. DOS combines sectors into allocation units depending on the capacity of the hard disk. For a 100-Mb disk, DOS combines four sectors, or 2048 bytes, into each allocation unit; for 200 Mb, each allocation unit is composed of eight sectors, or 4096 bytes.

File Allocation Table

The location of each part of the file, as well as which cluster it is in, is recorded in the File Allocation Table (FAT) so the computer has no trouble finding it. Usually, the larger the hard-disk partition, the more sectors are assigned to each cluster or allocation unit.

A 500-Mb hard disk would actually have 524,288,000 bytes. Dividing this number by 512 bytes to find the number of actual sectors gives 1,024,000 sectors. If each allocation unit is made up of four sectors, there would only be 256,000 of them; if eight sectors are used, then the operating system would only have to worry about the location of 128,000 allocation units. If it had to search through 1,024,000 entries in the FAT each time it accessed the hard disk, it would slow things down considerably. The FAT is updated and rewritten each time the disk is accessed. A large FAT would take a lot of time and disk space.

On one of my older machines, I had a 500-Mb hard disk that was divided into three logical disks: one 100-Mb and two 200-Mb. The 100-Mb logical disk used four sectors per allocation unit, so it has 51,219 clusters or allocation units. The 200-Mb ones used eight sectors per allocation units, so they each had 51,283 allocation units, about the same number as the 100-Mb disk. (A 500-Mb disk is not nearly enough today. I recently removed this disk and gave it to a nephew. I replaced it with a 4.3-Gb drive.)

The FAT is very important. If it is damaged or erased, you will not be able to access any of the data on the disk. The heads just won't know where to look for the data. The FAT is usually written on track 0 of the hard disk. Because it is so important, a second copy is also made near the center of the disk so that if the original is damaged, it is possible to use the copy.

DOS 3.3 and earlier versions could only handle hard disks up to 32 Mb. If you bought a 40 Mb hard disk, you could only use 32 Mb of it unless you used special software such as DiskManager. DOS 4.0 and later versions of DOS and Windows allow very large partitions, up to two gigabytes. Windows 95 allows you to format very large disks as a single partition, or to make very large partitions in large disks. At the DOS C: prompt, when you type *FDisk*, this message will come up:

```
This version of Windows includes improved support for large disks,
resulting in more efficient use of disk space on large disks, and
allowing disks over 2 Gb to be formatted as a single drive.
IMPORTANT: If you enable large disk support and create any new drives
on this disk, you will not be able to access the new drive(s) using
other operating systems, including some versions of Windows 95 and
Windows NT, as well as earlier versions of Windows and MS-DOS. In
addition, disk utilities that were not designed explicitly for the
FAT32 file system will not be able to work with this disk. If you
need to access this disk with other operating systems or older disk
utilities, do not enable large size drive support.
Do you wish to enable large disk support (Y/N) [N].
```

Unless your business or situation needs a very large single drive, I would recommend not using the large disk support. If you have a large drive, such as a 6-Gb drive, or even two such drives, you can format them as several 2-Gb logical drives.

If there are several partitions on a disk and one of them fails, you might be able to recover the data in the other partitions. If your disk is one large partition and it fails, you might not be able to recover any of the data, especially if the FAT is destroyed. Norton Utilities can be set up to make a mirror image of the FAT. If the primary FAT is destroyed, you can still use the mirror image.

One of the disadvantages of creating large logical drives is that the larger the drive, the more sectors are used to create each cluster or allocation unit. Remember that a sector is 512 bytes. If you have a lot of small files, it might waste a lot of disk space. Table 6-1 shows how DOS and Windows set up the allocation-unit size.

The figures in Table 6-1 are for FAT16 systems, which use 16 bits to store FAT entries. One reason for making the clusters or allocation units larger was to cut down on the amount of space in which the FAT would need to be stored. Also, remember that the larger the number of FATs the system has to search, the more it slows down the system.

Because of today's much faster systems and much larger disk drives, a version of Windows 95 released in 1996 gives you the choice of using a FAT32 system. The FAT32 system allows more FATs to be stored and allows very small clusters.

TABLE 6-1 Cluster or Allocation Sizes

Partition Size	Cluster Size
16—128 Mb	2 Kb (4 sectors)
128—256 Mb	4 Kb (8 sectors)
256—512 Mb	8 Kb (16 sectors)
512 Mb—1 Gb	16 Kb (32 sectors)
1—2 Gb	32 Kb (64 sectors)

Cylinders

Just like the floppy, each same-numbered track on the top and bottom of a disk is called a *cylinder.* Since a hard disk may have ten or more platters, the concept of cylinders is even more realistic. Incidentally, some BIOS chips in some of the older computers would not allow you to install a hard disk that had more than 1024 cylinders and 63 sectors, which is about 504 Mb. It was possible to install a disk larger than 500 Mb by using special driver software such as Disk Manager from the Ontrack Corporation.

Head Actuators or Positioners

Like the floppy, a head motor or head actuator moves the heads on a hard drive from track to track. The head actuator must move the heads quickly and accurately to a specified track, then detect the small variations in the magnetic fields in the specified sectors. Some less expensive and older hard disks use a stepper motor similar to those used on floppy disk drives to move the head from track to track. Most newer hard disks use a *voice coil* type of motor, which is much smoother, quieter, and faster than the stepper motors.

The voice coil of a loudspeaker is made up of a coil of wire that is wound on a hollow tube attached to the material of the speaker cone. Permanent magnets are then placed inside and around the outside of the coil. Whenever a voltage is passed through the coil of wire, it causes magnetic lines of force to be built up around the coil. Depending on the polarity of the input voltage, these lines of magnetic flux will be either the same or opposite the lines of force of the permanent magnets. If the polarity of the voltage, for instance a plus voltage, causes the lines of force to be the same as the permanent magnet, then they will repel each other, and the voice coil will move forward. If they are opposite, they will attract each other and the coil will move backwards.

Most of the better and faster hard disks use voice coil technology with a closed-loop servo control. They usually use one surface of one of the disks to store data and track locations. Most specification sheets give the number of heads on a drive. Since all the heads are on the same spindle, they all move as one. When the servo head moves to a certain track and sector, the other heads follow. Feedback information from the closed-servo loop positions the head to the exact track very accurately.

Figure 6-3 shows a Seagate hard drive with the cover removed to show the heads and disks. The voice coil actuator is the section in the top left corner of the drive. It can quickly and accurately swing the arm and head to any track on the disk.

Speed of Rotation and Density

As the disk spins beneath the head, a pulse of voltage through the head causes the area of the track that is beneath the head at that time to become magnetized. If this pulse of voltage is turned on for a certain amount of time, then turned off for some amount of time, it can represent the writing or recording of ones and zeros. The hard disk spins much faster than a floppy, so the duration of the magnetizing pulses can be much shorter at a higher frequency.

The recording density depends to a great extent on the changes in magnetic flux. The faster the disk spins, the greater the number of changes. This allows much more data to be recorded in the same amount of space. Most hard disks spin at a rate between 3600 to 7200 RPMs. Seagate's Cheetah spins at 10,000 RPMs. They have two models, a 1-inch-high model with four platters that has a capacity of 4.55 Gb and a 1.6-inch-high model with eight platters that has a capacity of 9.1 Gb. The Quantum Atlas is also 1.6 inches high and has a capacity of

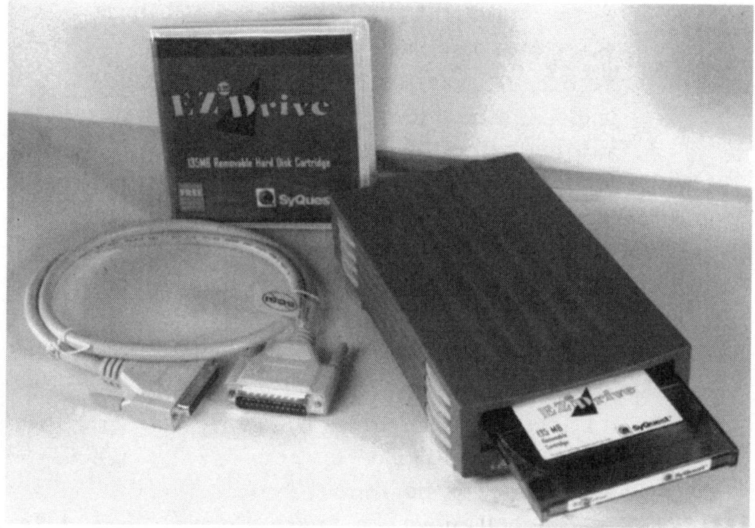

Figure 6-3
A Seagate hard drive with the cover removed. (Photo courtesy Seagate.)

9 Gb, but it has 10 platters. With the two extra platters, it should have more capacity than the Seagate, but the Quantum spins at 7200 RPM.

Areal density is the number of bits per inch times the number of tracks per inch. The areal density continues to be improved. At the present time, some manufacturers are achieving one billion bits per square inch. Within a couple of years, it should reach 10 billion bits per square inch.

Timing

Everything that a computer does depends on precise timing. Crystals and oscillators are set up so that certain circuits perform a task at a specific time. These oscillating circuits are usually called *clock circuits*. The clock frequency for the old, standard, Modified Frequency Modulation (MFM) method of reading and writing to a hard disk is 10 MHz per second. To write on the disk during one second, the voltage might turn on for a fraction of a second, then turn off for the next period of time, then back on for a certain length of time.

The head sits over a track that is moving at a constant speed. Blocks of data are written or read during the precise timing of the system clock. Because the voltage must go plus or zero, that is, two states, in order to write ones and zeros, the maximum data transfer rate is only 5 megabits per second for MFM, just half of the clock frequency. RLL systems transfer data at a rate of 7.5 megabits per second. Some of the ESDI drives have a transfer rate of 10 megabits per second or more. (Note that these figures are bits; remember that it takes eight bits to make one byte.) SCSI and IDE systems have transfer rates as high as 10 to 13 megabytes or more. So, an SCSI or IDE system that can transfer 10 megabytes/second is eight times faster than a 10 megabit/second ESDI.

You have probably seen representations of magnetic lines of force around a magnet. The magnetized spot on a disk track has similar lines of force. To read the data on the disk, the head is positioned over the track and the lines of force from each magnetized area cause a pulse of voltage to be induced in the head. During a precise block of time, an induced pulse of voltage can represent a one; the absence of an induced pulse can represent a zero. Pulses of voltage through the head cause a magnetic pulse to be formed, which magnetizes the disk track. When reading the data from the track, the small magnetic changes on the recorded track cause voltage to be produced in the heads. It is a two-way system. Forcing voltage through the heads causes magnetism to be produced; bringing a magnetic field into the area of the head when reading can cause a voltage to be produced.

Head Spacing

The amount of magnetism that is placed on a disk when it is recorded is very small. It must be small so that it will not affect other recorded bits or tracks near it. Magnetic lines of force decrease as you move away from a magnet by the square of the distance, so it is desirable to have the heads as close to the disk as possible.

On a floppy disk drive, the heads actually come in contact with the diskette. This causes some wear, but not very much because the rotation is fairly slow and the plastic disks have a special lubricant and are fairly slippery. However, heads of the hard-disk systems never touch the disk. The fragile heads and the disk would be severely damaged if they made contact at a speed of 3600 to 10,000 RPMs. The heads fly over the spinning disk, just microinches above it. Hard disks are sealed, and the air inside them is purified. The air must be pure because the smallest speck of dust or dirt can cause the head to crash. You should never open a hard disk.

Speed or Access Time

Speed or access time is the time it takes a hard disk to locate and retrieve a sector of data. This includes the time that it takes to move the head to the track, settle down, and read the data. For a high-end, very fast disk, this might be as little as 9 milliseconds (Ms). Some of the older drives and systems required as much as 100 Ms. An 85-Ms hard drive might have been fine for an old, slow XT. A 9-Ms drive might not be fast enough for a Pentium II. Some of the newer drives have an access time of less than 6 Ms.

Disk Platters

The surface of the hard-disk platters must be very smooth. Because the heads are only a few millionths of an inch, or microinches, away from the surface, any unevenness could cause a head crash. The hard-disk platters are usually made from aluminum, which is nonmagnetic, and lapped to a mirror finish. They are then coated or plated with a magnetic material. Some companies are using tempered glass as a substrate for the platters.

The platters must also be very rigid so that the close distance between the head and the platter surface is maintained. The early $5^1/_4$-inch hard disks had to be fairly thick to achieve the necessary rigidity. Being thick, they were heavy and required a fairly large spindle motor and lots of wattage to move the large amount of mass. If the platter is made smaller, it can be thinner and still have the necessary rigidity. If the disks are thinner, then more platters can be stacked in the same area. The smaller disks also need less power and smaller motors. With smaller-diameter disks, the heads don't have to travel as far between the outer and inner tracks. This improves the access time tremendously.

Avoid any sudden movement of the computer or any jarring while the disk is spinning because it could cause the head to crash onto the disk and damage it. Most of the newer hard-disk systems automatically move the heads away from the read/write surface to a parking area when the power is turned off.

Physical Sizes

One of the first hard drives I ever owned was a full-height 10-Mb drive. *Full height* meant that it was over 3 inches high, 6 inches wide, and 8 inches deep. The original full-height floppies were the same size. Later, half-height drives were developed for both hard drives and floppies. The drives were physically large and clunky and operated at a very slow 100 Ms. They were also expensive. A 20-Mb hard disk cost as much as $2500—back when $2500 was worth about three times what it is today.

Today, you can buy a 2-Gb hard disk for less than $200. A modern 2-Gb drive is only 1 inch high, 4 inches wide, and 6 inches deep, yet it has 100 times greater storage capacity, operates ten times faster at about 10 Ms, and is $2300 less expensive than a large 20-Mb drive was ten years ago.

If you weren't around in those early days, you can't begin to appreciate the advances in the technology. We have come a long way.

How They Can Make Smaller Drives

One of the reasons they can make the hard disks smaller now is because they have developed better plating materials, thinner disks, better motors, and better electronics.

Zone Bit Recording

There are several reasons why the old hard drives were physically so much larger than the newer drives. The old MFM drives divided each track into 17 sectors. A track on the outer edge of a $5^1/_4$-inch platter would be over 15 inches long if it were stretched out. You can determine this by using the simple math formula for Π times the diameter. So Π, or 3.14159, times 5.25 is 16.493 inches in length. A track on the inner portion of the disk may only be 1.5 inches times Π, or 4.712 inches in length.

The MFM system divided each track into 17 sectors, no matter whether it was 16 inches long or only 4 inches long. Obviously, you should be able to store more data in the outer longer tracks than in the short inner tracks. That is exactly what the newer drives do. One reason the newer drives can be made so much smaller with so much more capacity is that they use *Zone Bit Recording* (*ZBR*). The platters are divided into different zones depending on the area of the disk platter. The inner tracks, which are shorter, have relatively few sectors. The number of sectors per track increases toward the outer and longer tracks.

Rotational Speed and Recording Density

The recording density or bits per inch (bpi) for each zone changes from the inner tracks to the outer tracks because the speed at the inner tracks pass beneath the heads faster than the outer tracks. The overall drive speed is still another way of increasing the amount of storage. The old MFM drives spun at 3600 RPMs. The newer drives have a rotational speed of 6300 to 10,000 RPMs or more.

One big factor in the amount of data that can be recorded in a given area is the frequency of the changing zeros and ones and the speed of the disk. The higher the speed of the disk, the higher the recording frequency can be. Of course, the rotational speed of the disk is also one of the factors that determines the seek, access, and transferal time. If you want to access data on a certain track, the faster the disk rotates, the sooner that sector will be available for reading.

Hard-disk technology has improved tremendously over the last ten years.

Mean Time Between Failures (MTBF)

Disk drives are mechanical devices. If used long enough, every disk drive will fail sooner or later. Manufacturers test their drives and assign them an average lifetime that ranges from 40,000 up to 150,000 hours. The larger the figure, the longer they should last (and the more they cost). These are average figures, much like the figures quoted for a human lifespan. The average man should live to be about 73 years old, but some babies die very young, and some men live to be over 100. Likewise, some hard disks die very young, some older ones become obsolete before they wear out.

I have difficulty in accepting some of the manufacturer's MTBF figures. For instance, to put 150,000 hours on a drive, it would have to be used eight hours a day, every day, for over 51 years. If they operated a drive for 24 hours a day, 365 days a year, it would take over 17 years to put 150,000 hours on it. Since hard drives have only been around about ten years, I am pretty sure that no one has ever done a 150,000-hour test on a drive.

Near Field Technology

The TeraStor Company of San Jose is working on a new technology called *Near Field Recording*. It combines facets of magneto-optical technology and standard hard-disk technology. It will be able to store over 20 Gb on a plastic disk about the size of a CD-ROM. TeraStor can be reached at 408-324-2110, or on the Web at www.terastor.com.

IBM's GMR Read Head

IBM has developed a *Giant Magnetoresistive* (*GMR*) read head that can double the capacity of hard disks. GMR read heads are twice as sensitive as a standard head and can read 2.69 Gbits per square inch areal density. They will be used on an IBM $3^1/_2$-inch disk that can store 16.8 Gb.

How the times have changed. I was ecstatic when I got my first hard drive with 10 Mb. Physically, the new $3^1/_2$-inch IBM drive is about half the size of my early hard drive. The smaller IBM drive can store 1680 Mb, compared to only 10 Mb for my early full-size drive. And they say there are only seven wonders in the world!

Cables and Connectors

The standard SCSI cable is a 50-wire flat ribbon cable. The standard connectors are Centronics types, but some devices may have a small miniature connector. Most devices have two connectors in parallel for attaching and daisychaining other devices. I have a Future Domain host adapter that has a miniature connector for external devices. In order to attach my Epson 800 Pro scanner, I had to buy a cable with the miniature connector on one end. It cost almost $40. I found out later that there are adapters for this purpose that cost about $5.00. Try some of the cable companies that advertise in *Computer Shopper* and other computer magazines.

Not all of the 50 wires in a flat ribbon cable are needed for data. Many of the wires are ground wires placed between the data wires to help keep the data from being corrupted. The better, and more expensive, cables are round cables with twisted and shielded wires. This type of cable may be necessary for distances greater than 6 feet.

Be aware that the advertised price of an SCSI device usually does not include an interface or cables. It might not even include any software drivers. Be sure to ask about these items whenever you order an SCSI device.

Installation and Configuration

If you are only installing a single IDE drive, the installation may be very simple. The drive should have jumpers set at the factory that makes it drive 1, or the master drive. Check your documentation and the jumpers, then just plug the 40-pin cable into the drive connector and the other end into a set of pins on the motherboard. Make sure that the colored side of the ribbon cable goes to pin 1 on the drive and on the interface.

If you are installing a second IDE drive, you will need to set some jumpers so that the system will know which drive to access. When two IDE drives are installed, the IDE system uses the term *master* to designate the C:, or boot drive, and the term *slave* to designate the second drive. The drives usually come from the factory configured with the jumpers as a single or master drive. If the drives are not configured properly, you will get an error message telling you that you have a hard disk or controller failure. You will not be able to access the drives.

There were no standards as to how the early IDE drives should be configured. Different manufacturers used different designations for the pins and sometimes different functions for the pins. So it was difficult—sometimes impossible—to install and configure two different, early IDE drives in a system. Later, a group of IDE manufacturers got together and agreed on an IDE standard specification. They called the specification *Common Access Method AT Attachment*, or *CAM ATA*. Almost all IDE drives now conform to this specification. You should have very little trouble connecting drives made by different companies, or drives of different capacities, if they conform to the CAM ATA specifications.

Most later models have three sets of pins for jumpers: for configuring the drive as a single drive, for a master and slave, or for a slave. Some drives have pins that can be jumpered so that they will be read-only. This is a type of write-protection that is similar to write-protecting a floppy. This could be used on a hard disk that had data that should never be changed or written over.

You should have received some documentation with your drive. Fig. 6-4 shows the small configuration jumper pins on a Maxtor drive. Your drive may be different. If you don't have the configuration information, call the company or dealer. You may also visit the company's Web site. Most computer hardware companies now have Web sites. Most of the Web sites have e-mail addresses of the various departments within the company. Here are some addresses and Web sites:

Conner
URL: www.conner.com
Tech Support Phone: 408-438-8222
Tech Support Fax: 408-438-8137
Fax Back Support: 408-438-2620
Automated Support: 800-732-4283

Figure 6-4
Jumpers for configuring an IDE drive. Jumpers on other drives may be in a different location.

Conner Peripherals is now a subsidiary of Seagate.

Iomega Corporation
URL: www.iomega.com
Tech Support Phone: 801-629-7610

Fujitsu
URL: www.fcpa.com
Tech Support Phone: 800-626-4686
Fax Back Support: 408-428-0456

Maxtor
URL: www.maxtor.com
Tech Support Phone: 800-2-Maxtor or 800-262-9867
Tech Support Fax: 303-678-2260
E-mail: Technical Assistance@Maxtor.com

Micropolis
URL: www.micropolis.com
Tech Support Phone: 818-709-3325
Tech Support Fax: 818-709-3408
Fax Back Support: 800-395-3748
E-mail Support: tom@earthlink.net

Quantum

URL: www.quantum.com
Tech Support Phone: 800-826-8022
Tech Support Fax: 408-894-3282
Fax Back Support: 800-434-7532

Samsung Electronics America
URL: www.samsung.co.kr
Tech Support Phone: 800-726-7864
Fax Back Support: 800-229-2239

Seagate
URL: www.seagate.com
Tech Support Phone: 408-438-8222
Tech Support Fax: 408-438-8137
Fax Back Support: 408-438-2620
Automated Support: 800-732-4283

Western Digital
URL: www.wdc.com
Tech Support Phone: 507-286-7900
Fax Back Support: 714-932-4300

I bought a 3.5 Gb Maxtor drive at a swap meet. The vendor didn't give me any documentation, so I went to the Maxtor URL and downloaded the following information about this drive and several others in this model family. Several other companies also provide information about their drives similar to that given by Maxtor. You might be surprised at the large amount of information and specifications about drives. The information here is an example of what you may find.

```
==============================================================
MAXTOR's CrystalMax_ Family of 3.5" Enhanced IDE Drives Models:
83500A, 83062A, 82625A, 82187A, 81750A, 81312A, 80875A
==============================================================
KEY FEATURES:
12ms Average Seek                 ATA-3 Compliant
Low Power Consumption             PIO Mode 4 / DMA 2 Interface
ATA Power Saving Commands         Zone Density Recording
Supports EPA Energy Star          S.M.A.R.T. Capability
Standards (Green PC Friendly)     Superior Data Throughput
>400,000 Hours MTBF               128k Cache with MaxCache
  3 Year Warranty                 Manager Algorithms
```

SPECIFICATIONS:

Model Number	Megabyte* Capacity	Disks	Surfaces & Heads	Sectors per Drive
83500A	3,500	4	8	6,936,400
83062A	3,062	4	7	6,096,350
82625A	2,625	3	6	5,202,300
82187A	2,187	3	5	4,335,250
81750A	1,750	2	4	3,468,200
81312A	1,312	2	3	2,601,150
80875A	875	1	2	1,734,100

CONFIGURATION:

Bytes per block :.......................... 512
Integrated Controller/Interface: .... AT
Actuator type: .... Rotary Voice Coil
Data Zones per Surface: 10
Servo: .... Embedded
Tracks Per surface (Cylinders): 5,446
Track Density: .... 5,376.5 tpi
Flux Density: .... 86 kfci
Recording Density: .... 115 kbpi
Encoding Method: .... RLL 1,7
Buffer Size: .... 128 k
Interleave: 1:1

PERFORMANCE:

Seek performance (including settling time and servo overhead)

Seek times:Track to track: .... 2 ms
Average: .... 12 ms
Maximum: .... 25 ms

```
Spindle speed ( +-0.1%): ................ 4,480 RPM
Average latency (ms): ................... 6.7 ms
Controller overhead: .................... 0.3 ms
Data transfer rate:
To/From Media: .......................... 5.2 - 10 MBs
To/from Host (without I/O CHRDY): ....... PIO Mode 3, 11.1 MBs
To/from Host (with I/O CHRDY): .......... PIO Mode 4, 16.7 MBs
DMA Transfers ........................... Mode 2, 16.7 MBs
Start time (0 - Drive Ready) Average .... <= 10.0 sec
Stop Time/Power Down: Average ........... <= 10.0 sec

POWER REQUIREMENTS (Average)
Mode +12VDC +-8% +5VDC +-5% Power
-------       -------    ------    --------
Active*        252 mA    529 mA    5.66 W
Idle*          184 mA    462 mA    4.52 W
Read/Write*    265 mA    546 mA    5.91 W
Spin-up       1700 mA    255 mA   13.0  W
Standby*      0.90 mA    138 mA    0.70 W
Sleep*        0.90 mA     95 mA    0.49 W
(* Total RMS Power Mode)
```

Definitions:

Active

The drive is spinning and most circuitry is powered on. The drive is capable of responding to read commands in shortest possible time. Read/Write heads are positioned over the data area.

Idle

The drive is spinning, the actuator is parked and powered off, and all other circuitry is powered on. The drive is capable of responding to read commands within 40 ms.

Read/Write

Data is being read from or written to the drive.

Spin-up

The drive is spinning up following initial application of power and has yet not reached full speed. Maximum current draw lasts one second.

Sleep

This is the lowest power state. The interface becomes inactive. A software or hardware reset is required to return the drive to Standby.

Standby

The spin motor is not spinning. The drive will leave this mode upon receipt of a command that requires disk access. The time-out value for this mode is programmable. The buffer is active to accept write data.

PHYSICAL:

Height: 1.00", 25.4 mm
Length: 5.75", 146.1 mm
Width: 4.00", 101.6 mm
Weight: 1.2 lb, 0.5 kg

RELIABILITY AND MAINTENANCE:

MTBF .... >400,000 hours
AFR .... <-1.7%
Preventative Maintenance .... None
Component design life .... 5 years (minimum)
Error Rate .... <1 per 10^{13} bits read
Start/Stop Cycles...................... >40,000
Quality Acceptance Rate .... 99.5% (<1,500 DPPM)

JUMPERS & CONFIGURATIONS

```
Jumper Designations |J50|J48|J46|J44|J42|
+-------------------------------------+---+---+---+---+---+---+
| Master/Slave                        |   |   |   |   |   |   |
| Only Drive in single drive system*  | J |   |   |   |   |   |
| Master in a dual drive system*      | J |   |   |   |   |   |
| Slave in a dual drive system        | 0 |   |   |   |   |   |
+-------------------------------------+---+---+---+---+---+---+
| Cable Select                        |   |   |   |   |   |   |
| Disabled*                           |   | O |   |   |   |   |
| Enabled                             |   | J |   |   |   |   |
+-------------------------------------+---+---+---+---+---+---+
| Write Cache                         |   |   |   |   |   |   |
| Enabled*                            |   |   | O |   |   |   |
| Disabled                            |   |   | J |   |   |   |
+-------------------------------------+---+---+---+---+---+---+
```

```
+-------------------------------------+---+---+---+---+---+---+
| Factory Reserved                    |   |   |   | O |   |   |
+-------------------------------------+---+---+---+---+---+---+
| 4092 Cylinder Option                |   |   |   |   |   |   |
| Disabled*                           |   |   |   |   | O |   |
| Enabled                             |   |   |   |   | J |   |
+-------------------------------------+---+---+---+---+---+---+
J=Jumpered O=Open *=Default

J1 IDE Connector
J2 Power
___________ ________1_________________________
| .................... || @ * *  o  |/         \
| .......... ......... || @ o o o o || o o o o |
|______________________||___________||_________|
                      | | | | |   | | | |
 J50 Master/Slave   —' | | | |   | | | `- +12V (Yellow)
   J48 Cable Select ——' | | |   | | `—+12V Return (Black)
     J46 Write Cache ———' | |   | `—— +5V Return (Black)
   J44 Factory Reserved ——' |   `——— +5V (Red)
   J42 4092 Cyl Limitation —'
@= Default Jumped Positions =5 "Spare" Jumper Position o =5
  Default Open Positions CMOS Configurations:
```

Model Number	Cylds	Hds	Write PreComp	Landing Zone	Sectors /Track	Megabyte* Capacity
83500A	6800	16	0	0	63	3,500
83062A	5948	16	0	0	63	3,062
82625A	5100	16	0	0	63	2,625
82187A	4248	16	0	0	63	2,187
81750A	3400	16	0	0	63	1,750
81312A	2548	16	0	0	63	1,312
80875A	1700	16	0	0	63	875

The Maxtor Web site has similar information about all of their drives, even those that were made a few years ago. Most of the other Web sites also have similar information and technical support for their drives.

Sources

Local computer stores and computer swap meets are a good place to find a disk drive. You can look them over and get some idea of the prices and what you want. Mail order is a very good way to buy a hard disk. There are hundreds of ads are in the many computer magazines. Check the list of magazines in Chapter 19.

CHAPTER 7

Backup and Disaster Prevention

Making backups is a chore that most people dislike, but if your data is worth anything at all, you should be making backups of it. You might be one of the lucky ones and never need your backups, but there are thousands of ways to lose data. Data might be lost due to a power failure or a component failure in the computer system. In a fraction of a second, data that might be worth thousands of dollars could be lost forever. It might have taken hundreds of hours to accumulate it, and it might be impossible to duplicate. Yet many unfortunate people have not backed up their precious data. Most of these people are those who have been fortunate enough not to have had a major catastrophe. Just as sure as we have earthquakes in California, if you use a computer long enough, you can look forward to at least one unfortunate disaster. But if your data is backed up, it doesn't have to be a catastrophe.

By far, most losses are the result of just plain dumb mistakes. I have made lots of mistakes in the past. And no matter how careful I am, I will make mistakes in the future. When the poet said, "To err is human," he could have been talking about me. And, possibly, thee.

Write-Protect Your Software

When you buy a software program, make a copy of it and store the original away. If you ruin the copy, you can always make a new copy from the original. The very first thing you should do before you make a copy is to write-protect the original floppies. It is very easy to become distracted and write on a program diskette in error. This would ruin the program. The vendor might give you a new copy, but it would probably take weeks of waiting and much paperwork.

You probably won't be using $5^1/_4$-inch floppy systems. They are practically obsolete, but you might still have $5^1/_4$-inch floppies with data on them. They are still good for some types of small backups. If you are still using $5^1/_4$-inch floppies, once you have recorded them, you should cover the square write-protect notch with a piece of opaque tape. Don't use Scotch or clear tape. The drive focuses a light through the square notch. If the light detector can sense the light, it will allow the diskette to be written on, read, or erased. If the notch is covered with opaque tape, the diskette can be read, but cannot be written on or erased.

If you are using $3^1/_2$-inch diskettes, you should move the small slide on the left rear side so that the square hole is open. The $3^1/_2$-inch write-protect system is just the opposite of the $5^1/_4$-inch system. The $3^1/_2$-inch system uses a small microswitch. If the square hole is open, the switch will allow the diskette to be read, but not written on or erased. If the slide is moved to cover the square hole, the diskette can be written on, read, or erased.

It takes less than a minute to write-protect a diskette, but it might save months of valuable time. Most major software programs are now distributed on CD-ROM discs, but there are still lots of smaller programs and special drivers that are distributed on $3^1/_2$-inch diskettes. If a program diskette is ruined because it was not protected, it might take weeks to get a replacement for the original. You might even have to buy a complete new program.

.BAK Files

Many word processors and some other programs create a .BAK file each time you alter or change a file. The .BAK file is usually just a copy of the original file before you changed it. You can call up a .BAK file, but you might not be able to edit it or use it unless you rename it. Usually, just changing the .BAK extension is all that is necessary. Most word processors and other programs such as spreadsheets and databases can be set up automatically to save any file that you are working on at certain times when there is no activity from the keyboard. If there is a power outage, or you shut the machine off without saving a file, chances are that there is a backup of it saved to disk.

Unerase Software

One of the best protections against errors is to have a backup. The second-best protection is to have a good utility program, such as Norton's Utilities from Symantec. DOS and Windows 95 also have undelete utilities. These programs can unerase a file or even unformat a disk.

When a file is erased, DOS goes to the FAT table and deletes the first letter of that filename. All of the data remains on the disk unless a new file is written over it. If you have erased a file in error, or formatted a disk in error, **do not do anything to it** until you have tried using a recover utility. To restore the files, most of the utilities ask you to supply the missing first letter of the file name.

Delete Protection

I assume that you are using Windows 95 now. If you delete a file, it is sent to the Recycle Bin. If you decide later that you still need that file, you can search through the bin and recover it. The Recycle Bin can take up a lot of disk space. If you don't have a lot of spare disk space, you might have to go to the Recycle Bin every so often and dump certain files that you know you won't need, or dump the entire bin. If you delete just portions of a file, while revising it, the original might still be saved in the Recycle Bin. If you decide that the revision is not what you wanted, you might be able to recover the original and start over.

I have Norton Utilities installed. Norton also has a Recycle Bin that has a few more utilities than the one that comes with Windows 95. Every few minutes, my word processor automatically saves copies of the file I am working on. Of course, every time it saves a file, it is the same as deleting it.

I just checked the Norton Recycle bin for this file that I am currently working on. There are several versions of this file in the bin. The bin gives the exact time that the file was updated and saved. I could go back and recover any of those earlier versions.

I am sure that many people are still using DOS. After all, it did just about everything we wanted for several years. Erasing or deleting files by mistake was so common in DOS that Microsoft licensed undelete technology from one of the major utility companies. They included an UNDELETE command in all late versions of MS-DOS. This command is available immediately from any DOS prompt and any directory. To find out more about it, type *HELP UNDELETE* at any DOS prompt.

The early versions of MS-DOS made it very easy to format your hard disk in error. If you happened to be on your hard disk and typed FORMAT, it would immediately begin to format your hard disk and wipe out everything. Later versions would not format unless you specified a drive letter. The early versions of DOS also let you copy over another file. If two files were different, but you told DOS to copy one to a directory that had the file with the same name, the original file would be gone forever. MS-DOS 6.2, IBM PC DOS 7.0, and Windows 95 now ask if you want to overwrite the file.

Jumbled FAT

The all-important File Allocation Table (FAT) was discussed in the previous chapter about disks. The FAT keeps a record of the location of all the files on the disk. Parts of a file may be located in several sectors, but the FAT knows exactly where they are. If for some reason track 0, where the FAT is located, is damaged, erased, or becomes defective, then you will not be able to read or write to any of the files on the disk.

Because the FAT is so important, a program such as Norton Utilities can make a copy of the FAT and store it in another location on the disk. Every time you add a file or edit one, the FAT changes, so these programs make a new copy every time the FAT is altered. If the original FAT is damaged, you can still get your data by using the alternate FAT. Norton Utilities from Symantec (408-253-9600) is an excellent utility software package. If you accept the defaults when installing Norton Utilities, it scans your disk and analyze the boot record, FAT, directory structure, and file structure, and checks for lost clusters or cross-linked files. It then reads the FAT and stores a copy in a different place on the hard disk.

Reason for Smaller Logical Hard Disks

Early versions of DOS would not recognize a hard disk larger than 32 Mb. Windows 95 can handle hard-drive capacities up to several gigabytes. Most programs seem to be designed to be installed on drive C:. You could have a very large drive C:, but if this large hard disk crashed, you might not be able to recover any of its data. DOS allows you to use the FDISK command when formatting your disk to divide it up and partition it into as many as 24 logical drives. If the same disk was divided into several smaller logical drives, and one of the logical sections failed, it might be possible to recover data in the unaffected logical drives.

Partition Magic and Partition-It

Think of a disk partition much like a room with four walls. When the house was built, some of the rooms might have been very small. It is sometimes possible to knock out some of the walls and make the room larger. You can do something similar with the partitions on your hard disk. You are probably using a hard disk that has already been formatted and has lots of data on it. Normally, the only way to change the size of the drive partitions is to back up everything, use the FDISK command to resize it, and then reformat it. However, both Partition Magic and Partition-It let you resize the partitions on your hard drive without having to back up all the data. They will automatically move the data, resize the partition, and move the data back into it.

A very fast way to back up is to copy the data from one logical drive partition to another. This type of backup is very fast and very easy, but it doesn't offer the amount of protection that a separate hard drive would offer. Still, it is much better than no backup at all.

Head Crash

The heads of a hard disk "fly" over the disk just a few microinches from the surface. They have to be close in order to detect the small magnetic changes in the tracks. The disk spins at 3600 RPMs on some older drives, and up to 10,000 RPMs on some of the newer drives. If the head contacts the surface of the fast-spinning disk, it can scratch it and ruin the disk. A sudden jar or bump to the computer while the hard disk is spinning can cause the heads to crash. Of course, a mechanical failure or some other factor could also cause a crash. You should never move or bump your computer while the hard disk is running. Most of the newer disks have a built-in safe park utility. When the power is removed, the head is automatically moved to the center of the disk where there are no tracks.

The technology of hard-disk systems has improved tremendously over the last few years, but hard disks are still mechanical devices. As such, you can be sure that eventually they will wear out, fail, or crash. I worked in electronics for over 30 years and am still amazed that a hard disk will work at all. It is a most remarkable mechanical device. It is made up of several precision components. The mechanical tolerances must be held to millionths of an inch in devices such as the flying head and the distances between the tracks. The magnetic flux changes are minute, yet the heads detect them easily and output reliable data.

Despite all of the things that could go wrong with a hard disk, most hard disks are quite reliable. Manufacturers quote figures of several thousand hours mean time between failure (MTBF). However, these figures are only an average, so there is no guarantee that a disk won't fail in the next few minutes. If a disk should fail and you get it repaired, it should last as long as their guarantee says before it fails again. A hard disk is made up of several mechanical parts. If the disk is used long enough, eventually it will wear out or fail.

Crash Recovery

Despite the MTBF claims, hard drives do fail. There are lots of businesses who do nothing but repair hard disks that have crashed or failed. A failure can be frustrating, time-consuming, and make you feel utterly helpless. In the unhappy event of a crash, depending on its severity, it is possible that some of your data can be recovered, one way or another. Some companies specialize in recovering data and rebuilding hard disks. Many of them have sophisticated tools and software that can recover some data if the disk is not completely ruined.

OnTrack Data International

If it is possible to recover any of the data, the Ontrack Data Recovery can probably do it. They can send you a floppy disk that can help in the event of a crash or disaster. Contact them at

OnTrack Data Recovery & Ontrack Data International
6321 Bury Drive
Eden Prairie, MN 55346
800-872-2599

Here is some information from their Web site (www.ontrack.com):

Diagnose a Data Loss Directly on Your Computer!

When you lose your valuable computer data, every second that passes equals time, money and effort lost to you or your company. Ontrack Data Advisor software reduces expensive downtime by providing you with an instant diagnosis of your data loss situation. Ontrack Data Advisor software will investigate your desktop, laptop or notebook computer to determine what is preventing you from accessing your data. This keeps your downtime to a minimum, helping you resume normal business functions as quickly as possible. Powerful Tools Provide a Comprehensive System Analysis

Ontrack Data Advisor software includes a complete set of hard disk drive and system diagnostic tools. These tools assess the read abilities of your hard-disk drive and determine if your drive is electromechanically stable. These tools also analyze your file systems and file structures, check your system memory, scan for computer viruses and more. Contained on a bootable diskette, Ontrack Data Advisor software can even diagnose your system when it cannot boot on its own!

The First Component of the Patent-Pending Ontrack Remote Data Recovery Process

Ontrack Data Advisor software is the first component of Ontrack Remote Data Recovery services, currently in development. This patent-pending process will allow Ontrack to perform remote data recoveries via communication link based on the test results provided by Ontrack Data Advisor software. It is yet another way to bring you the fastest data recovery services available.

DriveSavers

A similar company is DriveSavers:

DriveSavers
400 Bel Marin Keys Boulevard
Novato, CA 94949
Phone: 800-440-1904 or 415-382-2000
Fax: 415-883-0780

Here are some tips from their Web site at www.drivesavers.com:

What to do before you call DriveSavers

If your disk is crashed, you can try the following suggestions before you contact DriveSavers. This document covers a few of the many kinds of problems that can occur when data recovery may be necessary.

The "oops" factor

Sometimes cables just wiggle loose. It's a good idea to check your cables when there's a problem accessing your drive. It's a good idea to do this anyway. Be sure to shut the system off and check both the power cable and ribbon cable(s). Make sure their connections are all secure. If need be, you can pull them off and then put them back on to be certain there's a secure connection.

The Disk Exhibits Unusual Noises (clicking, grinding or metal scraping)

This typically indicates a serious hardware problem such as a head crash or major media damage. In such a case it is best to copy all accessible data from the drive immediately. The longer the drive runs in this condition the more damage can occur making the data irretrievable. It is best to send the drive directly to DriveSavers so we may disassemble it in a special clean-room environment and extract the data for you.

Using utility programs

Use utility programs with caution. They are best used to clean up minor problems on drives that have already been backed up. These programs can do a fine job of helping you out of a tight spot...or they can "fix" your data beyond recoverability! If you do use one of these, please heed the following cautions.

Utility programs like Symantec's Norton Utilities and MS-DOS's Scandisk allow you the opportunity to save "undo" files if the repair doesn't work out. It's very important because saving an undo file can help you back out of a bad "fix." Save your undo file to a floppy disk, not your hard disk. It's a good idea to have a few formatted diskettes handy for the program to write to.

If your drive is sounding or acting "funny" in any way, it's extremely important that you avoid the use of these utilities altogether. These symptoms can include any rattling, buzzing, or scraping sounds the disk drive might be emitting. In these circumstances, it's best to back up your data immediately or shut the drive down as further use may well cause damage. If the drive is completely crashed your best chance for recovery is to contact us here at DriveSavers.

"Invalid Drive Specification" error message

A common problem that occurs, especially with older 386 systems, is a system's propensity to lose track of its CMOS drive setup. When you turn on your system, it goes through its memory countdown, etc., and then just sits there, asks for a system disk, or drops into BASIC (on true-blue IBM systems). When you put in a boot floppy, and ask for drive C:, you get the "invalid drive specification" message. In such a circumstance, first check your CMOS setup. Most systems will allow you to enter the CMOS setup at startup time with a key stroke or two, such as [Del], [Esc], or [Cntrl]-[Esc]. Some systems, such as Compaq, NEC, Mitsubishi, and many laptops and notebooks, require a setup or diagnostic diskette to change the CMOS drive setting. Tab to the appropriate field for drive settings and enter in the correct settings for your drive. (It's a good idea to keep these settings on a note attached to your computer for future reference.) Most modern systems will let you "Auto" sense the drive. This will usually be successful. You should then reboot your PC. If this works, great! Back up your system and get a replacement battery from your dealer. If not, it may be time to give DriveSavers a call.

Removable Cartridge or other SCSI drive gives "Invalid Drive Specification" error

If a removable cartridge (SyQuest, magneto-optical or Iomega) or SCSI hard disk refuses to mount, the device driver may be damaged, or the CONFIG.SYS file may have been changed. Look for lines in your CONFIG.SYS files that look something like: "DEVICE=ASPIDISK.SYS."

If no such line exists, check the manual or README file on your installation disk for the cartridge drive or SCSI Host Adapter manual. Try another cartridge that is known to be good. This will help you identify whether the problem is with the cartridge or the drive mechanism. If the same problem occurs with another cartridge check that your SCSI cables are firmly attached and the termination is correct.

You might also isolate the drive on the SCSI bus by disconnecting other devices. With most systems, the first SCSI drive must have an SCSI ID of 0 (zero), and the first removable media drive must have a SCSI ID of 2.

Another company that specializes in recovery is

Total Recall
2462 Waynoka Road
Colorado Springs, CO 80915

Cost of Recovery

The cost for recovery services can be rather expensive, but if you have data that is critical and irreplaceable, it is well worth it. Still, it is a whole lot cheaper to have a backup. Look in the computer magazine ads for more companies who specialize in data recovery.

Preventing Hard Disk Failures

During manufacturing, the hard-disk platters are coated or plated with a precise layer of magnetic material. It is almost impossible to manufacture a perfect platter. Most hard disks end up with a few defective areas after being manufactured. When the vendor does the low-level format, these areas are detected and marked as bad. They are locked out so that they cannot be used. There might, however, be areas that are borderline bad and won't be detected. Over time, some of the areas might change and lose some of their magnetic characteristics. The disk might then lose some of the data that is written to it.

Several companies that manufacture hard disk utilities that can perform rigorous tests on the hard disk. These software programs can exercise the disk and detect any borderline areas. If there happens to be data in an area that is questionable, the programs can usually move the data to another safe area.

The SCANDISK command in MS-DOS 6.2 basically does what some of the stand-alone utilities do. It does a surface test of the hard disk and will report on any areas that are questionable. It can move any data from those areas to safer areas. It will then mark the questionable areas as bad.

The bad areas are listed in the FAT just as if they were protected files that cannot be written to or erased.

A Few Reasons Why People Don't Back Up and Why They Should

Here are a few of the lame excuses used by some people don't back up their software:

- *Don't have the time*—This is not a good excuse. If your data is worth anything at all, it is worth backing up. It takes only a few minutes to back up a large hard disk with some of the newer software. It might take just seconds to copy all of the files to a directory on another logical drive of the disk or to another hard drive.
- *Too much trouble*—It *can* be a bit of trouble to do a backup unless you have an expensive, automated, tape backup system or a second hard disk. If you back up to floppies, it can require a bit of disk swapping, labeling, and storing. With a little organization, however, it can be done easily. If you keep all of the backup disks together, you don't have to label each one. Just stack them in order, put a rubber band around them, and use one label for the first one of the lot. Although it is a bit of trouble to make backups, consider the trouble it would take to redo the files from a disk that had crashed. Compared to that, the trouble that it takes to make a backup is infinitesimal.
- *Don't have the necessary disks, software, or tools*—If you use floppy disks, depending on the amount of data to be backed up, and the software used, you might need 50 to 100 disks. It might take only a few minutes and just a few disks, however, to make a backup of only the data that has been changed or altered. In most cases, the same disks can be reused the next day to update the files.
- *Failures and disasters only happen to other people*—People who believe this are those who have never experienced a disaster. There is nothing you can say to convince them. They just have to learn the hard way.

Outside of ordinary care, there is little you can do to prevent a general failure. It could be a component on the hard disk's electronics or in the controller system—or any one of a thousand other things. Even things such as a power failure during a read/write operation can cause data corruption.

Theft and Burglary

Computers are easy to sell, so they are favorite targets for burglars. It would be bad enough to lose a computer, but many computers have hard disks that are filled with data that is even more valuable than the computer. Speaking of theft, it might be a good idea to put your name and address on several of the files on your hard disk. It would also be a good idea to scratch identifying marks on the back and bottom of the case. You should also write down the serial numbers of your monitor and drives.

I heard of a story where a man took a computer to a pawn shop. The dealer wanted to see if it worked, so he turned it on. A name came up on the screen that was different from the name the man had given to the dealer. The dealer called the police, and the man was arrested for burglary. The owner of the computer was very happy to get it back. He was also quite fortunate. Most burglaries don't have a happy ending.

Another good idea is to store your backup files in an area away from your computer. This way, there is less chance of losing both computer and backups in case of a burglary or fire. You can always buy another computer, but if you had a large database of customer orders, files, and history, how could you replace that?

An article in a recent issue of *Information Week* magazine says that PC theft has increased over 400% in the last few years. (*Information Week* is free to qualifying subscribers. See Chapter 17 for the address.)

Archival

Another reason to back up is for archival purposes. No matter how large a hard disk is, it will eventually fill up with data. Quite often, there will be files that are no longer used or that might only be used once in a great while.

I keep copies of all the letters that I write on disk. I have hundreds of them. Rather than erase the old files or old letters, I put them on a disk and store them away.

Data Transfer

There are often times when it is necessary to transfer a large amount of data from one hard disk on a computer to another. It is quite easy to use a good backup program to accomplish this. Data on a disk can be used to distribute data, company policies and procedures, sales figures, and other information to several people in a large office or company. The data can also be easily shipped or mailed to branch offices, customers, or to others almost anywhere. If more companies used disks in this manner, we could save thousands of trees that are cut down for paper.

Types of Backup

There are two main types of backup: *image* and *file-oriented.* An image backup is an exact bit-for-bit copy of the hard disk copied as a continuous stream of data. This type of backup is rather inflexible and does not allow for a separate file backup or restoration.

The file-oriented type of backup identifies and indexes each file separately. A separate file or directory can be backed up and restored easily. It can be very time-consuming to have to back up 40 Mb or more each day, but with a file-oriented system, once a full backup has been made, it is necessary only to make incremental backups of those files that have been changed or altered.

DOS stores an archive attribute in each file directory entry. When a file is created, DOS turns the archive attribute flag on. If the file is backed up by using DOS BACKUP or any of the commercial backup programs, the archive attribute flag is turned off. If this file is later altered or changed, DOS turns the attribute back on. At the next backup, you can have the program search the files and look for the attribute flag. You can then back up only those that have been altered or changed since the last backup. You can view or modify a file's archive attribute by using the DOS ATTRIB command.

There are several very good software programs on the market that let you use a 5¹/₄-inch or 3¹/₂-inch disk drive to backup your data. Again, you should have backups of all your master software, so you don't have to worry about backing up that software every day. Since DOS stamps each file with the date and time it was created, it is easy to back up only those files that were created after a certain date and time. Once the first backup is made, all subsequent backups need only be made of any data that has been changed or updated.

Most backup programs can recognize whether a file has been changed since the last backup. Most of them can also look at the date that is stamped on each file and back up only those within a specified date range. It might take only a few minutes to make a copy of only those files that are new or have been changed. And, of course, it is usually not necessary to back up your program software. You do have the original software disks safely tucked away, don't you?

Windows 95 Backup Accessory

Windows 95 has a very good built-in backup program. To use it, click the Start button, then choose Programs, Accessories, System Tools, and Backup. The Microsoft Backup Wizard will be displayed. Just follow the simple directions.

XTree

XTree is an excellent shell program for disk and file management. It has several functions that make computing much easier. You can use it to copy files from one directory or disk to another very easily. I often use it to make backups when I only have a few files to back up. XTree is now a division of Symantec at 408-253-9600.

Tape

There are several tape backup systems on the market. Tape backup is easy, but it can be relatively expensive. A drive unit can cost $250 to over $500, and tape cartridges $10 to $20. Some systems require the use of a controller that is similar to the disk controller, so they will use one of your precious slots. There are some SCSI systems, however, that can be daisychained to an SCSI controller. There are also enhanced IDE tape systems that can be controlled by an EIDE interface.

Unless the tape drives are external models, they will also require the use of one of the disk mounting areas. Since it is only used for backup, it will be idle most of the time. Some tape systems run off the printer parallel port. These systems don't require a controller board that takes up one of your slots. Another big plus is that they can be used to back up several different computers by simply moving the tape drive from one to the other.

Like floppy disks, tapes have to be formatted before they can be used. Unlike a floppy disk, it might take over two hours to format a tape. You can buy tapes that have been preformatted, but they cost quite a bit more than the unformatted tapes. Tape systems are very slow, so the backups should be done at night or during off hours. Most systems can be set up so that the backup is done automatically. If you set it on automatic, you won't have to worry about forgetting to back up, or wasting the time doing it.

Another disadvantage of tape is that data is recorded sequentially. If you want to find a file that is in the middle of the tape, the drive has to search until it finds it. Since disk systems have random access, they are much, much faster than tape both in recording and reading.

DAT

Several companies offer digital audiotape (DAT) systems for backing up large hard disks. DAT offers storage capacities as high as 1.3 Gb on a very small cartridge. DAT systems use a helical-scan type of recording similar to that used for video recording. DAT tapes are 4 millimeters wide, which is about 0.156 inches.

Removable Disks

One of the better ways for data backup and data security is to back up to a disk that can be removed and locked up. There are several different systems and companies that manufacture such systems.

Iomega Zip Drive The Iomega Zip drive uses a $3^1/_2$-inch disk that is similar to a floppy, but this disk can store 100 Mb. This system is much less expensive than the Bernoulli. At this time, the Zip drives cost less than $200 and the disks cost less than $20. With a few disks, you would never have to worry about running out of hard drive space. The Zip system is ideal for backup or for any type of data storage.

LS120 Floppy System Compaq, 3M, and Matsushita-Kotubuki have developed a 120-Mb floppy system. The very high-density drives are downward compatible so that they can also read and write to the 720-Kb and 1.44-Mb format. These drives are ideal for backup. Several vendors are now offering the high-capacity floppy drive. For more details, refer back to Chapter 5.

Sony 200-Mb Floppy System The Sony Corporation and Fuji Film have developed a 200-Mb floppy system. It is also discussed in Chapter 5.

SyQuest Corporation The SyQuest Corporation (800-437-9367) manufactures drives with removable disks that can store up to 1.5 Gb. Data compression can be used to almost double this amount of storage. Each cartridge is actually a single hard-disk platter. SyQuest also has a 230-Mb EZ230 drive that costs less than $300. Each removable cartridge costs about $40. Any of these drives could be used to make an excellent backup system.

Magneto-Optical Drives Magneto-optical (M-O) drives are rather expensive, but the removable cartridges are fairly low-cost. They are a good choice for use as a normal hard drive and for backup.

Pinnacle Micro (800-553-7070) has a 4.6-Gb removable M-O drive system they call the Apex. It is almost as fast as a standard hard disk. The cartridges can be erased and rewritten up to 10 million times. A standard magnetic disk begins to deteriorate almost immediately after it has been recorded. It should be refreshed every two or three years. M-O disks have a minimum lifetime of more than 30 years without degradation of data. The Apex system would be ideal for backing up or archiving a large amount of data.

Recordable CD-ROM

When they first came out, the recordable CD-ROM systems were very expensive. at about $10,000. Many companies are now selling recordable CD-ROM systems for less than $500. and the prices are still dropping.

If you have a lot of data that needs to be permanently backed up, a CD-ROM can store over 650 Mb. An advantage of CD-ROM over magnetic systems is that data on a CD-ROM will last for many years. Magnetic data deteriorates and might become useless within ten years. Unlike the magnetic systems, the data on a CD-ROM cannot be erased, changed, or altered. If the data needs to be changed, just record it onto another disc. The blank discs cost about $6 each.

WORM

Write Once, Read Many (WORM) are laser optical systems that are similar to recordable CD-ROMs. One difference is that the WORM systems usually have larger disks and can store up to several gigabytes. They are great for backing up and archiving data.

With a good document-management system and a scanner, vast amounts of paper files can be stored on a WORM. This type of system even has earned its own acronym, *COLD*, which means *Computer Output to Laser Disc*. A WORM recording should last for over 100 years. Ordinarily, even paper will deteriorate in less time.

Second Hard Disk

The easiest and the fastest of all methods of backup is to have a second hard disk. It is very easy to install a second hard disk. An IDE interface can control two high-capacity hard disks; the EIDE interfaces can control up to four hard drives. You can add as many as seven hard drives to an SCSI interface. A good system is to have an IDE drive for the C: boot drive and one or more SCSI drives. You can back up several megabytes of data from one hard drive to another very easily and quickly. The chances are very good that both systems would not become defective at the same time. So, if the same data is stored on both systems, it should offer very good RAID-like protection.

At one time, tape backup systems were much less expensive than hard disks, but the cost of hard disks have come way down. One of the advantages of using a hard disk for backup is that, unlike tape, any file is available almost immediately.

LapLink

LapLink allows you to connect two computers together and access either one. It is very simple to use the parallel port cables that come with the package and transfer files from one computer to the other. LapLink allows you to update only those portions of a file that has changed. If you are updating or backing up files that are already on the disk, it takes very little time. LapLink can also be used over a modem. If you are on the road and need to back up a laptop, you can easily send the data back to the desktop.

RAID Systems

RAID is an acronym for *Redundant Arrays of Inexpensive Disks*. Some data is absolutely critical and essential. In order to make sure that it is saved, data is written to two or more hard disks at the same time. Originally, five different levels were suggested, but only three levels, 1, 3, and 5, are in general use today.

Some RAID systems allow you to *hot-swap* or pull and replace a defective disk drive without having to power down. You don't lose any information because the same data is being written to other hard-disk drives. To prevent data losses due to a controller failure, some RAID systems use a separate disk controller for each drive. A mirror copy is made of the data on each system. This is called *duplexing*. Some systems use a separate power supply for each system. And all systems use uninterruptible power supplies.

RAID systems are essential for networks or any other area where the data is critical and must absolutely be preserved. No matter how careful you are and how many backup systems you have, however, you might still occasionally lose data through accidents or some other act of God. You can add more and more to the backup systems to make them fail-safe, but eventually you will reach a point of diminishing returns. Depending on how much is spent and how well it is engineered, the system should be system fault tolerant (SFT), that is, it will remain fully operational regardless of one or more component failures.

Uninterruptible Power Supplies

Uninterruptible power supplies (UPSs) are very important to backup. If you have a power failure or brownout while working on a file, you could lose a lot of valuable data. In areas where there are frequent electrical storms, it is essential that you have a UPS.

The basic UPS is a battery that is constantly charged by the 110-V input voltage. If the power is interrupted, the battery system takes over and continues to provide power long enough for the computers to save the data that might happen to be in RAM, then shut down. Several companies manufacture quite sophisticated UPS systems for almost all types of computer systems and networks. Of course, for a single user, you only need a small system. On a network or for several computers, you will need a system that can output a lot of current.

There are several UPS companies. Here are just a few:

American Power Conversion
888-289-APCC, extension 8172
www.apcc.com

Best Power Technology
800-356-5794

Sola Electric
800-289-7652

Tripp-Lite Mfg.
312-329-1777

Again, if your data is worth anything at all, it is worth backing up. It is much better to be backed up than to be sorry.

CHAPTER 8

CD-ROM

CD-ROM drives are an essential part of modern computers. Most computers sold today have a CD-ROM as standard equipment. It has become almost as necessary as a hard-disk drive. It makes one wonder how we got along without them for so long.

A CD-ROM offers some very important benefits to the user for entertainment, education, business, and industry. There are thousands and thousands of CD-ROM disc titles that cover just about every subject imaginable.

CD-ROM Drives

It would be impossible for me to try out and test all the CD-ROM drives that are on the market, but I subscribe to a lot of magazines who do tests and evaluations. In most cases, there is really not that much difference in similar models from different companies. In some instances, one drive might have a fraction of a second better statistics than another. I don't worry too much about fractions of a second, though. Since most of the similar-model drives are equivalent, the first thing I look at is cost.

One of the best ways to look for CD-ROMs and do some comparisons is to visit the corporate Web pages. Of course, you should expect to find a lot of PR hype at the company sites, praising their products. Here are the URLs and telephone numbers of a few companies who make CD-ROM drives:

Diamond
800-468-5846
www.diamondmm.com

NEC
800-632-4636
www.nec.com

Panasonic
800-742-8086
www.panasonic.com

Pioneer
800-444-6784
www.pioneerusa.com

Plextor
800-886-3935
www.plextor.com

Samsung
800-726-7864
www.samsung.com

Sony
800-352-7669
www.sony.com

TEAC
800-888-4293
www.teac.com

Toshiba
800-678-4373
www.toshiba.com

UMAX
800-562-0311
www.umax.com

Visit these companies' Web sites or call them for brochures and spec sheets.

Here is an example of information at Toshiba's Web site for their CD-ROM XM-6102B 12, a 24-speed, ATAPI drive:

> PC manufacturers and resellers will find that Toshiba's XM-6102B 12X-to-24X ATAPI internal CD-ROM drive delivers industry-leading performance. The XM-6102 boasts the industry's fastest access time of 90ms and an 85ms random seek. The new 12X-to-24X XM-6102B drive speeds through data at a sustained maximum data transfer rate of 3.6 MB/sec.
>
> To enhance its industry-leading specifications, the drive employs Partial Constant Angular Velocity (PCAV) technology to obtain the highest transfer rates when reading data from anywhere on a disk. The Toshiba quality and reliability are evident with the drive's MTBF of 100,000 hours.
>
> Like other Toshiba CD-ROM drives, the XM-6102 employs the Active Wide Range playback system, which allows the drive to read data at +/—80 percent of a specific rotational speed—allowing the drive to access data on the disc at almost any time.
>
> Data Transfer Rate:
>
> Sustained Mode 150 KBytes/sec (1X)

3600 KBytes/sec (24X) Burst (ATAPI)
16.7 MBytes/sec (PIO Mode 4)
Buffer Cache Size 256K
ACCESS TIME:
Average Random Seek (12-24X) 85 ms
Average Random Access (12-24X) 90 ms, Full Stroke 145 ms
Compatible CD-ROM Format Red-Book, Yellow-Book, ISO9660 and High Sierra (Logical Formats), CD-ROM XA, CD-I BRIDGE (Photo CD, Video CD), CD-I, CD-I READY, CD-G and Multisession (Photo-CD), CD EXTRA, CD-RW, CD-R
AUDIO: Output 1.0V (rms TYP) Distortion 0.04% Max. (at 1 kHz w/20 kHz LPF)
Error Rates: Unrecoverable—Mode 1 < 1 in 1015
Unrecoverable—Mode 2 < 1 in 1012
Seek< 1 in 106

CD-ROM Titles

A short time ago, CD-ROM titles were very expensive, but every day there is more and more competition. There are just too many titles to even try to review them in a book like this. There are several CD-ROM magazines and PC magazines that can help you learn what is available. Here are just a few:

New Media Magazine
800-253-6641
vanessas
@newmedia.com
www.hyperstand.com
(This magazine is sent free to qualified subscribers. Almost anyone with a business connection can qualify.)

EMedia Professional
800-806-7795
emediasub
@online.com
www.online.com/emedia

CD-ROM Today
415-696-1688

CD-ROM Power
800-328-6719

CD-ROM Multimedia
800-565-4623

Mr. CD-ROM (catalog)
800-444-6723

Because of the thousands of companies that are producing CD-ROM titles, the enormous amount of competition is forcing the prices down. Some CD-ROM titles that cost as much as $100 a few months ago can now be bought for as little as $5 or $10—and the prices are still going down. It is great for the consumers.

I subscribe to several magazines. For some time, every magazine would have a 3½-inch floppy disk with AOL signup software. Now, though, CD-ROMs are so inexpensive that AOL and many other companies are sending out their sample software, ads, and demos on CD-ROMs. The plastic CD-ROM disc doesn't cost as much as a floppy disk, and it is much quicker and less expensive to stamp out a CD-ROM disc than to record a 3½-inch floppy.

Home Entertainment

A large number of CD-ROM titles are designed for entertainment for both young and old. There are titles for arcade-type games, adventure games, and chess and other board games. There are titles for music, opera, art, and a large variety of other subjects to entertain you. Many of the titles are educational as well as entertaining.

Home Library

At present, only one side of the CD-ROM discs are used for recording, but this single side can hold over 650 Mb of data. You can have a multitude of different programs on a single CD-ROM disc and a world of information at your fingertips. More books and information can be stored on just a few CD-ROM discs than you might find in an entire library. A 21-volume encyclopedia, for example, can be stored in just a fraction of the space on one side of a single CD-ROM disc. When data compression is used to store text, several hundred books can be stored on a single disc. It might take only seconds to search through an entire encyclopedia or through several hundred books to find a subject, a sentence, or a single word.

Easier Way to Learn

Text, graphics, sound, animation, and movies can be stored on CD-ROM discs. We have several avenues to the brain. The more avenues used to input information to the brain, the easier it is to learn and to remember. We can learn by reading, but we can learn much better if sound is added to the text.

You have undoubtedly heard the old saying that a picture is worth a thousand words. It is so very true. We learn much better and retain more if graphics and motion are added. Rather than trying to remember just dry text, the many advantages of CD-ROM can make learning fun and pleasurable. Schools can use CD-ROM for teaching. Businesses can use CD-ROM to train their personnel.

Lawyers

Lawyers might have to spend hours and hours going through law books to find precedents, to find some of the finer points of the law, or to find loopholes. A few CD-ROM discs could replace several law clerks.

Health and Medicine

The human body is a fantastic machine. There is more written about medicine and computers than any other subject. There are several CD-ROMs published for the home user, such as the Family Doctor, published by Creative Multimedia Corporation (503-241-4351), and the Mayo Clinic Family Health Book, published by Interactive Ventures (507-282-2076).

A doctor must keep abreast of all of the scientific advances, new drugs, and treatments. A busy doctor can't possibly read all of the published papers. A CD-ROM can help. The American Family Physician is the official journal of the American Academy of Family Physicians. It is available from the Bureau of Electronic Publishing at 800-828-4766. The A.D.A.M. (for *Animated Dissection of Anatomy for Medicine*) Software Company (800-755-2326) has developed several discs that show the various parts of the anatomy, both male and female. This CD-ROM is very good for students and families to learn about the human body. If you are a bit prudish, you are given an option to cover certain parts of the anatomy with fig leaves.

How CD-ROM Works

CD-ROM is an acronym for *Compact Disc-Read Only Memory.* The system was first developed by Sony and Philips using lasers for recording and playing back music. (*Laser* is an acronym for *Light Amplification by Stimulated Emission of Radiation.*) Almost all CD-ROM drives can also play audio compact discs. Most of the drives have a plug for earphones and an audio connector on the back so that it can be plugged into a sound card. You can set up a very good hi-fi system using a CD-ROM and a computer. Basically, the audio compact disc systems are quite similar to the CD-ROM systems, but the CD-ROM drives are usually more expensive.

When a CD-ROM disc is created, a powerful laser is turned on and off in response to data zeros and ones, which burns holes in the disc material. When the beam is switched on to create a hole, it is called a *pit;* when left off, the area of the track is called a *land.* When played back, a laser beam is focused on the track. The pits do not reflect as much light as the lands, so it is easy to distinguish the digital data.

High Sierra/ISO 9660

The Philips and Sony companies developed the audio CD in 1982. It wasn't long before the importance of the technology was recognized and adopted for CD-ROMs.

It was a fast-growing technology, but there were no standards. Every company wants to make their products a bit different, so there were several different formats. In 1985, a group of industry leaders, including Microsoft, met at a hotel in Lake Tahoe to hammer a set of standards. The standard that they devised defined the table of contents and directory structure. It also defined the logical, file, and record structures. Microsoft provided their Microsoft Compact Disc Extensions (MSCDEX) software, a driver that allows DOS to access the CD-ROM through conventional DOS commands. All CD-ROMs used in PCs use the Microsoft MSCDEX driver.

Several other specifications were adopted at this meeting. Since they were meeting at Tahoe, which is in the Sierra Mountain range, they called the new standard the High Sierra Specification. The specification was later adopted, with minor modifications, by the International Organization for Standards as ISO 9660. Unless otherwise stated, all CD-ROM drives and discs conform to ISO 9660.

Besides the standards set forth in ISO 9660, several other standard specifications have been developed. There are thousands of pages of specifications in each of four books. Some of these books are more than a foot thick. The specifications were originally issued in books with different colors. The standards have been named for the color of the original book. Sometimes, a disc will have specifications from two or more books. For instance, if the disc contains text, audio, and graphics, it might conform to specifications from the Red Book, the Yellow Book, and the Green Book.

The Red Book sets forth the standards for audio or compact-disc digital audio (CD-DA). The Yellow Book sets forth the ISO 9660 standards for storing files that can be translated to DOS, Apple, or Amiga files. Microsoft's MSCDEX driver is used to accomplish the translation. (Of course, every time someone uses the MSCDEX drivers, they are making Bill Gates a little bit richer.)

The Green Book covers CD-Interactive (CD-I) and CD-ROM extended architecture (CD-ROM/XA). The Orange Book covers WORM drives and magneto-optical (M-O) drives. It also covers the multisession Photo CD drives.

How the Discs Are Made

Data that is to be stored on a CD-ROM disc is usually assembled and organized, then copied onto a large-capacity hard disk. The data can be copied onto the large hard disk from floppies, hard disks, tape, or almost any medium. A table of contents, an index, error-detection and correction, and retrieval software is usually added to the data.

A one-off disc is made from the organized data. A CD-ROM recorder similar to the Philips CCD 521 can be used to make this first test disc. The disc is tested and tried, and if it meets the clients specifications, then the data will be laser etched onto a glass master disc. All of the duplications will come from this disc.

All CD-ROM discs are pressed much like vinyl phonograph records, except that a disc that is pressed from the original master would be a mirror image of it. The pits and the lands on the copy would be just the reverse of those on the master. To make it identical to the master, a copy of a copy is made. The pits and lands are then in the proper order. The first copy of the master is called a *mother*. The working copy that is made from the mother is called the *father*. Virgin blank discs are pressed against the father to make all of the commercial discs.

The blank discs are 120 millimeters (about 4 inches) in diameter and are made from a polycarbonate plastic. Each blank disc costs less than one dollar. After being pressed, the discs are coated with reflective aluminum. This coating is 1 micron thick. The discs are then coated with a thin layer of lacquer to prevent oxidation and contamination. The same process is used for both audio compact discs and CD-ROM discs.

Laser Color

As you know, white light encompasses all of the colors of the rainbow. Each color has its own frequency of vibration; the slower frequencies are at the dark red end. The frequencies increase as the colors move toward the violet end. The particles that make up ordinary light are incoherent, that is, they are scattered in all directions. Lasers are possible because a single color of light can be sharply focused and amplified. All of the particles of one color are lined up in an orderly coherent fashion.

The laser effect can be obtained from several different gases and materials. Most current CD-ROM lasers use light at the lower-frequency, dark end of the spectrum, such as red or yellow. The Samsung Company has developed a green laser that has a shorter wave length and higher frequency. They claim that by using this laser and their proprietary compression techniques, they can store up to 110 minutes of MPEG 2 video on a disc, five times as much as usual. (*MPEG* is an acronym for *Moving Pictures Experts Group,* who developed a set of methods for video compression.) An experimental blue laser has also been developed. It will have an even higher frequency than a green laser. At the time of this writing, neither the green nor the blue laser has been incorporated into available units.

A hard disk may have several thousand separate concentric tracks, with each track divided into several sectors. Usually, each sector can store 512 bytes. A CD-ROM disc has a single spiral track that begins in the center and winds out to the outer edge. If the track were stretched out, it would be several miles long. The track is similar to the groove on a phonograph record except that the groove on a phonograph record begins on the outer edge and winds to the center. An old question is how far does the needle on a phonograph travel when it plays a large record? The answer is about six inches. The needle moves from the outer edge to the center while the record spins beneath it.

The long spiral track of a CD-ROM disc is divided into about 270,000 sectors, each sector with 2048 bytes. The sectors are numbered and given addresses according to the time in minutes, seconds, and hundredths of a second. For instance, the first sector starting from the center is 00:00:00, the second sector is 00:00:01. Remember that the hard disk has a head actuator motor that moves the head to the various concentric tracks. The CD-ROM has a similar small motor that moves the laser beam to whatever sector on the spiral track needs to be read.

Rotational Speed

The CD-ROM uses a system that constantly changes the speed of the drive. The drive electronics speed the disc up or slow it down depending on what area of the disk it is reading. The original 1x (single speed) drive spun at about 200 RPM, and up to 530 RPM. This is called *constant linear velocity* (CLV). The double-speed (2x) CD-ROMs rotate at 400 RPM to 1,060 RPM; quad-speed drives double these figures again, from 800 to over 2000 RPM; 6x drives range from 1200 to over 3000 RPM; 8x range from 1600 to over 4000 RPM.

At 4000 RPM, there may be quite a lot of vibration from the spindle motor. The plastic disc is somewhat flexible. At the higher speeds, a slight imbalance can cause the spinning disc to wobble and vibrate. Even if the label is not properly placed on the disc, it can cause an imbalance at the high speed. This might cause errors in reading the small pits and lands.

Because of its importance, several companies have developed label-printing machines and installers. Many people are now using CD-recordable machines to make their own CD-ROMs. Here are some companies who sell CD labeling kits:

Mediastore
800-555-5551
www.mediastore.com
(Mediastore also sells CD-R recorders, CD-blanks and other electronic products.)

One-Off Label System
800-340-1633
www.oneoffcd.com

NEATO CD Labeler Kit
800-648-6787

CD-R Gold Label Applicator
800-255-4020

PressIT CD Labeling Kit
800-203-6727

Prosource
800-903-1234

Look in CD-ROM magazines for other dealers and other components.

The Speed Limit

Because of the vibration and other problems, when they came out with the 8x CD-ROM drive, many people thought that this was the absolute speed limit. Technology does not stand still, however. I just bought a 24x drive from Panasonic for $115. By the time you read this, there will probably be 32x units available. Actually, the discs will not rotate much faster than the 12x speed. They achieve the transfer rate of a higher speed without spinning that fast by using a combination of constant linear velocity (CLV) and constant angular velocity (CAV).

The 1x and 2x drives are as obsolete as 360-Kb floppy drives. Just a short time ago, the double-speed drives were selling for over $400. No one is even making them today.

Transfer Speed

The transfer speed, or the amount of time that it takes to read a track on the original 1x, and all of the audio CDs, was 75 sectors per second. A sector is 2048 bytes (2 Kb) times 75, which is equal to 150 Kb per second.

Doubling the speed of the 1x drive doubles the transfer rate to 300 Kb per second. A quad-speed drive will transfer data at 600 Kb/s; the 6x drives can transfer data at 900 Kb/s. Faster transfer times allow video and motion to be displayed in a smooth fashion. The faster drives can read all of the CD-ROM discs that the slower drives can read, but read them faster.

The audio files must still be played back at the 150-Kb rate. When playing audio, the speed must drop down to the original speed of 200 to 530 RPMs.

Data Buffers

The faster drives usually have a fairly large buffer system, which also helps to smooth out video and motion and speed up the transfer rate. The buffer memory is located on chips on the drive. The firmware (software embedded on chips) portion of the buffer system decides which information will be used most often and stores it in the buffer. For instance, the contents of the disk directory might be stored in the buffer. Many of the newer drive systems have from 128 Kb up to 2 Mb of DRAM for cache memory buffers.

Access or Seek Time

The *access* or *seek* time is the time necessary to move the laser head to find a certain block or sector on the spiral track and begin reading it. The original MPC specification was that the drive should be able to find any block in 1000 milliseconds (Ms), or 1 second. Most of the older drives had access times of 300 to 400 Ms. The faster rotational speed yields a faster access speed, but not in direct proportion. For instance, the best quad-speed dives have an access rate of 150 Ms. The best eight-speed drive still has a rate of 150 Ms. The best 12- or 24-speed drive is a little better at 90 Ms.

Generally, the transfer rate or speed is more important than the access speed. In most cases, the transfer rate is proportional to the rotational speed.

CD-ROM Differences

There are several different types of CD-ROM drives. Some mount internally, some are external, some use SCSI for an interface, some use an enhanced IDE interface, and of course, they operate at various speeds. There are also a lot of different prices. External drives may cost up to $100 more than internal ones because they need a power supply and cables.

As always, what you should buy depends on your needs.

Interface Systems

Some of the earlier systems had their own proprietary interface. Often, the interface was built in on sound cards. Almost all drives today are either SCSI or EIDE. The EIDE interface is built in on many of the Pentium-type motherboards.

If you are buying an SCSI drive, the interface card and cable might not be included in the price of the system. Read the ads carefully if you are buying by mail order. The interface card will be plugged into one of the bus slots.

Before plugging the card in, make sure that any jumpers or switches on the board are set properly. The board must be configured so that it does not conflict with the address or interrupt (IRQ) of any of your other devices. Check your documentation. Always turn your computer off before unplugging or changing the settings of any card. Never plug in or unplug a card, cable, or device while the power is on.

If your system does not conform to the Plug-and-Play (PnP) specification, a CD-ROM drive interface might be difficult to set up and configure. It must be set to a specific IRQ and memory address location. If the board conflicts with any other device in your system, it will not work.

Enhanced IDE Interfaces The Enhanced IDE (EIDE) interface can handle up to four devices. This can be any combination of EIDE hard drives and EIDE CD-ROMs or EIDE backup tape drives. The IDE CD-ROM systems are considerably less expensive than the SCSI. Your motherboard will probably have a built-in EIDE interface. If not, you will have to buy one. They are fairly inexpensive and may cost from $20 to $60. The interface can be plugged into any one of the 16-bit ISA slots.

Remember that the ISA system operates at 8 to 10 MHz. For high-end work, you might want to buy a PCI IDE interface, which would be considerably faster and, of course, more expensive. IDE CD-ROM drives cost from $50 to $100 less than equivalent SCSI CD-ROM drives.

SCSI Interfaces More and more companies are now manufacturing drives for the SCSI interface. If you have other SCSI products, such as an SCSI hard drive or tape backup, you already have an interface card. SCSI interface cards can drive up to seven different devices. It is amazing how quickly the slots get used up. SCSI can save having to install a separate interface for up to seven different devices. Most SCSI devices have two connectors, one for the input cable and an identical connector for the next item.

If you don't already have an SCSI interface, you might have to pay $100 to $200 extra for the interface. Again, these interfaces plug into the 16-bit

ISA slots and operate at 8 to 10 MHz. If you are doing high-end work, you might want to buy a faster and more expensive PCI SCSI interface.

Parallel Printer Port The parallel printer port has become a popular method to attach peripherals. It all started with tape backup drives that could be attached to one system, then removed and used on another. Soon, many hard-disk drives were doing the same thing. It saves time and saves not having to open the system or buy an interface board or controller, and the peripheral can be used on multiple machines. Some companies are now using the parallel printer port for attaching CD-ROMs. It is a very easy way to go.

Multidisc Systems

Even though you have over 600 Mb on a disc, there will be many times when it doesn't have the programs or information that you need at the moment. For instance, I have a telephone directory of the whole country on five discs from PhoneDisc (800-284-8353). Each disc covers a certain section of the country. Ordinarily, to change discs, you have to eject the disc, unload the caddy, and put the new disc in. To solve this type of problem, several companies have developed multidisc systems. Panasonic has a 12x Big 5 system that holds five CD-ROM discs. You can then switch to any one of the five.

Here are a few other companies who make multidisc systems. Call them for a brochure or visit their Web sites:

Alps Electric
800-825-2577
www.alpsusa.com

NEC Technologies
800-632-4636
www.nec.com

Panasonic Computer Peripherals
800-742-8086
www.panasonic.com

Pioneer New Media
800-444-6784
www.pioneerusa.com

Smart & Friendly Co.
800-959-7001
www.smartandfriendly.com

There will probably be many more companies who offer multidisc systems by the time you read this.

Multidrive Systems

There are several companies who manufacture multidrive systems for network servers and other high-end users. Of course anything that is high end is usually highly expensive. They may have four to 14 drives or more and may cost from $2,000 up to $18,000 or more. Here are some of the companies who offer multidrive systems:

JVC
800-828-1582
www.jvc.com

Logicraft
800-308-8750
www.logicraft.com

Meridian
800-755-8324
www.mtc.com

NSM Jukebox
630-860-5100
www.nsmjukebox.com

Plasmon IDE
612-946-4100
www.plasmon.com

JVC has several changers and network devices. Their CL-100 CD-Library gives you access to 100 different discs. The NSM Mercury Jukebox (800-238-4676) gives you access to up to 150 discs.

Build Your Own Multidrive/Multidisc System

You can build your own system and save a bundle. The cost of CD-ROM drives is coming down every day. I just bought a 24x drive for $115. They will no doubt cost less than that by the time you read this. Your Pentium II or socket-7 motherboard with built-in IDE interfaces allows you to easily install two CD-ROM drives in your system. If you need more CD-ROM drives, you can set up a SCSI system and have up to seven drives. By plugging a second SCSI adapter into the first adapter, you could get six drives on the first adapter, then seven on the second adapter. Theoretically, you could have up to 49 units on SCSI adapters.

There aren't any CD-ROMs available at the moment for the Universal Serial Bus (USB), but there will probably be several by the time you read this. The USB system allows up to 128 peripherals to be attached. That would probably be all that you could possibly need, especially if you have a small office or home office (SOHO).

Some of the multidisc drives are selling for just a little more than $300. (Prices quoted are for comparison only, and will be less by the time you read this.) You can put together a system with three or four of the multidisc drives for a whole lot less than $2000.

Caddies

Some CD-ROM drives just have a tray to hold the disc. You push a button and a tray comes out, you drop the disc in with the label facing up, and push the tray back in. Be very careful in handling the discs to prevent fingerprints, scratches, coffee stains, or other damage to the bright side of the disc. Try to handle them by the edge.

Some CD-ROM drives use a caddy to hold the disc, as shown in Fig. 8-1. The caddy has a clear plastic hinged cover. The caddy encloses the disc and protects it from dirt, dust, and unnecessary handling. When the caddy is inserted into the drive, a metal sliding door moves to one side for the head access. It is similar to the 3½-inch floppies.

If your CD-ROM drive uses a caddy, you can buy several caddies, load them up, and not have to handle the discs thereafter. The caddies cost about $3.00 each and are available from several places. Look in the computer magazines.

CD-ROM Recorders (CD-R)

Several companies are now manufacturing CD-ROM recorders. When they were first introduced, they were very expensive, at around $10,000 for a system. Some companies are now offering the CD recorders for less than $500. The blank discs cost from $5 to $7 at this time. In 1989, Taiyo Yuden of Japan developed an organic dye that could be combined with a reflective gold plating on a blank disc. A laser could then be used to

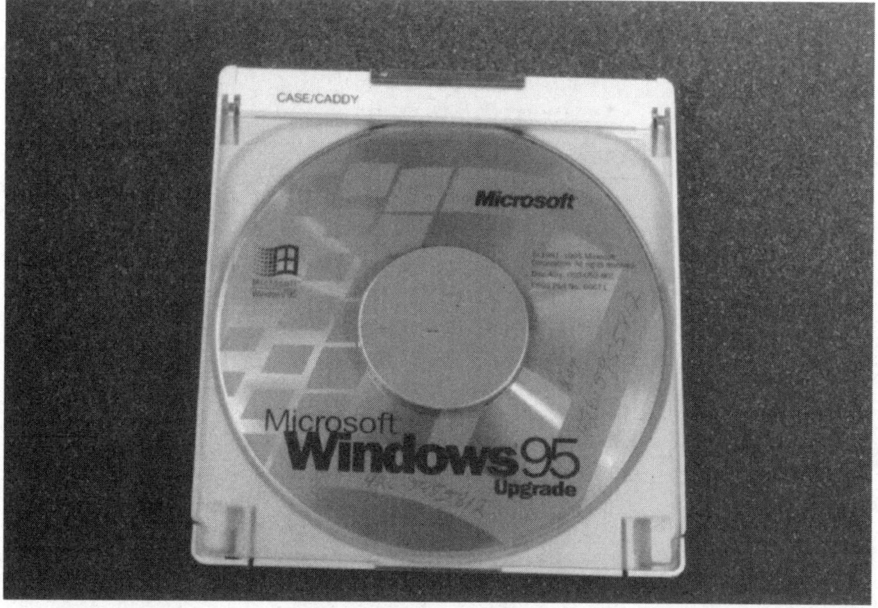

Figure 8-1
A CD-ROM disc caddy. Not many systems use the caddy anymore. They just have a sliding tray to hold the disc.

burn pits in the disc, and it would have the same qualities as a standard CD-ROM disc. In addition, this disc offered the capability of multisession, that is, data could be added from time to time. When a disc is stamped out at a factory, nothing further can be added. The data on the recordable disc has the same reflective characteristics as that of a standard disc.

Recordable CD-ROMs

There are several advantages to recordable CD-ROMs. If only one or two discs are needed, they can be made for the cost of the media. The disc is available immediately. You might have to wait for a week or more to have a disc made up at a factory. Of course, if a large number is needed, it would be better to have a factory master made to replicate them. Even then, however, it would be advisable to record a single disc, check it for accuracy and content, then have a master made.

Another reason to record the disc in house is to guarantee the security of the data. Recording a small number of discs in-house from time to time is much less expensive than having them mastered and replicated. Some large businesses have huge databases of customers, invoices, prices, and other information. Businesses might also have large parts catalogs that must be updated frequently. They can use a single disc to replace the parts catalogs. A CD-ROM disc can store millions of part numbers, descriptions, drawings, costs, locations, and any other pertinent information.

In addition to paperwork records that are stored, some businesses must keep and archive important records that should never be changed. If the records and data are stored on magnetic tape and floppy disks, they could be lost or destroyed. The magnetic properties of tape, floppy, and hard disks gradually deteriorate. The data might be good for less than 10 years. It is also very easy for magnetic material to be erased, either accidentally or purposefully. A CD-ROM disc should last for 75 to 100 years or more. It is much, much easier to search and find an item on a CD-ROM disc than on a backup tape or in a stack of paperwork.

Large organizations may have acres of file cabinets, overflowing with paper. Some studies have shown that 90% of the files are never looked at again after they are stored. What a terrible waste of space and paper! If businesses replaced the millions of file folders and cabinets with CD-ROM discs, they could regain millions of square feet of office space. We could save thousands of trees if businesses saved documents electronically on CD-ROM discs instead of putting everything on paper. CD-ROM recordings are ideal for data that should never be changed. CD-ROM discs are an excellent way to make backups, and to store and archive data. CD-ROM makes it very easy to share large files with other computers across the room, across the nation, or anywhere in the world. A CD-ROM disc can be shipped for a very nominal price, and you won't have to worry too much about it being erased or damaged. The discs can be read by any standard CD-ROM drive.

Most of the CD-ROM recordable systems record at 2x or 4x. Faster systems are being developed and will be available by the time you read this. They usually record at a fairly low speed, but play back at a higher speed. With a 2x CD-R, you could record 74 minutes of music in 37 minutes. With a 4x CD-R, it would only take half that time, about 18½ minutes. Most CD-R systems will let you have multisession recording. If you don't have enough data to completely fill a disc, you can record as much as you have, then come back later and record more. This is also the system used for Photo CDs.

When you send data to CD-R, it will probably be from a hard disk. Either the hard disk or the CD-R should be SCSI. If both drives are IDE, there might be some conflict and slowing of data transfer. There won't be as much of a problem if both of them are SCSI.

Organizing Data

There are systems that can be used to scan information into a computer and then compress it. It can then be indexed, so that any item can be quickly found and accessed. The data can then be stored on a CD-ROM disc, a WORM disc, or other storage device.

COLD is a recent acronym for Computer Output to Laser Disk. With a good COLD system and the proper hardware and software, millions of documents can be placed on a few small discs. To learn more about this technology, subscribe to the following imaging magazines, which are free to qualified subscribers:

Imaging Business Magazine
301-343-1520

Advanced Imaging
445 Broad Hollow Road
Melville, NY 11747-4722

Managing Office Technology
1100 Superior Avenue
Cleveland, OH 44197-8092

If you are in any kind of business at all, you should be able to qualify. There are several other magazines listed in Chapter 19.

Here are just a few of the many companies who offer recordable CD-ROM systems:

Alos
800-431-7105
www.alosmc.com

CMS Enhancements
800-327-5773
www.cmsenh.com

Consan Storage
800-229-3475
www.consan.com

Creative Labs
800-998-5227
www.creativelabs.com

DataDisc
800-328-2347
www.datadisc.com

DynaTek Automation
800-461-8855
www.dynatek.ca

Eastman Kodak
800-235-6325
www.kodak.com

Hewlett-Packard
800-810-0134
www.hp.com/go/storage

JVC
714-261-1292
www.jvcinfo.com

Microboards Technologies
800-646-8881
www.microboards.com

MicroNet Technologies
714-453-6100
www.micronet.com

Optima Technologies
800-411-4237
www.optimatech.com

Philips Professional
800-235-7373
www.pps.philips.com

Pinnacle Micro
800-553-7070
www.pinnaclemicro.com

Pioneer New Media
800-444-6784
www.pioneerusa.com

Plasmon
800-451-6845
www.plasmon.com

Smart & Friendly
800-366-6001
www.smartandfriendly.com

Sony
800-352-7669
www.sel.sony.com

TEAC America
213-726-0303
www.teac.com

Several companies manufacture blank discs for the CD-R systems. The ProSource Company (800-903-1234) offers blank discs from several companies. The discs cost from $6 up to $9 each. They also have several other items that are needed for recording, such as labels and label applicators.

A group of hardware manufacturers, led by Philips and IBM, are working on a CD-Erasable (CD-E) format.

Kodak Photo CD

Eastman Kodak (716-742-4000, www.kodak.com) has developed a system that will display photos on a television set or computer monitor. A person can take a roll of film to a developer and have the photos copied onto a CD-ROM disc. The Kodak CD recorder is much too expensive for most small photo-finishing labs, so they have to send them out to be done. It usually takes about a week to get the disc back. It costs about $20 for a disc, and the cost for putting 24 photos onto a CD disc is about $20. If later you decide to add more photos to the disc, you can take it back to the lab and they will load them on.

One advantage of the Photo CD system is that the photos can be recorded at a resolution of 128×192 and up, as high as 4000×6000 pixels. There are no televisions or even computers that would allow you to view photos at 4000×6000. At this resolution, less than 100 photos in the 4-inch-×-5-inch format can be recorded on a disc. The lower the resolution and the smaller the photo, the more photos that can be stored on a disc. Most photos will be stored at 480×640. At a resolution of 128×192, as many as 6000 small, thumbnail-size photos can be stored on a disc. The 128×192 format is often used to make a small copy of each photo on the disc. These small copies are then used as an index or catalog for all photos on the disc. If you are using a computer, you can use a mouse to point and click on any of the small images to bring up the large photo.

The Kodak Photo CD player can be connected directly to a television or computer. The photos can be displayed and enlarged on the screen, rotated, mirrored, flipped, cropped, copied to a computer file, printed out. or exported. The Kodak Photo CD player is a great tool for business presentations. It would be much more versatile than using a slide projector. It is also a high-fidelity player for audio CD.

Digital Videodisc (DVD)

It takes a tremendous amount of memory to store digital images. Just one digitized frame of a movie can require over 25 Mb to store. At this rate, you could only store a few seconds of a movie on a standard CD-ROM disc. It is now possible, however, to store up to three hours of movies on the digital videodisc (DVD) systems. The discs for this system are the same size as CD-ROM discs, but instead of 650 Mb, DVD discs store up to 17 Gb.

At this time, not very many titles are available. The film industry has held up the production of DVD because of their insistence that absolute copy-prevention be installed on all units. The copy-prevention must be built into the hardware, which is rather expensive because of engineering and manufacturing problems.

Besides being able to store complete movies, the new system will be great for business use. There is always the need for more information. Chances are, though, even with 4.7 Gb of data, what you are looking for will be stored on some other disc. Several companies have developed CD-ROM systems that can have four or more discs loaded in the drive. If what you want is on another disc, it can easily and quickly switch to that disc. These companies should be able to do the same with the DVD system.

The DVD system will be able to read all current CD-ROM discs, but today's CD-ROM drives will not be able to read the new DVD discs. There will be several companies manufacturing DVDs by the time you read this. Here are just a few:

Creative Labs
800-998-5227
www.creativelabs.com

Quantex
800-896-4898
www.quantex.com

STB
888-234-8750
www.stb.com

Toshiba
714-457-0777
www.tais.com/taisdpd/

Rewritable DVD

Several companies are working on DVD-R (write once) technology, but the Hitachi Company (800-448-2244, www.hitachi.com) has developed a DVD rewritable system that can be erased and rewritten several times. They call it DVD-RAM. The discs can store 2.6 Gb on each side. They are available as IDE or SCSI units and are backward-compatible with DVD systems.

DVD Movie Rentals

You might have heard about Divx, a company that plans to revolutionize the movie rental business by "renting" DVD movie discs for as little as $5. The discs can only be played once, then thrown away. Their sophisticated scheme requires special DVD-ROM or TV set-top box players that can dial out (via modem) in order to process financial transactions. There has not been a lot of information about the product. Some of the videotape movie rental companies are definitely not too happy about the new product.

The first Divx-capable DVD products will be available from Matsushita/Panasonic, Thompson Consumer Electronics, and Zenith in the summer of 1998.

Installing CD-ROM Drives

The rest of this chapter describes the steps for installing a CD-ROM drive in your computer.

Step 1: Remove the Computer Cover

There are two main types of CD-ROM drives at this time, IDE and SCSI. The first step in installing either of these drives is to remove the cover from your computer. Then, make sure that you have a standard 5¼-inch bay that is accessible from the front panel. Use two small screws on each side to mount the drive.

Step 2: Set Any Jumpers or Switches

You should have received some sort of documentation and installation instructions with your drive. If you are installing more than one IDE CD-ROM drive or an IDE hard disk on the same cable, they must be configured as master and slave.

IDE CD-ROM Drives Most Pentium-type motherboards have a secondary EIDE interface built in as a set of upright pins. The EIDE interface can support up to four devices. Set any necessary jumpers or switches, then follow the instructions below for plugging in cables and boards. IDE CD-ROM drives come with driver software, so they are fairly easy to install.

SCSI CD-ROM Drive You may have up to seven SCSI devices installed, but each device must be assigned a logical unit number (LUN) between 0 and 6. The LUN is usually determined by a set of jumpered pins. Check your documentation. If you already have other SCSI devices installed, you must determine which LUNs are assigned to them and configure the CD-ROM drive for a number not being used.

Step 3: Install the Cables

There should be two sets of 40 upright pins on the motherboard for IDE devices. One set will be marked *primary* and the other set *secondary*. The primary set is used for the hard disk that will be the boot drive and a second hard drive, if you have one. The CD-ROM will use the secondary pins.

The IDE CD-ROM drives should have a flat, 40-wire ribbon cable. It is the same type of cable used for IDE hard drives. It should have a connector on each end and one in the middle. Some motherboards provide a shell around the pins with a cutout so that the cable can only be plugged in properly. Without the shell, the connector can be plugged in backwards. Make sure that the colored wire on the ribbon cable goes to pin 1 on the motherboard.

For SCSI drives, you will have a 50-wire ribbon cable that connects to the back of the CD-ROM, and then to an SCSI interface board. Most SCSI interface boards have provisions for two cable connections. If you have more than two SCSI devices, you might need to buy a cable with two or more connectors in the center. Like the IDE cables, the SCSI flat ribbon cable will also have a different colored wire on one side. This wire will go to pin 1 of the connectors. Most SCSI connectors have a shell with a square slot on one side. The cable connector will have a square elevation that fits in the slot so that it can only be plugged in correctly. Otherwise, look for an indication of pin 1 on the CD-ROM drive and on the interface board.

If you plan to use your CD-ROM drive with a sound card, and I strongly recommend that you do, you will have to install a small audio cable. There is no standardization for audio cables and sound cards. Since CD-ROM drives and sound cards are made by different manufacturers, you must tell the vendor which sound card you are using to get the proper audio cable. Since there are so many variations, many vendors don't include the audio cable unless you specifically ask for it. The cable may cost an additional $5.

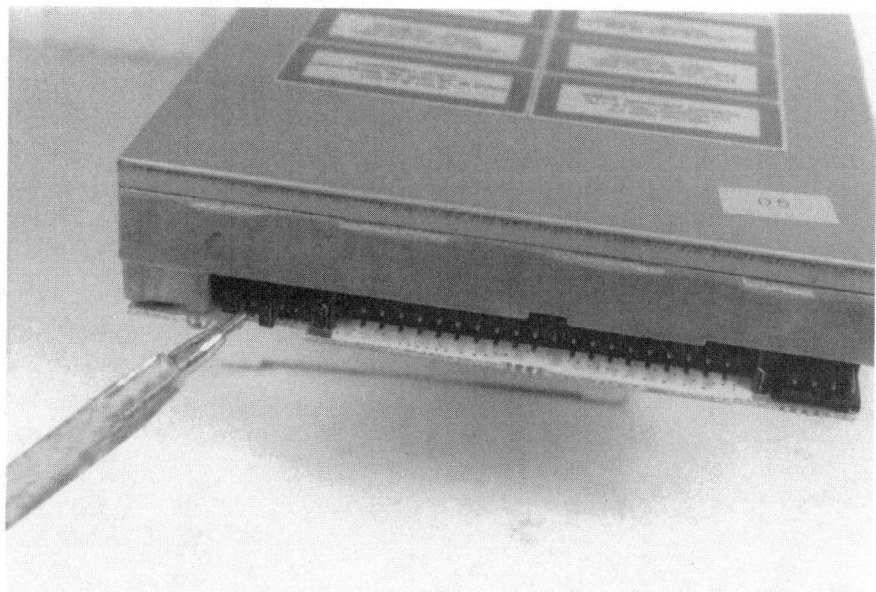

Figure 8-2
The pen points to jumpers on an SCSI CD-ROM. These jumpers are used to set the Logical Unit Number (LUN) of the device.

Figure 8-2 shows a 50-pin SCSI connector on a CD-ROM drive. To the left of this connector are jumper pins for setting the LUN of the drive. There is also a small connector for attaching the audio cable.

Step 4: Install the Drive Power Cable

Plug in one of the four-wire power cables to the drive. The connector can only be plugged in one way.

Step 5: Install Software Drivers

All of the drives should come with some sort of installation and driver software, usually on a floppy disk. The vendor might not provide it unless you ask for it. If you have other SCSI devices already installed, then you probably have SCSI driver software such as the Corel SCSI. If not, then you should contact your vendor for SCSI driver software. Once the SCSI software is installed, it will automatically recognize the new drive when you boot up.

Step 6: Test the System

Test the system with a CD-ROM disc. If everything works, reinstall the computer cover.

Sources

There are several companies and vendors for CD-ROM and DVD-ROM drives. There are thousands of CD-ROM disc titles. At this time, there are not many DVD-ROM titles, but there should be lots of them very soon. Just look in any computer magazine and you will see dozens of ads. Check the magazines listed earlier.

CHAPTER 9

Monitors and Adapters

You will need a good monitor to go with your new system. What you intend to use your computer for helps determine what type and size monitor to buy. You must also consider what type of adapter to buy. A very expensive monitor won't do you much good unless you have a good adapter to drive it.

You should buy the biggest and best monitor you can afford. You will spend all of the time you are at the computer looking at the monitor. Try to get the best.

There are lots of 15-inch monitors available now. Most of them are very good, but for just a few dollars more, you can get a 17-inch or 19-inch model. Even the 20- and 21-inch models are fairly reasonable now. Several companies manufacture large screen monitors. Here is contact information for just a few:

ADI Systems
800-228-0530
www.adiusa.com

CTX International
800-888-2120
www.ctx.com

Eizo Nanao Technologies
800-800-5202
www.eizo.com

Mitsubishi Electronics America
800-843-2525
www.mitsubishi-display.com

Princeton Graphic Systems
800-747-6249
www.prgr.com

Sony Electronics
800-352-7669
www.sony.com/technology

Viewsonic
800-888-8583
www.viewsonic.com

You can call the companies and ask them to send a brochure. If you have access to a computer, it might be better to visit their Web sites for information and specifications. Viewsonic has a "Monitor 101" type of article for those who are new to monitors. They also list some of the features that are desirable in choosing a monitor.

Flat-Panel LCD Monitors

Manufacturers are making bigger and bigger Liquid Crystal Display (LCD) monitors for laptops. They are also called *Thin Film Transistor* (*TFT*) displays. They are also now making them for desktop computers. These monitors use a liquid crystal sealed between two pieces of polarized glass. The polarity of the liquid crystal is changed by an electric current to vary the amount of light that can pass through.

LCDs are still rather expensive. They require a separate transistor for each pixel. Depending on the size of the display or monitor, it might require several million transistors. If some of the transistors prove to be defective after the panel has been made, there is no way to repair it. There will be a blank spot in the screen wherever the defective transistor is. If there are only three or four defective transistors and if they are not clumped together, they might not be noticeable. If there are several in one area, however, the screen must be rejected. A large number of displays are rejected. Of course, this drives the price up.

Several companies have developed LCD panels from 12 inches to as large as 20 inches, measured diagonally. Some are as thin as 2.5 inches, up to about 7 inches deep, and weigh about 20 pounds. They can sit on the desktop or can easily be hung on a wall. The LCD panel supports 24-bit color at a resolution of 1280×1024. It requires no special adapter, but, of course, it works best with the better ones. Figure 9-1 shows a flat-panel monitor.

Many people worry about the radiation from the monitor. Over 25,000 volts bombard the back of the monitor face constantly. There has been no good evidence that any radiation produced can harm one, but a few companies have made a lot of money selling special shields for the monitor. The LCD uses a very low voltage, so there is not any concern about radiation. The bad news is that at this time, a 20-inch LCD monitor costs almost $8000. They will eventually be more reasonable. There are companies who have smaller ones for less cost. Viewsonic has a 14-inch LCD that is 2.5 inches thick for $2199. Prices will be different by the time you read this.

Some companies are developing projection-screen monitors. They work on the same principle that large television screens use. Several of the companies who make monitors also manufacture LCD projection devices for presentations. A fairly small screen can be projected onto a much larger screen at the same resolution. It is possible that a similar technology could be used for large projection-screen monitors.

We are now becoming more and more energy conscious. Most of the cathode ray tube (CRT) monitors are real wattage hogs. Most of them

Figure 9-1
A flat-panel monitor using Thin Film Transistor technology (TFT). At the present time, they are very expensive.

now have an energy saving mode, but they might still require from 100 to 175 watts. The largest LCD monitors require only 40 watts.

The basic CRT technology is over 100 years old. There doesn't seem to be much room for further improvements. Eventually, LCD technology will replace the CRT for most applications.

Many of the companies who manufacture CRT type monitors also manufacture LCD displays. Check the Web sites listed earlier in this chapter, as well as the following ones:

Buffalo, Inc.
www.buffinc.com

NEC Technologies
www.nec.com

Sharp Electronics Corporation
www.sharp-usa.com

USB Monitors

Many of the new monitors, the standard CRT and the newer LCDs, are now able to connect to the computer by the Universal Serial Bus (USB).

You will also be able to connect your keyboard, mouse, scanner, printer, and any of several other peripherals to the USB bus. Instead of having seven or eight cables going to the computer, everything will be attached to the USB and it will be the only connection. Many of the newer monitors act as a USB hub and provide up to five or more connections for a USB-compatible device.

AGP Adapters

Accelerated Graphics Port (AGP) was discussed in some detail in Chapter 2 on motherboards. One of the prime uses for AGP is for high-end graphic designers. The other major use is for games. Games are big business, especially 3D games. It takes a lot of memory and CPU power to make them realistic. Many of the newer Pentium II motherboards have a special slot for the AGP.

3D Adapters

Much of the newer software for games and animation is now 3D. Several companies are manufacturing special adapters for 3D. At present, there are no standards for 3D software or hardware, but Microsoft, Creative Labs, and several other companies are working to create a standard.

Lightwave 3D
NewTek
800-847-6111

Microsoft 3D
Movie Maker
800-426-9400

A couple of 3D adapter companies are:

3D Blaster
Creative Labs
800-998-1000

Edge 3D
Diamond Multimedia
800-468-5446

Here are a couple of virtual-reality products:

SimulEyes VR
Stereo Graphics
800-746-3937
Virtual I-Glasses
Virtual I-O
800-646-3579

Many other companies are working on 3D hardware and software. There are usually articles about their progress in several magazines, such as *New Media Magazine, CD-ROM Today,* and *Virtual Reality.* More sources are listed in Chapter 17.

PCI Bus Adapters

You could use an old 8- or 16-bit ISA adapter on your Pentium Pro, but it would be about like hitching up a horse to pull a Cadillac. Many of the 486 and Pentium motherboards have either a VL bus or a PCI bus. The PCI offers some advantages over the VLB, so the VLB is obsolete. Most Pentium-class motherboards now have three or four PCI connectors and three or four ISA plug-in slot connectors. The PCI bus adapters are much faster than the older graphics and accelerator boards because they have a 32- or 64-bit path that is used to communicate directly with the CPU. This direct path also allows them to communicate at the CPU's speed or frequency. The ISA I/O systems are limited to the 8- or 16-bit bus and operate at a speed of 8 to 10 MHz, no matter how fast the CPU is.

Some Windows programs, most graphics programs, and many other applications require a lot of interaction with the CPU. Many of the true-color adapters, therefore, are made for motherboards with a PCI bus. Most of the newer adapters are now designed for 64 bits, and a few even operate at 128 bits, such as the Number Nine Imagine 128 Pro.

Video Accelerator Boards

The fixed-function cards have accelerator chips with several built-in graphics functions. Because they have built-in functions, they can handle many of the Windows-type graphics tasks without having to bother the CPU. Newer and better boards are being developed every day to meet the strenuous demands of multimedia for digital video, 3D technology, and full motion. Most of these boards are available for the PCI bus.

The graphics accelerator boards can handle graphics and play digital video from several different formats, such as Indeo, Motion JPEG, and MPEG. (*JPEG* is a set of standards set up by the Joint Photographers Expert Group; *MPEG* is a similar set of standards set up by the Motion Picture Expert Group. Both standards concern compression of video and motion pictures.)

3D Video Cards

If you do a lot of game playing, a 3D graphics card will make the games much more realistic. 3D graphics cards are also needed for animation, simulation, 3D Web authoring, CAD, and other graphics applications. The 3D cards need a lot more memory than standard graphics cards, at least 4 Mb for games and at least 8 Mb for good CAD work. Vendors usually provide one or more drivers for the cards. Vendors usually provide updated drivers that can be downloaded from their Web sites. The 3D cards will provide good 2D as well 3D.

Video Memory

Having memory on the adapter board saves having to go through the bus to the conventional RAM. Some adapter boards even have a separate plug-in daughterboard for adding more memory. With the older, dumb, frame-buffer type of cards, even with a lot of memory, the adapter had to go back and forth over the 16-bit bus to communicate with the CPU. Many of the applications, especially under Windows, became painfully slow.

A PCI accelerator card with lots of onboard memory can speed up the processing considerably. You should have at least 2 Mb of memory to display 256 colors in 1024×768 resolution. The more colors displayed and the higher the resolution, the more memory is required. For 24-bit true color, you need a minimum of 4 Mb.

Adapter Memory Chips

Many of the high-resolution adapters have up to 4 Mb or more of video RAM (VRAM) memory on board. The VRAM chips look very much like the older DRAM DIP memory chips, but they are not interchangeable with DRAM. The DRAM chips have a single port; they can only be accessed or written to through this port. VRAM chips have two ports and can be accessed by one port while being written to in the other. This makes them much faster and a bit more expensive than DRAM.

Some of the less expensive adapters use DRAM memory. I am looking at an ad for a Diamond Stealth 3D with 4 Mb of EDO memory for $69. The same Diamond Stealth 3D with 4 Mb of VRAM is $139, double the cost. If you expect to do lot of heavy graphics, VRAM is worth it. Many of the ads do not specify the type of memory. If the price is fairly low, then it is probably DRAM or EDO memory.

Many less-expensive adapter boards are sold with only 512 Kb of memory or less. They often have empty sockets for adding more memory. Some cards have space to install as much as 40 Mb of DRAM. It is not likely that you would need that much for ordinary use. It is very easy to install the memory chips in the sockets. Just be sure that you orient them properly. They should be installed the same way as other memory on the board. Make sure that all legs are fully inserted in the sockets.

Sources

There are hundreds of adapter manufacturers. I hesitate to mention models because each manufacturer has dozens of different models with different features and resolutions, and they are constantly designing, developing, and introducing new models.

I have used several different models of the Diamond adapters and I think they are one of the best. Several computer magazines have tested and rated the following to be among the best. Call or visit the Web sites for brochures and more information.

ATI Technologies
905-882-2600
www.atitech.ca

Boca Research
561-997-6227
www.bocaresearch.com

Diamond Multimedia Systems
800-468-5846
www.diamondmm.com

Matrox Graphics
800-361-1408
www.matrox.com

Number Nine Imagine 128
800-438-6463
www.nine.com

Orchid Technology
510-683-0300
www.orchid.com

STB Powergraph 64
214-234-8750
www.stb.com

Adapter Software

Most adapter cards will work with any software that you have. Many adapter vendors provide special software drivers, however, that are necessary for high resolution and speed with certain applications. Make sure that the adapter has drivers for all popular graphics software.

MPEG Boards

The Motion Pictures Expert Group (MPEG) devised a specification for compressing and decompressing graphics and video. Ordinarily, a single frame in a moving picture requires about 25 Mb to digitize and store. The MPEG system allows a compression up to 100 to 1, so that it is possible to store as much as 72 minutes on a 650 Mb CD-ROM.

Several companies have developed plug-in boards that allow you to capture and play back video from several different sources, such as a VCR, camcorder, CD-ROM, TV, laser disk, and others. Some cards have built-in sound systems, and some can even be supplied with a TV tuner so that you can watch TV on your monitor.

A few feature movies have been compressed to the MPEG specifications. With an MPEG board, you can watch the movies on your high-resolution monitor. It is possible that as the MPEG system becomes more widespread, the PC might become the home entertainment center. The following are a few companies who manufacture MPEG boards. Contact them for brochures and information:

Diamond Multimedia Systems
800-468-5846
www.diamondmm.com

Genoa GVision DX
800-934-3662
www.genoasys.com

Orchid Kelvin MPEG
510-651-2300
www.orchid.com

Sigma Real Magic Rave
510-770-0100
www.realmagic.com

Using a TV as a Monitor

For some applications, such as presentations or playing some games, it would be nice to have a large-screen such as a 32-inch TV or even a projection-screen TV to use as a monitor. You can't just plug your PC output into a TV, however, and have it work. There are adapter boards that will let you do it. The ATI Technologies All-In-Wonder graphics board allows output to a TV and even brings a TV signal back to the PC. The All-In-Wonder is a full-featured 2D/3D video accelerator that will work on your standard monitor or on a TV. It has a TV tuner so that you can watch TV on your standard monitor. This board also accepts the output of a VCR for your standard monitor.

You should not expect the resolution of a TV to be equal to even the poorest monitor. There are other companies who manufacture similar graphics boards that will allow you to use the TV. Here are some Web sites:

ATI Technologies
All-In-Wonder
www.atitech.com

Matrox Graphics
Rainbow Runner
www.matrox.com

STB Systems
TV PCI
www.stb.com

If you are using a TV as a monitor, you might want to be a few feet away from it. Most keyboards have about a 4-foot cable, but several companies make wireless keyboards that work off the same principle as the TV remote control.

The Silitek Corporation, at www.silitek-corp.com, has a wireless keyboard that is rather inexpensive. Wireless Computing, at www.wireless computing.com, also has a wireless keyboard, but it is a bit expensive.

Monitor Basics

There are many different types of monitors with many different sizes, qualities, and, of course, prices. A few monitor basics are discussed here to help you make a better decision in buying your monitor.

The CRT

A monitor is similar to a TV. The main component is the cathode ray tube (CRT), or picture tube. In some respects, the CRT is like a dinosaur; it is a relic of the vacuum-tube era. Before the silicon age of semiconductors, vacuum tubes operated almost all electronic devices. Like all vacuum tubes, CRTs use enormous amounts of power and generate lots of heat.

Vacuum tubes have three main elements: the cathode, the grid, and the plate. These elements correspond to the emitter, the base, and the collector of the transistor. In a vacuum tube, the cathode is made from metallic material that causes electrons to be boiled off when heated. The filament is made from resistive wire similar to that used in lightbulbs. Also, very much like lightbulbs, the filaments burn out, which causes the tube to fail. Burned-out filaments are the single greatest cause of failure in vacuum tubes. The filaments of computer CRTs are designed a bit better now, so that they don't burn out as often as in the early days.

If a positive direct-current (dc) voltage is placed on the plate of a vacuum tube, the negative electrons boiled off from the heated cathode will be attracted to the plate. A control grid is placed between the cathode and plate. If a small negative voltage is placed on the grid, it will repel the negative electrons and keep them from reaching the plate. Zero voltage, or a small positive voltage, on the grid will let them go through to the plate.

As the analog voltage swings up and down on the grid, it acts as a switch that allows a much larger voltage to pass through the vacuum tube. A voltage as small as a millionth of a volt on the grid of a vacuum tube can create a much larger exact voltage replica on the output of the plate. With the proper voltages on the emitter, base, and collector, a transistor operates much like a vacuum tube, acting as a switch or as an amplifier. A vacuum tube can take a small signal and amplify it. A vacuum tube is quite large, requires a lot of space and energy, and produces a lot of heat. A transistor can amplify the same signal, but it requires much less power and space and produces very little heat. The Pentium II has 7.5 million transistors in a very small enclosure. If you had 7.5 million vacuum tubes, it would fill a large warehouse.

Like the vacuum tube, the CRT has a filament that heats up a cathode to produce electrons. It also has a grid that can shut off the passage of the electrons or let them pass through. The corresponding plate of the CRT is the back of the picture screen, which has about 25,000 volts on it to attract the electrons from the cathode. The back of the screen is coated with a phosphor. Because of the high attracting voltage, the electrons slam into the phosphor and cause it to light up and glow.

A very small, thin beam of electrons are formed. This electronic beam acts very much like a piece of iron in a magnetic field. If four electromagnets are placed around the neck of the CRT, one on top, one on the bottom, and one each side, the beam of electrons can be directed to any area of the screen by varying the polarity of the voltage fed to the electromagnets. If you wanted the beam to move to the right, you would increase the plus voltage on the right magnet. If you wanted the beam to move up, you would increase the plus voltage on the top magnet. With these electromagnets, you can move the beam to any spot on the screen.

The small input-signal voltage on the grid of the CRT turns the electron beam on and off to cause portions of the screen to light up. The beam can be caused to move and write on the screen, just as if you were writing with a pencil. Alphabetic characters or any kind of graphics can be created in an exact replica of the input signal.

Present-day CRTs are like the ancient dinosaur. Many laptops and notebook computers have excellent color screens using transistors. The active-matrix type of laptop monitor uses millions of transistors, one to light up each individual pixel. Eventually, we will have large, low-energy LCD screens that will produce good, high-resolution pictures. Even the television CRTs will be replaced with flat screens that can be hung on a wall.

Monochrome Versus Color

In a monochrome TV or monitor, there is a single "gun" that shoots the electrons toward the back of the screen. Color TVs and color monitors are much more complicated than monochrome systems. During the manufacture of color monitors, three different phosphors, red, green, and blue (RGB), are deposited on the back of the screen. Usually, a very small dot of each color is placed in a triangular shape. If you use a magnifying glass and look at a color monitor or color TV, you can see the individual dots.

The different phosphors used to make color monitors are made from rare earths. They are designed to glow for a certain period of time after they have been hit by an electron beam. In a color TV or monitor, there are three guns, each shooting a beam of electrons. The electrons from each gun have no color, but each gun is aimed at a particular color, one to hit only the red dots, one the blue dots, and one the green dots. They are very accurately aimed so that they will converge or impinge only on their assigned color dots.

To make sure that the beams hit only their targets, they must go through the holes of a metal shadow mask. Being hit by stray electrons causes the shadow mask to heat up. The heat can cause fatigue and loss of focus. Many of the newer monitors use shadow masks made from Invar, an alloy that has good heat resistance. By turning the guns on or off to light up and mix the different red, green, and blue dots of phosphor, any color can be generated.

The Sony Trinitron monitors and TVs use a system that is a bit different. Their three guns are in a single housing and fire through a single lens. Instead of a shadow mask, the Trinitron uses a vertical grill that allows the beams to pass through. The Trinitron system was actually invented in the United States, but no one in the TV industry was interested until Sony adopted it.

Dot Pitch

If you look closely at a black-and-white photo in a newspaper, you can see that the photo is made up of small dots. There will be a lot of dots in the darker areas and fewer in the lighter areas. The text or image on a monitor or a television screen is also made up of dots, very similar to the newspaper photo. You can easily see these dots with a magnifying glass. If you look closely, you can see spaces between the dots. This is much like the dots of a dot-matrix printer.

The more dots and the closer together they are, the better the resolution. A good, high-resolution monitor will have solid, sharply defined characters and images.

Also, the more dots and the closer together they are, the more difficult it is to manufacture a CRT. The red, blue, and green dots must be placed very accurately and uniformly in order for their specific electron beam to hit them. Most standard monitors have a dot pitch of 0.28 millimeters (mm). The better monitors have dots that are as close as 0.24 mm. Some of the low-cost color monitors might have from 0.39 mm up to 0.52 mm. Such monitors might be all right for playing games, but they wouldn't be very good for anything else.

Pixels

Resolution is also determined by the number of picture elements (*pixels*) that can be displayed. A pixel is the smallest unit that can be drawn or displayed on the screen. A pixel can be turned on or off with a single bit, but to control the intensity and color depth might take several bits per pixel.

The following figures relate primarily to text, but the graphics resolution will be similar to the text. Most monitors are designed to display 80 characters in one row, or line, across the screen. By leaving a bit of space between each row, 25 lines of text can be displayed from top to bottom. The old color graphics monitor (CGA) could display 640×200 pixels. If we divide 640 by 80, we find that one character will be eight pixels wide. There can be 25 lines of characters, so 200/25 = 8 pixels high. The entire screen will have 640 × 200 = 128,000 pixels.

The EGA monitor has 640×350 pixels, so each cell is eight pixels wide and 14 pixels high. The Video Electronics Standards Association, (VESA) chose 640×480 to be the VGA standard, and 800×600 to be the Super VGA (SVGA) standard. SVGA is 800/80 = 10 pixels wide, and 600/25 = 24 pixels high. Many of the newer systems are now capable of 1024×768, 1280×1024, 1664×1200, and more. With a resolution of 1664×1200, you would have 1,996,800 pixels, or almost 2 million pixels that could be lit up. We have come a long way from the 128,000 pixels possible with CGA.

Painting the Screen

To put an image on the screen, the electron beam starts at the top left corner. Under the influence of the electromagnets, it is drawn across to the right of the screen, lighting up a very thin line as it moves. Depending on what the beam is depicting, it will be turned on and off by the grid as it sweeps across the screen. When the beam reaches the right side of the screen, it is turned off and sent back to the left side. It drops down a bit and begins sweeping across the screen to paint another line.

On a TV set, it paints 262.5 lines in $\frac{1}{60}$ of a second. These are all of the even-numbered lines. It then goes back to the top and *interlaces* the other 262.5 odd-numbered lines in between the first 262.5. It does this fairly fast, at a frequency of 15,750 Hz. (15750 divided by 60 = 262.5). Therefore, it takes $\frac{1}{30}$ of a second to paint 525 lines. This is called a *frame,* so 30 frames are written to the screen in one second.

When you watch a movie, you are seeing a series of still photos, flashed one after the other. Due to persistence of vision, it appears to be continuous motion. This same persistence-of-vision phenomenon allows us to see motion and images on television and video screens.

Scan Rate

It is obvious that 525 lines on a TV set, especially a large screen, leaves a lot of space in between the lines. If there were more lines, the resolution could be improved. At the time this is being written, the FCC and the TV industry are trying to decide on a standard for a High Definition TV that would have from 750 to about 1200 lines at 30 frames per second. At 750 lines, it would paint 375 lines in $\frac{1}{60}$ of a second and 750 in $\frac{1}{30}$ of a second. For 750 lines, the horizontal frequency would be 22,500 Hz. For 1200 lines, the horizontal frequency would be 36,000 Hz.

The Vertical Scan Rate

The time that it takes to fill a screen with lines from top to bottom is the *vertical scan rate.* This may also be called the *refresh rate.* The phosphor might start losing some of its glow after a period of time unless the vertical scan refreshes it in a timely manner. Some of the multiscan, or multifrequency, monitors have several fixed or variable vertical scan rates. The Video Electronics Standards Association (VESA) specifies a minimum of 70 Hz for SVGA and 72 Hz for VGA systems.

Multiscan

Multiscan monitors can accept a wide range of vertical and horizontal frequencies. This makes them quite versatile and flexible. Many of the early multiscans could accept both digital and analog signals. Almost all monitors sold today are the analog type.

The VGA system introduced by IBM on their PS/2 systems in 1987 used a fixed frequency instead of a multiscan adapter and monitor. A multiscan design costs more to build, so many of the low-cost VGAs were designed to operate at a single fixed frequency. They are not as versatile or flexible as the multiscan, but the resolution can be as good as the multiscan.

Adapter Basics

An adapter is just as important as the monitor. You can't just plug a monitor into your computer and expect it to function. Just as a hard disk needs an interface with the computer, a monitor needs an adapter to interface with the computer.

A computer monitor is a bit different from a TV. A TV usually has all of its controlling electronics mounted in the console or case and is assembled and sold as a single unit. A computer monitor might have some electronics within its case, but its main controller, the adapter, is usually on a plug-in board on the PC motherboard. This provides more versatility and utility because you can use different or specialized adapters if needed. A TV is usually much less expensive than a comparable-sized computer monitor. One reason is because it doesn't provide the resolution that a computer monitor does.

There are several manufacturers who make monitor adapters, so there is quite a lot of competition. This has helped to keep the prices fairly reasonable. Most monitors can operate with several different types of adapters. Adapters can cost as little as $40 up to $1000 or more. Monitors can cost as little as $200 up to $3000 or more. It would be foolish to buy a very expensive monitor and an inexpensive adapter, or vice versa. Try to match the capabilities of the monitor and the adapter.

Most monitor adapters have text character generators built onto the board, which is similar to a built-in library. When you send an *A* to the screen, the adapter goes to its library and sends the signal for the preformed *A* to the screen. Each character occupies a cell made up of a number of pixels. The number of pixels depends on the resolution of the screen and the adapter. In the case of the VGA, if all the dots within a cell were lit up, there would be a solid block of dots 10 pixels or dots wide, and 24 pixels high. When an *A* is placed in a cell, only the dots necessary to form the outline of the *A* will be lit up. It is very similar to the dots formed by a dot matrix printer when it prints a character.

With the proper software, a graphics adapter can allow you to place lines, images, photos, various text fonts, and almost anything you can imagine on the screen. Almost all adapters sold today have both text and graphics capability.

Analog vs. Digital

Most monitors and adapters sold today are analog systems. Until the introduction of the PS/2 with VGA, most displays used the digital system, but the digital systems have severe limitations.

Digital signals are of two states, either fully on or fully off. The signals for color and intensity require separate lines in the cables. It takes six lines for the EGA to be able to display 16 colors out of a palette of 64. The digital systems are obsolete.

SVGA Colors

The number of colors that an SVGA card can display is dependent on the resolution displayed. Here are the numbers for a low cost SVGA:

- 16.7 million colors at 640×480
- 64,000 colors at 800×600
- 16 colors at 1280×1024

Of course, there are adapters that can display a much greater number of colors than that listed here, but they are also more expensive.

True Colors

Most of the standard, low-cost VGA cards are capable of only 16 colors. True colors or pure colors requires video boards with lots of fast memory, a coprocessor, and complex electronics. *True color* means that a video board can drive a monitor to display a large number of shades in separate, distinct hues or pure colors.

Remember that a pixel can be turned on or off with a single bit, but for color intensity or shades and depth, it may take several bits per pixel. A good adapter for true color might cost more than the monitor. Table 9-1 lists the number of bits needed for true color.

TABLE 9-1
Pure Color

Bits	Shades	Depth
4 or 2^4	16	
8 or 2^8	256	
15 or 2^{15}	32,768	5:5:5
16 or 2^{16}	65,536	5:6:5 or 6:6:4
24 or 2^{32}	16.7 million	8:8:8

Depth

True color usually refers to displays with 15-, 16-, or 24-bit depth. *Depth* means that each of the individual red, green, or blue pixels will have a large amount of information about each color. The 15-bit system will have five bits of information for each of the three colors. The 16-bit system may have six bits for red, six bits for green, and four bits for blue, or a combination of 5:6:5. The 24-bit system will have eight bits for each color.

Table 9-2 can give you an idea of how much memory is needed for the various resolutions and colors.

TABLE 9-2
Memory and Resolution

Bits/Pixel	Color	640×480	800×600	1024×768
4	16	150 Kb	234 Kb	386 Kb
8	256	300 Kb	469 Kb	768 Kb
16	35,536	600 Kb	938 Kb	1.536 Mb
24	16,777,216	900 Kb	1.406 Mb	2.304 Mb

Dithering

If a board doesn't have enough power to display the true, distinct colors, it might use *dithering* to mix the colors to give an approximation. Dithering takes advantage of the eye's tendency to blur colors and view them as an average. A printed black-and-white photo uses all black dots, but several shades of gray can be printed depending on the number of black dots per inch. Similarly, a mixture of red dots with white ones can create a pink image. Gradual color transitions can be accomplished by using dithering to intersperse pixels of various colors.

Anti-aliasing

Some low-resolution systems have a "stair-step" effect when a diagonal line is drawn on the screen. Some adapters have the ability to use anti-aliasing to average out the pixels so that a smooth line appears.

Choosing a Monitor

The primary determining factors for choosing a monitor should be what it is going to be used for and the amount of money you have to spend. Try to get a good, 15-inch monitor as a minimum. If you can afford it, buy a large, 21-inch monitor with super high resolution and a good SVGA board to drive it. Look for monitors with a refresh rate of at least 72 Hz or higher. Look for a dot pitch of at least 0.28 mm; 0.26 mm or 0.24 is even better, but more expensive. The resolution should be at least 800×600; 1024×768 is better.

Make sure the controls are near the front and easily accessible. The stated screen size of a monitor is very misleading and almost fraudulent. The stated size is a diagonal measurement. There is a border on all four sides of the screen. For example, the usable viewing area on a 14-inch monitor is about 9.75 inches wide and about 7.75 inches high. One reason for this difference is because the screen is markedly curved near the edges on all sides. This curve can cause distortion, so the areas are masked off and not used.

If you expect to do any kind of graphics or CAD/CAM design work, you will definitely need a good, large-screen, color monitor, with very high resolution. A large screen is almost essential for some types of design drawings so that as much of the drawing as possible can be viewed on the screen. You will also need a high-resolution monitor for close tolerance designs. For instance, if you draw two lines to meet on a low-resolution monitor, they might look as if they are perfectly lined up, but when the drawing is magnified or printed out, the lines might not be anywhere close to one another.

Most desktop publishing (DTP) is done in black-and-white print. The high-resolution paper-white monochrome monitors might be all you need for these applications. These monitors can usually display several shades of gray. Many of these monitors are the *portrait* type; that is, they are higher than they are wide. Many of them have a display area of $8^1/_2$ by 11 inches. Instead of 25 lines, they have 66 lines, which is the standard for an 11-inch sheet of paper. Many have a phosphor that will let you have black text on a white background so that the screen looks very much like the finished text. Some of the newer color monitors have a mode that lets you switch to pure white with black type.

Most monitors are wider than they are tall. These are called *landscape* styles.

What to Look for

If possible, go to several stores and compare various models. Turn the brightness up and check the center of the screen and the outer edges. Is the intensity the same in the center and the outer edges? Check the focus, brightness, and contrast with text and graphics. There can be vast differences even in the same models from the same manufacturer. Ask the vendor for a copy of the specs. Check the dot pitch. For good, high resolution it should be no greater than 0.28 mm, even better would be 0.26 mm or 0.24 mm.

Check the horizontal and vertical scan frequency specs. For a multiscan, the wider the range, the better. A good system could have a horizontal range from 30 KHz to 40 KHz or better. The vertical range should be from 45 Hz to 70 Hz or higher.

Controls

You might also check for available controls to adjust the brightness, contrast, and vertical/horizontal lines. Some manufacturers place them on the back or some other difficult area to get at. It is much better if they are accessible from the front so that you can see what the effect is as you adjust them.

Glare

If a monitor reflects too much light, it can be like a mirror and be very distracting. Some manufacturers have coated the screen with a silicon formulation to cut down on the reflectance. Some have etched the screen for the same purpose. Some screens are tinted to help cut down on glare. If possible, try the monitor under various lighting conditions. If you have a glare problem, several supply companies and mail-order houses offer glare shields that cost from $20 up to $100.

Cleaning the Screen

Since there are about 25,000 volts of electricity hitting the back of the monitor face, it creates a static attraction for dust. This can distort and make the screen difficult to read.

Most manufacturers should have an instruction booklet that suggests how the screen should be cleaned. If you have a screen that has been coated with silicon to reduce glare, you should not use any harsh cleansers on it. Usually, plain water and a soft paper towel will do fine.

Monitor Radiation

Almost all electrical devices emit very low frequency (VLF) magnetic and electrical fields. There have been no definitive studies that prove that this radiation is harmful to a person. In some cases, the emissions are so weak that they can hardly be measured. However, the government of Sweden developed a set of guidelines to regulate the strength of emissions from video display terminals (VDTs). Several people in this country are also concerned that VDT radiation might be a problem, so many monitor manufacturers now add shielding to control the emission. If you are worried about VDT emissions, look for monitors that are certified to meet MPR II specifications.

Incidentally, if you use a hair dryer, you will get much more radiation from that than from a monitor.

Green Monitors

A monitor might use 100 to 150 watts of energy. The EPA Energy Star program demands that the energy be reduced to no more than 30 watts when the monitor is not being used.

I sometimes sit in front of my monitor for 10 or 15 minutes, doing research, or more likely dealing with writer's block. All this time, the monitor is burning up lots of watts of energy. Many of the new monitors meet the Energy Star specifications, so when there is no activity, they go into a sleep mode, where they use very little energy. A small amount of voltage is still applied to the monitor and it will come back online almost immediately.

Software for Monitor Testing

If you are planning to buy an expensive, high-resolution monitor, you might want to buy a software program called DisplayMate for Windows from Sonera Technologies (908-747-6886, www.displaymate.com). It is a collection of utilities that can perform several checks on a monitor. It lets you measure the resolution for fine lines, clarity of the image, and distortion, and has gray and color scales, and a full range of intensities and colors. The software can actually help tweak and finetune your monitor and adapter. The setup also helps you set the controls for the optimum values. About 40% or more of the cost for a computer system is for the monitor. It could be well worth it to test the monitor first.

The following information is from the DisplayMate Web site at www.displaymate.com:

> The DisplayMate Utilities are designed to help you achieve the highest possible image quality and picture quality on any computer monitor, LCD display, video projector, television, HDTV, or any type of display device that can be connected directly or indirectly to a computer. DisplayMate guarantees to improve the image and picture quality on any display. You can use DisplayMate to compare and evaluate displays you're thinking of buying. Our video diagnostic products will thoroughly test including your entire video system for performance and compatibility, the monitor, video board and video BIOS. DisplayMate's rich set of color and grayscale patterns are also essential for accurate printer setup and calibration. DisplayMate is the only utility in the world that is devoted to monitors and video boards. The product is easy to use. There is no learning time.

DisplayMate works by presenting a slide show of special highly sensitive test screen images. You simply look at them and follow the easy step-by-step instructions and expert online advice and guidance. The result is a complete video system Tune-Up with your display performing at its absolute best. Here are some monitor tips from the DisplayMate Web site:

1. How Picky Are You?

No video display is perfect, including the best and most expensive monitors, so be prepared to accept some compromises in image and picture quality. Remember, you may be looking at that monitor for several thousand hours! Every single major computer magazine in the USA uses DisplayMate to test and evaluate monitors. You can gain similar insight into monitor performance and capabilities by taking along a copy of DisplayMate when you go monitor shopping.

2. Know What Bothers You the Most

Different people are bothered by different image quality imperfections. It's important to identify the ones that bother you, and then prioritize them. The most common problems that bug people include: color misregistration, fuzzy image, Moire patterns in the image, geometric distortion, tilted image, flicker, glare and screen reflections. Look for monitors with controls that can adjust the imperfections that bug you the most: for example, look for convergence controls if color misregistration is at the top of your list.

3. The More Controls on Your Monitor, the Better

Monitors are now coming with more and more end-user accessible controls that allow you to adjust and correct problems in the image. Besides the mandatory Brightness, Contrast, Size, and Position controls, you may find Focus, Convergence, Tilt, Pincushion, Keystone, Moire, Color Temperature, RGB Color Drive and Cutoff, and Manual Degaussing controls. Advanced controls found on only a few monitors include: Dynamic Focus, Dynamic Convergence, Color Purity, Pincushion Phase, and Pincushion Balance. They're all very useful. The more controls you have, the better the image and picture quality on your monitor will be. Don't worry if you don't know how to adjust some of the more obscure controls, DisplayMate can show you how.

4. The More Controls on Your Video Board, the Better

Controls on the video board can be used to correct some problems in the monitor's image. For example, as demonstrated within DisplayMate, certain combinations of video board and monitor control adjustments may be able to reduce or eliminate certain forms of geometric distortion. Controls that are especially helpful in a video board are: Vertical and Horizontal Size, Vertical and Horizontal Position, Horizontal Scanning

Frequency, and Vertical Refresh Rate. Some of the video board controls may only be accessible using obscure DOS utilities that came on the video board's drivers disk, so look over the list of files carefully. In other cases the controls are only accessible through supplementary utilities available from the manufacturer's BBS.

5. Watch Out for Sample-To-Sample Variations

There is generally a significant sample-to-sample variation between monitors of the same make and model, even among the best brands. Monitors are actually delicate precision analog instruments. They are affected by variations in components, assembly and factory calibration. They are also particularly affected by how much they bounce around during shipment and handling. If you're buying from a store rather than mail order, then check out the actual monitor you're getting with DisplayMate before you pay for it and take it home. If you're buying mail order, then try to get an exchange capability in case there is a problem.

6. Carefully Set All the Controls on Your Monitor and Video Board

Many users don't know how to adjust some of the controls on their monitor or video board. If you don't take the time to properly set every control, then they'll actually make matters worse rather than better. DisplayMate includes specialized Test Patterns to precisely adjust every one of the controls to its optimum value. Detailed online information and instructions explain what to look for and what to do. For example, setting the Brightness and Contrast Controls is straightforward, but requires four separate Test Patterns in DisplayMate to do it accurately. The payoff is obtaining an optimum gray-scale with optimum contrast.

7. Take Advantage of the Inherent Image Quality Trade-Offs Between Controls

Most of the monitor's image parameters are interdependent. Changing one control will often directly or indirectly affect another. While this is a complication, it's also an opportunity, because some things can be improved at the expense of others, based on your own preferences. For example: the higher you set the refresh rate, the lower the image flicker, but the fuzzier the image is likely to appear due to limitations in video bandwidth. Setting the refresh rate to the highest values allowed by your monitor and video board is not likely to be the best visual compromise setting. DisplayMate tells you which are the important trade-offs and provides Test Patterns that let you decide what the best overall visual compromises are. There are hundreds of suggestions on improving image quality.

8. Make Sure You Get a Sharp Video Board

Image quality and image sharpness vary significantly among video board brands and models. Try out different boards with the same monitor to compare the differences.

9. If You Need Good Color Accuracy and Color Matching, Get a Good Video Board

The color matching controls found on most high-end monitors can only adjust the monitor's White Point or Color Temperature. To perform detailed color matching or to correct color tracking errors you need a video board that lets you adjust the RGB Color Transfer Functions, sometimes incorrectly referred to as the Gamma Correction curves. This can be accomplished by downloading new RGB tables into the board's hardware RAMDAC, or alternatively performed in software by the Windows driver. Check for these capabilities. If you need them but don't understand the terminology or how to calibrate the colors and grayscale, DisplayMate explains how and leads you through the calibration procedures in a detailed step-by-step fashion.

10. Keep the Monitor in Good Tune

Many users will set the controls as best as they can when the monitor and video board are first installed, and then forget about them. Monitors drift as they warm up, they'll drift a bit during the day, and they'll age over a period of weeks and months. Environmental factors such as room lighting are also important, and can vary because of changing sunlight. How often you need to adjust the monitor controls depends upon how stable your hardware is, the nature of your application, and how discriminating you are. Once you become aware of image quality issues, you'll become sensitized to them. Things that you glossed over or tolerated before will no longer be acceptable.

Installation

Installing a monitor and adapter is usually fairly easy. Just plug the adapter board into an empty slot, and plug in the monitor cable. Then run any software drivers that might have come with the board. Virtually all monitors and adapters now conform to the PnP standard, so they are very easy to install and set up. Windows 95 lets you easily customize your display. Just click the right mouse button anywhere on the desktop, then choose Properties. The Properties window has four different tabs:

- Background lets you set or change the desktop's pattern or wallpaper
- Appearance lets you modify the color scheme
- Screen Saver and Settings let you change the color depth, resolution, and drivers for the monitor and adapter

Glossary of Monitor Terms from Princeton Graphics

The following glossary is from the Princeton Graphics Web site at www.prgr.com. It defines specific terms used to describe monitor characteristics and performance.

Active timing—This is defined as the portion of the Video Signal that carries the actual Video information. Surrounding this region, is the front porch and back porch.

Actual Image Size—The size of the display on the screen is dependent upon the timing signals provided by the video card. The displayable diagonal linear measurement can vary based on the graphic mode being generated and how the monitor responds to the characteristics of the signal.

Aspect ratio—The ratio of height to width. Typical aspect ratio for a monitor is 4 to 3 or 1.33. Example: 640/480 = 1.33

Bandwidth—This is a qualitative term used to describe the monitor's Video Amplifier potential performance. The higher the pixel rate (or format number), the higher the Bandwidth required of the Video Amplifier.

Barrel—An outward bowing of the picture.

Brightness—Light output measured at the face plate of the CRT; typically measured in foot lamberts (Fl). A minimum brightness level of 20Fl when viewing at full page size is considered acceptable.

Character matrix—The total number of Horizontal and Vertical spaces required per character.

Color Balance—The ability of the monitor to show and maintain the same color when switching or varying the intensity of the screen.

Convergence--The ability of the electron beam to hit precisely the correct phosphor dot.

CRT—This abbreviation stands for Cathode Ray Tube, also known as picture tube or screen. The picture tube in a home TV is also a CRT.

Degauss—Removes random color swirls caused by changes in the earth's magnetic field. To avoid putting a strain on your monitor wait at least 10 minutes before pressing the degauss button a second time.

Diagonal Linear Measurement— "Official" screen size is the diagonal measurement of the CRT before it's mounted in the monitor cabinet. Some monitor CRT category sizes are 14″, 15″, 17″, 19″, and 21″.

Dot Pitch—The distance between the one phosphor dot and the nearest dot of the same color in the line above or below.

Driver—A special configuration file written to control a specific device.

Flicker—Lit condition of the display caused by mismatch of phosphor and Vertical refresh when the phosphor begins to decay prior to being refreshed giving the display the appearance of "flashing."

Focus—Sharpness of a pixel or series of pixels on the CRT face plate. Also measured as the spot size.

High voltage regulation—Ability of the high voltage to respond to changes in beam current. Good high voltage regulation means a stable display even when changing between different intensity levels.

Horizontal Frequency—This indicates how long it takes to scan each of the Horizontal lines that make up the display. The unit of measurement is kilohertz (KHz). It is directly related to the number of lines and the Vertical Refresh (Frequency) so that the higher the Vertical Refresh or the number of lines, the higher the Horizontal Frequency required.

Interlaced—Method of significantly increasing data densities at conventional Horizontal scan rates. Half the image is refreshed (every other scan line) to produce a field. Two fields are refreshed at rates of 87 Hz forming one 43.5 Hz frame. Causes flicker on the display.

Linearity—Comparison of a character size to the size of adjacent characters.

Magnetic Field Effects—As described in the paragraph "Rotation Control," the Monitor is affected by magnetic fields. If your screen develops wrong colors in areas or the picture becomes distorted you must check what is near to your Monitor. If your Monitor is positioned near a steel cabinet, on a steel desk or bench, or a steel girder imbedded in a wall or ceiling, then all of these things could be magnetized and therefore interfering with the picture tube's Electron Beams. Try moving the Monitor two to three feet away from the suspected source of magnetic field and see if the picture improves. If the picture only looks colored or distorted during certain times check if you have any speakers near the Monitor because these could radiate magnetic fields strong enough to distort the picture when they are powered-up.

Maximum Viewing Area—The actual maximum viewing area is dependent upon the size of the plastic or bezel around the CRT. Typically, the maximum possible for a "17-inch monitor" is actually 15.75 inches plus or minus $^1/_2$ inch. In other words, plus or minus 0.25 inches at the ends of the diagonal measurement.

Moire—An interference pattern generated by the interaction of the electron beam and the shadow mask.

MPRII—The Swedish National Board for Measurement and Testing (SWEDAC) require that products sold in Sweden comply with a set of safety standards known as MPRII, that covers the levels of magnetic and electrical fields in both the VLF and ELF ranges. It is worth noting that there are no scientific studies that conclude that measurements above MPRII levels are hazardous. To measure emissions, a sophisticated testing area that screens out background radiation needs to be in place. Since distance to the CRT and orientation of the measuring device effects measurement, precise placement of the measuring device is essential and difficult to repeat. For the MPR standards, 48 different locations around the monitor need to be measured. In addition, the actual image displayed can have an impact on emissions so that a given set of measurements may not predict the emissions a user would actual encounter.

Orthogonality—A deviation from true perpendicular of the vertical.

OSD—OSD stands for On Screen Display. Most monitors today have on-screen menus that will allow you to configure and manipulate settings.

Parallelogram—A deviation of the sides from the true vertical.

Persistence—Phosphor characteristic consisting of the ability to emit light after excitation current of electron beam is removed.

Phosphor—Chemical compound that emits light while being excited by electrons.

Pincushion—An inward bowing of the video image. All monitors experience slight amount of pincushion distortion. The manufacturer has a guideline on what the specification is for each model. The pincushion changes per resolution and also according to the size of the image. Pincushion is similar to bowing or barrel distortion.

Purity—The ability of the electron beam to hit precisely the correct phosphor color dot. If a full page of red color is shown on the display, impurity would result in a purple or greenish color region. This impurity can occur if the shadow mask has been damaged or if the screen has become magnetized. Degaussing the screen may fix the problem.

Real World Screen Size—Starting out with a 17″ monitor, adding the bezel, and then having a border around the actual video image may result in a diagonal picture size of only 14″. With new technology, there is a way to increase the viewing size but there are some limitations.

Recommendations for Comfortable Viewing

1. Sit at least an arm's length away from the screen. It will reduce eye strain and the low levels of magnetic and electrical fields referred to above reduce by the square of the distance, i.e., if you increase the distance by two you reduce the field by four.

2. Leave a distance of at least 2 or 3 feet from the back of a neighboring monitor if this is possible. The fields are lower at the front than at the rear of the monitor.
3. Adjust the Contrast and Brightness Controls for comfortable viewing for three reasons. One, it reduces eye fatigue, two, the picture tube will last longer, and three, all field and emission strengths are related to the brightness of the picture.

Refresh rates—An ergonomic issue that is directly related to long term ease of use. A higher refresh rate translates to a more "flicker" free display. Bandwidth, horizontal, and vertical scanning rates depict a monitor's ability to provide a higher resolution and refresh rate.

Resolution—The number of pixels or dots per linear distance, dots per inch (DPI).

Tilt—The angle of the CRT with respect to the horizontal mounting bracket of the chassis. Tilt can vary depending on the monitor's orientation to the Earth's magnetic poles. Monitor manufacturers orient and align their products in the Eastern direction. When the monitor is facing a north/south direction, there may be a slight rotation of the image.

Uniformity—Comparison of one area's brightness to an adjacent area. In general, the brightest part of the image will be in the center area. When moving out to the edges, the intensity of image will vary in a nonlinear function. This means that one corner of the screen will not be the same brightness as another corner of the screen. A typical CRT manufacturer's specification may call for up to a 30 percent difference between the center area and the corners.

Vertical frequency—This indicates how many times per second the monitor can draw all the lines on an entire screen. A higher Vertical frequency or Refresh rate will produce less flicker.

Other Resources

A monitor a very important part of your computer system. I couldn't possibly tell you all you need to know in this short chapter. One of the better ways to keep up on this ever-changing technology is to subscribe to one or more computer magazines. They frequently have articles about monitors. Of course, they also have many ads for monitors and adapters. I have listed several computer magazines in Chapter 19.

CHAPTER 10

Input Devices

Before you can do anything with a computer, you must input data to it. There are many ways to input data, such as from a keyboard or a disk; by modem, mouse, or scanner; with barcode readers, voice recognition, fax; or online from the Internet, a bulletin board, a mainframe, or a network. This chapter discusses a few of the ways to input data to a computer.

Keyboards

By far the most common way to get data into the computer is by way of the keyboard. For most applications, it is impossible to operate the computer without a keyboard. The keyboard is your most personal connection with your computer. If you do a lot of typing, it is very important that you get a keyboard that suits you. Not all keyboards are the same. Some have a light, mushy touch, while others are heavy. Some have noisy keys, others have silent ones with very little feedback.

A Need for Standards

Typewriter keyboards are fairly standard. There are only 26 letters in the alphabet and a few symbols, so most QWERTY typewriters have about 50 keys. However, I have had several computers over the last few years, and every one of them have had a different keyboard. The main typewriter characters aren't changed or moved very often, but some of the very important control keys like Esc, Ctrl, PrtSc, \, the function keys, and several others are moved all over the keyboard. For the past few years, most keyboards have had 101 keys. Windows 95 and multimedia functions have caused several more keys to be added. Keyboards may now have up to 109 or more keys. The extra keys provide application shortcuts for Windows 95 and other functions.

There are well over 400 different keyboards in the United States. Many people make their living by typing on a keyboard. Many large companies have systems that count the number of keystrokes that an employee makes during a shift. If the employee fails to make a certain number of keystrokes, then that person can be fired. Can you imagine the problems if the person has to frequently learn a new keyboard? I am not a very good typist in the first place. I have great difficulty using different keyboards.

There definitely should be some sort of standard. Innovation—creating something new that is useful and needed and makes life better or easier—is great. That type of innovation should be encouraged everywhere. Many times, however, changes are made just for the sake of differentiation without adding any real value or functionality to the product. This applies not only to keyboards, but to all technology.

Windows 95 Keyboards

It appears that we may be nearing a standard of sorts. Most newer keyboards now have three or four extra keys. A couple of them usually have the Microsoft logo on them. If you have one of the new keyboards with the Microsoft logo, pressing one of those keys lets you switch from one program to another. It will put the program in the task bar while you work on another program. When you are ready to come back to the original program, you just point to the program and Windows brings you back to the same place you were when you switched.

It is a very good utility. Quite often, I need to stop writing and look up something on the Internet. I can press one of the Windows keys, access the Web, then come back exactly where I left off.

Carpal Tunnel Syndrome

Businesses spend billions of dollars each year for employee health insurance. Of course, the more employee injuries, the more the insurance costs. Carpal tunnel syndrome (CTS) has become one of the more common complaints. CTS causes pain and/or numbness in the palm of the hand and the thumb, and in the index and ring fingers. The pain can radiate up into the arm. Any movement of the hand or fingers becomes very painful.

CTS is caused by pressure on the median nerve where it passes into the hand through the carpal tunnel and under a ligament at the front of the wrist. Either one or both hands might be affected. Treatment often requires expensive surgery, which might not relieve the pain.

CTS most commonly affects those people who must use a computer for long periods of time. Keying in data is a very important function in this computer age. It is the job of many employees, eight hours a day, every day. CTS is usually caused by the way the wrist is held while typing on the keyboard. Several pads and devices are available to help make typing more comfortable. I have a foam rubber pad (Fig. 10-1) that is the length of the keyboard and about 4 inches wide and $^{3}/_{4}$ inch thick. I can rest and support my wrists on this pad and still reach most of the keys. Many vendors give these pads away at shows like COMDEX.

Repetitive Strain Injury (RSI) is about the same as CTS. Many employees are asking for worker's compensation insurance and taking companies to court because of RSI. At the time of this writing, there are several cases in court against IBM, Apple, and several other large computer manufacturers. CTS and RSI injuries have cost millions of dollars in loss of work days. They have become serious problems. Worker's compensation programs in California alone cost millions of dollars. In 1997, a law was passed requiring all employers with more than 10 employees to provide special training to injured workers and others doing similar work. Employers must try to identify and combat potential injury hazards with corrective action. Possible steps are adjusting desks for typists with sore wrists or providing more rest breaks. The law also addresses those who might be lifting heavy weights or other repetitive tasks that could be injurious.

Before the computer revolution, thousands and thousands of people, mostly women, sat at typewriters eight or more hours a day typing on keyboards that are similar to computer keyboards. Yet there were few, if any, cases of CTS or RSI ever reported. It is a disorder that

Figure 10-1 A foam rubber wrist pad that can help prevent Carpal Tunnel Syndrome (CTS) or Repetitive Stress Injury.

has become prevalent only in the last few years. Last year, 308,200 cases were reported. It could be that typewriter keyboards have more slant and were usually placed at a different height. Another factor might be that the typewriter limited the typist's speed and repetition. With the computer, some data-input workers can type as many as 13,000 keystrokes per hour.

To help prevent RSI and CTS, pause frequently and stretch your hands and upper body. Also, your desk and chair should be adjusted so that both feet rest easily on the floor.

Ergonomic Keyboards

The Key Tronic company developed an ergonomic keyboard for Microsoft. Like most products with a brand name, it is a bit expensive, at $99. Several other companies have developed similar ergonomic keyboards for less than half that price.

ALPS Electric (800-825-2577), Cirque Corporation (800-454-3375), and Northgate (800-548-1993) all have *glidepoint* keyboards with pads that can take the place of mouse. They have a square pad below the arrow keys. You use your finger on the pad to move the cursor. To click, you just tap the pad with your finger or press one of the three nearby buttons. The Northgate OmniKey is ergonomically shaped, with the keys separated and angled similar to the Microsoft Natural keyboard. Mitsumi (800-648-7864) also has a low-cost ergonomic keyboard.

Figure 10-2 shows a clone ergonomic keyboard with a touchpad. It is quite similar to the keyboards mentioned above. This clone sells for about half the cost of Microsoft and other brand name keyboards. It has a PS/2-type connector, which is much smaller than a standard AT keyboard connector, but it comes with an adapter so that it can be used on either system. The touchpad must be connected to one of the serial ports, just like a normal mouse. This port connector and cable are part of the keyboard cable. One of the advantages of the touchpad is that it eliminates the mouse cable from the desktop. Also, it does not require desktop space for a mouse pad. The keyboard has a switch that allows you to switch off the touchpad and use a standard mouse if you want to.

This clone keyboard has the extra Windows 95 keys. It also has an extra Tab and Backspace key. Most of the other keys are the same as the standard 101 keyboard, but they are angled, separated, and raised in the center.

Figure 10-2 An ergonomic keyboard that can help prevent CTS and RSI.

It has taken me a bit of time to become accustomed to an ergonomic keyboard. Although some of them are a bit expensive, they are a lot less expensive than having to go to a doctor for a painful operation that might not be successful. The alternative to surgery for CTS is to rest the hands and miss several months of work. A large company might save money by installing these ergonomic keyboards. Many people are now suing companies for CTS and RSI injuries. Of course, the insurance companies are increasing their rates to help pay for any damages that might be awarded.

How a Keyboard Works

The keyboard is actually a computer in itself. It has a small microprocessor with its own ROM. The computerized electronics of the keyboard eliminate the bounce of the keys, can determine when you hold a key down for repeat, can store up to 20 or more keystrokes, and can determine which key was pressed first if you press two at a time. In addition to the standard BIOS chips on your motherboard, there is a special keyboard BIOS chip. Each time a key is pressed, a unique signal is sent to this BIOS. This signal is made up of a dc voltage that is turned on and off a certain number of times, within a definite time frame, to represent zeros and ones.

Each time a 5-volt line is turned on for a certain amount of time, it represents a one. When it is off for a certain amount of time, it represents a zero. For example, in the ASCII code, if the letter *A* is pressed, the code for 65 will be generated, 1000001.

Reprogramming Key Functions

Most word processors, spreadsheets, databases, and other software programs designate certain keys to run various macros. A *macro* is a command or several commands that can be input by pressing one or more keys. By pressing a certain key combination, you could, for example, input your name and address or any other group of words that you use frequently.

These programs also use the function keys to perform various tasks, such as moving the cursor, underlining, and bolding. The problem is that there is no standardization. Changing from one word processor or software program to another is about like having to learn a new foreign language. It sure would be nice if you could go from one program to another as easily as you can drive different automobiles.

Keyboard Sources

Keyboard preference is strictly a matter of individual taste. The Key Tronic Company of Spokane (509-928-8000) makes some excellent keyboards. They are the IBM of the keyboard world. Their keyboards have set the standards. The Key Tronic keyboards have been copied by the clone makers, even to the extent of using the same model numbers.

Quality keyboards use a copper-etched printed circuit board and keys that switch on and off. The keys of quality keyboards have a small spring beneath each one to give it a uniform tension. Key Tronic offers several models. On some models, they can even let you change the little springs under the keys to a different tension. The standard is 2 ounces, but you can configure the key tension to whatever you like. You can install 1-, 1.5-, 2-, 2.5-, or 3-ounce springs for an extra fee. The company also lets you exchange the positions of the CapsLock and Ctrl keys. Key Tronic keyboards have several other functions that are clearly described in their large manual. Call them for a copy.

Many of the less-expensive keyboards use plastic with conductive paint for the connecting lines instead of an etched-copper printed circuit board. Instead of springs beneath each key, they use a rubber cup. The bottom of each key is coated with a carbon conductive material. When the key is depressed, the carbon allows an electrical connection between the painted lines. The keys are part of, and are attached to, the main plastic board by strips of flexible molded plastic. These low-cost keyboards might have as few as 17 parts, but they work fairly well.

I recently saw new, clone keyboards being sold at a swap meet for $10 each. The keyboards looked very much like the Key Tronic 101-key types. The assembly snapped together instead of using metal screws. They also had several other cost-saving features. However, there are quite a lot of electronics in a keyboard. I don't know how they can possibly make a keyboard that sells for $10. At that price, you could buy two or three of them. If you ever had any trouble with one, you could just throw it away and plug in a new one.

There are several keyboard manufacturers and hundreds of different models with many different special functions. Prices range from $10 up to $400 or more. Look through any computer magazine for more information.

Specialized Keyboards

Several companies have developed specialized keyboards. For example, quite often, I need to do some minor calculations. The computer is great for calculations. Most word processor, database, and spreadsheet programs have built-in calculator functions. In order to use these calculators, however, most of these programs require that the computer be on and be using a file. There are some keyboards that have a calculator built into the number pad. It has a battery so that it can be used whether the computer is on or not.

All newer keyboards now have the extra Windows 95 keys, even the $10 clones that I saw at the swap meet. You don't really need the extra keys to run Windows 95. I have several older keyboards that work just fine with Windows 95.

The Maxi Switch Company (520-746-9378), NMB Technologies (800-662-8321), and SC&T International (800-408-4084) have multimedia keyboards that come with a microphone, speakers, input jacks, and volume control.

Another Key Tronic model has a barcode reader attached to it. This can be extremely handy if you have a small business that uses barcodes. This keyboard would be ideal for a computer in a point of sale (POS) system.

If you have been in the computer business for a while, you might remember the PCjr from IBM. It had a wireless keyboard that used an infrared system similar to a TV remote control. The Casco Products Company (800-793-6960) thinks this is still a good idea. They have developed the LightLink, a wireless keyboard that communicates by infrared with a small receiver that plugs into the motherboard keyboard socket. One use for this keyboard is for presentations, since you can operate the computer from across the room.

The Cherry Electrical Products Company (800-510-1689) has developed several different keyboards. They now have one that can accept a Smart Card. The Smart Card is similar to a credit card, except that the Smart Card has a certain amount of money encoded on it from your bank. Each time you use the card, your purchase is deducted from the card. It has been used in Europe for some time and is expected to become very popular here. The one thing that some people might not like is that you must have the money on the card. With a credit card, you can charge an item and not worry about paying for it until the bill comes. Then you might only have to pay a portion of it, and finance the rest of it.

Some companies have developed keyboards that have scanners built into them. This is a good idea because there are many times when you need to scan in a letter or information. It can save a lot of typing.

Mouse Systems

One of the biggest reasons for the success of the Macintosh is that it is easy to use. With a mouse and icons, all you have to do is point and click. You don't have to learn a lot of commands and rules. A person who knows nothing about computers can become productive in a very short time. The people in the DOS world finally took note of this and began developing programs and applications such as Windows for the IBM and compatibles.

There are now dozens of companies who manufacture mice. Some mice may cost up to $100 or more; others cost less than $10. What is the difference between a mouse that costs $100 and one that costs $10? The answer is $90. The low-cost mouse does just about everything that most people would need from a mouse. After all, how much mouse do you need just to point and click? Of course, if you are doing high-end drafting, designing, or other very close-tolerance work, you definitely need a mouse that has a high resolution.

Ball-Type Mice

Most mice have a small, round, rubber ball on the underside that contacts the desktop or mousepad. As the mouse is moved, the ball turns. Inside the mouse, two flywheels contact the ball, one for horizontal and one for vertical movements. The flywheels are mounted between two light-sensitive diodes. The flywheels have small holes in their outer edge. As the flywheels turn, light shines through the holes or is blocked where there are no holes. This breaks the light up into patterns of ones and zeros, which then controls the cursor movement.

Mouse-Ball Cleaning

The mouse ball picks up dirt. If the dirt builds up on the flywheel rollers, it may cause the mouse to be erratic or skip and not work properly. On most mice, the ball can be easily removed and the rollers cleaned. If you turn the mouse over, there is usually a round twist-off retainer plate that allows you to remove the ball. One of the best ways to clean the rollers is to use a cotton swab and alcohol. I told one woman this, and she asked me whether she should use bourbon or scotch! Either one will work fine, but it would be a terrible waste. I suggest just plain old rubbing alcohol.

Mouse Interfaces

You can't just plug in a mouse and start using it. The software, whether Windows, WordPerfect, or a CAD program, must recognize and interface with the mouse, so mouse companies develop software drivers to allow the mouse to operate with various programs. The drivers are usually supplied on a disk. The Microsoft Mouse is the closest to a standard, so most other companies emulate the Microsoft driver. Most mice drivers are now included in Windows 95. Most mice today come with a small switch that allows you to switch between the Microsoft emulation or the IBM PC. If the switch is not in the proper position, the mouse might not work.

The Microsoft type of mouse plugs into a serial port, either COM1 or COM2. This might cause a problem if you already have two serial devices using COM1 and COM2. DOS also allows for COM3 and COM4, but these two ports must be shared with COM1 and COM2, so you need special software in order to use them. Most mice do not like to share COM ports.

The serial ports on some systems use a DB25-type socket connector with 25 contacts. Others use a DB9 socket with nine contacts. Many mice now come with the DB9 connector and a DB25 connector adapter. The DB25 connector looks exactly like the DB25 connector used for the LPT1 parallel printer port, except that the serial port connector is a male connector with pins, while the LPT1 printer port is a female with sockets.

Most motherboards now come with upright pins for the COM1 and COM2 and printer connections. Short cables with connectors plug into the upright pins. The connector assembly is then installed in one of the spaces on the back panel. There might be times when you have a cable that is a male when what you need is a female, or vice versa. (A male connector is one that has pins, a female connector has sockets.) You can buy DB25 "gender bender" adapters that can solve this type of problem.

If you simply need an extension so that you can plug two similar cables together, straight-through adapters are also available. There are many different kinds of combinations. The Cables To Go Company (800-225-8646) has just about every cable and accessory that you would ever need. The Dalco Electronics Company (800-445-5342) also has many types of cables, adapters, and electronic components. Before you buy a mouse, check the type of serial port connector you have and order the proper type. If necessary, you can buy an adapter for about $3.

PS/2 Mice

Many of the newer Pentium, Pentium II, AMD, and Cyrix motherboards have PS/2 connectors for the mouse and keyboard. You can use either connector to plug in the keyboard or the mouse. The PS/2 connector saves having to use one of the COM ports, but it does require the use of one of the precious IRQs, usually IRQ 12. Even the fastest, most powerful computers still only have 16 IRQs, and most of them are used by the system. If you need to install a sound board, modem, mouse, network card, SCSI device, or any of many other peripherals, you might not have enough IRQs. There are some devices that will share IRQs, but most of them are selfish and will not share.

Instead of a connector, many of the newer motherboards have a set of six upright pins alongside the connector for the keyboard. You need a special cable with a connector for the motherboard and a PS/2 connector on the other end. Not many stores have these connectors at this time. This cable is not usually supplied with the motherboard. You might have to order it from one of the cable companies who advertise in magazines such as *Computer Shopper*.

Wireless Mice

One of the disadvantages of operating a keyboard such as the wireless LightLink mentioned earlier is that you also need a wireless mouse. Several companies have developed wireless mice. They operate with infrared rays similar to the remote control of a TV. Some operate using a radio frequency, such as the wireless mouse made by Mitsumi Electronics (800-648-7864). Logitech (800-231-7717) also has wireless models. Although they are wireless, they still need a receiver and an interface to connect to a serial port.

Trackballs

A trackball is a mouse that has been turned upside-down. Like the mouse, the trackball requires a serial port. One advantage of the trackball is that you don't need the square foot of desk space that a mouse requires. Trackballs are usually larger than the ball in a mouse, so it is possible to have better resolution. They are often used with CAD and critical design systems.

Constant use of a mouse can also lead to CTS and RSI. The Itac Systems at 800-533-4822 claim that their ergonomically designed trackball, MouseTrak, can help prevent those injuries. Several companies manufacture trackballs. Look through the computer magazines for ads.

Touch Screens and Light Pens

Some fast-food restaurants now have a touch screen with a menu of several items. You merely touch the item that you want, and the order is transmitted to the executive chef (usually a high-school kid). The same type of system is sometimes found in kiosks in shopping malls and large department stores. Some systems use an image of a keyboard, so that you can touch the various keys almost as if you were typing. The touch system is accurate, saves time and money, and is convenient. Its operation is similar to using a mouse and pointing.

Most touch screens have a frame installed on the bezel of the monitor. Beams of infrared light crisscross the front of the monitor screen. For ordinary text, most monitors are set up so that they have 80 columns from left to right and 25 rows from top to bottom. Columns of beams originate from the top of the frame and pass to the bottom of the frame. Rows of beams originate from the left of the frame and pass to the right of the frame. If one of the beams is interrupted by an object such as a finger or pencil, the computer can determine exactly what happens to be in that portion of the screen.

Joysticks

Joysticks are used primarily for games. They are serial devices and need an interface. Many of the multifunction boards that have COM ports also provide a game connector for joysticks. Joysticks are fairly reasonable, costing from $10 up to $30. There are usually several ads for them in magazines such as *Computer Shopper.*

Digitizers and Graphics Tablets

Graphics tablets and digitizers are similar to a flat drawing pad or drafting table. Most of them use some sort of pointing device that can translate movement into digitized output to the computer. Some are rather small, while others may be as large as a standard drafting table. Some cost as little as $150, others over $1500. Most of them have a very high resolution, are very accurate, and are intended for precision drawing. Some of the tablets have programmable overlays and function keys. Some work with a mouselike device, a pen light, or a pencillike stylus. The tablets can be used for circuit design, CAD programs, graphics designs, freehand drawing, and even for text and data input. The most common use is with CAD software. The Wacom Technology Corporation also has a digitizer pad that uses a cordless, batteryless, pressure-sensitive pen.

Most of the tablets are serial devices, but some of them require their own interface board. Many of them are compatible with the Microsoft mouse system.

Pressure-Sensitive Graphics Tablets

Several companies have developed pressure-sensitive tablets. Wacom has developed several different models. The Wacom tablets use an electromagnetic resonance system. This allows the use of a special stylus that requires no wires or batteries. The tablet has a grid of embedded wires that can detect the location of the stylus and the pressure that is applied. The tablets sense the amount of pressure and draw a thin line or a heavy line in response. These tablets can be used with different graphics software programs to create sketches, drawings, designs, and art. Here are some of the companies who manufacture pressure-sensitive tablets:

Wacom Technology
800-922-6613

Communication Intelligence
800-888-9242

Kurta Corporation
602-276-5533

Summagraphics
800-337-8662

Contact them for brochures or more information.

Scanners

Scanners with Optical Character Reader (OCR) software can scan a line of printed type, recognize each character, and input that character into a computer just as if it were typed in from a keyboard. A beam of light sweeps across the page, and the characters can be determined by the absorption and reflection of the light. One problem with early scanners was that they could only recognize a few different fonts, and they could not recognize graphics at all. The machines today have much more memory and the technology has improved to where the better scanners can recognize almost any font or type.

Scanners have been around for several years. When they first came out, they cost from $6000 to more than $15,000. Many full-page flatbed scanners are now fairly inexpensive, starting at about $500. Scanners have the ability to recognize a large number of fonts, and they can copy and digitize color graphics and images. Many of the early scanners had a resolution of 100 dpi (dots per inch). Later ones had 300 to 400 dpi. Many of the newer high-end ones have a dpi as high as 800.

Some of the early, low-cost color scanners had to make three passes, one for each primary color. Most of the newer and more expensive ones can scan all three colors in one pass.

Many flatbed scanners have a resolution of 24-bit color. Some of the newer ones have 30- to 36-bit resolution. The 36-bit resolution means that 12 different bits of information are stored for each of the three primary colors. Some high-end, very high-resolution scanners used for color graphic image-processing and publishing cost from $12,000 up to $95,000.

Flatbed scanners have a glass panel similar to those found in copy machines. The sheet to be scanned is laid on the glass panel. and the machine sweeps the scanning heads across the sheet from top to bottom. Scanners have a lot in common with copy machines, printers, and fax machines. Many companies now manufacture multifunction machines that includes the capability to scan, copy, print, and fax. These machines are discussed in more detail in Chapter 15.

Personal Scanners

Several companies are manufacturing small-page, pass-through, compact scanners such as the Logitech PageScan shown in Fig. 10-3. (Note: The photo shows my computer with the cover off. I do lots of changing and trying out new boards and devices on my computers. I never bother to replace the covers. It might look messy, but they actually run cooler.)

This scanner is quite versatile. It attaches to the parallel port of the computer, so it doesn't need a separate board. It can scan in text, drawings, or even photos into the computer. If you need a copy of a page, scan it into the computer, then print it out. It can input printed text, signatures, drawings, or graphic images to a fax/modem board or to a hard disk. The PageScan can also handle color very well. If you happen to be on the Internet, you can scan in a photo of yourself and send it to someone as e-mail. It is very simple.

Here are a few of the compact scanner vendors:

Delrina
WinFax Scanner
800-268-6082

Envisions
Personal PageVacuum
800-365-7226

Epson Personal Document Station
800-626-4686

Logitech
ScanMan PowerPage
800-231-1717

Figure 10-3 A Logitech PageScan Personal Scanner, a very handy tool.

Microtek Lab
PageWiz
800-654-4160

Plustek USA
PageReader
800-685-8088

Umax Technologies
PageOffice
800-562-0311

Visioneer
PaperPort
800-787-7007

What to Look for When Buying a Scanner

What to look for when buying a scanner depends on what you want to do with it, and of course, how much you want to pay. There are several manufacturers of scanners and hundreds of different models, types, resolutions, bus types, and prices. A monochrome scanner is fine for text. Many of the monochrome scanners are relatively inexpensive, and can recognize text and graphic images in up to 256 different shades. If you are buying a color scanner, there are many more options to consider. Some of the lower-priced color scanners might have to make three passes, once each for red, green, and blue. For each pass, the light is sent through filters that can recognize 256 levels of red, green, or blue.

The less-expensive scanners might have a resolution of only 300 or 400 dpi, but might use interpolation software to fill in the spaces between the dots, giving two or three times the true resolution. As you might expect, some ads list the interpolated resolution in large letters and the true resolution in small letters if it is mentioned at all.

The more expensive color scanners capture all three colors in one pass. They usually also scan at a true 24-bit color depth to yield 16.7 million colors. That means that there can be eight bits of color information about each of the red, green, or blue colors.

Try to find a system that conforms to the TWAIN specification. *TWAIN* is an acronym for *Technology Without an Interesting Name.* (Mark Twain would have appreciated this acronym.) It is an Application Programming Interface (API) specification that was jointly developed by Aldus, Caere, Eastman Kodak, Hewlett-Packard, and Logitech. A different device driver is needed for each of the hundreds of different printers. Before TWAIN, you needed a different device driver from every manufacturer for each model and type of scanner. TWAIN helps to standardize some of the device drivers. (We really need something like TWAIN for printers.)

Some of the less expensive scanners use a proprietary interface board. It is much better to buy one that uses the SCSI interface.

There are many manufacturers of scanners and, of course, many different prices. Look at the ads in any of the computer magazines listed in Chapter 17.

OCR Software

The OCR capabilities of a scanner allow it to recognize each character of a printed document, and input that character into a computer just as if it were typed in from a keyboard. Once the data is in the computer, a word processor can be used to revise or change the data, then print it out again.

Faxes are received as graphical documents. It requires a lot of disk space to store a fax. However, a scanner can convert faxes to text, which takes up much less disk space. Some OCR software programs, such as OmniPage Pro, support over 100 different scanners. In most cases, it can match text to the original fonts. It can read degraded text by reading it in context. It has a large internal dictionary that helps in this respect. It yields excellent OCR accuracy. OmniPage Pro can automatically convert scanned text into any of the most popular word processor formats. It has Image Assistant, an integrated 24-bit color editor for graphic editing. OmniPage Pro 6.0 is one of the better OCR packages available. If you have any earlier version of OmniPage or WordScan, you can upgrade for a nominal cost.

Surplus Software at 800-753-7877 advertises earlier versions of many software packages for a very low price. If you are an owner of a previous version of software, many companies will let you upgrade to the latest version for a very reasonable price. A software package that might cost as much as $600 originally might cost less than $100 as an upgrade. (See Chapter 16 for more about Surplus Software and other low-cost, early versions of software that can be traded in for current versions.)

Once data is entered into a computer, it can be searched very quickly for any item. Many times, I have spent hours going through printed manuals looking for certain items. If the data had been in a computer, I could have found the information in just minutes. Several companies have developed advanced software to work with their scanners, and in some cases, those manufactured by other companies.

Here is a brief list of companies who have OCR software:

Caere Corporation
800-535-7226
OmniPage Professional

Logitech Corporation
510-795-8500
Catchword Pro

Ocron, Inc.
408-980-8900
Perceive

Recognita Corporation
408-241-5772
Recognita Plus

Delrina Company
408-363-2345
WinFax PRO

COLD

About ten years ago, just about everyone began installing computers in their offices. There was lots of excitement about the forthcoming age of the paperless office. Instead of reducing the large stacks of paper, however, the amount of paper increased. The reason was that most people insisted on having paper printouts along with the files on disk. A discouraged vice president of a large company made the observation that we would probably see paperless offices at about the same time we had paperless bathrooms. He was right, but we are making a bit of progress.

Most large companies have thousands of file cabinets overflowing with memos, manuals, documents, and files that must be saved. Most of the documents will never be needed again, but from time to time, a few items stored in these files must be retrieved. Even with a good indexing system, it might take lots and lots of time to find a particular item. A good filing system and document-management system using scanners, OCR, and a Computer Output to Laser Disc (COLD) system can be very helpful. Acres of file cabinets can be replaced by just a few small, optical disks. As an added bonus, a good COLD system can help you find and retrieve any document within seconds.

Business-Card Scanners

If you depend on business cards to keep in contact with prospective buyers or for other business purposes, you might have several rolodexes full of cards. You can take each card and enter the information into your computer database, but there is an easier way. Some companies have developed card scanners that can read the information off a business card and input it to a computer.

At this time, business-card scanners are still a bit expensive, but if you depend on business cards, they are well worth it. Like most computer products, the prices will come down very soon. Here are three companies that offer these scanners:

CypherTech, Inc.
CyperScan 1000
408-734-8765

Microtek Labs
Scan-in-Dex
800-654-4160

Cognitive Technology
Cognitive BCR
415-925-2367

Pacific Crest Technology
CardGrabber
714-261-6444

Large-Format Scanners

Several companies manufacture large-format scanners that are similar to large plotters. They may be up to 4 feet wide and stand about 3 feet high. These scanners can be used to copy and digitize blueprints, CAD drawings, architectural drawings, and even large signs and color images.

These scanners are rather expensive and are often used with high-end workstations. Here are a few companies who manufacture them:

ANAtech
303-973-6722

Ideal Scanners
301-468-0123

Intergraph
205-730-8008

Scangraphics
610-328-1040

The WideCom Group
905-712-0505

Vidar Systems
703-471-7070

Installing a Scanner

Most scanners, especially the high-end, color ones, use an SCSI interface. You should get some sort of installation documentation and driver software with your scanner.

Some scanners come with a plug-in board and software drivers. Some of them are serial type devices, so they will require the use of one of your COM ports and one of your motherboard slots. You might have to set switches or jumpers to configure the board so that it does not conflict with other devices in your system.

Voice Recognition Input

Another way to input data into a computer is to talk to it with a microphone. Of course, you need electronics that can take the signal created by the microphone, detect the spoken words, and turn them into a form of digital information that the computer can use.

The early voice data-input systems were very expensive and limited. One reason was that voice technology required lots of memory. The cost of memory has dropped considerably in the last few years, though, and the technology has improved in many other ways. Eventually, voice-input technology will replace the keyboard for many applications.

Voice technology usually involves "training" a computer to recognize words spoken by a particular person. When you speak into a microphone, the sound waves cause a diaphragm, or some other device, to move back and forth in a magnetic field and create a voltage that is analogous to the sound wave. If this voltage is recorded and played through a good audio system, the loudspeaker will respond to the amplified voltages and reproduce a sound that is identical to the one input to the microphone.

A person can speak a word into a microphone that creates a unique voltage pattern for that word and that particular person's voice. The voltage is fed into an electronic circuit, and the pattern is digitized and stored in the computer. If several words are spoken, the circuit will digitize each one of them and store them. Each one of them will have a distinct and unique pattern. Later, when the computer hears a word, it will search through the patterns that it has stored to see if the input word matches any one of its stored words.

Once the computer is able to recognize a word, you can have it perform some useful work. You could command it to load and run a program, or perform any of several other tasks.

Because every person's voice is different, ordinarily, the computer would not recognize the voice of anyone who had not trained it. Training the computer might involve saying the same word several times so that the computer can store several patterns of the person's voice. Some of the new systems now recognize the voices of others who have not trained the computer.

Uses for Voice Recognition

Here are just a few uses for voice recognition: letters, reports, and complicated business and technical text. Voice recognition can be used by doctors, nurses, lawyers, reporters, loan officers, auditors, researchers, secretaries, business executives, language interpreters, and writers.

Computer voice recognition is very useful whenever you must use both hands to do a job, but still need a computer to perform certain tasks. Voice recognition is also useful on production lines, where the person does not have time to manually enter data into a computer. It can also be used in a laboratory, where a scientist looking through a microscope cannot take his or her eyes off the subject to write down the findings or data. There might be times when the lighting must be kept too dim to input data to a computer manually. In other instances, a person might have to be several feet from the computer and still be able to input data through the microphone line or even with a wireless microphone. The person might even be miles away and be able to input data over a telephone line.

Voice recognition and a computer can help many of those who have physical limitations become productive and independent. There are a few systems that allow a person using English to call someone who speaks a different language and have the spoken conversation instantly translated and understood. The system recognizes the spoken word, then uses computerized speech to translate it, so the two parties are actually talking to a computerized, mechanical interpreter. The same type of system has been built into small, handheld foreign-language interpreters. Speak an English word into the machine, and it gives you the equivalent spoken foreign word. Many luxury automobiles now come with cellular phones with voice-activated dialing. This lets the driver keep his or her eyes on the road while the number is being dialed.

Designers of computers are constantly looking for new ways to differentiate and improve their product. In the very near future, you can be sure that many of them will have voice recognition built in.

Chips that use very large-scale integration (VLSI) are combining more and more computer functions onto single chips. They are making computers smaller and smaller. We now have some very powerful computers that can fit in a shirt pocket. One of the big problems is that there is not room for a decent keyboard. To fit them all on a keyboard, the keys have to be very small. Some of them use a stylus to press each key. Some let you use a single finger to type on the keyboards. If your fingers are large, you might end up pressing two keys at once. One solution would be to build in voice recognition so that the keyboard would not be needed. At this time, however, voice recognition requires a lot of transistors and hardware, perhaps more than can fit into a small handheld computer.

Limitations

For most systems, the computer must be trained to recognize a specific, discrete, individual word, so the computer's vocabulary is limited to what it is trained to recognize, the amount of memory available, and the limitations imposed by the software and hardware. There are many basic systems available today that are very good at recognizing discrete words, but ordinarily, when we speak, many words meld together. Some systems, such as Dragon Systems's Naturally Speaking and IBM's Via Voice, can recognize some continuous speech. Dragon System is at 800-437-2466, www.dragonsys.com. IBM is at 800-426-3333, www.software.ibm.com/is/voicetype.

Another problem is homonyms, or words that are pronounced the same, and sometimes spelled the same, but have different meanings. For instance, *him, hymn, hem* are all pronounced similarly but have very different meanings. Another instance is the words *to, too,* and *two.* Many people misspell and confuse the words *there* and *their, your* and *you're,* and *it's* and *its.*

A lot of our words have many different meanings, such as the word *set, run, round,* and *date.* One of the solutions to this problem would be to have software and hardware with enough intelligence that it could not only recognize the words, but recognize the meaning due to the context in which they are used. That requires more intelligence than some human beings have.

Security Systems

The voice of every person is as distinct and different as a fingerprint. Voice prints have been used to convict criminals. Since no two voices are alike, a voice-recognition system could be used to practically eliminate the need for keys. Most automobiles already have several built-in computerized systems. You can be sure that sometime soon, you will see cars that have a voice-recognition system instead of ignition keys. Such a system could help reduce the number of car thefts and carjacking. A voice-recognition system could also be used for anyplace that required strict security. If they installed voice recognition at Fort Knox, they could probably eliminate many of their other security measures.

In most of the older systems, the computer had to be trained to recognize a specific word. Memory limitations and computer power were such that the vocabulary was quite limited. Today, we have computers with hundreds of megabytes of memory and lots of power. Since every word is made up of only 42 phonemes, several companies such as IBM, Verbex Voice Systems, and Dragon Systems are working on systems that will use a small sample of a person's voice that contains these phonemes. Using the phonemes from this sample, the computer could then recognize any word that person speaks.

Basic Systems

Verbex Voice Systems has developed a fairly sophisticated system that makes the keyboard almost obsolete. Their Listen for Windows uses special software and a 16-bit plug-in board with a Digital Signal Processor (DSP) on it. After a bit of training, this system can recognize continuous speech. Of course, it is still not perfect, so there are times when you will have to slow down to discrete words and make corrections for words it does not understand. Call Verbex at 1-800-275-8729 or visit the Verbex Web site at www.verbex.com for more information and current pricing.

Computers and Devices for the Handicapped

Several computer devices have been developed that can help the disabled person live a better life. Just because they have a physical impairment, doesn't mean disabled people have a brain impairment. Nature often compensates. For instance, the hearing and tactile senses of many blind people are much more acute than those who can see.

There are devices that allow the blind, the deaf, the quadriplegic, and other severely disabled people to communicate. There are special braille keyboards and keyboards with enlarged keys for the blind. The

EyeTyper from Sentient Systems Technology of Pittsburgh, has an embedded camera on the keyboard that can determine which key the user is looking at. It then enters that key into the computer. Words Plus, of Sunnyvale California, has a sensitive visor that can understand input from a raised brow, head movement, or eye blinks. The Speaking Devices Corporation (408-727-5571) has a telephone that can be trained to recognize an individual's voice. It can then dial up to 100 different numbers when the person tells it to. The same company has a tiny earphone that also acts as a microphone. These devices would be ideal for a person who can speak, but cannot use their hands.

Devices for the disabled can allow many people to lead active, useful, and productive lives. Some have become artists, programmers, writers, and scientists. These communication devices have allowed them a bit of freedom from the harsh prison of their disabilities. IBM has a number of products that they call the Independence Series, designed to aid people with physical disabilities. Their DOS-based utility, AccessDOS, can be used to add functions to the keyboard, mouse, and sound boards. Call IBM at 800-426-4832 for more information.

Windows 95 includes a bit of help for disabled persons. Click on the Start button, highlight Settings, click on Control Panel, then double-click on the Accessibility Options. You will see five window tabs:

- StickyKeys lets you press one key at a time instead of having to press two or three such as Ctrl, Alt, Del. FilterKeys tells Windows 95 to disregard keystrokes that are not held for a certain length of time.
- SoundSentry lets you substitute a visual cue for an audible alert. ShowSounds can be used with programs that use digitized speech to display captions on screen.
- Display is an option that allows you to select colors, fonts, and high contrast.
- MouseKeys lets you control the cursor with the numeric keypad instead of a mouse.
- The SerialKey option makes it easy to attach special equipment to the serial port.

Braille

I correspond frequently on the Internet with a friend who has been blind since early childhood. He has a computer with a braille reader and printer and a text-to-speech (TTS) recognition program. He has never considered his blindness a handicap. He figures that he can do almost anything that anyone else can do. Here is his signature:

"bud keith Ph.D., blind cross-country skier, tandem biker, returned Peace Corps volunteer and retired civil servant, currently surviving prostate cancer in arlington virginia."

Despite all of his problems, he has never lost his sense of humor. Sometimes, he becomes a bit philosophical about how his blindness can allow him to see things better and differently than others. He is a delightful person to know. One thing that his text-to-speech program will not do, however, is recognize graphics. Someone sent him a drawing of a turkey on Thanksgiving and he said his program went crazy trying to recognize it.

Here are some other companies who supply devices for the handicapped:

- Wrist and arm supports:
  - Bucky Products (800-692-8259)
  - DeRoyal/LMB (800-541-3992)
- Miniature keyboards:
  - InTouch Systems (800-332-6244)
  - TASH (800-463-5685)
- Programmable keyboards:
  - Don Johnston (800-999-4660)
  - IntelliTools (800-899-6687)
- Onscreen keyboards:
  - Don Johnston (800-999-4660)
  - Words+ (800-869-8521)
- Wands and pointers:
  - Extensions for Independence (619-423-1478)
  - North Coast Medical (800-821-9319)
- Electronic pointers:
  - Ability Research (612-939-0121)
  - Madenta (800-661-8406)
- Switches:
  - AbleNet (800-322-0956)
  - Toys for Special Children (800-832-8697)
- Touch screens:
  - Edmark (800-426-0856)
  - MicroTouch Systems (800-642-7686)

- Voice recognition:
  - Dragon Systems (800-825-5897)
  - Speech Systems (303-938-1110)

Speech Technology is a free magazine to qualified subscribers. If you are in any kind of business that involves speech, you probably qualify. Call 203-834-1430 for information and a qualifying form, or e-mail Speechmag@AOL.COM.

Several organizations can help in locating special equipment and lending support. If you know someone who might benefit from the latest technology and devices for the handicapped, contact these organizations:

AbleData
800-344-5405

Accent on Information
309-378-2961

Apple Computer
408-996-1010

Closing the Gap, Inc.
612-248-3294

Direct Link for the Disabled
805-688-1603

Easter Seals Systems Office
312-667-8626

IBM National Support Center
800-426-2133

American Foundation for the Blind
212-620-2000

Trace Research and Development Center
608-262-6966

National ALS Association
818-340-7500

Some of these organizations will be glad to accept your old computers. Of course, you can write it off your income tax as a donation. You will be helping them and yourself. And you will feel better helping someone else.

CHAPTER 11

Communications

One of the most important properties enjoyed by human beings is our many ways to communicate. Since the first time people yelled at the top of their lungs or beat on a hollow log, we have been constantly striving to improve our methods of communicating. We have come a long way since that first hollow log. Today, we have more means of communicating than at any time in history. The reason for communications is to share information. We need information for pleasure, health, business, and every aspect of our daily lives.

Some people think that today we have too much information, that it is overwhelming. Someone has coined the term *infoglut* to describe this idea. Whether you like it or not, infoglut is going to continue to grow. What we all need is enough information to be able to determine what we need without being overwhelmed.

Telephones

Telephones are one of the most important communications devices ever invented. They can be a critical part of personal life as well as almost all businesses. By adding a modem to your computer, you can make the telephone even more useful and important. You can use your computer and the telephone line to access online services, use bulletin boards, telecommute, surf the Internet, and communicate with anyone else in the world who also has a computer and modem.

Many modem boards are now integrated with fax capability. A modem board with a fax might not cost much more than the modem alone. Communicating by fax is fast and efficient.

Reaching Out

There are about 200 million computers installed in homes, offices, and businesses worldwide. About half of them have a modem or some sort of communications capability. This capability of the computer is one of its most important aspects. If your computer has a modem, you can access over 10,000 bulletin boards in the U.S. You can take advantage of electronic mail, faxes, up-to-the-minute stock market quotations, and a large number of other online services such as home shopping, home banking, travel agencies, business transactions, many databases, data services, and even dating services.

For some types of work, a person can use a modem and work from home. This is called *telecommuting*. It is a whole lot better than commuting by car and sitting in traffic jams on the crowded freeways.

Communications covers a wide range of activities and technologies. Many books have been written that cover all phases of communications. Just a few of the many technologies will be discussed in this chapter.

The Internet and World Wide Web

One of the hottest topics at the moment is the Internet and World Wide Web (WWW). The Internet is so important that Chapter 14 is devoted to it.

Modems

A modem is an electronic device that allows a computer to use an ordinary telephone line to communicate with other computers that are equipped with modems. *Modem* is a contraction of the words *modulate* and *demodulate*.

The telephone system transmits voice and data in analog voltage form. Analog voltages are sine waves that vary continuously up and down. (Check back to Fig. 1-4 to see what a sine wave looks like.) Computer data is usually in a digital voltage form, which is a series of on and off voltages. The modem takes the digitized bits of voltage from the computer and modulates, or transforms, them into analog voltages in order to transmit them over the telephone lines. At the receiving end, a similar modem demodulates the analog voltage and transforms it back into a digital form.

Transmission Difficulties

Telephone systems were originally designed for voice and have a very narrow bandwidth. A person with perfect hearing can hear from 20 to 20,000 Hz (cycles per second). For normal speech, we only use about 300 to 2000 Hz.

Telephone analog voltages are subject to noise, static, and other electrical disturbances. Noise and static take the form of analog voltages. So do most of the other electrical disturbances, such as electrical storms and pulses generated by operating electrical equipment. The analog noise and static voltages may be mixed in with any analog data voltages that are being transmitted. The mixture of static and noise voltages with the data voltages can corrupt and severely damage the data. The demodulator might be completely at a loss to determine which voltages represent data and which is noise.

Baud Rate

These problems, and the state of technology at the time, limited the original modems to about five characters per second (CPS), or a rate of 50 baud. The term *baud* is from Emile Baudot (1845—1903), a French inventor. Originally, the baud rate was a measure of the dots and dashes in telegraphy. It is now defined as the actual rate of symbols transmitted per second. For lower baud rates, it is essentially the same as bits per second.

Remember that it takes eight bits to make a character. Just as we have periods and spaces to separate words, we must use one start bit and one stop bit to separate the on/off bits into characters. A transmission of 300 baud means that 300 on/off bits are sent in one second. For every eight bits of data that represent a character, we need one bit to indicate the start of a character and one bit to indicate the end. We then need another bit to indicate the start of the next character. So, counting the start/stop bits, it takes 11 bits for each character. If we divide 300 by 11, it gives us about 27 CPS. Some of the newer technologies might actually transmit symbols that represent more than one bit. For baud rates of 1200 and higher, the CPS and baud rate can be considerably different.

There have been some fantastic advances in modem technologies. A few years ago, 2400-baud systems were the standard. Today they are obsolete. The industry leaped over the 4800 and 9600 baud systems to the 14.4 Kb systems, then doubled to 28.8 Kb, then 33.6 Kb, and now the 56 Kb.

When communicating directly with another modem, both the sending and receiving units must operate at the same baud rate and use the same protocols. Most of the faster modems are downward compatible and can operate at the slower speeds. If you use a modem frequently, a high-speed modem can quickly pay for itself. We have sure come a long way since those early 50-baud standards.

56 Kb Modems

I am sure you have seen the ads for 56 Kb modems. At the time of this writing, in early 1998, you might be better off waiting for a while. There are two competing systems, Rockwell/Lucent K56flex and U.S. Robotics X2. (U.S. Robotics is now a part of the 3Com Corporation.) The two systems are incompatible and cannot communicate with each other.

It would be nice if the two companies sat down and determined which were the best features of each system, then agreed on a standard, but the two sides are at war with each other, each claiming that theirs is the only system that is worthwhile. The chance of a peaceful agreement is about as likely as peace in the Middle East. The International Telecommunications Union (ITU) will have to make a decision as to which system to choose as a standard. If you buy one of the 56 Kb units now, both companies promise to offer an upgrade to whatever standard that is chosen. Both systems work fairly well when downloading graphics and large files on the Internet, but the fastest they can upload files is the same as what you probably have now, the standard 33.6 Kb.

ISDN (Integrated Services Digital Network) is faster than the 56 Kb systems; you can have two 64 Kb systems. However, it requires an expensive special-line installation and a fairly high monthly fee. One good thing about the 56 Kb technology is that you do not have to have new lines installed, and there is no increase in telephone charges.

How 56 Kb Modems Work

Originally, the Public Switched Telephone Network (PSTN), a fancy name for our Plain Old Telephone System (POTS), was all analog. Today, once the telephone message gets from your telephone line to a central office, in most instances, it is converted to digital information and transmitted by radio relay to the next station. When it gets to the central office closest to where you are calling, the digital message is converted back to analog data and transmitted by wire to the telephone.

All modems are analog systems. The digital bits of data from the computer are transformed into an analog voltage, which is transmitted to the receiving modem, which transforms it back to digital bits. The 56 Kb modems take advantage of the fact that most data is transmitted from the central offices as digital data. However, the data from a computer to the central office must still be sent there as analog data over the phone lines, so it is limited to the 33.6 Kb speed.

On the download side, Internet Service Providers and large companies can install special equipment that can bypass the analog loop and send the message as digital data directly to the central office. It still must come from the nearest central office as analog data to your modem, however, then converted back to digital for the computer. If the lines are dirty and noisy between the central station and your computer, you might not be able to enjoy the full 56 Kb transmission. Even with the best conditions, you might never get more than 48 Kb.

Like the standard systems, whenever a high-speed connection is not possible, the 56 Kb systems fall back to the next lower speed that is reliable, so you shouldn't be surprised if it drops to as low as 28.8 Kb at times.

The ITU was supposed to make a decision as to which system to recognize as the standard by the end of 1997, but it didn't happen. Hopefully, by the time you read this, we will have a single standard.

How to Estimate Connect Time

You can figure the approximate length of time it will take to transmit a file. For rough approximations of CPS, you can divide the baud rate by 10. For instance, a 33.6 Kb modem would transmit at about 3360 CPS. Look at the directory and determine the number of bytes in the file. Divide the number of bytes in the file by the CPS to give a rough approximation of download time. For instance, to transmit a file with 336,000 bytes at 3360 bytes per second, it would take about 100 seconds.

Protocols

Protocols are procedures that have been established for exchanging data, along with the instructions that coordinate the process. Most protocols can sense when the data is corrupted or lost due to noise, static, or a bad connection. The protocol will automatically resend the affected data until it is received correctly. A protocol transmits a block or packet of data along with an error-checking code, then waits for the receiver to send back an acknowledgment. It then sends another packet, and waits to see if it got through okay. If a packet does not get through, it is resent immediately.

Both the sending and receiving modems must use the same protocol and baud rate. However, faster modems are able to shift down and send or receive at the lower speeds.

ITU Recommended Standards

The communications industry is very complex, so there have not been many real standards. There are many different manufacturers and software developers, and of course all of them want to differentiate their hardware or software by adding new features. A United Nations standards committee was established to help create worldwide standards. If every country had different protocols and standards, it would be very difficult to communicate. The original committee was called the Comite Consulatif International de Telephone et Telegraphique (CCITT). The name has now been changed to the International Telecommunications Union (ITU). This committee has representatives from over 80 countries and several large private manufacturers. The committee makes recommendations only. A company is free to use or ignore them, but more and more companies are now adopting the recommendations.

All ITU recommendations for small computers have a *V* or *X* prefix. The V series is for use with switched telephone networks, which is almost all of them. The X series is for systems that do not use switched phone lines. Revisions or alternate recommendations have *bis* (second) or *ter* (third) added. The V prefixes can be a bit confusing. For instance, a V.32 modem can communicate at 4800 or 9600 bits per second (bps). It can communicate with any other V.32 modem. A V.32bis modem can communicate at 14,400 bps. The V.32bis standard is a modulation method, not a compression technique. The V.34 standard is for 28.8K modems.

The V.42bis standard is a method of data compression plus a system of error-checking. A V.42bis modem can communicate with another V.42bis at up to 57,600 bps by using compression and error-checking.

Low-Cost Communication Software

If you buy a modem or modem/fax board, many companies include a basic communications program. If you subscribe to one of the large online services such as Compuserve or Prodigy, they provide special software for their connections.

Netscape and Microsoft Internet Explorer are well known as browsers, but they also handle e-mail and have several other utilities. You can get copies of communication shareware programs from bulletin boards or from any of the several companies who provide shareware and public-domain software.

Shareware is not free. You may try it out and use it, but the developers ask that you register the program and send in a nominal sum. For this low cost they usually provide a manual and some support. Some shareware companies are listed in Chapter 16. You should be very careful and check for viruses when downloading or using any public-domain or shareware programs.

Basic Types of Modems

There are two basic types of modems, the external desktop and the internal modem. Each type has some advantages and disadvantages. A disadvantage of the external type is that it requires some of your precious desk space and a voltage source. It also requires an external cable from a COM port to drive it. The good news is that most external models have LEDs that light up and let you know what is happening during your call.

The external and most of the internal models also have speakers that let you hear such things as the phone ringing or a busy signal. The internal modem, however, might have a very small speaker, so you might not be able to hear the dial tone and the ringing. Some external models have a volume control for the built-in speaker.

The internal modem is built entirely on a board, usually a half, or short, board. The good news is that it doesn't use up any of your desk real estate, but the bad news is that it uses one of your precious slots. It also does not have the LEDs to let you know the progress of your call. Of course, not being able to see the LEDs flashing might not be that important to you. The only thing most people care about is whether it is working or not. The fewer items to worry about, the better.

External modems cost up to $50 or more than an equivalent internal modem. By far, the most popular modems are the internal types. External modems might also require an external 110-volt power source.

One of the most popular early modems was made by Hayes Microcomputer Products. This company became the IBM of the modem world and established a de facto standard. Now there are hundreds of modem manufacturers. Except for some of the very inexpensive ones, almost all of them are Hayes compatible.

Installing a Modem

The first thing to do when installing a modem (or any device) is to check your documentation to see if there are any jumpers or switches needed to configure the device. There probably will not be any. The older modems usually had jumpers or small switches that had to be set to enable COM1, COM2, COM3, or COM4. Under Windows 95 and Plug-and-Play devices, there might not be any jumpers to set.

Find an empty slot and plug the board in. At this time, most modems are still ISA-type 16-bit boards. Some of the newer, faster ones will be for the PCI type. Normally, most systems only allow for two ports, COM1, which uses IRQ 4, and COM2, which uses IRQ 3. However, COM1 and COM3 can share IRQ 4, and COM2 and COM4 can share IRQ 3, if the software or hardware will allow it.

One of the biggest problems of installing serial-type hardware such as modems, fax boards, network cards, mice, sound cards, serial printers, and plotters is that there just aren't enough IRQs. Every computer, even the most powerful Pentium II, only has 16 IRQs, and most of them are reserved for other uses. The interrupt requests cause the BIOS and CPU to stop whatever they are doing and give their attention to the current request. The IRQs have a hierarchical arrangement, so that the lower numbered IRQs have priority. Table 11-1 shows how my IRQs are arranged.

TABLE 11-1
IRQ Arrangement

IRQ Number	Users
0	Timer Click
1	Keyboard
2	Second 8259A
3	COM2:, COM4
4	COM1:, COM3
5	LPT2
6	Floppy Disk
7	LPT1
8	Real-Time Clock
9	Redirected IRQ2
10	(Reserved)
11	(Reserved)
12	(Reserved)
13	Math Coprocessor
14	Fixed Disk
15	(Reserved)

You can use any of the IRQs marked *Reserved* for things like sound boards and network cards, but serial devices such as mice and modems must be connected to one of the COM ports. A PS/2 mouse does not use a COM port, but it does require an IRQ, usually IRQ 12.

If you are using Windows 95 and want to see how your IRQs are assigned, click on the My Computer icon, then click on Control Panel, then the System icon, then the Device Manager tab. This will bring up a list of all the items in your computer. At the top of the list is Computer. Double-click on Computer, and it will show you a list of all your IRQs that are being used. It will not show those that are not currently being used. Some that might be open are 10, 11, 12, and 15.

If you are installing an external modem, you must go through this procedure to make sure the COM port is accessible and does not conflict. If you have a mouse, a serial printer, or some other serial device, you will have to determine which port they are set to. You cannot have two serial devices set to the same COM port unless you have special software that allows them to share the port. It is not always obvious that an interrupt is in use.

It is a crying shame that even the fastest, most powerful computers still only have 16 IRQs, and most of them are used by the system. If you need to install a sound board, modem, mouse, network card, SCSI device, or any of many other peripherals, you might not have enough IRQs. Some devices will share IRQs, but most of them are selfish and will not share.

Plug-and-Play

The Pentium-class motherboards have a Plug-and-play (PnP) BIOS. Almost all modems are now manufactured to the PnP specification. When you plug in a modem board, Windows checks to determine which IRQs are free and automatically sets itself so that there is no conflict.

It is not always that easy, however. In order to write this book, I bought a 266-MHz Intel Pentium II, a 233-MHz AMD K6 and a Cyrix 6x86MX PR200. (Actually, the book was a good excuse to move up to the more powerful systems.) I removed a 120-MHz Pentium motherboard from one of my systems and installed a new motherboard with the Cyrix 6x86MMX PR 200. Everything worked great except for my modem. I opened the Windows 95 Control Panel and clicked on Modems. A window came up and said that my modem, a Diamond

SupraExpress 33.6, was installed. I clicked on the tab marked Diagnostics. A display showed that the modem was connected to COM3, interrupt 11, address 3E8. I then clicked on More Info. A message was displayed, saying that Windows would test the modem. An error message was then displayed that said, "The modem failed to respond. Make sure it is properly connected and turned on. If it is an internal modem and is connected, verify that the interrupt for the port is properly set." On my old motherboard, the modem had been set for COM1, but COM3 should be okay. I didn't know why it would not work.

I was a bit unhappy. I wasted a whole day trying to install the modem. I thought there might be something wrong with the new motherboard, so I tried the modem on my Intel 266-MHz Pentium II. It would not work there either. I then thought that perhaps I had somehow damaged the modem when I removed it from the 120-MHz motherboard. I reinstalled it on the old motherboard, and it worked perfectly. I then thought that perhaps the modem was just not capable of working at the higher frequencies.

I called the long-distance support number and, after pushing about 15 different buttons for choices and options, I was put in a queue for technical support. I was told that I would have to wait about 20 minutes for a technician. I have a speaker telephone just for this sort of occasion. When the technician finally came on, he had me go back to the Control Panel and check Modem, then Diagnostic, and More Info, just as I had already done. He then had me click on the System Icon, then on Device Manager. Then he had me click on Modem, then on my SupraExpress 336i. A window came up and he had me click on Properties. Another window came up and he had me click to delete the checkmark for Automatic settings. He then had me click on Change Settings, then on Resources. A window came up that said "Edit Interrupt Requests."

The interrupt, number 11, that was presently being used was displayed. Below that was a box that said this interrupt was not conflicting with any other interrupt—but evidently it was lying. At this point, I could enter a specific interrupt number or use the up-down arrows to install any interrupt that was not being used. Interrupt 15 said it was free and would cause no conflicts. I chose 15, then went back and clicked on Modems and Diagnostics, then had Windows try to communicate with the modem. Again, an error message came up that the modem was not responding. Back to Systems and Device Manager, then Change Settings, then a selection of interrupt 12. Then I went back to Modems and Diagnostics, then More Info, and had Windows try to communicate with the modem. Although Windows had said there was no conflict, I still got an error that said the modem failed to respond.

I went back to Systems and Device Manager to try the one remaining IRQ that was free, number 10. This one worked like a charm. I have no idea why the others did not work. Windows said that they were free and that there was no conflict. I believed Windows when it first told me that there was no conflict with interrupt 11, which Windows had automatically assigned to the modem. I also believed it when it told me that there was no conflict with interrupt numbers 15 and 12. But again, Windows was lying. It was only telling the truth when it said there was no conflict on IRQ number 10.

Because I believed it when it said there was no conflict with the automatically assigned IRQ 11, I thought there must be some other problem. Therefore, I never thought to try the other IRQs.

I still had one more problem, however. My AOL and Prodigy software was set for a modem that operated on COM1. This one was now operating on COM3. It was fairly easy to use the Setup option on the AOL and Prodigy sign-on screens and reassign the modem COM ports from COM1 to COM3.

Connecting to the Line

Unless you expect to do a lot of communicating, you might not need a separate dedicated line, but you might need some sort of switching device, such as those from Command Communications (800-288-6794). This company has several different devices that can recognize an incoming voice, modem, or fax signal and route the call.

There should be two connectors at the back of the board. One might be labeled *Line in* and the other *Phone*. Unless you have a dedicated telephone line, you should unplug your telephone, plug an extension into the modem Line, then plug the telephone into the jack marked *Phone*. After you have connected all of the lines, turn on your computer, and try the modem before you put the cover back on.

Fax/Modem Software

Most fax/modems come with several communication software packages. The fax/modem that I had been using for the last couple of years died on me. I bought a new one and installed it, along with some communication software that came with it. It screwed up my system completely. I could no longer access Prodigy or CompuServe. I sweated for half a day before I discovered that the software was Terminate and Stay Resident (TSR). It loaded itself into memory each time I booted up. With that software in memory, I could not access AOL or Prodigy.

You can find out if there are any TSRs loaded into memory on your computer when in Windows 95 by pressing the Ctrl+Alt+Delete once. (If you do it twice, it will shut the computer down.) This will show you a list of any TSR programs in memory. You can then highlight them, press the Enter key, and they will be closed. You will always see Explorer in the list. Don't close it. If you do, it will shut your computer down.

There are thousands of little things that can go wrong when installing serial hardware such as a modem. PnP goes a long way to help solve some of the problems, but it can't possibly solve all of them.

Bulletin Boards

If you have a modem, you have access to several thousand computer bulletin boards. At one time, most bulletin boards were free of any charge. You only had to pay the phone bill if they were out of your calling area. Since then, however, a lot of lowdown scum have uploaded pirated software and software with viruses to them, posted stolen credit-card numbers, and engaged in many other loathsome and illegal activities. Because of this, the sysops (systems operators) have had to spend a lot of time monitoring their BBSs. Many of the bulletin boards now charge a nominal fee to join; some just ask for a tax deductible donation. Many bulletin boards are set up to help individuals. They usually have lots of public-domain software and a space where you can leave messages for help, for advertising something for sale, or for just plain old chit-chat.

If you are just getting started in computer communications, you probably need some software. There are all kinds of public-domain and shareware software packages that are equivalent to almost all of the major commercial programs. The best part is that public-domain software is free, and shareware is practically free. Another good source of software is the Surplus Software Company at 1-800-753-7877. Call them for a free catalog. You can save hundreds of dollars on essential software.

At one time, bulletin boards were very popular, but today, most people use the Internet instead. Many companies still maintain their bulletin boards, however, to provide help to their customers.

Viruses

A few years ago, you could access a bulletin board and download all kinds of good public-domain or shareware software. You never had to worry about the software destroying your data. Because a few sick psychopaths have created computer viruses, however, you now have to use safeguards. You must be quite selective and very careful about where you get your software and whom you get it from. Since bulletin boards are not very popular anymore, the scum who write viruses have moved to the Internet.

There are all kinds of people in this world, but I cannot imagine why anyone would be so mean and dastardly as to harm someone they don't even know. I wouldn't condone it, but I might be able to understand doing harm to someone as revenge for some wrong received. But the no-good &"&%$@# people who write viruses seem to get their jollies by harming people they have never met or will never know. (Note: The *&"&$@#* is shorthand for some very dirty words that can't be used in a book like this.)

A computer virus is not a live thing. It cannot harm you, only the data in a computer or on a disk. You might have invested a large part of your life creating that data, however. A computer virus is usually a bit of program code, hidden in a piece of legitimate software. The virus is usually designed to redirect, corrupt, or destroy data. A computer virus resembles an organic virus in that it can cause a wide variety of virus-type symptoms in the computer host.

The virus code might be written so that it can replicate or make copies of itself. When it becomes embedded on a disk, it can attach itself to other programs that it comes in contact with. Whenever a floppy disk is inserted into the drive, it can come away with a hidden copy of the virus.

Infected software might appear to work as it should for some time. Eventually, however, it contaminates and might destroy many of your files. If a virus gets on a workstation or network, it can infect all of the computers in the network. Here are some of the companies who have good antivirus software:

Norton AntiVirus
Symantec
www.symantec.com

PC-cillin
TouchStone
www.checkit.com

McAfee
Antivirus
www.mcafee.com

Visit their Web sites for information and downloads.

The U.S. Department of Energy has established the Computer Incident Advisor Capability (CIAC). It has lots of information about viruses. There are thousands of viruses, some just slight variations of an original. The CIAC lists some of the more infamous of them. Visit the Web site at http://ciac.llnl.gov

Virus Hoaxes

A group of #@%%&"& scum has surfaced recently who are almost as bad as the virus writers. These are people who broadcast virus hoaxes. A person has to have a good knowledge of programming and computer technology to be able to write a computer virus, but it takes no technical knowledge to be able to devise a virus hoax.

Once the hoax has been posted on the Internet, others with good intentions pick it up and rebroadcast it. A hoax that has been on the Internet several times is that if you read a certain e-mail, it will infect your system. Many people have started chain letters about this phony virus. Just reading your e-mail, however, will not affect your system. When you open e-mail to read it, you are reading it from an ISP's (Internet Service Provider's) server. Unless you download the e-mail to your own hard disk, it remains on the ISP server.

These hoaxes have become so prevalent that many antivirus companies have placed information about them on their Web pages. Of course, they also provide information about real viruses. The U.S. Government Department of Energy's CIAC Web site compiles a list of virus hoaxes and updates them often. Visit the Web site at http://ciac.lln.gov.

Online Services

Bulletin boards are not nearly as popular today as the Internet and online services. (See Chapter 14 for more about the Internet.)

Online services provide forums for help and discussions, mailboxes, and a large variety of information and reference services. Subscribers to a service can search the databases and download information as easily as pulling the data off their own hard disks. The major online services have phone numbers in most areas in the larger cities, so that there is not even a toll charge. They have an impressive list of services, including home shopping, home banking, airline schedules and reservations, stock market quotations, and medical bulletin board.

Banking by Modem

Many banks offer systems that let you do all your banking with your computer and a modem from the comforts of your home. With such a system, you would never again have to drive downtown, hunt for a parking space, then stand in line for a half-hour to do your banking. Intuit's (415-322-0573) Quicken is an excellent financial software program. Intuit also offers CheckFree, a service that lets you pay all of your bills electronically. It also allows you to print your checks from your computer on a laser printer. This requires special checks that are imprinted with your account number in magnetic ink.

CheckFree costs about $10 a month, but if you spend about four hours a month paying bills, the $10 is not very much compared to the time spent. Another advantage to CheckFree is that the bills are paid automatically, but not until they are due. This lets your account accrue interest until the last moment. If you ordinarily write a lot of checks, CheckFree and Quicken can quickly pay for themselves.

Intuit is now merged with ChipSoft (602-295-3070). ChipSoft is the developer of TurboTax, one of the better software packages for doing your taxes. The marriage of these two companies means that they can offer the most complete financial software available for your computer system. With a good financial program, you can get rid of the shoeboxes full of canceled checks. The data that is in your computer can automatically flow onto the TurboTax forms, making the onerous task that occurs on April 15 each year a bit easier to accomplish.

Facsimile Machines

Facsimile (fax) machines have been around for quite a while. Newspapers and businesses have used them for years. The early machines were similar to the early acoustic modems. Both used foam rubber cups that fit over the telephone receiver-mouthpiece for coupling. They were very slow and subject to noise and interference.

Fax machines and modems have come a long way since those early days. A page of text or a photo is fed into the facsimile machine and scanned. As the scanning beam moves across the page, white and dark areas are digitized as ones and zeros, then transmitted out over the telephone lines. On the receiving end of the line, a scanning beam sweeps across the paper. The dark areas cause it to print as it sweeps across the paper. The finished product is a black-and-white image of the original.

When a text file is sent by modem, the digitized bits that make up each character are converted from digital voltage to analog voltage. A modem sends and receives bits that make up each character. A fax machine or board sends and receives scanned whole pages of letters, graphics, images, signatures, etc. Since a modem recognizes individual characters, a computer program can be sent over a modem, but not over a fax. A fax sends and receives the information as digitized graphic data. A modem converts the digital information that represents individual characters into analog voltages, sends it over the line, then converts it back to individual digital characters.

There are times when a modem or fax is needed. Unfortunately, both units could not be in use at the same time on the same phone line. There are millions of facsimile machines in use today. Almost every business can benefit from the use of a fax. It can be used to send documents that includes handwriting, signatures, seals, letterheads, graphs, blueprints, photos, and other types of data around the world, across the country, or across the room to another fax machine. Express mail costs from $8 to $10 or more. A fax machine can deliver the same letter for about 40 cents, and do it in less than three minutes.

Many software programs let you delay sending a fax until late at night to get the best rates. Depending on the type of business and the amount of critical mail that must be sent out, a fax system can pay for itself in a very short time. If you have a fax/modem board, it might be even less expensive to send e-mail.

Most fax machines use thermal paper for printing, especially the lower-cost machines. Thermal paper does not provide very good resolution and fades when exposed to light. The better, and more expensive, fax machines use inkjet or laser technology and print on plain paper. They are usually a bit slow, but almost all of the fax machines can be used as a copier.

Fax machines have a lot in common with copy machines, scanners, and printers. Several companies have added these features to their machines so that one machine can do the work of several.

Fax/Modem Computer Boards

Several companies have developed fax systems on circuit boards that can be plugged into computers. Most of the fax boards are now integrated with a modem on the same board. The modem and fax combination costs very little more than either board separately. This combination also saves having to use an extra plug-in slot.

For some time, the standard baud rate for fax was 9600, but many of the newer fax/modem boards are capable of a 14,400-baud speed for both modem and fax. However, just like with modem connections, both the sender and receiver of the fax must be operating at the same speed. Also like the modem, the fax can shift down to match the receiver if it is slower.

Special software allows the computer to control the fax boards. Using the computer's word processor, letters and memos can be written and sent out over the phone lines. Several letters or other information can be stored or retrieved from the computer's hard disk and transmitted. The computer can be programmed to send the letters out at night, when rates are lower.

Computer fax boards have one disadvantage compared to regular fax machines: They cannot scan information such as signatures, graphics, or drawings. With a scanner, however, this information can be stored as a file on a hard disk, then added to a document that is to be faxed. There are several scanners that can be used to input data. With the proper software, a computer can receive and store any fax. The digitized data and images can be stored on a hard disk, then printed out.

Fax-on-Demand

Several companies have set up fax machines that can supply information to you 24 hours a day. You simply call them with your voice phone, tell them what documents you want, give them your fax number, and the documents will be sent immediately. Most of the companies have a catalog that lists all of their documents and the document number. You should first ask to have the catalog faxed to you. You can then determine which documents to order.

The FaxFacts Company (708-682-8898) publishes a small booklet that lists several companies who have fax-on-demand or faxback capability. They list topics such as medical, computers, travel, and trade shows. Most faxback information is free, but some companies such as Consumer Reports (800-766-9988) ask for a credit card number and charges a fee for articles you request.

Here are just a few of the other companies who offer faxback or fax-on-demand:

- Borland TechFax: 800-822-4269
- Cyrix Direct Connect: 800-215-6823
- IBM: 800-426-4329
- Novell Support Line: 800-638-9273
- Symantec Corporation: 800-554-4403

When you call, ask for their new users' instructions and navigation map. If you prefer, most will send the information to you by mail rather than by fax.

Fax/Modem/Phone Switch

Having the modem and telephone on the same line should cause no problems unless someone tries to use the telephone while the modem is using it. Life will be a lot simpler, though, if you have a switch that can detect whether the incoming signal is for fax, modem, or voice. Fax and modem signals transmit a high-pitched tone, called the CNG (CalliNG) signal. A fax/modem switch can switch and route the incoming call to the proper device.

Be aware that there are a few old fax systems that do not use the CNG signals. My Command Communication system will let me manually transfer the call in that case. If I know the incoming call is a fax, I can press 11 and it will be switched to the fax machine. If it is a modem call, I can press 22 and it will be switched to the modem. Of course, I have to be there to answer such a call. One solution to this problem for those people who have machines without the CNG signal is to have them punch in the 11 or 22 on their end after they dial the number. I can also put this instruction on my answering machine if I am not available.

Fortunately, not many of the old systems without the CNG signals are still in existence. There is another solution for the problem of those people who have machines without the CNG signal. The telephone company can set up two or more numbers with different and distinctive rings on a single line. The Command Communications switchers can be programmed to recognize the distinctive ring and route the call to the proper device. The South Tech Instruments Company at 1-800-394-5556 has a FoneFilter device that can recognize the distinctive rings and route the call to a fax, modem, or answering machine. Of course, there is a charge by the telephone company for the extra numbers added to your line. At this time, in the Los Angeles area, it costs $7.50 to set up a separate distinctive ring on your line and then $6.00 a month thereafter. This is still less expensive than adding a second line.

If you still have one of the older fax machines, I would suggest that you scrap it and buy a later model. Most of them are now very inexpensive, but they are faster and handle paper much better. If you do a lot of faxing, they will pay for themselves quickly.

Command Communications at 800-288-6794 has several different switchers that are suitable for homes, small offices, and large businesses. They have connections for a telephone answering device (TAD), telephone extensions, a fax machine or fax board, and a connection for an auxiliary or modem.

The alternative to a switcher is to install a dedicated telephone line for the fax machine, another line for the modem, and another line for voice. If you don't do a lot of transmissions by fax and modem, you can get by with a single telephone and a good switcher. It can pay for itself many times over. Many of the standalone fax machines have a built-in detector that can determine if the incoming call is for voice or fax.

Telephone Outlets for Extensions

You need a telephone line or extension to hook up a computer modem or a fax. You might also want telephone outlets in several rooms, at one or more desks, or at another computer. You can go to almost any hardware store, and even some grocery and drug stores, and buy the telephone wire and accessories needed, but you might have trouble running telephone wires to the computer, desks, and rooms. It can be a lot of work cutting holes in the walls and running the wires up in the attic or under the floor.

There is a much simpler way. Just use the 110-volt wiring of the building. The Phonex Company (801-566-0100) developed special adapters that plug into any wall outlet. The system requires at least two adapters, one for the telephone input line, the other for where you want the extension. More adapters can be plugged into any other 110 volt outlet to provide as many telephone extensions as needed. If you need an extension in another location, just unplug an adapter and plug it into another nearby wall outlet. You could even use a standard electrical extension cord and a Phonex adapter to provide a telephone extension. Electronic circuitry in the adapters blocks the ac voltage from getting into the telephone lines, but allows voice and data to go through. The device is being marketed and sold by Comtrad Industries at 800-704-1211.

Combination Devices and Voice Mail

Fax machines, copiers, printers, and scanners all have a lot in common. Several companies are now taking advantage of this commonality and offering combination devices.

Some companies are starting to use color for fax. If you have one of the combination devices with a color scanner, the Laser Today International (415-961-3015) has software that will let you send and receive color faxes. The Compex International Company (800-626-8112) has an all-in-one fax, scanner, printer, and copier. The Speaking Devices Corporation (408-727-2132) has a unit with a fax, fax/phone switch, scanner, voice mail, and caller ID.

Boca Research's (407-997-6227) Multimedia Voice Modem has up to 1000 password-protected voice and fax mailboxes, private and public fax-on-demand, remote message and fax retrieval, professionally recorded greetings and voice prompts, and personalized greetings for individual mailboxes. Tiger Software (800-888-4437) publishes a catalog that has hundreds of software and hardware items. They advertise the Vomax 2000, which is a fax, voice, and modem system. It has 1 Mb of digital storage, which can store up to 20 minutes of voice mail messages or up to 50 sheets of faxes. It has message forwarding, so that it can call another number and play your messages. It can also call your pager and relay messages. Call Tiger Software for a catalog and more information.

I recently upgraded my 14.4 Kb fax/modem to a U.S. Robotics Sportster Vi 28.8K v.34 system. This system has personal voice mail that can be used as an answering machine. It also came with a book on the World Wide Web and several software packages for exploring the Web. AnyWhere Associates (617-522-8102) has software that allows you to send e-mail to faxes. Delrina's WinFax 7.0 integrates fax, e-mail, and voice mail. Cylink (408-735-5800) and Syntel Sciences (800-499-1469) have software that lets you encrypt faxes so that your nosey neighbor will not be able to read them.

Telecommuting

Millions of people risk their lives fighting frustrating traffic every day. Many of these people have jobs that could allow them to stay home, work on a computer, then send the data to the office over a modem or a fax. Even if these people had to buy their own computers, modems, and faxes, it might still be worth it. Telecommuting saves the cost of gasoline, auto maintenance, and lower insurance. Thousands are killed on the highways. Telecommuting can be a lifesaver.

Being able to work at home is also ideal for those who have young children and for the handicapped. It is expected that about half of all PCs sold in 1996 will be for home use. A large percentage of those computers will be used for telecommuting.

One other very big plus for working at home in that you can be an "open-collar" worker instead of a blue-collar or white-collar worker. Many women spend thousands of dollars buying new outfits so that they can wear a different one to work each day of the week. They can save that money if they work at home. Men won't save as much because few people notice if they wear the same clothes more than once a week. A man can wear the same shirt two or three times in the same week if he wears a tie so that no one can see the ring around the collar. (This is one of the best reasons I know of for wearing a tie.) If you are working at home, though, you can wear any old clothes as often as you like. If you are living alone, you don't have to wear anything at all—but you probably should remember to put on a robe or something when answering the door for the UPS or Fedex delivery person.

Several technological tools, such as the new fast modems/fax/voice/whatever machines, remote-access software, conference-calling software, and cellular telephones can make working from home almost like being at the office. A telecommuter can have a first-class virtual office in a bedroom or den. A plus for the company is that it will be saving office space, parking space, and wear and tear on the coffee machine.

There are a few disadvantages to telecommuting. You might miss the face-to-face interaction with your coworkers. In some cases, you might be overlooked when it comes time to hand out raises and perks. Out of sight, out of mind. On the other hand, you might be required to wear a beeper and stay close to a telephone or computer. You might feel like you are on a short leash. Generally, though, the advantages far outweigh the few disadvantages. Telecommuting or virtual offices will be adopted by more and more companies.

Remote-Control Software

If you are on the road or working from home and have a computer at the office, it is often necessary to access the data on that computer. Several software packages allow you to connect from remote locations. You can be sitting in a distant hotel room or at a PC at home and dial up a computer at the office. You can take control across a phone line or across a network and work just as if you were sitting in front of the office computer. You can review documents, update files, edit reports, produce printouts, or download files.

For many years LapLink (800-343-8088) has had one of the best ways to connect a laptop to a desktop or to connect any two computers together. Their software usually comes with a cable for linking computers together. LapLink for Windows 95 does all the good things it did in the past, in addition to being one of the better ways to remotely access and connect two or more computers. Its SmartXchange lets you transfer only those files that have been changed. You can also update a file by sending only that portion of it that has changed, which can save a lot of connect time. You can connect via cable, modem, Internet, a network or even with infrared. It comes with a cable for the parallel port or for the serial port.

Here are a few other software packages for remote control:

- Carbon Copy from Microcom
- Close-Up from Norton Lambert
- CO/Session from Triton
- Norton pcAnywhere from Symantec
- Reachout, from Ocean Isle (800-677-6232)

You should be able to find this software at most software stores or in software catalogs such as MicroWarehouse (800-367-7080) or DellWare (800-847-4051).

All of these packages will only work if the computer is turned on and booted up. Server Technology sells a product called Remote Power On/Off + AUX. This device plugs into the power line between the computer and the wall plug. The telephone line plugs into this device. When the device detects an incoming call, it will automatically turn on and boot up the PC. When the call is ended, it can turn off the PC. It can even let you reboot if the computer hangs up for some reason. Some companies bundle the Remote Power On/Off with pcAnywhere and other remote software. It is available from Dellware, MicroWarehouse, and other discount catalog stores.

Telephony

There have been some important advances in computers and telephones in the last few years. Even greater changes can be expected soon. All of the items listed here can be used in a large business or a small office or home office (SOHO). The SOHO has become a very important element of business today.

Computer Telephony is a magazine that is devoted entirely to telephone computer technology and computer-telephone integration (CTI). The magazine is free to qualified subscribers. If you work for a company or for yourself and use a telephone or computer, then you can probably qualify for a free subscription. Call 800-677-3435 and ask them to send you a qualifying form.

The telephony business has become so important and widespread that computer telephony conferences and expositions are being held twice a year. The conferences are sponsored by *Computer Telephony*. At these shows, hundreds of vendors display and demonstrate the latest computer and telephone technology, and you can attend dozens of informative seminars. For the next show date and location, call 800-677-3435.

Another free magazine that deals with telephony is *InfoText* at 218-723-9437. A free catalog that is devoted to telephone products is Hello Direct (800-444-3556). A current issue has 72 pages full of descriptions of telephone-related products, such as all kinds of telephones, headsets, and computer and telephone integration products. A couple of items actually do away with a standard telephone. The telephone line is plugged into your computer, then, with a headset and microphone, you can use a mouse to point to an address list or dial a phone number by pressing the keys of the keyboard. There are several different models with different features. The products handled by Hello Direct are rather expensive, but they have many items that are difficult to find elsewhere.

The Universal Serial Bus (USB) is a new standard that allows telephones and other telephone technologies to be connected to computers and operate at up to 12 Mbits per second.

Several companies provide hardware and software for Interactive Voice Response (IVR) that can be used in many different business functions. The computer industry is rife with hundreds of acronyms. The CTI portion of the industry has greatly increased the number.

Telephone Conference

It is very simple to have a telephone conference with as few as two people or as many as several hundred. In conference calls, everyone who is on the line can talk to anyone else on the line. You can have teleconferences anywhere, in a home, small office, large office, or even a pay telephone booth.

U.S. Robotics (800-949-6757) has developed a PC-adaptable conference speakerphone, the ConferenceLink CS 1500. It can be connected to a computer as a speakerphone for teleconferences or for videoconferencing, or for use in Internet telephony applications.

Fax Conferences

If you have a fax machine, you can send out a graphic design, plans, or any number of business papers, have other people review the document, make changes or sign it, and return it. You can have an interactive meeting with others in the same building, or almost anywhere in the world, over a simple telephone line. One disadvantage is that it is not in real-time. You have to send the fax, then wait for a reply.

Modem Teleconferences

With a computer modem, you can have a desktop conference. You send data, graphics, and other materials over the telephone line to other computers over a local area network (LAN), in the same building or almost anywhere in the world. Other people sitting at their computers can view the text, spreadsheets, graphics, and other materials. These people can change the material or interact with the other people on the line in real-time.

One of the better products that can help with a desktop conference is called TALKShow, from Future Labs (415-254-9000, fax 408-736-8030). This small, simple program works under Windows. Each person in the conference must have a copy of TALKShow installed on their computer. TALKShow connects everyone together and automatically handles all of the computer communications. The same data appears on all the computer screens that are on the line.

Many live conferences use a large whiteboard in front of the conference room. The leader writes on the board while the attendees watch, and perhaps make comments for changes. With TALKShow, each computer screen becomes a whiteboard. Each individual can suggest changes or additions to the material on the screen. Of course, if it is the president of the company who is leading desktop conference, you might have to be careful of what you suggest.

With TALKShow, anything that appears on the screen can be saved on hard disk or printed out.

Educational Uses

Several universities, colleges, and specialized training facilities are using telecommunications to offer many different courses. Some courses might lead to degrees, others might be for specialized training for a large company. You could sit at home in front of your computer and take a course from a college or training facility on the other side of the country.

National Telephone Directories

I live in the Los Angeles area. In Los Angeles and Orange Counties, there are over 100 suburban cities with over 12 million people. Can you imagine a single telephone directory that would list all of these people? How about a telephone directory that would list all of the millions of people in New York, Boston, or San Francisco? Believe it or not, there are such directories, and they are smaller than one that you might find in a small town.

These national directories are small because they are on CD-ROM discs. ProPhone, from New Media Publishing (617-631-9200) has seven CD-ROM discs, six discs for the "white pages" and one disc for businesses in the U.S. There is over 600 Mb of data on each disc, which lists telephone numbers, addresses, and zip codes. The separate disc for businesses makes it very easy to look up a company anywhere in the country.

PhoneDisc, from Digital Directory Assistance (800-284-8353), is a similar product on five CD-ROM discs. It has over 90 million listings of residences and businesses. It does not have a separate business disc, but lists businesses along with the general population in the white pages. Not every person in the country is listed on the discs. And, of course, many people move and change phone numbers.

Most phone companies only update their directories once a year, but these CD-ROM disc directory companies do quarterly updates. Once you are a registered owner, the updates are very reasonable. If you are in a business where you have to contact a lot of people, then you need these two directories. You might also need them if you live in the Los Angeles area.

ISDN

ISDN is an acronym for *Integrated Services Digital Network*. ISDN is a system that can transmit voice, data, video, and graphics in digital form rather than the present analog form. Most ISDN networks are made up of fiber-optic cable.

Eventually, the whole world will have telephone systems that use this concept. When this happens, we can scrap our modems. ISDN is already installed in several cities, but don't throw your modem away just yet. This new service might not be available at all locations for some time, and it will be rather expensive.

Cable Modems

At present, ISDN allows modems to operate at up to 128 Kbits per second, which is more than four times faster than a 28.8 Kb modem. Still, this is not nearly as fast as communicating over coax cable, which can operate at up to 10 Mbits. Many Internet Web sites have lots of graphics.

It might take several megabytes to create a good graphic image. Over the plain old telephone service (POTS), it might take several minutes to download a graphic. With a cable modem, it would only take seconds. At the time of this writing, Congress has just passed a law giving cable TV companies the right to enter the phone business, and vice versa. You can expect to see a lot of competition from the cable and telephone companies for your business. Motorola and several other companies are busy making new cable modems.

Sources

I have not listed the names and manufacturers of modems and faxes because there are so many. Look in any computer magazine and you will see dozens of ads. A recent copy of *Computer Shopper* had ads for about 200 modem/fax boards from several different companies. One modem company that I do want to mention is U.S. Robotics. They manufacture a large variety of modems, especially the high-end, high-speed type. They will send you a free 110-page booklet that explains just about all you need to know about modems. For a free booklet, call 800-342-5877.

I suggest that you subscribe to several of the computer magazines listed in Chapter 19. A good magazine that is free to qualified subscribers is *Telecommunications*. Almost anyone can qualify, especially if you fudge a little on the questionnaire form. For a qualification form, call them at 617-769-9750 or write to

Telecommunications
P.O. Box 850949
Braintree, MA 02185

CHAPTER 12

Upgrading an Older PC

There are several things that you can do to an older computer to make it run better, including adding more memory, adding a new motherboard, adding new hard drives, and adding other peripherals.

Why You Should Do It Yourself

There are shops and mail-order stores who will upgrade your computer for you. Of course, these stores cannot stay in business unless they make a profit, so it can be a bit expensive. It can also take a lot of time and cause a considerable amount of problems. First, you have to find someone who will do it for you at a reasonable price. Then, you have to lug the computer down to the shop during business hours, or package it up and send it off to a mail-order store.

If you send it to a mail-order store for an upgrade, there can be a problem of communications. Just what do you want done to your computer? How much do you want to spend? How busy is the store? How reliable is it? Can you get a firm price for the total cost and a date as to how soon they can get it back to you? How long can you wait for it? If the shop is very busy, it might take longer than promised to get it out.

What If It Is Too Old to Upgrade

A computer is never too old to be enhanced or upgraded in some manner. You can add new monitors, large-capacity hard drives, and many other peripherals to almost any of the older computers. Still, although I hate to say this, depending on what type of upgrade you want or what you want to do with your computer, it might be better to buy a new computer. You can buy a less expensive one, then add to it to suit your needs. If you decide that you don't want to upgrade your older computer,what do you do with it?

You might decide to try to sell it, but you probably won't be able to sell the computer for what you think it is worth. The computer that you paid $2500 for a few years ago might not be worth $100 today. Besides, you might not want to go through the bother and hassle of advertising and selling it, especially if you live in a city like Los Angeles. A news story reported that a gang would go to a person's house who had advertised a computer for sale. The gang would tie the person up, then take all of the computers and software that they could find. It would be bad enough losing a computer, but it would be disastrous if I lost all of my software. If you live near a larger city, there might be computer swap meets every so often. Usually, there will be a consignment table at these meets where you can sell your old hardware, but don't expect to make a lot of money off your old components.

Still another alternative is to pass your old computer on to a relative or someone who is just getting started in computers. You can also keep it and use it for word processing, for a dedicated printer server on a network, or for voice mail. Several perfectly good DOS software packages, such as WordPerfect 6.0, WordStar 7.0, Microsoft Works, and dBASE IV, work very well on 286 computers. Most standard DOS programs also run very well on an XT. The DOS programs will run a bit slower on an XT or 286 than they would on a Pentium II, so you might have to wait a few seconds or a few minutes. If you are not exactly wealthy, perhaps you can afford to waste a bit of time rather than spend money for an upgrade.

Another alternative might be to donate your old computer to a school, church, or charitable organization. Depending on your tax situation, you might come out ahead by donating it and deducting it as a gift on your income tax return.

Upgrading to a New Hard Disk

It seems like every program wants to be loaded on drive C:. Pretty soon, that drive is bursting at the seams. Some programs are temporarily loaded onto the hard disk while being run, especially if you don't have a lot of memory. If you don't have enough space on your hard disk, you will not be able to run the programs.

Parallel Printer Port Drives

One of the easiest ways to upgrade to a new hard disk is to install one of the drives that plugs into the printer port. You can plug the drive cable into the port. There will be an extra connector for the printer cable so that both can be plugged into the same port.

Most of these drives have removable cartridges. The SyQuest 270 is one such drive. It is made by SyQuest at 800-245-2278, www.syquest.com. Iomega (801-778-1000, www.iomega.com) also has large parallel-port drives up to 2 Gb.

IDE Drives

If you have a fairly new system, you have provisions for hooking up four IDE drives. This can be four hard disks, or better yet, two hard disks and two CD-ROM drives.

There are two sets of upright pins on the motherboard for connecting the IDE drives. One set is marked *Primary* and the other is marked *Secondary*. You will have two cables similar to that in Fig. 12-1. Each cable has a connector on each end and one in the middle. Small jumpers, as shown in Fig. 12-2, are used to configure each drive. The two drives on the primary set of pins are configured as master and slave. The master drive on this cable should have drive C:, which is your boot drive. The two drives on the secondary set of pins are configured as secondary master and slave. The two drives may be a CD-ROM and a hard drive or any other IDE device.

SCSI Drives

If you already have an SCSI device, you can easily add a second one. If not, you need to buy an SCSI host adapter. You can attach six SCSI devices to the host. The devices will have a set of jumper pins so that

Figure 12-1 A 40-wire ribbon cable for attaching two IDE drives.

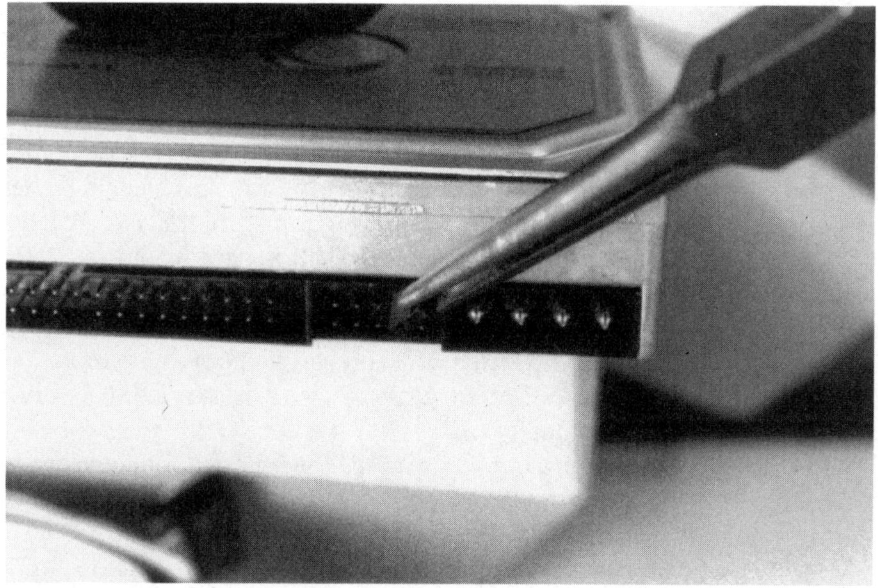

Figure 12-2 Small jumpers used to configure the IDE drive as a master or slave.

each device can be set to a Logical Unit Number (LUN). The devices can be hard drives, CD-ROM drives, scanners, or any other SCSI device.

Formatting and Transferring Files

You probably have lots of files and stuff on your old hard disk that you want to save. Before you can even think of transferring any files or even using your new computer, the hard disk must be partitioned and formatted. You might have bought it from a dealer who has already formatted it and installed Windows 95 on it. It is great if this has already been done, but if it has not been done, then you must do it. Instructions for partitioning and formatting a hard disk are in Chapter 13.

Once the hard disk (or disks) has been formatted, you can install software or transfer it from your old machine. If you have lots of floppies, you could copy your entire hard disk onto floppies and transfer it to your new system's hard disk, but it can take a whole lot of time and be a lot of trouble. Also, some programs and files will not fit on a 1.44-Mb floppy. This is a good reason to have something like the SyQuest 270-Mb drive that plugs into a printer port. You could plug it into your old system, copy all the files, then plug it into your new system and transfer it. Another disadvantage in copying files is that Windows 95 adds many files to your programs, even if they are DOS programs. Many of these files are hidden and scattered all over your disk. It is almost impossible to copy them all.

LapLink

One of the best solutions for transferring files is to use LapLink. LapLink, from Traveling Software (800-662-2652, www.travsoft.com), has software and cables that allow you to plug into the printer connection of each computer, then easily transfer all your files. Once you have connected the cables, the software allows you to see the entire directories on both machines. You can just point the mouse and click on a file or a whole directory, and it will be immediately transferred to the other computer.

LapLink was originally developed for transferring data back and forth between laptop and desktop computers, but Traveling Software has improved the software tremendously. It can even be used over modem for remote file transfers. The software can also let you set up a very simple network by connecting two computers with the furnished cabling.

DriveCopy

Another solution for transferring data from one hard drive to another is to use the DriveCopy software from PowerQuest (801-226-8977, www.powerquest.com). When you buy a new hard disk, DriveCopy lets you easily copy everything to the new drive and make a much larger drive C:. It maintains your file and directory structure so that your new drive operates the same as the old one.

You will be very happy to have a lot of extra disk space. You can then reformat your old drive and use it as a second drive or as a backup for your critical files.

Buying a Used Computer

You might find some very good bargains in buying a used computer. You can then upgrade it to suit your needs. Try looking around in your area and checking the classified ads.

If you work for a large company, chances are that they are in the process of buying new, more powerful systems to meet their added business needs. (A basic law, based on Parkinson's laws, is that the need for more and larger computer systems grows in a logarithmic fashion each year that the company is in business, whether or not the business increases.) Try to find out what the manager of the computer-procurement department is doing with the old computers. Some companies pass them down to secretaries and other people who are low on the totempole. Many companies sell them to their employees for a good price. Remind the manager how much goodwill such a practice can buy for the company.

Buying a Barebones System

Several companies advertise barebones systems. A barebones system usually includes a case, power supply, motherboard, and CPU. Sometimes, it includes memory and a monitor adapter. The price depends primarily on the CPU that you choose. The barebones bundle usually costs less than what it would cost to buy each component separately. Here is an example from an ad in a recent issue of *Computer Shopper.*

Intel 430TX motherboard, 512K pipeline burst cache, 32Mb EDO RAM, PCI 3D monitor adapter with 2Mb, 7 Bay Tower Case with power supply. The cost with various CPUs:

1. AMD K6 166:	$389	6. Cyrix 6x86MX 233:	$609
2. AMD K6 200:	$449	7. Intel Pentium 166MMX:	$399
3. AMD K6 233:	$599	8. Intel Pentium 200MMX:	$499
4. Cyrix 6x86MX 166:	$349	9. Intel Pentium 233MMX:	$609
5. Cyrix 6x86MX 200:	$389		

To find companies who offer barebone systems, look in computer magazines. Here are a few companies who advertised in a recent *Computer Shopper:*

- American Micro Professionals at 800-857-3223
- Target USA at 888-311-4455
- Cyberspace Computers at 800-772-2305
- Micro Time at 800-834-0000

As with all ads, read them carefully to make sure what they include. I am looking at an ad that lists several components at a very good price, but they do not include a CPU.

The barebones systems usually do not include a floppy or hard disk, keyboard, mouse, and other essential things that you will need.

Upgrading to a New Computer

I hate to admit it, but there are some companies who advertise computer systems for less than I could build one. So it spoils my "Save A Bundle" title. Vendors who advertise low-cost machines do it by being able to purchase in high volume at good discounts. Some of these low-cost machines might not have all that you would like in a computer, but you can always add to them.

If you have bought a barebones system or a low-cost new machine, you might already have a modem, a floppy drive, a hard-disk drive, a CD-ROM, a printer, or any of several other components and boards that you would like to install in your new machine.

In most cases, you can just install them, plug them in, and let Windows recognize and install the software. In some cases, you have to go to the BIOS setup and tell it what you have installed. Most systems give you the opportunity to run the BIOS setup when you first turn on the computer. Usually, you have to press a key such as the Del, or a combination of keys, to have the setup displayed. You can then set the time and date, tell the system what type of floppy drives you have, and input the hard drive information. (This might not be necessary for some drives, since some of the more recent BIOS systems automatically recognize a hard drive's characteristics.)

You will be given several other options for setting up and configuring your system. You should have received some documentation that explains these options. If you are transferring a CD-ROM, the controlling software from your old disk should be copied onto your new hard disk. If not, you should have the original software that came with the drive so that you can install it.

If you are transferring a CD-ROM, floppy drive, or hard drives from an older machine to the new one, leave the cables connected to the drives. The other end of the cables will be connected to the motherboard. There will be sets of pins for the floppy drive and for the IDE drives. When plugging the connectors onto the upright pins, make sure that the colored-wire side goes to pin 1 on the motherboard. There is usually some marking on the motherboard.

Ordinarily, if the upright pins are side by side, pin 1 on the floppy connection and pin 1 on the IDE connection and printer connection will be in the same direction. For instance, in most cases, if pin 1 on any connector is toward the rear of the motherboard, pin 1 on all connectors will be toward the rear. Be very careful. It is very easy to plug the connectors in backwards. If you do so, you could possible damage the drive or the motherboard electronics. It is also possible to plug the connector in so that some of the pins are outside the connector. Figure 12-3 shows a 40-wire IDE connector being plugged into a set of upright pins.

Some of the newer motherboards have a shell around the upright pins. They have a cutout that is keyed so that the connectors can only be plugged in properly. Figure 12-4 shows a 34-wire floppy drive cable being connected to a set of pins that have a shell around them.

Minor Upgrades

Even if you just bought it yesterday, in many ways, your computer is obsolete. There is no way it could have all the things that could be installed in it. There are hundreds of ways that a computer can be configured and upgraded. Computers are made up of various components that just plug together. You can add hundreds of different boards, components, and peripherals to a computer. When we speak of upgrading, we usually think about hardware, but software upgrades are every bit as important. Some of the essential software upgrades are discussed in Chapter 16.

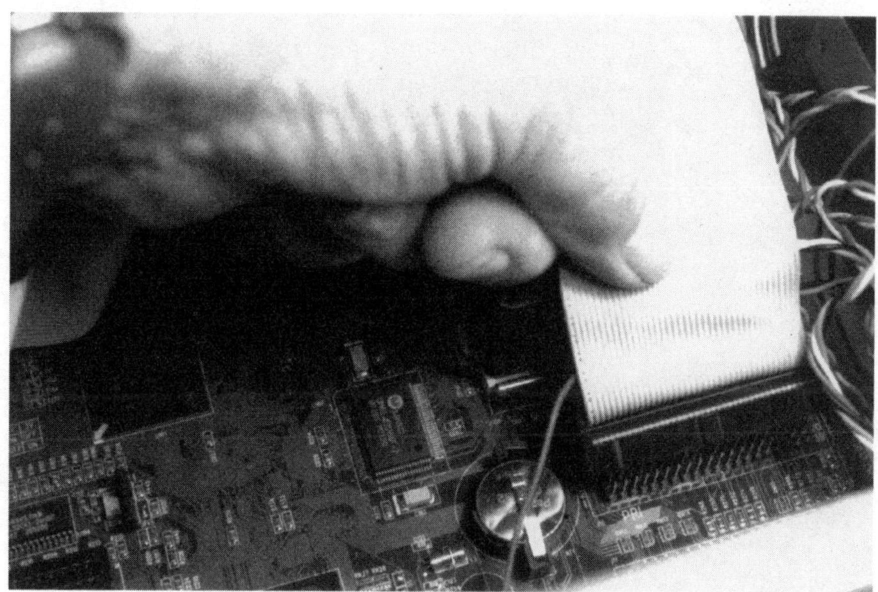

Figure 12-3
An IDE cable being connected to the motherboard interface pins. The cable can be plugged in backwards, or so that not all pins are connected. Be careful that the colored-wire side of the cable goes to pin 1 on the motherboard pins.

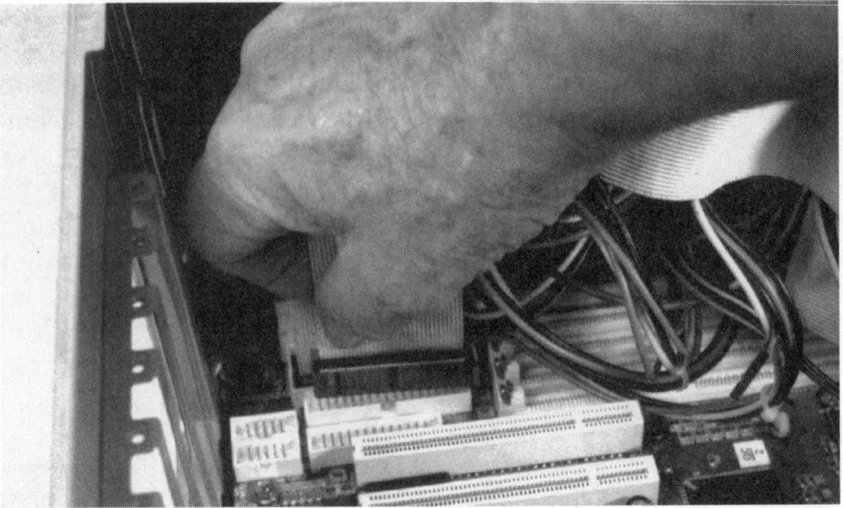

Figure 12-4
Connecting a 34-wire ribbon cable to a set of motherboard pins that have a shell around them. Many of the newer motherboards have these shells. The shell has a cutout that matches the cable connector, so that it can only be plugged in properly.

Memory Upgrade

When a program is being processed or operated on, it is loaded into Dynamic Random Access Memory (DRAM). Most programs today are very friendly, but the friendlier they are, the larger they are, so you will need a lot of DRAM.

One very useful feature of Windows 95 is that it lets you have two or more programs open and running at the same time. You can go from one to the other, swap files, compare and edit them, and much more. If they are large programs, you need lots of memory. Most programs today need at least 16 Mb of DRAM to run well, but the more you have, the better. At one time memory was rather expensive, but the prices have dropped considerably in the last few months and will probably be even less by the time you read this.

Adding memory is very easy to do. Just open your computer and plug in the new memory. Before you rush out to buy more memory, though, open your computer and check to see what kind you have installed. If you have a manual, it might tell you. You need to buy the same type of memory as you already have. If you have an older computer, it is possible that you have rather slow and outdated memory. In that case, it is perfectly okay to install faster memory. At one time, there was a large differential between the slower memory and the faster. Today, there is very little difference.

You might never need all the memory you have available, but it is nice to have. It is something like having a car with a 427-horsepower engine. You might not ever need all the power, but if you ever run large programs or have several programs in memory at the same time, it is sure nice to have it when you do need it.

Figure 12-5 shows SIMMs (Single Inline Memory Modules) being installed. It is very easy. Just lay them in the slot, and pull them forward until the latches on each end lock them in. There are cutouts on the SIMMs so that they can only be installed properly. Refer back to Chap. 4 for more about memory and installation instructions.

Upgrading the CPU

One of the best upgrades is to install a new motherboard and CPU. I hesitate to mention this, but you might not have to buy a new motherboard if your old one has the Pentium socket 7 for the CPU. (The different types of CPU sockets are discussed in Chap. 2. Also see Table 12-1.) You might be able to just install a new AMD K6, Cyrix 8x86MX, or an IDT Centaur C6 CPU. This would be a fairly inexpensive way to move up to a more powerful computer.

Before you rush out and buy a new CPU, however, make sure your motherboard can handle it. The newer CPUs operate at different frequencies and at different voltages. Newer motherboards have jumpers that can be used to configure them for almost any CPU. However, even some of

Figure 12-5
Installing SIMM memory chips. Lay them in on a slant, then pull forward until the latches on each end lock them in.

the late-model motherboards cannot handle the latest, high-frequency CPUs. I responded to an ad in one of the computer magazines and ordered a Tyan S1570 motherboard with an AMD 233-MHz CPU. I tried for some time to get it to work, but I had no luck. I wasn't sure whether it was the CPU or the motherboard. I called Tyan and they told me that the S1570, even though it was socket 7, it was not designed to operate at 233 MHz. They sent me a model S1571 and it worked perfectly.

It is very important that you match the right motherboard with the CPU. All this talk about sockets might be a bit confusing; Table 12-1 should help.

TABLE 12-1
CPU Sockets

CPU	Socket Number	Chipset
Intel 75 to 233 MHz	7	Intel 430TX
AMD, Cyrix, IDT	7	Intel 430TX
Pentium Pro	8	Intel 440LX
Pentium II	SEC 1	Intel 440LX

Replacing the Motherboard

Upgrading an older computer to a Pentium II is not much different than upgrading any other computer. It is even easier and much less expensive to upgrade to one of the CPUs that uses the motherboards with socket 7. The AMD K6, Cyrix 6x86MX, and IDT Centaur C6 all use socket-7 motherboards. Figure 12-6 shows a socket-7 motherboard with an AMD K6 233-MHz CPU beneath the fan and heatsink.

You can upgrade an old computer—a 486, 386, or even a 286—to a fast and powerful top-of-the-line socket-7 clone or a Pentium II. If you are upgrading to a socket-7 clone, you will still be able to use your old case, hard disks, floppy disk, keyboard, and other peripherals. If you upgrade to a Pentium II, you will have to buy a new case and power supply.

Until recently, the standard case has been about 6 inches wide. Because of the new fan and mounting arrangement of the CPU, however, Pentium II cases are now about 8$^1/_2$ inches wide. Figure 12-7 shows a Pentium II case on the left and a standard case on the right. The standard case is taller, but not as wide. It is possible to install a Pentium II motherboard in a standard case, but you need an ATX

Figure 12-6
A socket-7 type motherboard. Note that the power connector for the CPU fan has a pass-through so that another device can be connected.

power supply. Also, the fan would not be as close to the Pentium II CPU, so it would not receive the cooling that is possible with a Pentium II case.

You might have to buy a new keyboard and mouse or buy some adapters so that you can use the PS/2-type connectors. (Refer back to Chap. 2 and Fig. 2-5 for more about adapters.) Figure 12-8 shows standard and PS/2 keyboard cable connectors. The standard keyboard connector is much larger than the PS/2 type. You should be able to use almost all of your other boards and peripherals. Of course, you might want to buy more memory chips and perhaps a higher-capacity hard drive. Upgrading to one of these machines merely involves removing the old motherboard and CPU and installing new ones. All PCs are very similar in the way they are assembled. They are all very simple.

Pentium II Motherboard with a 300-MHz MMX CPU

If money is no object, then you should buy a Pentium II 300-MHz CPU and motherboard. With this motherboard and CPU, it should be some time before your system becomes obsolete. At the moment, there

Figure 12-7
A wide Pentium II case on the left, and a standard tower case on the right.

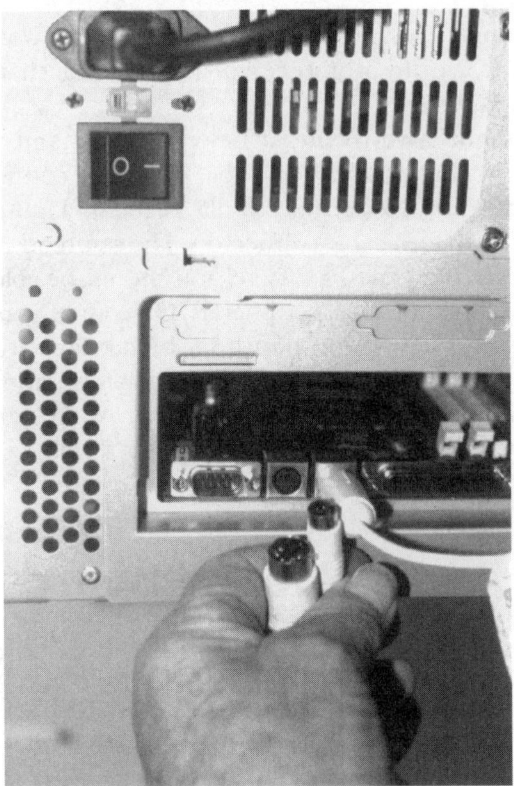

Figure 12-8
A standard keyboard connector and a smaller PS/2 type used on the Pentium II motherboard.

is little or no software that can take advantage of the speed and power. Software development always lags behind the hardware. Of course, this CPU and motherboard will be rather expensive. You can probably buy two 233-MHz AMD, Cyrix, or IDT Centaur CPUs and motherboards for what one Pentium II 300-MHz would cost.

The original Pentium was introduced in March 1993. It had 3.1 million transistors and operated at either 60 or 66 MHz. It was a fantastic advance at that time. The Pentium 75+ was introduced in March 1994. it had 3.3 million transistors and originally operated at 75 MHz, but was soon boosted to 100, 120, 150, and now 200 MHz. The Pentium Pro, with 5.5 million transistors, was introduced in September 1995. Originally, it operated at 150 MHz, but was soon boosted to 200 MHz.

Intel redesigned some of their 166-MHz and 200-MHz Pentiums and added a set of 57 multimedia extension (MMX) instructions to the chip. The MMX technology has given new life to the Pentium. It runs most normal software programs much faster. Programs whose graphics, video, and multimedia are written to take advantage of the MMX can be processed much faster.

The Pentium II is the next generation of the Pentium Pro. Intel added the 57 MMX instructions to the CPU. The fastest Pentium Pro runs at 200 MHz. The new Pentium II runs at 233 MHz, 266 MHz, and 300 MHz. Eventually, the Pentium II will run as high as 400 MHz. Soon after that, the AMD, Cyrix and IDT Centaurs will also be running at the same speed.

Back to Reality

Realistically, for most applications, the 233-MHz AMD, Cyrix, and IDT CPUs will do just about everything the Pentium II will do—and for a whole lot less money. If you are really strapped for money and don't mind waiting a few microseconds for a program to be processed, they are practically giving away the 166-MHz and 200-MHz CPUs. These CPUs will do just about everything you need, especially for home offices and small businesses.

Owning a Pentium II is almost like owning an expensive automobile that can go 150 miles an hour, but there is no place where you could drive that fast except on a racetrack. At this time, unless you have some high-end applications, you might be much better off buying an AMD, Cyrix, or IDT 200-MHz MMX CPUs and investing the money saved on peripherals and other goodies.

Another alternative would be the 200-MHz Pentium Pro. If you don't need to do a lot of multimedia, this CPU does just about anything that you need. In January of 1996, I paid $2500 for my first 200-MHz Pentium Pro motherboard and CPU. By January of 1998, you could get the same motherboard and CPU for less than $700. The Pentium Pro does not have the MMX instructions and must have a special motherboard with socket 8, while Intel's Pentium 200-MHz CPU with MMX instructions can be installed in the standard, socket-7 motherboards.

I am looking at an ad for the 200-MHz Pentium Pro CPU with a 256-Kb cache for $498. The same company is offering an Intel 200-MHz MMX CPU for $266. They offer an Intel 200-MHz without MMX for $218. A Cyrix 6x86MX 200-MHz is advertised for $139. I almost cry every time I look at an ad for the Pentium II 266-MHz CPU. In June of 1997, I paid $870 for one. Less than four months later, it was selling for $620. Sometimes, if you can get by with a CPU that is not quite as fast, you can save a lot of money. (The prices listed here are for comparison only. They will be less by the time you read this.)

Steps to Replace a Motherboard

There are just seven steps to replacing a motherboard. Before you begin, however, a word of caution is in order.

Caution

Before you handle any boards or chips, be sure to discharge yourself of any static electricity. You can build up an electric charge on your body of 3000 to 4000 volts. You might have experienced a shock after walking across a carpet and then touching a doorknob. Most of the transistors and semiconductors in your computer and peripherals are very fragile. You could fry them if you are not careful. To discharge yourself, just touch any metal object that has a power cord plugged into a wall outlet.

Step 1: Remove the Case Cover

To replace the motherboard, unplug the power cord and remove the case cover. The case probably has six to eight screws that hold it in place. The screws are usually in the back along the edge of the case cover.

If it is a tower case, you will probably see four screws near the top of the case. These screws are to hold the power supply in place. Do not remove them. If it is a desktop case, the power-supply screws are located in the right rear corner. Again, remove only the screws that hold the cover in place. On tower cases, the cover usually slides off to the back. On desktop cases, it probably slides off to the front.

Step 2: Make a Diagram

Once the cover is removed, make a drawing of where all the boards are plugged in and the cables that are connected to the boards. Once you have made your diagram, remove the boards and power cables that are plugged into the motherboard. Label and remove the several wires that go to the speaker and the front panel.

Step 3: Disconnect Cables and Remove Boards

Disconnect all of the cables and plug-in boards from the motherboard. If possible, leave the cables connected to the plug-in boards. For most of the cables, the other ends will be connected to your disk drives. There should be no reason to disconnect the drives or remove them. Just lay the cables and boards aside. See Fig. 12-9.

For the cables connected to the rear panel, use some tape or some sort of marking to identify them and where they were connected. You will probably only have four or five cables connected to the rear panel. In most cases, the connectors will all be different, so that there will no problem reconnecting them.

Step 4: Remove the Motherboard

There will probably be a single screw in the front of the motherboard and one in the rear, usually in the center. Once the two screws are removed, pull the motherboard toward you. It has plastic standoffs that fit in the slots of the case. When you pull the motherboard toward you, the slots are wide enough to allow you to lift the motherboard out. See figure 12-10.

Figure 12-11 shows the back of the motherboard with the slots and the white standoffs. When the screw is removed, the motherboard can be moved to the wide portion of the slots and lifted out.

Figure 12-9
Cables and boards disconnected from the motherboard while preparing to remove and replace the motherboard. Leave the cables connected to the plug-in boards and to the drives.

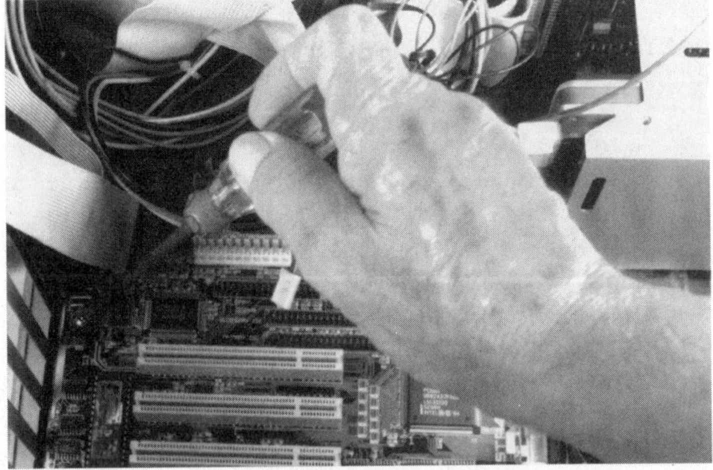

Figure 12-10
Removing one of the two screws that holds the motherboard in place.

Step 5: Configure the New Motherboard

Before installing the new motherboard, make sure that all of the jumpers and/or switches have been set properly for the CPU that you are going to use. It is very important that you get some kind of documentation with your motherboard. Most motherboards today can be configured to work with dozens of CPUs, but they usually have lots of jumpers that must be set. Without the documentation, it is almost impossible to configure a motherboard. Figure 12-12 shows a motherboard that has the jumper settings stamped on it.

You should install your memory now, since it might be a bit difficult to get to it after the motherboard is installed. Again, check your documentation. Your memory slots are banks. You must fill the lowest-numbered bank first. Memory is also usually installed in pairs.

Once the jumpers have been set, remove the plastic standoffs from your old motherboard and install them on your new one. You will need a pair of pliers to remove the plastic standoffs. They are flared so that when they are pushed through the hole in the motherboard, two sections flare out to hold them in place. If you do not have a pair of pliers handy, you can take a ballpoint pen, such as a Bic, and remove the pen. You can then press the plastic shell down over the flared standoff, and it will allow you to remove it easily. See Fig. 12-13.

Figure 12-11 The back side of the case showing the slots and white plastic standoffs. Once the two screws are removed, slide the motherboard to where the standoffs are in the wide portion of the slots. The motherboard can then be lifted out.

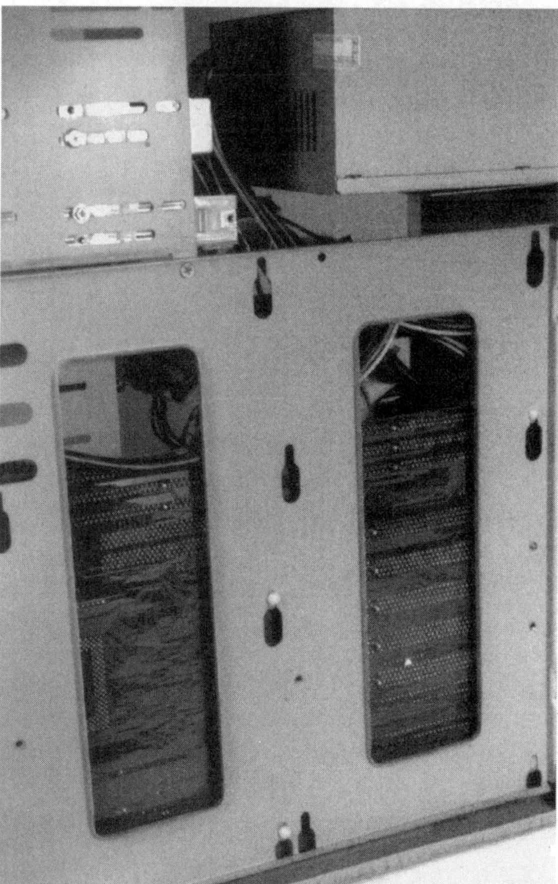

Figure 12-12 The configuration jumper settings are stamped on this motherboard—handy if you lose your documentation manual.

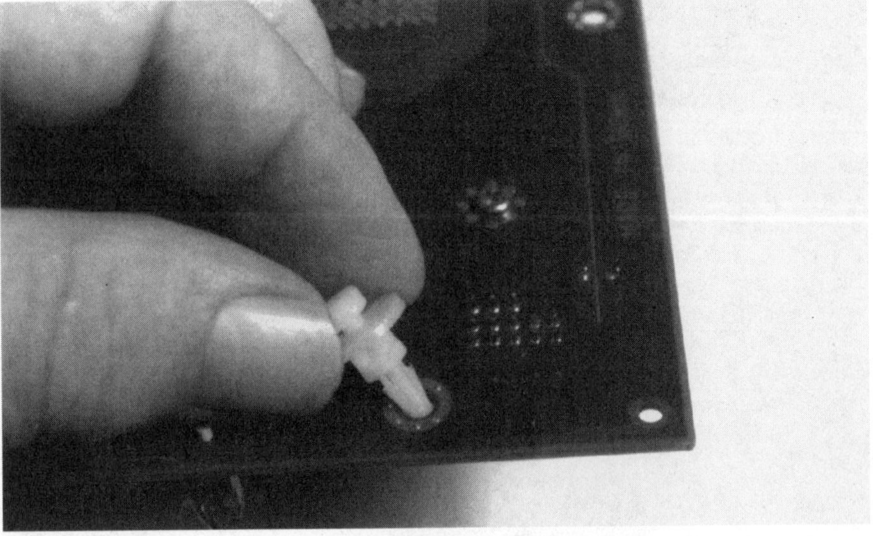

Figure 12-13 A close-up of a plastic standoff.

There will be several holes in the motherboard and in the case. Find the proper holes and install the standoffs. See Fig. 12-14.

Place the motherboard in the case so that the standoffs drop in the wide portion of the slots, then push it until it locks in. Place a screw in the rear center of the board and one in front.

Step 6: Reinstall Boards and Cables

Once the motherboard is in place, reinstall all the boards and cables. The first thing to connect is the motherboard power. If you have one of the old-style systems, your motherboard's power supply will be a set of two cables. They are usually marked P8 and P9. There are six wires in each connector. When plugged into the motherboard properly, the four black wires will be in the center. See Fig. 12-15. Some motherboards have both the ATX-type connector and the old style. If you have an ATX power supply, it can only be plugged in properly.

Next, you will have to plug the hard and floppy disk cables in the upright pins on the motherboard. Some motherboards have a shell around these pins so that the cable can only be plugged in properly. You will also have sets of upright pins for the printer and mouse cables. These short cables have a bracket on one end that mounts in the back panel for external connections. If your motherboard does not have the shell around the upright pins, you will have to make sure the cables are plugged in properly. There should be an indication on the motherboard as to which is pin 1. Your flat ribbon cables will have a different-colored wire on one side, either red, black, blue, or red stripes, that indicates pin 1. Make sure that the side with the different-colored stripe goes to pin 1.

You will also have wires for the small speaker and several wires for the front-panel LEDs. If you left the boards connected to the cables, it should be no problem reinstalling them. The ISA boards can be plugged into any ISA slot, and the PCI into any PCI slot.

Figure 12-14
The back of a motherboard, showing the plastic standoffs installed.

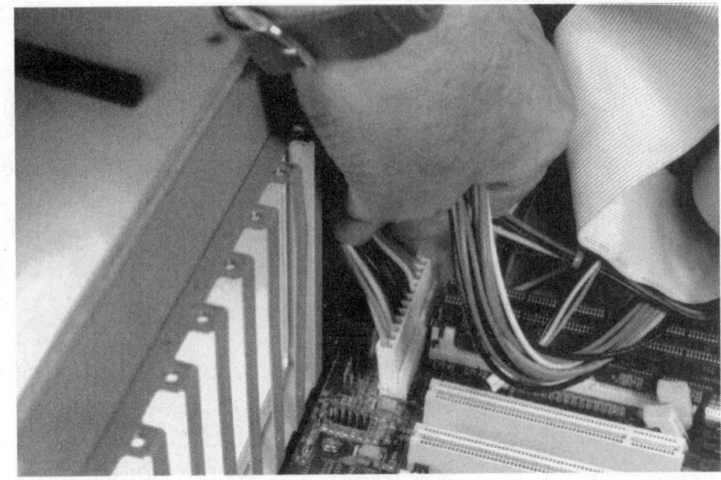

Figure 12-15
The power connection to the motherboard. It can be plugged in incorrectly, so make sure the four black wires are in the center.

After all the cables and boards are installed on the motherboard, connect all the cables to the back panel. You should have a power cord, a keyboard cable, a cable for the monitor, a printer cable, a mouse cable, a telephone line to the modem, and a wire for your speakers from the sound card. See Fig. 12-16.

Step 7: Turn on the Power and Test It Out

If everything was done properly, your system should boot up immediately. If it works okay, you can replace the cover. Then congratulate yourself for saving a bundle on your new computer.

There Is No End to Upgrade Possibilities

There are many other things you can do to improve and enhance the performance and capabilities of your computer. It is impossible to list them all. One reason is that new hardware and software is being developed and introduced every day. We could never have a complete list of all possible upgrades.

Figure 12-16
The back panel, showing all cables reattached. The power cord is at top, then the keyboard, then the printer and mouse, then the monitor, then the telephone line for the modem.

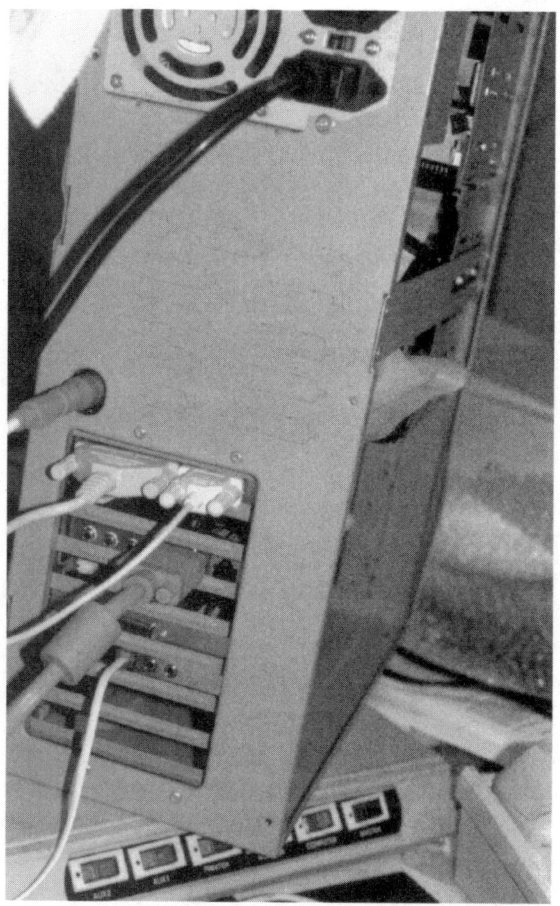

CHAPTER 13

Assembling Your Computer

This chapter is primarily about assembling a computer from scratch. It lists the recommended components and how to assemble them, as well as how to format and configure hard disks once they are installed.

Needed Components and Tools

You should have all of your components ready for installation. Here is a list of what you should have:

- Case and power supply
- Motherboard CPU and cooling fan
- Hard drive
- Floppy drive
- CD-ROM drive
- Monitor
- Monitor adapter
- Sound card
- Modem card
- Keyboard
- Mouse
- IDE cables
- Floppy drive cables
- CD-ROM Drive audio cable
- Windows 95 or Windows 98 software
- A bootup floppy disk

Before you start, gather all of your components and tools. You will need a Phillips and a flatblade screwdriver, and a pair of long-nose pliers. The long-nose pliers will be needed to place the small configuration jumpers over pins. If you don't have a pair of long-nose pliers, you can use a pair of tweezers.

Static Electricity Warning

Caution! Before touching any of the components, make sure that you discharge yourself of any static electricity. If you have ever walked across a carpeted room and got a shock when you touched a doorknob, then you know what static electricity is. It is possible for a person's body to build up 3000 volts or more of static electricity. If you touch any sensitive electronic components, that static electricity could be discharged through them. This static electricity could destroy or severely damage some of the fragile components.

When you touch a metal doorknob, you can discharge the static electricity. A much better discharge occurs if you touch something that goes directly to ground, such as a water pipe. Since you probably don't have a water pipe near your computer, the next best thing is to touch a bare metal part of your computer.

Most boards and components have a static-electricity warning label on the packaging. In most cases, you have to break that warning label in order to open the package. It is a good idea to discharge yourself by touching something that is metal and grounded before handling any electronic component or board, especially if you have walked across a carpeted room.

Assembly Steps

When I assemble a computer, I usually gather all of the components and assemble them on a benchtop or kitchen table. I then turn on the power and try it before I install it in the case. If there is any problem or trouble, it is fairly easy to find it while the component is still in the open. Note that the back of motherboards and other plug-in boards have sharp projections from the cut and soldered component leads. I usually lay a couple of newspapers on the table or benchtop to prevent scratching or marring the table or bench.

Detailed steps for assembly are listed below, but in a few words, here is a basic benchtop assembly:

1. Plug the power-supply cables into the motherboard. If you are using the old style power supply, make sure that the four black ground wires are in the center. If you are using an ATX type motherboard and power supply, there will be a socket and the cable connector can only be plugged in properly.
2. Connect the keyboard, floppy drives, hard-disk drives, and monitor.
3. Apply power, boot the computer up, and see if it works.

Quite often, I go through all the steps listed in the following sections, except that I do not install it in the case until I know that everything works right. It is much easier to find a mistake or something not connected right if it is out in the open. It will not hurt to run the system outside the case.

The Motherboard, Case, and Power Supply

The AMD K6, Cyrix 6x86MX, and IDT Centaur C6 are designed to use motherboards with the CPU socket 7. (To save a bit of typing, when I speak of the socket-7 type of CPUs, I will just call them socket-7 clones.) Intel Pentium MMX CPUs are also designed for motherboards with socket 7. The Intel Pentium Pro, however, is designed for a motherboard with socket 8.

The Pentium II is quite a bit different from other systems in several ways. One difference is that the power-supply fan is reversed. On the standard systems, the fan in the power supply draws air in from the grill in the front of the case and pulls it over the components, then exhausts it out the back to the system. The ATX power supply draws air in from the back of the computer and pushes it over the components and out of the front of the case. The newer cases have been redesigned so that the power-supply fan will be directly above the Pentium II CPU.

Until recently, all CPUs mounted in a socket. Now, the Pentium II CPU is mounted on a board and plugs into a slot on the motherboard. Intel calls it slot 1. The board and CPU assembly rises about 4 inches above the motherboard when plugged into slot 1. Because of the CPU assembly and the reversed fan in the power supply, you need to order a wider case for the Pentium II. The standard case is $6^3/_4$ inches wide. The Pentium II case that I bought is $8^5/_8$ inches wide. It is possible to mount a Pentium II motherboard in a standard case, but I would not recommend it. It would not get the cooling that it should have, and without proper cooling, the CPU might fail.

When I bought my 266-MHz Pentium II CPU, it cost $870 plus $27 for the special fan and 8.25% California state tax, for a total of $971. (They cost less now.) I could have bought a standard case for $40. A special case with the ATX power supply cost me $71. The extra $31 that the special case cost was worth every penny. I sleep better at night knowing that my $971 Pentium II CPU is not going to overheat tomorrow.

Configuring the Motherboard

If you bought your motherboard and CPU as a unit, the jumpers on the motherboard might already be set and configured for your CPU. You should still use your documentation and check to make sure. If you bought a socket-7 CPU separately, then you must use the motherboard manual that came with it and set all the jumpers for that particular CPU.

Dozens of different CPUs can be used with the motherboards. The jumper blocks are very small, so you will need the long-nose pliers or tweezers to install them. Figure 2-7 in Chap. 2 shows some jumpers. The small jumpers are used to configure the motherboard for CPU voltage, frequency, bus speed, memory type and voltage, as well as several other functions.

Be very careful when setting the jumpers. For instance, most motherboards offer an option of several different CPU core voltages. The Tyan S1571S offers settings for 16 different voltages from 2.0 to 3.5 in steps of 0.1 volts. If the voltage is set too high, it might burn up the CPU.

Installing the CPU

It is very easy to lift the ZIF (Zero Insertion Force) lever and drop the CPU in the socket. You will notice that there might be a dot on one corner of the CPU, and the corner will be cut at an angle. This indicates pin 1. Be very careful—the pins are very fragile. The CPU will not drop in unless the pins are lined up properly. Once the CPU drops in, pull the lever down and then install the fan on top of the CPU. The fan usually has a clip that fits over the projections on the socket. Figure 3-4 in Chapter 3 shows a fan and heatsink assembly.

If you are installing a Pentium II, you must first install a *cradle*, or *retainer*, on the motherboard to hold the CPU assembly. See Fig. 13-1. Since it rises so high above the motherboard, the motherboard is usually shipped with the cradle uninstalled. It is installed over the slot-1 connector. Four screws hold it in place. The Pentium II, heatsink, and fan are also separate items, as shown in Fig. 13-2. There are clips on the heatsink that are inserted into square holes on the CPU assembly. See Fig. 13-3.

Once the heatsink and fan are assembled to the CPU, the Pentium II CPU assembly is inserted into slot 1 and locked, as shown in Fig. 13-4.

Figure 13-1
The Pentium II CPU retainer or cradle. You will have to install it with four screws.

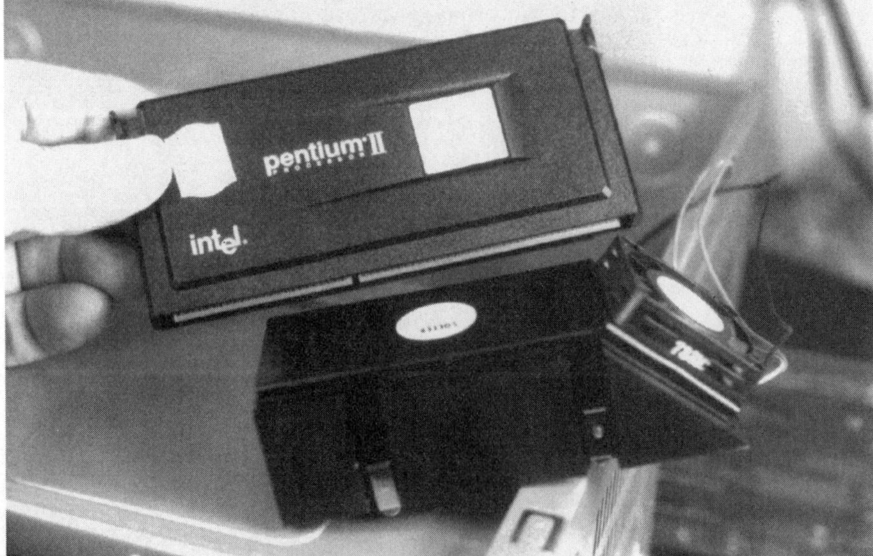

Figure 13-2
The Pentium II CPU, heatsink, and fan assembly.

Memory Installation

You should next install the memory chips. The memory slots might not be plainly labeled. Use your motherboard documentation to determine which slots to fill.

Memory is very easy to install. The slots are designed so that it can only be installed correctly. For SIMMs, just lay the assembly slantwise in the slot and pull it toward you until the retainers on each end snap. Once the motherboard is installed, the memory slots are often in an area that is difficult to get to, so it is usually much better to install memory on the motherboard before installing the motherboard.

Figure 13-5 shows a 32-Mb DIMM assembly being installed. DIMMs are installed a bit differently from SIMMs. SIMMs are laid in the socket on a slant, then pulled up until they are latched in place. DIMMs are pressed straight down until the holders on each end can be closed. Make sure the memory is seated properly. If it is not properly seated,

Figure 13-3
Clips are used to attach the heatsink and fan assembly to the CPU.

Figure 13-4
The Pentium II motherboard with the CPU assembly installed. The retainer has latches that lock the CPU assembly in place.

Figure 13-5 Installing a 32-Mb DIMM. The module is seated in the slot, then latches are used to lock it in place.

the computer will not boot up. Usually, when something is wrong, you will get an error beep. If the memory is not seated properly or is defective, you might get no error beep or message at all.

Motherboard Standoffs

When you buy a case, you will get a plastic bag with screws and standoffs that will be needed. The old XT used brass standoffs to mount the motherboard in the case. Beginning with the 286, however, most motherboards use white plastic standoffs. Most of them also use one or two brass standoffs to make sure the motherboard makes good ground contact with the case.

Check the plastic bag to make sure all of the standoffs, screws, and other hardware that you will need are there. Your motherboard will have several holes for the plastic standoffs. There will be several slots in the case for the standoffs. You might not need to use all the holes. You should lay the motherboard in the case and see which holes line up with the slots. Three standoffs along each side of the motherboard, and one in the center, should be all that is needed. Use the brass standoff in the front center and one in the back center to ground and secure the motherboard. For mounting a socket-7 clone motherboard in a case with the white standoffs, refer back to Chapter 12.

The case that I bought for my Pentium II did not have the slots for the standoffs. It had a bag of hardware with a few plastic standoffs, but it also had several brass standoffs. Since it had no slots, I had to use the brass standoffs. Brass standoffs are a bit more substantial, but they do require a bit more time to install, and they are not really necessary. The plastic standoff system is much easier to install. Figure 13-6 shows the brass standoffs.

Installing the Drives

Here is a copy of an e-mail that I received:

> Dear Mr. Pilgrim,
>
> I intend to build a computer and have purchased your book. There's just one thing I need to know. I am building a midi tower so do I just turn everything sideways or is it more complicated than that?

At first I thought the letter was a bit humorous. But then I realized that there are a whole lot of things that I take for granted that a person who is new to computers would not know.

I am sure that the writer was mostly concerned about the disk drives, which can be mounted on the side. You could even mount them upside-down, but this is not recommended. For some hard drives, it might be difficult to determine which is the right side up. The top usually has a cover over it. The bottom might have some exposed electronic components. Figure 13-7 shows a CD-ROM, a floppy drive, and a hard drive from the rear.

Figure 13-6
Except for a single plastic standoff, the Pentium II motherboard uses brass standoffs.

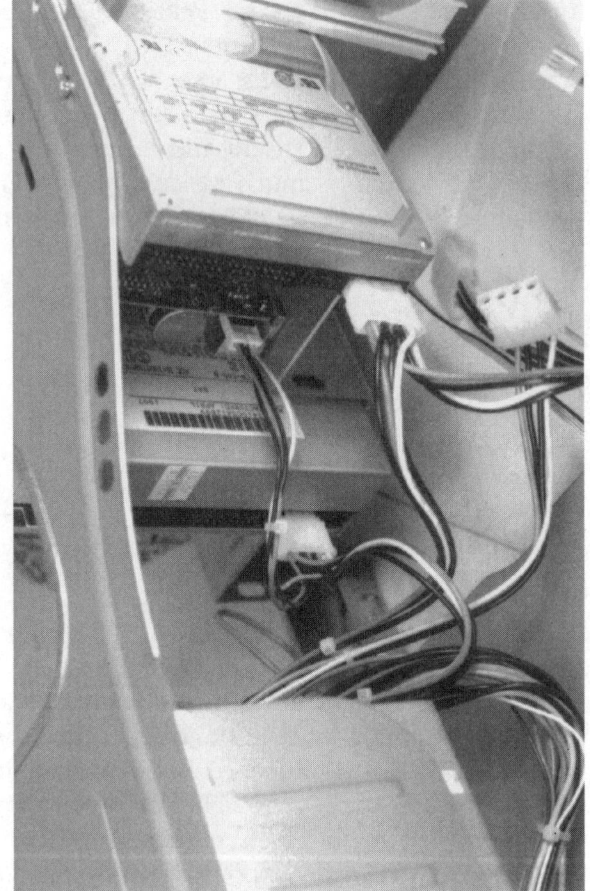

Figure 13-7 The rear of the drives installed in the Pentium II. On top is a hard drive, then a $3^1/_2$-inch floppy drive and a CD-ROM drive. The power cables have been connected. When mounted right-side-up, the power cables will be on the right side, looking at the drives from the rear.

Most drives, when mounted properly, have a large four-pin power connector on the right side. When I started installing the drives in my Pentium II case, I noticed that there was no way to access the screw holes on the right side. They were completely blocked by the large metal panel that held the motherboard. I was quite unhappy, until I noticed that the large metal panel was designed so that it could be moved. If I pulled up on the back panel, I could slide the motherboard out so that I could easily add components or work on it. This is an excellent idea. The case had no instructions or manual of any kind to tell me about this feature. I only discovered it by accident. Figure 13-8 shows the case with the panel slid out, offering plenty of room to work on or add to the motherboard, as well as easy access for installing drives.

Before the drives are installed, they must be configured. If you are only installing a single IDE drive, the installation might be very simple.

The drive should have jumpers set at the factory that makes it drive 1 or the master drive. Figure 13-9 shows the top of a Western Digital 2.5-Gb hard disk, showing all the jumper information you need to configure the disk. It also lists the drive parameters in smaller letters at the top. It has 4960 cylinders, 16 heads, and 63 spt (sectors per track), and is 2559.8 Mb.

Check your documentation and the jumpers, then just plug the 40-pin cable into the drive connector and the other end into a set of pins on the motherboard. The drive connectors have a shell around the connector with a cutout so that they can only be plugged in properly. If there is no shell around the pins, make sure that the colored-wire side of the ribbon cable goes to pin 1. It should be connected to the motherboard set of pins marked Primary. See Fig. 13-10.

If you are installing a second IDE drive, you need to set some jumpers so that the system will know which drive to access. When two IDE drives are installed, the IDE system uses the term *master* to designate the C: or boot drive and *slave* to designate the second drive. The drives usually come from the factory configured with the jumpers as a single or master drive. In Fig. 13-11, the jumper pins can be seen to the right of the connector. If the drives are not configured properly, you will get an error message that might tell you that you have a hard disk or controller failure. You will not be able to access the drives.

There will be a second set of upright pins on the motherboard for IDE drives, which will be marked *Secondary*. If you install more than two

Figure 13-8 On this Pentium II case, the panel that holds the motherboard slides out to provide access to the bays for installing drives. It also provides access to the motherboard.

Figure 13-9
The top of a Western Digital hard drive. It provides all the information needed to configure and install the drive.

IDE drives, they will be installed on the secondary pins. Again, one of the two drives should be configured as the master and the other as the slave. To recap, you can have a master and a slave on the primary set of pins, and a secondary master and slave on the second set of pins.

If you are installing an SCSI hard drive or SCSI CD-ROM drive, you will have to set some jumpers to assign a Logical Unit Number (LUN) to each device. This also should be done before installing the drives. The cables for the SCSI drives usually have a keyed shell around the connector so that they can only be connected properly. Not many motherboards have the SCSI interface built in, so you will probably have a plug-in board for the SCSI host interface. The hard-disk cable will be connected to it. The cable may have one or more connectors in the middle for other SCSI devices. The interface board will also probably have an external connector on the back panel for external SCSI devices, such as a scanner.

The CD-ROM drives have a small audio cable that is usually difficult to get to once it is installed. It is best to connect it before the drive is installed. Figure 13-12 shows an audio cable from the CD-ROM to the sound board.

Bench Test

I usually hook everything up on the bench and try it out before I install it in the case. Figure 13-13 shows a benchtop test. If I have made

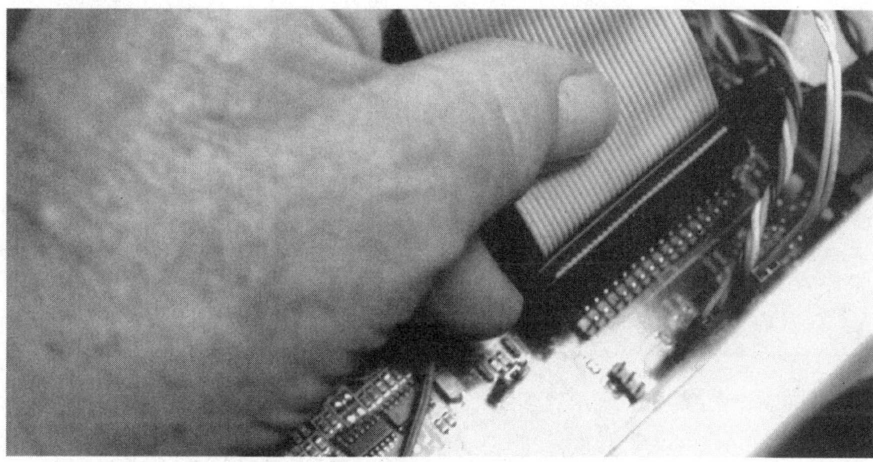

Figure 13-10
Connecting an IDE cable to the motherboard's interface pins. Make sure that the colored-wire side goes to pin 1. Also make sure the connector is seated properly, and that it fits over all the pins.

Figure 13-11
Connecting a 40-wire ribbon cable to an IDE hard drive. The cutout on the shell around the drive connector ensures that it can only be plugged in properly. Note the white jumper and pins at the right of the connector. The jumper configures the drive as a master or slave.

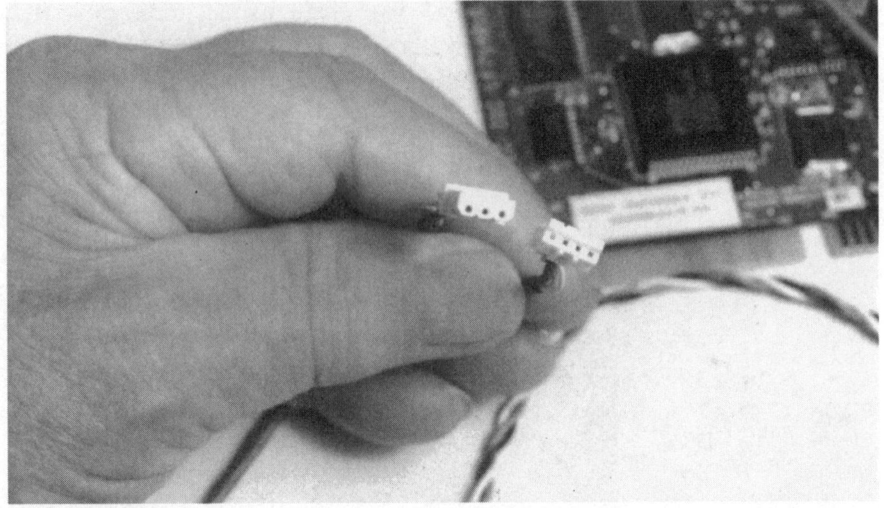

Figure 13-12
An audio cable from the CD-ROM drive to the sound card.

Figure 13-13
All components connected on the bench, ready for a test.

an error or did not connect something, it is much easier to find on the benchtop. Once I am sure a component works, I install it in the case.

Install in Case

I usually leave the cables connected to the drives when I install them in the bays. There is not much room between some of the drives and the power supply, as shown in Fig. 13-14. The power supply is the rectangular box in the top left corner. The four-wire power cables for the drives are usually accessible. They can only be plugged in properly. The power cable for the small fan that is mounted on the CPU also needs to be connected to a power cable. Some motherboards have a small connector near the CPU for the fan. You might not have enough of four-wire connectors for the drives, so most fans have a short cable with a Y so that it does not utilize one of the power cables.

Most cases are like that shown in Fig. 13-14. You can see by the slots that there are bays that will accept five or more $3^1/_2$-inch drives. In the top section, there is room for three or four more bays for $5^1/_4$-inch drives, such as CD-ROMs or old floppy disks.

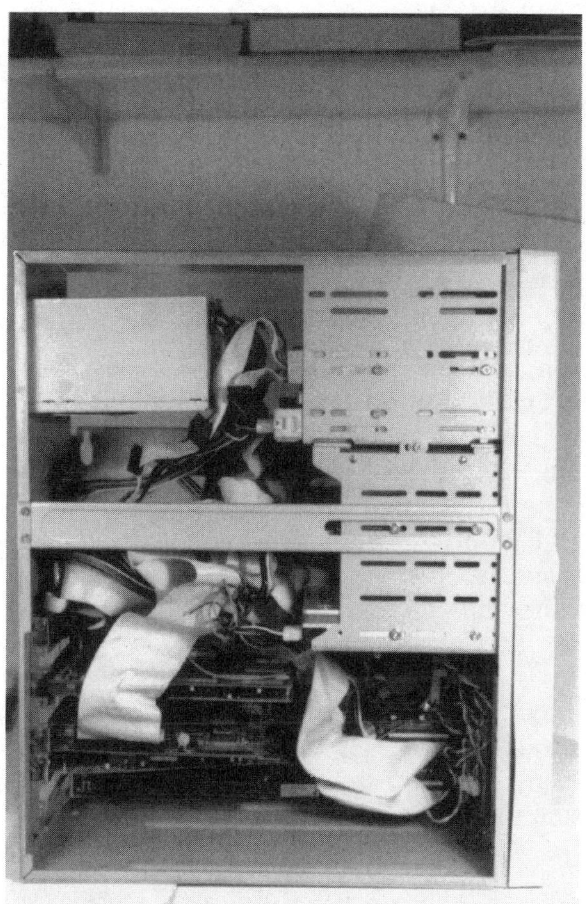

Figure 13-14 It is best to connect the cables to the drives before installing them in bays. There is not much room between the power supply on the top left and the drives, once installed.

Most computer cases have two or three $3^1/_2$-inch bays that are accessible from the front for floppy disk drives. Of course, for the hard drives you don't need front-panel access. In the upper part of the case, the $5^1/_4$-inch bays are accessible from the front for CD-ROM drives or old floppy disk drives. The screw holes in almost any drive can match up with the slots. You should use two screws on each side of the drive.

Be careful not to overtighten the screws. The frames of most drives are made from soft-cast aluminum, and will strip out very easily. Also, be very careful not to use screws that are too long. If too long, they might protrude into the electronics on the drive.

Install Plug-in Boards

Once all the cables are connected, install the plug-in boards. I have an SCSI board for one of my hard drives. I also have an adapter board for the monitor, a sound board, and a modem/fax board.

Installing Brackets and Cables for External Connections

There will be sets of upright pins for COM1, COM2, the printer, a PS/2 mouse, and USB. You will probably get short cables attached to a bracket that mounts on the rear panel for these devices. Figure 13-15 shows cables and bracket for a standard mouse and printer.

At present, there is no standardization for the connection of the PS/2 mouse. On some socket-7 motherboards, there might be a set of five upright pins, arranged with three pins on one side and two on the other. Figure 13-16 is a PS/2 mouse connector that plugs into a set of five pins. Another motherboard that I have has a set of four pins in one line. Still other motherboards use the small, round, DIN-type connector. This type connector is also used for the keyboard. Some motherboards have two of these connectors side by side, or one on top of the other. Figure 2-6 shows my Pentium II motherboard with the two PS/2 connectors side by side. Either connector can be used for the PS/2 mouse or the keyboard.

Most Pentium II motherboards use a PS/2-type small connector for the keyboard and mouse. Many of the new keyboards have this small connector. Sometimes, the keyboard will have the old style and a PS/2 adapter so that it can be used on either system. If you are buying a new

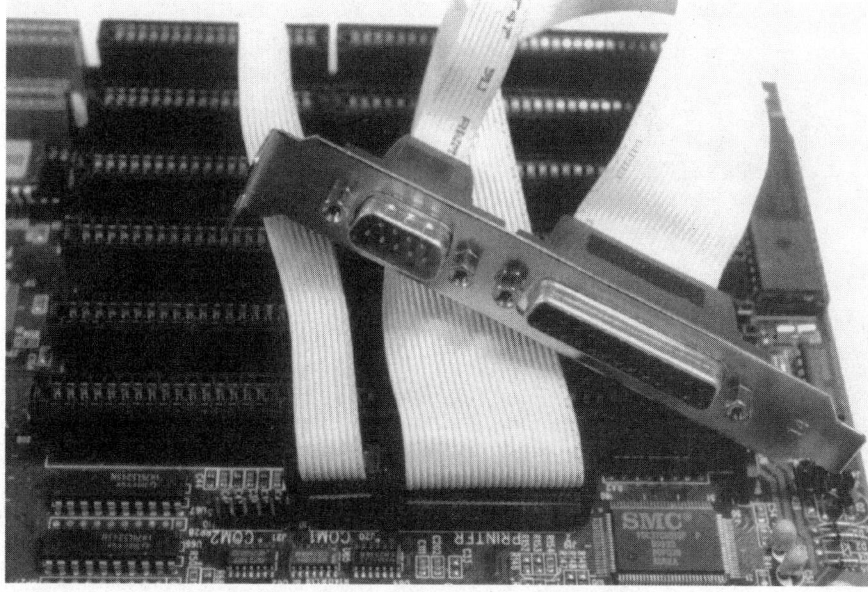

Figure 13-15
A bracket and short cables with a standard mouse and printer connectors for external connections. Again, when connecting to the motherboard, make sure the colored-wire side of cable goes to pin 1.

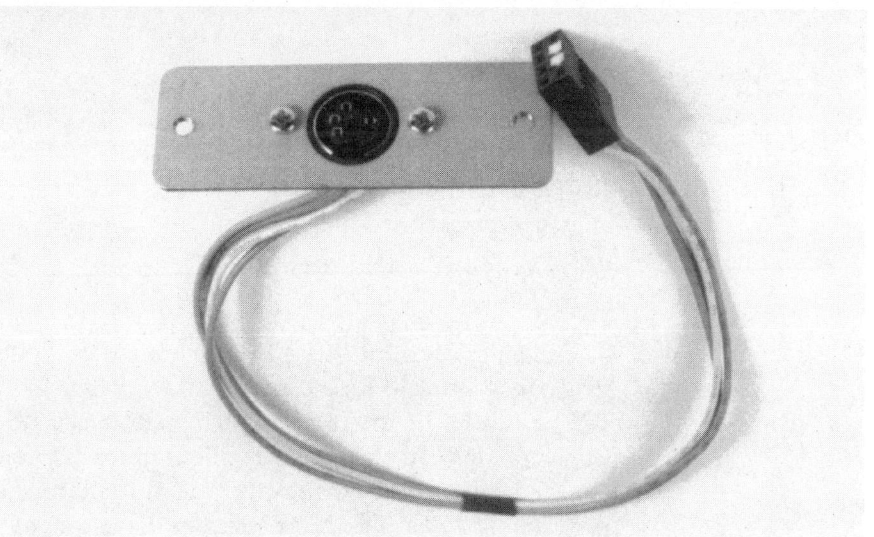

Figure 13-16
A PS/2 mouse connector, cable, and bracket for an external connection. Not all motherboards have the same connector. This one has a five-pin connector arranged in three and two pins. The white dot on the connector keys it so that it can only be plugged in properly. Some motherboards have five pins in line.

keyboard, make sure that it has the PS/2 connector. If you already have a standard keyboard and mouse that you want to use, it is possible to buy PS/2 adapters. If you want to use your standard mouse, it can be connected to COM1 or COM2. The only benefit of the PS/2 mouse is that it does not use one of the COM ports, but it does require the use of one of the precious IRQs.

Here is a chart showing the difference in the wiring in the standard keyboard and mouse connector pins and the PS/2 connector pins:

Signal	Standard Pin	PS/2 Pin
Clock	1	5
Data	2	1
Ground	4	3
+5 VDC	5	4
Not used	3	2 and 6

As you can see, there is a difference in the pin assignments for the two systems. An adapter will have the wires crossed and wired so that the proper signal will be present on the proper pin. The adapters are available from most major computer stores or from several of the companies who specialize in cables and connectors. The adapters cost from about $3 to $5 each.

Here are some companies who carry the adapters:

Cables to Go
800-506-9605
www.cablestogo.com

ABL Electronics
800-726-0610
sales@ablcables.com

QVS Computer Connectivity
800-622-9606

There are several other similar companies. Look for ads in computer magazines, and call for a catalog.

The motherboard might also have a socket for the Universal Serial Bus. This bus can theoretically allow up to 128 components to be daisy-chained and attached. At present, not many USB components and peripherals are available, but there will be lots of them in a very short time. The USB has many advantages over the SCSI bus. The cable companies listed above also carry cables and connectors for the USB system.

Connecting Wires for the Front-Panel LEDs

A good feature of the Pentium II case that I bought is that the wires going to the front-panel LEDs are in a ribbon cable. The connectors and the motherboard are all clearly marked, as shown in Fig. 13-17. Most earlier cases had twisted pairs of wires with connectors that were not well marked. Quite often, I never bothered to connect the wires to the motherboard. It was just too much trouble trying to trace the twisted wires back to the various LEDs and switches.

Turn on the Power and Boot up

Make one last check to see that all the cables are connected properly, then turn on the power and boot up. If everything was connected properly, the system should boot up. You will need a floppy disk that can boot up your system. If you are using Windows 95, you will have a $3^1/_2$-inch floppy boot disk. Once you have booted up, it will lead you into installing the CD-ROM drive so that the Windows program can be copied onto the hard disk. (Before installing Windows, the hard disk must be partitioned and formatted, as explained later.)

I often try out new boards and parts. Quite often, I will install something, than reassemble everything and put the cover back on, only to find that it doesn't work. Sometimes, it is because I did not check my cables or didn't do something that I should have. So, if I have installed something new, I usually try it out first to make sure it works before I replace the

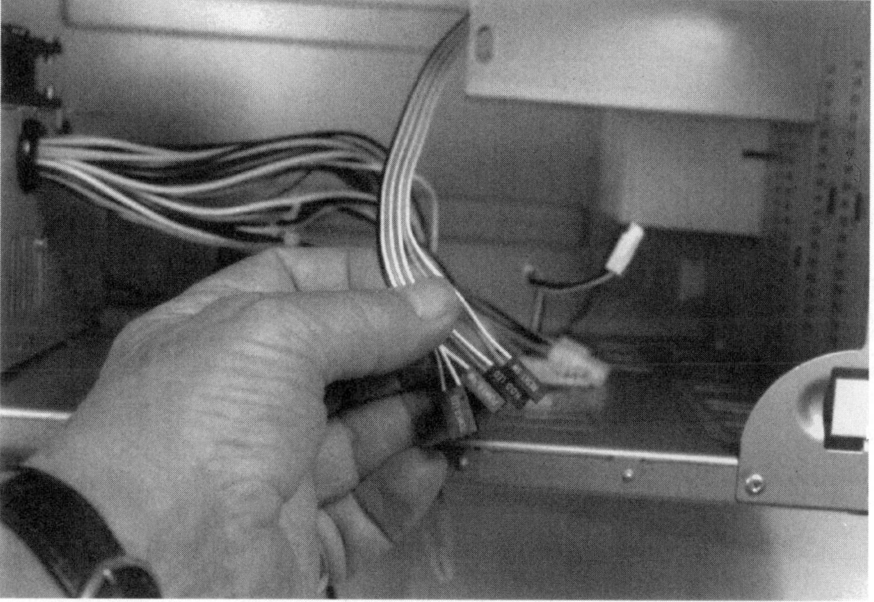

Figure 13-17 The wires for the front-panel LEDs on my Pentium II. The wires are in a ribbon cable and are very easy to install.

cover. Often, I just leave the covers off my computers. Other than the messy look, it doesn't cause any problem. Actually, besides saving me time and trouble, leaving the covers off allows the system to run cooler.

Software Installation and Formatting

You can't do anything with your hard drives until they have been formatted. Windows 95 comes on a CD-ROM that can hold up to 660 Mb of data. It has several Help files, including a brief message about formatting floppy disks, but you won't find any help for formatting a hard disk. I don't understand why Microsoft neglected this very important aspect of computing. I suppose they expect you to buy your system with the hard disks already installed and formatted. But what if you wanted to add a second hard disk? You just have to buy a book like this one.

Once the drives are installed and connected, you can turn on the power, boot up the computer, and enter the drive type into your CMOS setup table. Boot up the computer from your floppy A: disk drive. Besides the system files for booting up, the floppy should have the Fdisk and Format commands on it.

Setup Routine

Once you have assembled your computer, you need to format and load your software on your hard disk (or disks). If you don't have a copy of Windows 95, you should buy one. The CD-ROM comes with a boot floppy disk that lets you start your system and format the hard disks. The floppy disk has Command.com, Fdisk, Format, Sys, Config.sys, Autoexec.bat, MSCDEX, and Chkdsk.

The first thing you need to do is use the Fdisk utility on the hard disk. This allows you to partition it into one or more logical drives. Your first drive should be your primary DOS system drive, or drive C:. You can only have one active primary drive in the system, so all other logical drives will be extended DOS drives.

When you install a hard disk, your BIOS must be told what type it is. The BIOS in your Pentium II, Cyrix 6x86 MMX, or AMD K6 will be able to automatically recognize your hard drive if it has been manufactured to the PNP specifications.

If you are installing a new drive, you must use the Fdisk utility to partition and format the drive before you do anything else. The format procedure is explained later in this chapter.

The BIOS also must know the number and type of floppies you have, the time, and date, the type of monitor, and other information. The setup routine asks several questions, then configures the BIOS according to your answers. This part of the BIOS configuration is in low-power CMOS semiconductors and is on all the time. Even when the computer is turned off, a small battery on the motherboard supplies power for the CMOS semiconductors.

The setup usually only allows you to enter two drives, C: and D:. I have two large IDE drives on one of my computers. One is partitioned into C:, D:, and E: drives. The second one is partitioned into F:, G:, and H: drives. My D: drive partition, then, is actually part of my C: drive. Just enter the information for your first drive, the C: drive, then enter the information under the D: drive for your second drive. The CMOS setup would be less confusing if it asked for information about hard drive number 1, then number 2, instead of C and D.

Booting from a Floppy

Caution! Never boot up with a floppy disk with a different version of DOS than the one used to format the hard disk. There is a short boot record on the hard disk. If a different version is used to boot up, you might lose all of your data on the disk.

Entering Drive Data into CMOS

If you have Windows 95 and a Plug-and-Play BIOS, it will automatically recognize the hard disk. To enter the drive, type information into the CMOS setup, turn on your system, and press the necessary key or keys to enter the setup.

Vendors use different keys to access the setup. The AMI setup is accessed during the bootup by pressing the Delete key. Some systems require you to press the ESC and Delete keys or some other combination during bootup. Your motherboard documentation should tell you which keys to press. If you don't have your documentation, you might be able to access the setup by holding down one of the keys on the keyboard during bootup. The system will beep at you and say that you have a keyboard error. It will then usually give you the option of pressing F1 to enter the setup. Once you access the setup, enter the type data for your drive.

The Purpose of Formatting

Formatting organizes the disk so that data can be stored and accessed easily and quickly. If the data was not organized, it would be very difficult to find an item on a large hard disk. I have about 3000 files on my two hard disks. Those files are on tracks and sectors that are numbered. A File Allocation Table (FAT) is set up to record the location of each track and sector on the disk.

Disk organization is similar to developing a piece of land. The developer lays out the streets and creates blocks, then partitions each block into lots and builds a house on each lot. Each house would have a unique address. A map of these streets and house addresses would be filed with the city. A track would be analogous to a street, and a sector number would be similar to a house number. The FAT is similar to an index in a street atlas or a book. When a request is sent to the heads to read or write to a file, it goes to the FAT, looks for the location of that file, and goes directly to it. The heads can find any file, or parts of any file, quickly and easily.

Formatting is not something that is done every day, and can be rather difficult in some cases. One reason the disks do not come from the manufacturer preformatted is that there are so many options. If you have a 2.5-Gb hard disk, you will probably want to divide or partition it into two or three different logical disks. For the old MFM-type drives, one reason manufacturers did not preformat the drive is that there were so many different controller cards. The controller cards were usually designed so that they would operate with several different Fdisk options. *Fdisk* means fixed disk or format disk. It is a DOS command on the boot disk that comes with your system when you buy a copy of Windows. You will not be able to use a hard disk until it has been partitioned with Fdisk, then high-level formatted.

DOS uses all of the alphabet letters for disk drives. It reserves A: and B: for floppy drives, and C: for the boot drive. If you have a very large disk, then, you can make up to 23 other logical partitions on drives D: through Z:.

Using Fdisk can be a bit confusing. Windows 95 comes on a CD-ROM that has a lot of help, but the Fdisk help is not much help. If Microsoft's manuals were well written, you would not need to buy an extra book to learn how to use the software. If I were a suspicious or distrustful person, I might think that the Microsoft manuals are deliberately poorly written so that you have to buy some Microsoft Press books on the software.

The older MFM, RLL, and ESDI hard disks had to have a low-level and a high-level format. Newer drives have the low-level format done at the factory. Many of the newer BIOS systems have a utility for doing a low-level format, but do not use it on an IDE or SCSI drive that has already been low-level formatted. If the low-level format has been done, you can do the high-level format. Boot up from your floppy disk drive with a copy of DOS and type

```
DIR C:. If the message "Invalid drive specification" comes up, put
a copy of DOS that has the Fdisk command on it in drive A:.
If you are using MS-DOS version 6.2 or later when you type Fdisk,
this message will be displayed:

FDISK Options
Current Fixed Disk Drive: 1
Choose one of the following:
1. Create DOS partition or Logical DOS Drive
2. Set active partition
3. Delete partition or Logical DOS Drive
4. Display partition information
5. Change current fixed disk drive (Option 5 is only displayed if
you have more than one drive).
Enter choice: [1]
Press ESC to exit FDISK
```

If you choose 1, and the disk has not been prepared, a screen like this comes up:

```
Create DOS Partition or Logical DOS Drive
Current Fixed Drive: 1
Choose one of the following:
1. Create Primary DOS partition
2. Create Extended DOS partition
3. Create logical DOS drive(s) in the Extended DOS partition
Enter choice: [1]
Press ESC to return to FDISK Options
```

If you want to boot from your hard drive (I can't think of any reason why you would not want to), then you must choose 1 to create a primary DOS partition and make it active. If you choose 1, a prompt will come up and ask

```
Do you wish to use the maximum size for a Primary DOS
partition and make the partition active (Y/N....?[Y})
```

If you type Y for yes, the entire drive will be made into one large C: drive. If you answer no, DOS will display the maximum disk size and ask what percentage or number of megabytes to assign as the primary drive. You can type in 50% or any number of megabytes. You can make the whole drive a single partition, but it is better to have two or more partitions.

After you create the primary partition, press the Esc key, and this screen will be displayed again:

```
Create DOS partition or Logical DOS Drive
Current Fixed Drive: 1
Choose one of the following:
1. Create Primary DOS partition
2. Create Extended DOS partition
3. Create logical DOS drive(s) in the Extended DOS partition
Enter choice: [2]
Press ESC to return to FDISK Options
```

Since you have already created the primary partition, choose option 2 to create an extended DOS partition. You will see the amount of space that is left over from the primary drive assignment. You cannot partition the drive at this point. Accept the figure given. If you try to partition the drive at this point, whatever you choose will be all that you can use. For instance, with option number 2, if you have 1500 Mb left and you try to divide it into two 750-Mb partitions, DOS will figure that the entire extended drive is to be only 750 Mb. You will not be able to use the other 750 Mb. You must tell it to use the 1500 Mb that is available. Then, press the Esc key to return to the options and choose option number 3, "Create Logical DOS Drives in the Extended DOS partition." You can now divide this partition into as many drives as you want.

DOS will tell you how much space is available for the extended partition. The default is the maximum amount of space shown. If you want to accept it and have a single primary drive and a single extended drive, just press Enter. Otherwise, type the number of megabytes or the percentage desired. If you type a percentage, follow with the percentage symbol, such as 25%. Continue creating logical drives until the entire disk is assigned.

You can press the Esc key to delete or revise any of the partitions that you have created.

Installing a Second Hard Disk

If you are installing a second hard disk, you will see this display:

```
FDISK Options
Current Fixed Disk Drive: 1
1. Create DOS partition or Logical DOS Drive
2. Set active partition
3. Delete partition or Logical DOS Drive
4. Display partition information
5. Change current fixed disk drive (Option 5 is only displayed if
you have more than one drive).
Enter choice: [5]
Press ESC to exit FDISK
```

Choose option 5 to change drives. The primary partition is only on the C: drive, and it contains the boot utility. Use the options to create more logical drives just as you did on the first drive.

High-Level Format

After the Fdisk options have been completed, return to drive A: and perform a high-level format on drive C:. Because you want to boot off of this drive, you must also transfer the system and hidden files to the disk as it is being formatted, so you must use the /S switch to transfer the files. Type

```
FORMAT C: /S. DOS will display the following message:
WARNING! ALL DATA ON NON-REMOVABLE DISK DRIVE C: WILL BE LOST!
Proceed with Format (Y/N)
```

If you press Y, the disk light should come on, and you might hear the drive stepping through each track. After a few minutes, DOS will display the following:

```
Format complete
System transferred
Volume label (11 characters, ENTER for none)?
```

You can give each partition a unique name, or volume label, if you wish to. You can test your drive by doing a warm boot, which means pressing the Ctrl, Alt, and Del keys at the same time. The computer should reboot.

Now that drive C: is completed, if you have other partitions or a second disk, format each of them.

DriveCopy

You might have just bought a new hard drive to add to your system. One reason you might have bought it is because your C: drive is bursting at the seams. It seems that every program wants to be loaded on C:. A hundred megabytes can be used up in a hurry.

It would be nice to be able to just copy all of the files from drive C: onto a new much larger drive, but Windows 95 has all kinds of hidden files that must be copied along with the parent files. Besides that, you need to create new directories before you can copy files into it. This process can be quite time-consuming. The DriveCopy program from PowerQuest Corporation does all of the work for you in a very short time. The program is rather inexpensive and is well worth the money. PowerQuest has a home page at www.powerquest.com. You can also e-mail drivecoy@powerquest.com or call 801-226-8977.

Partition Magic

In addition to DriveCopy, PowerQuest also makes PartitionMagic. PartitionMagic 3.0 is the revolutionary utility that lets you resize your drives and reclaim wasted disk space. It also lets you safely boot and run multiple operating Systems and organize and protect your data.

Everyone wants to get the most they can out of their hard drive. But up to 40% of your hard drive might be totally wasted due to inefficient storage methods. PartitionMagic 3.0 increases your usable disk space by shrinking large FAT partitions and restructuring cluster sizes to reclaim up to hundreds of megabytes of lost disk space.

Partition-It

Partition-It is another relatively inexpensive utility that lets you partition large hard drives into smaller, more manageable drives. Partition-It can do this without having to back up. It is all automatic. It scans the drive and calculates what the optimum cluster size should be for maximum storage. Partition-It is made by Quarterdeck Corporation (www.quarterdeck.com, info@quarterdeck.com, 800-683-2391).

LapLink

If you have just built a new computer and need to transfer files from your old one, one of the best ways to do it is to use LapLink from Traveling Software (800-527-5465, www.travsoft.com). It transfers all the directories and files, and saves an enormous amount of time.

As the name implies, LapLink was first developed for connecting laptops to desktops to transfer information and data, but LapLink also has several other excellent utilities. The software comes with cables so that you can connect two computers together through the printer ports. The cables could even be used as an inexpensive peer-to-peer network.

Install in the Case

If you have assembled your computer on the benchtop and everything works okay, turn the power off and install it in the case. Turn the power on and check it again to make sure it still works, then install the cover.

Congratulations

Go ask your spouse or somebody to pat you on the back and congratulate you. You deserve it.

CHAPTER 14

The Internet

Never before in the history of the world has there been so much information available. Almost all of it is no farther away than your fingertips. The one thing that makes it possible is the Internet, specifically the World Wide Web (WWW).

The Internet started off as ARPAnet, a government project in 1973 with the Advanced Research Projects Agency (ARPA), an agency of the Department of Defense (DoD). It was a network designed to facilitate scientific collaboration in military research among educational institutions. ARPAnet had some similarities to peer-to-peer networking. It allowed almost any system to connect through an electronic gateway. This network is no longer primarily concerned with military research and is now known as the Internet. It is possible to access the Internet or WWW from several of the larger online services. Here are some telephone numbers:

- Prodigy: 800-776-3449
- America Online (AOL): 800-827-6364
- Microsoft Network: 800-386-5550
- CompuServe: 800-848-8199

Note that CompuServe is now a part of AOL. Besides these large online service providers, there are thousands of smaller *Internet Service Providers* (ISPs). The Los Angeles California edition of *Computer Currents* magazine lists several local ISPs each month. They have an overall listing of over 200 ISPs in the greater Los Angeles area. The smaller ISPs connect to a network of a National Service Providers (NSPs).

You can access anyone on the Internet from any of the online providers or ISPs. There are now millions of people who access the Internet. There is something on the Internet for everyone. You can find encyclopedias, up-to-the-minute news, people chatting with another, online romance, and X-rated photographs. You can post notes or send e-mail. You can send a message to anyone in the world for just the cost of the dial-up connection and your hourly rate from the ISP. I frequently send e-mail messages to friends in England, Australia, Canada, Germany, and other parts of the world for the same price that it would cost to call my next door neighbor.

At one time, the larger online companies had a higher hourly or monthly rate than the smaller ISPs. The smaller ISPs began cutting their rates in order to attract customers. The larger companies began cutting their rates to match the small companies. Most of the small ISPs in the Los Angeles area charge $20 a month for unlimited hours. Some are as low as $10 or $12 per month. Almost all of the large companies now offer a flat rate of $19.95 per month for unlimited usage. This is an excellent example of competition working to our benefit.

The lowered rates and unlimited time has caused some problems, however. Before the unlimited time was instituted, a person would watch the clock and get on and get off as quickly as possible. Now, people can log on and chat or surf for hours because of the flat rate.

AOL instituted a very aggressive ad campaign and signed up over 8 million subscribers. Unfortunately, this was more than they could handle. Many people spent hours trying to get online, only to get a busy signal. AOL has since increased its number of phone lines, but it can still be difficult to get on at certain times of the day. AOL recently took over CompuServe and their 3 million subscribers. It is estimated that AOL now has over 12 million subscribers. Many people go online after they have dinner, so it might be difficult to sign AOL during the hours from 5 PM until 10 PM. This usually isn't too much of a problem with most of the other ISPs.

Voice and Video on the Internet

Several companies are now making software and hardware that lets you use voice over the Internet. The telephone companies are a bit worried. If a person can make a long-distance call to anywhere in the world by just dialing a local access number, then the telephone companies stand to lose some money. One of the software packages for Internet voice is WebTalk from Quarterdeck at 310-309-3700.

Some of the voice systems require that the ISP have special equipment. The ISP then usually charges for calls made, usually around 12 cents a minute. Also, at present, the voice quality is not as good as the Plain Old Telephone System (POTS).

Diamond Multimedia (www.diamondmm.com) has developed a kit that allows you to send voice and video over the Internet. The $199 kit includes a camera, microphone, hardware, and software to make this possible. The Diamond system does not require that the ISP provide any special equipment. It can be used just as if you were using your modem for the Internet. Several other companies have developed similar video and voice systems that can be used on the Internet.

Since there is such a large amount of information on the Internet, search and browsing software is essential. The most popular navigational software at this time is Netscape Navigator, but Microsoft is giving away their Internet Explorer 4.0, so it might catch up to Netscape.

The vast majority of people on the Internet are good and honest. When you get a lot of people communicating with one another, however, there will always be a few who will try to take advantage of others. Lots of people are now using the Internet for business purposes. Most of them are honest and have something of value to offer. Again, however, there are a few who will do or say anything in order to get their hands in your pocket. Just be careful and watch your wallet.

Modems and Access Numbers

At the time when there were only three or four major access providers, most people were using 1200- and 2400-baud modems. It took quite a lot of time for downloads or to send messages. When the 14.4 Kb modems came out, the access companies figured that they would be losing a lot of money because people would not be online as long. To make up for the lost revenue, if you used a high-speed modem, they charged you extra.

Now, there is no difference in the charge for faster modems. The access numbers that you call must be able to handle the faster modems. Most companies have been very good at providing numbers for the faster modems. Of course, they also still provide numbers for the older 14.4 Kb band even the old 2400-baud systems. Most faster modems will drop down and operate at the lower speed. Since you are paying a flat monthly rate, it is advantageous to use a 14.4 Kb number. It might also be easier to get on during the busy hours. If you are just chatting or sending a short e-mail, it won't make much difference what speed you use. If you are browsing Web sites, especially ones with a lot of graphics, you definitely need a fast modem.

When you sign up with most of the companies, they will ask for your telephone area code and number, then provide a list of numbers in your area. They will list them by speed, such as 28.8 Kb, 14.4 Kb, and even 2400 baud. The major ISPs now also offer 56 Kb or X2 service in many cities. You are usually allowed to choose two numbers, a primary number and an alternate number. If the primary number that you choose is busy, the software will usually have the modem try the alternate number. Hopefully, the numbers offered will be toll free. If the numbers offered require a toll charge, you will have to pay it. Unfortunately, some parts of the country do not have local service. It is in your best interest to check with several ISPs to find out if there are any local numbers available.

At present, two companies have developed 56 Kb technology. The two systems are incompatible. The International Telecommunications Union (ITU) has not yet decided which technology to adopt. It will probably be a mix of the two. Both companies claim that their product will still be usable no matter which is adopted. If you do a lot of downloading of graphics or access a lot of Web sites with graphics, it might be a good idea to buy a 56 Kb modem. If you are on AOL, to find out if the X2 or 56 Kb is available in your area, go to AOL KEYWORD and type in X2. You will then be prompted to type in your area code, state, and city. AOL will display a list of access numbers in your area. Those that are 56 Kb will have an X2 beside the number.

Modems operate by taking the digital signals from the computer, then turning them into analog signals for transmission over the phone lines. Several factors limit the speed of analog signals. One big factor is noise and static, which are analog type signals. Digital signals are not affected by noise and static.

When using high-speed modems, the standard analog signal is sent to the main router. The signal is then broken up into packets and transmitted digitally to the next station, where it is again converted back to analog. This analog signal is then fed to your modem, which converts it back to digital. So the signal is converted from digital to analog then to digital, then back to analog then back to digital. The Integrated Service Digital Network (ISDN) will make life a lot better, but it has been very slow to be installed in most cities. It is also rather expensive. ISDN is discussed a bit later in this chapter.

Free ISP

Unlike other Internet service providers, the Juno Online Services Company (800-654-JUNO, www.juno.com) provides Internet service without charging a monthly fee. They can do this because they have signed up several advertisers. If you are on a tight budget and don't mind a few commercials, Juno could be all that you need. They don't offer all of the goodies that you would find on AOL, but they provide e-mail and most of the other essentials.

You can access anyone on the Internet or WWW from any of the online providers or ISPs. Unfortunately, if you travel a lot, you might not be able to find a local number for a smaller ISP. The larger companies have local numbers near most cities.

Services

There is something on the Internet for everyone. There are encyclopedias, up-to-the-minute news, people chatting with another, and online romance. You can send a message to anyone in the world for just the cost of the dial-up connection and your hourly rate from the ISP. I recently sent several e-mail messages to a friend in England for less than it would have cost me to send a letter. It is as easy to chat with someone in Australia or France or England as it is to chat with your next-door neighbor.

Since there is such a large amount of information on the Internet, search and browsing software is essential. The two most popular navigational browsers at this time are Netscape Navigator and Microsoft Internet Explorer. Prodigy, AOL, and CompuServe provide browsers as part of their service.

Most Internet services also provide search engines to help you find specific items. A search utility that works with most of the browsers is ZooWorks Research software. It can help you find almost any information on the Internet or on an intranet. One good feature of it is that it records keywords and tracks where you have been so that you can easily return. For more information, contact Hitachi Computer Products (America), at 408-986-9770, www.hitachisoft.com/research. Yahoo (www.yahoo.com) is another search engine that can search the whole net.

Most of the larger service providers offer either Netscape or Microsoft Explorer with their programs. These two browsers have more or less become the double standard. Most of the systems also include search engines such as Yahoo, Magellan, and Lycos.

There are very few businesses today who do not have a Web site. You might not need a search engine to look up the addresses for most of them. For the larger companies, to access a particular Web site, try typing www.*companyname*.com.

All of the major ISPs offer chat rooms, Instant Messaging, home pages, member searches, and many other services. Many offer private chat rooms where two or more people can go to chat or do almost anything they want behind the closed doors. One reason AOL is so popular is because of their many chat rooms and areas. They also offer a "Buddy List." You can add your friends to this list, and whenever one of them signs on, it will show up on the list. You can then send an Instant Message (IM) to the buddy, and it will reach him or her wherever they are. You can even ask to locate the member and AOL will tell you if they are in a private room or a chat room or just online doing IMs. If they are in a chat room, it will ask if you want to join them or send them an IM.

AOL has made its Instant Message utility available so that anyone on any other network can send and receive IMs to any member of AOL. If you have friends on other networks, just have them point their browsers to www.aol.com and download the free software.

I have been a member of Prodigy for over 10 years. It is fine for e-mail and a few business things, but it can't come close to AOL for fun and games. To its credit, Prodigy has changed quite a lot. They still have the old classic Prodigy, but they now have Prodigy Internet. The old classic has an old, very slow browser. Prodigy Internet uses Netscape for a browser. Prodigy added a few features to Netscape which makes it look a little bit like AOL.

There are millions of people who are lonely, have no one to talk to or visit with. About 8 million of these people have discovered AOL. One person called Prodigy that stodgy old Prodigy. Compared to AOL, it fits.

On Prodigy, without any input from me, any time that I make a post to one of the lists or send e-mail, my name is emblazoned at the top as MR. AUBREY PILGRIM. Because my name is in all capitals, which means shouting on the Internet, several people have written to me and asked if I was on an ego trip or something. I had nothing to do with it; Prodigy set it up that way. Hopefully, they will have made some changes by the time you read this. They are trying hard to catch up to AOL.

AOL and several other services will let you choose a unique screen name. On AOL I am simply "Apilgrm." If I get tired of using that name, I can have up to five aliases. I can log on as someone else, play out any fantasies, and do it anonymously. I don't have to worry that my dignity or reputation will be marred by something that I might say or do, because nobody would know it was me. No matter how mousy or wimpy someone might be in real life, he or she one can assume any identity, persona, or personality, and play out the wildest fantasies online.

The downside of the anonymity is that there are always people who will become obnoxious. They might be crude, rude, or disruptive. It can sometimes take all the fun out of it. Some of them will join a chat room and use special programs they have created that will completely take over the screen and prevent anyone from participating. The senior scene room on AOL seems to be a favorite target. It is suspected that it is younger people just showing off.

AOL usually provides a host to facilitate the chat sessions. The host can remind the disruptive person of the rules of netiquette, but that might not dissuade some of them. Of course, these people can be reported to the AOL Terms of Service (TOS) Advisors, which can warn them or even deny them service. The disruptive people usually hit and run, however, so it is difficult to catch them. These people are a lot like those who write virus programs to harm other people. They take great pleasure in causing problems to others whom they have never met.

AOL has many, many different chat rooms for various topics. There is a senior scene room, a married with children room, a lesbian room, a twenty something room, and many, many more. Often, there are as many as 20 to 25 people in these rooms. When one fills, the host will open another one similar to the one that is filled. It is not required, but members are invited to post a profile of themselves. This is a brief statement, such as whether you are male or female, your interests, and anything else you would like to say about yourself. Of course no one is going to verify the statements, so some of them might be just a bit exaggerated. The names of the members who are in a room are displayed in a box alongside the chat screen. You can double-click on any member's name and a box comes up that lets you read his or her profile.

With AOL's Instant Message utility, you can click on the IM button, type in a person's name, and it will tell you whether the person is online and available. It can even tell you if the person is in a particular chat room. You can type in a message and it will be sent to the person immediately. The person can then respond or ignore you. Many people just spend time IMing each other or chatting without going to a room. It is very private; no one else can see what is going on. Maybe it is better that no one sees the typed words that are exchanged in these sessions, especially if one is easily shocked.

There are also private rooms where two or more people can go and chat behind closed doors. All kinds of things can happen behind these closed doors. The Internet can be dangerous to some marriages. Although it is strictly fantasy, some spouses take a very dim view of their mate having a cyber affair with someone else. I heard of one woman who didn't trust her husband. She went next door and used her friend's computer. She signed on with an assumed name and made up a very sexy profile. She then sent IMs to her husband and enticed him into a private room. After leading him on to see just how far he would go, she stopped, went home, and confronted him. It very nearly led to a divorce.

I read once that someone had determined that there were 726 sins. But that was before cybersex. There must be many more than that now.

Lest you get the wrong idea, AOL and the Internet are not all just sex. Many lasting friendships are made on the Internet. It is a godsend to many lonely people, especially those who can't sleep at night. There are also informational and special-interest groups who meet on the Internet. Some services do require legitimate identification. One such place is the Well at www.well.com.

One other disadvantage of the Internet is addiction. The Canadian Medical Association and the University of Pittsburgh have defined a disorder they call the Internet Addiction Disorder (IAD). They claim that it is a maladaptive pattern of Internet use that can lead to clinically significant impairments and increased levels of distress. They say it might be as serious as alcoholism.

I know one woman who has been on the Internet for about six months. Her telephone company bills her by the minute. One month she logged 12,000 minutes. She has used her keyboard so much that the most used letters are completely worn off, so a person who was not a touch-typist would not be able to use her computer. In another case, a woman was recently arrested and charged with child endangerment. She had locked her three young children in a separate room while she chatted and surfed the Internet for hours. The children were dirty, hungry, and neglected. Her ex-husband had often found them in this condition when he came to pick them up for his weekend visits. He finally turned her in for child neglect.

A support group, much like the Alcoholics Anonymous, has been formed to help these type of people. Of course, to participate, you have to be on the Internet. This is something like an AA member taking a bottle along to a meeting. If you would like to find out more about the Internet Addiction Disorder (IAD) Support Group, point your browser to www.iucf.indiana.edu/~brown/hyplan/addict.html

House-Wiring Intranet

The Phonex Company (801-556-0100) has developed special telephone adapters that plug into any wall outlet. The system requires at least two adapters, one for the telephone input line, the other where you want the extension. More adapters can be plugged into any other 110-volt outlet to provide as many telephone extensions as needed. If you need an extension in another location, you can just unplug an adapter and plug it into another nearby wall outlet. You could even use a standard electrical extension cord and a Phonex adapter to provide a telephone extension. Electronic circuitry in the adapters blocks the AC voltage from getting into the telephone lines, but allows voice and data to go through. The device is being marketed and sold by Comtrad Industries (800-704-1211).

The Adaptive Company (617-497-5150, www.adaptivenetworks.com) has developed a similar system using ordinary house or factory wire as cabling to form networks. Some of their products operate at up to 100 Kbps. Eventually, these products should allow you to plug your computer or several computers and modems into any outlet in the house and access the Internet.

E-Mail

To me, one of the most useful and worthwhile benefits of the Internet is e-mail. It is so much better than snail mail in dozens of ways. An e-mail message is almost instantaneous, and it is cheap. You can send hundreds of e-mail letters for the cost of one 32-cent stamp. E-mail that you receive can be answered immediately, saved to a hard disk, printed out, or deleted. I subscribe to several health-related sites. Besides personal messages, I usually get 100 or so health messages in my mailbox every day. I have set up directories and files on my hard disk for the messages that I want to save. I usually save them in a word processor format. If I compose a message offline with my word processor, I have to convert it to ASCII format before it can be sent. Most word processors let you do that.

Some e-mail programs designed for the Internet have several management tools. Eudora (www.eudora.com) is a very powerful e-mail program. It can receive your messages, separate them, and automatically send them to various folders and directories. Eudora has multiple formatting tools to let you send or receive stylized text, fonts, graphics, sound bytes, video clips, or any data file. It lets you read and compose mail offline, and also has a built-in spelling checker. Eudora has a lot more utilities and functions than the e-mail that comes with AOL, Prodigy, or CompuServe. Unfortunately, however, Eudora will not work with these large companies. It works fine with most of the smaller ISPs, such as Juno.

J-Mail and Spamming

One of the disadvantages of being on the Internet is being bombarded with junk e-mail. Some one has called this "j-mail." The reason there is so much j-mail is because it is so cheap and easy to do. There are organizations who sell e-mail addresses. You can get over a million addresses for as little as $25 and up to $100. You could send a message to every one of those million people for less than the cost of a single postage stamp.

Boot Magazine is a new computer magazine that is rather irreverent and much like the old hippie stuff. One of their writers, Tom Halfhill, said in one issue that if just 3% of the people who get the j-mail responded, it would be enough to give the direct-mail marketer an orgasm.

There are no laws against spamming. Even if there were, they would probably be unenforceable. The crush of spam material can clog a small ISP and even some of the larger ones. I have gotten unwanted mail on AOL, but when I reply and try to complain to the sender, it is sent back to me as undeliverable. They have ways of sending the stuff without revealing their whereabouts. There are a few resources on the Web for dealing with spammers. First, try http://www.compulink.co.uk/~net-services/spam/. This site says

> Hit back at the Spammers!
>
> Get lots of e-mail offering you get-rich-quick schemes? Want to hit back? "Spam Hater" (Now at V2.03) is free Windows software that helps you respond effectively and makes it hot for these people. This program:
>
> Analyzes the Spam
>
> Extracts a list of addresses of relevant Postmasters, etc.
>
> Prepares a reply
>
> Choice of legal threats, insults or your own message
>
> Appends a copy of the Spam if required
>
> Puts it in a mail window ready for sending
>
> Tool to help keep you out of spammers databases
>
> Analyzes Usenet spam
>
> Context sensitive help - right mouse click on the item concerned
>
> Shows a sample of the spam its analyzing
>
> Generates a "WHOIS" query to help track the perpetrator
>
> Generates a "TRACEROUTE" query to help track the perpetrator's upstream provider.

Another site, which tells you how to do it yourself, is http://www.cci-web.com/iway7/spam4.html.

One small ISP has sued one of the spammers, but it has not gone to court yet. Spammers are making so much money that they will gladly pay any fine and continue doing business as usual. One way to stop them would be to ignore them and not buy their products.

Connections

You should try find the fastest modem possible. Technology does not stand still. Newer and faster methods are being developed every day.

ISDN

Integrated Services Digital Network (ISDN) is about the fastest connection method available at the moment. However, you need a special ISDN modem and your ISP must be able to interface with ISDN. Another disadvantage of ISDN is that it is not available in all areas of the country. Even where it is available, it can be rather expensive, adding from $25 to over $200 to your phone bill. If you are a large business that does a lot of videoconferencing and other business over the telephone and Internet, it might be well worth it.

ADSL

Asymmetric Digital Subscriber Line (ADSL) is a very fast line that can provide data at a speed as high as 6.14 Mbps (megabits per second). That is about 200 times faster than a 28.8-Kbps modem. It will be ideal for videoconferencing, video-on-demand, networking, fax, and voice. It is still being tested and developed, but should be available in some parts of the country by the time you read this. The original hardware will cost about $300 to $500. The service will cost about $100 a month.

Cable

Some companies have developed cable modems that can operate off the cable lines. They can operate as high as 10 Mbps. The hardware cost might be $300 to $500, plus an extra $30 to $40 a month on your cable bill.

Cable-TV Internet

If you can't afford a computer and a modem, a few companies have developed keyboards and set-top boxes that let you access the Internet over your cable TV. Instead of a computer monitor, it uses the TV screen. The keyboard uses a wireless infrared system similar to that used in standard TV remote controls. These systems do most of what you can do with a computer as far as the Internet goes. You can surf the Internet, access all the Web sites, send and receive e-mail, perform financial transactions, search for desired information, and visit chat rooms.

Of course, you will not have many of the advantages of a computer, such as a hard disk, printer, scanner, or CD-ROM drive. Another disadvantage is that most of them are very slow. If you have been exposed to a fast computer, using one of the set-top boxes might not satisfy you. Most of the systems require you to purchase the set-top boxes and keyboards for a nominal price. Then, accessing the Internet usually costs about $29.95 for unlimited hours. Here are some companies who provide set-top boxes:

- Inter-Con/PC: 612-975-0001
- Interactive Media Systems: 408-245-8283
- Interlink Electronics: 800-340-1331
- NetLink Sega Saturn: 800-733-7288, www.sega.com
- Philips Magnavox Internet TV: 888-813-7069, www.magnavox.com
- Web-i: www.pmpro.com
- WebTV: 888-772-7669, www.sony.com

Distance Learning

California's state universities, and I am sure many others, are using the Internet for teaching courses. It doesn't matter where you are, you can sign up for a course and receive college credit for it just as if you were sitting in class. Anyone can access the classes, but to receive credit, you might have to pay some fees and actually go to the classroom for tests.

Quite often, when I was attending San Jose State University, I would try to get a class, but if it was filled, I was just out of luck. It made it very difficult if it was a class that was required for graduation. With the Internet, there will be no problem of denial because of filled classes.

Another problem that I faced was that I was working full-time and had to take my classes when I could arrange them around my work schedule. I sure wish Internet classes had been available at that time. With the Internet, you can do your classwork at any time that suits you.

You might be surprised to know that the company that published this book also provides significant distant-learning opportunities. Point your browser to www.mhcec.com or call 888-649-8648, extension 2621.

Here is a sampling of the information you will find there:

McGraw-Hill World University is a unique distance education provider. The curriculum of the University's AAS degree program was written by experienced college professors and the unique CyberCampus was designed by a team of industry experts. The educational, ethical, and business standards of McGraw-Hill World University have met the rigid requirements of the Distance Education and Training Council. McGraw-Hill World University is fully accredited as a distance education provider.

Online Catalog and Bookstore

The McGraw-Hill Online Catalog and bookstore at www.mcgraw-hill.com/books.html has 9,000 in-print titles in areas such as business, computing, engineering, science and medicine from imprints such as Osborne, Schaum's, International Marine, and Ragged Mountain Press. The catalog includes all titles published by the McGraw-Hill College Division, with titles to be added from our recently acquired Irwin, Dushkin, and WCB publishing units.

The McGraw-Hill Bookstore

Professional books of all publishers with more than 30,000 titles in areas such as business, computing, technical, professional, and reference. The site puts the spotlight on a Book of the Week and features new arrivals, forthcoming titles, bestsellers and special promotions—all available through secure electronic transactions.

Warning! The following is an unabashed commercial: Of course, you will find all of the books that I have written in the McGraw-Hill bookstore. Be sure to look for the "Save a Bundle" series.

McGraw-Hill has several good books on the Internet, such as *The Internet for Everyone: A Guide for Users and Providers,* by Richard Wiggins. Some of their other Internet-related books include the following:

- *America Online for Busy People*
- *Great American Websites*
- *Internet and Web Yellow Pages*
- *Internet Complete Reference*
- *Internet Essentials and Fun List*

- *Internet Explorer 4.0: Browsing and Beyond*
- *Internet Kids and Family Yellow Pages*
- *Internet Yellow Pages*
- *McGraw-Hill Encyclopedia of Networking*
- *Official America Online Yellow Pages*
- *Official AT&T WorldNet Web Discovery Guide*
- *Web Publishing with Corel WordPerfect 8 Suite: The Official Guide*
- *Web Publishing with Netscape for Busy People*
- *Webmaster's Toolkit*
- *World Wide Web for Busy People*

These books can be found in the McGraw-Hill Bookstore mentioned above, Or you can contact Osborne/McGraw-Hill at 800-227-0900 or www.osborne.com, and they will send you a current catalog.

If you are just getting started, the *Internet Complete Reference* would help you immensely. It has over 800 pages of information about getting on the Net. It has addresses and numbers of hundreds of local, state, national, and international access gateways. There are valuable helpful hints on almost every page. There are several other books about the Internet, published by companies other than McGraw-Hill.

Another excellent place to buy books online is Amazon, at www.amazon.com. Amazon claims to be the world's largest online bookstore. They carry all of my books. They have a search engine that can quickly locate any book that they carry. If you search on *Pilgrim*, you will see all of the computer books that I have written.

Internet Magazines

Most computer magazines have at least one article about the Internet in each issue. several magazines are devoted entirely to the Internet. Most of the magazines have reviews and listings of Web sites. There are thousands of sites. The magazines can be very helpful in telling you where to look. Here are a few Internet magazines:

- *Boot Magazine*—Many of *Boot Magazine*'s issues include a CD-ROM disc with lots of programs and games. I enjoy the magazine for its new and fresh outlook. If you would like to subscribe, call 415-468-4869 or send e-mail to subscribe@bootnet.com. They have a Web site at www.bootnet.com.

- *NetGuide*—To access *NetGuide* online, point your browser to www.netguidemag.com or send e-mail to netguide@palmcoastd.com. You can also contact them by mail or phone:

P.O. Box 420400
Palm Coast, FL 32142-9232
800-829-0421

- *Internet World*

P.O. Box 7461
Red Oak, IA 51591-2461
800-573-3062
iwservice@iw.com
www.iw.com

- *The Web*—For online subscriptions, point your browser to www.webmagazine.com/webmag.html. Otherwise, contact

P.O. Box 56943
Boulder, CO 80323-6943
800-932-6241
www.webmagazine.com

- *ZD Internet*—For online subscriptions, point your browser to http://subscribe.zdimag.com/service. Otherwise, contact

P.O. Box 55483
Boulder, CO 80323-5483

Magazines are an excellent way to know what is available on the Web. They also have some very interesting and informative articles in each issue.

Your Own Web Page

Many of the large providers such as Prodigy and AOL give you space on their site for your own Web page. It is usually just a few megabytes. If you want more, it will cost you. Most large, corporate Web pages have been constructed by professionals who are familiar with the Hypertext Markup Language (HTML). There are books that can show you how to create your own professional-looking site. WordPerfect 7 and Microsoft Word 97 can convert text to the HTML format.

Web Hosting

A recent issue of *NetGuide* had dozens of ads from companies who will set up a site for you and give you 20 to 25 Mb of space. Additional space is usually available in 5-Mb blocks. These companies will take care of the business of registering you for one or more domain names. They will set up unlimited e-mail for you, set up anonymous FTP (File Transfer Protocol), and many other services. Most of the companies charge from $19.95 to $25.

If you have a company or larger business, there are professional designers who will develop a complete site for you. For a large job, you might have to bring in an ISP rep, a graphics designer, a programmer, network integrators, and many others. It can be very expensive to set up a large site. The Corel Company at www.corel.com has WebMaster Suite software that can be used to create a professional Web Site. The suite of programs contains Web page authoring, Web site management, graphics, database publishing, Web site hosting services, and much more.

Sex on the Web

There has been a lot of concern about young people accessing the many Web sites that feature nudity and sex. Most of the sites ask if the person is over 18 or not. If someone admits to being under 18, he or she will not be allowed to access the site. But how many teenagers do you suppose will say that they are under 18? In Scandinavian countries, they don't worry too much about young people seeing depictions of the sex act, but they do ban young children from movies that have lots of killing and gore. Our children are exposed to an unbelievable amount of killings and blood and guts on television and in the movies. I think the Scandinavians are right.

The government is worried about pornography on the Net and has spent a lot of time trying to come up with laws that would control it. They really shouldn't worry too much. Almost every one of these sites will show a fairly modest teaser for free, but if you want to see the "good stuff," they ask for a credit card number. Unless your children have their own credit cards, you probably don't have to worry too much.

The Future

The Internet is still in its infancy, but it is growing faster than the weeds in my front lawn. Thousands of new sites are being put up every day. There are millions of Web pages. Just about everything that anyone could possibly want is on the Internet. Maybe even more than what you want.

There will be even more tomorrow.

Emoticons and Acronyms

There are several ways to communicate with the symbols on the keyboard. You might have to turn your head sideways to see them properly. Here are a few:

:-) Happy or a smiley face
:-o Writer is surprised
:-# Writer's lips are sealed
;-) Winking
:-@ Screaming
:-(Frowning or unhappy
>:-> Angry
:/) Not funny
{ } A hug
{{{{ HUG }}}} Lots of hugs
:* A kiss
:**: Kissing
:-)*(-: Also kissing
:-& Tongue-tied

There are also some shorthand acronyms that are used in addition to or in place of emoticons. Here are a few:

brb—Be right back or bathroom break
LOL—Laughing out loud or lots of love
ROFLOL—Rolling on floor laughing out loud
ROFLMAO—Rolling on floor laughing my __ off
$$%^&—Dirty words
Snail-mail—U.S. Postal Service

CHAPTER 15

Printers

For the vast majority of applications, a computer system is not complete without a printer. There are several manufacturers of computer printers and hundreds of different models. You will have a vast number of options and choices when choosing a printer.

One of the least expensive printers is the inkjet. Even color inkjet printers are very inexpensive. If you have a small office/home office (SOHO), you might want to buy one of the multifunction machines that can print, copy, scan, and fax. If you expect to do a lot of heavy-duty printing, then you should look at laser printers.

This chapter discusses some of the features and functions of those different types. There are many different printer manufacturers and hundreds of different models. Almost every company now has a Web site that is frequently updated. I have listed several vendors and their Web sites. Visit these sites for more information. All of the computer magazines also have articles and ads for printers. You can easily compare types, models, and prices by looking through the magazine ads.

Printer Life Expectancy

Printers usually have a long life. I have an HP LaserJet III that I bought in May, 1990. It has a self-test utility that tests and prints out all of the various fonts and graphics that it can do. It also prints out a record of how many pages it has printed. As of today, it has printed out 28,520 pages. It has had only one major problem. I had to replace the fuser assembly at 26,000 pages, at a cost of $120. I thought that it would cost me several hundred dollars to get it repaired. To tell the truth, I was just a little bit disappointed that it didn't cost more to repair it. Deep down, I was looking for an excuse to buy a new printer. There have been some fantastic advances in the last few years. The new lasers are faster, have much better resolution, and are much less expensive.

Although printers usually last a long time, like most other industries, the printer manufacturers constantly work to obsolete the printer that you might already have so that you will buy a new and improved model. There are dozens and dozens of printer companies. Each company produces dozens of different models. Because the models change so frequently, when I mention a product here, I don't usually mention the model name.

Inkjets

An inkjet is about the least expensive printer you can buy, yet inkjets can produce an output that is close to that of an expensive laser. A disadvantage of inkjets is that they are much slower than a laser. Hewlett-Packard developed the first inkjet printer. Now, many companies manufacture them, including Brother, Canon, Epson, Texas Instrument, and Lexmark. Some companies call them by a different name, such as Canon's Bubble Jet, but they are all basically inkjets.

Most inkjet manufacturers have one or more color models. Those models that can print in color usually have a *C* in the model number, such as the HP DeskJet 660C or the Canon Bubble Jet BJC-70.

Inkjet printers use a system that is similar to dot-matrix printers, but instead of pins that press a ribbon onto the paper, they use a matrix of small inkjets that sprays dots of ink on the paper. They also have a much larger number of inkjets; the dot matrix may have from 9 to 24 pins, while the inkjet may have from 48 to 128 small jets. The head moves across the paper much like the dot-matrix system, and dots of ink are sprayed onto the paper to form text or graphics. To print color, the printer has three or more color inkjets. Of course, those printers with a larger number of jets produce more and smaller dots, yielding higher resolution.

Most inkjet printers come with one or more fonts, but they might be able to use several more that are available on plug-in font cartridges. Some inkjets can use scalable fonts. Like the dot matrix, the speed of inkjets is measured in characters per second. Depending on the type of print, the average speed is about two pages per minute.

Inkjet Color

Most inkjet printers sold today are color. Since black is used most often, most of them have a large black cartridge along with the three primary color cartridges. It is now possible to buy color inkjet printers for less than $200. Some of the color machines can be very slow. About the best they can do is two pages per minute, printing black text. Lasers can print four to eight pages per minute. A color graphics printout might take several minutes on an inkjet machine.

Inkjet color printers use a system of three different-colored ink cartridges, cyan, magenta, and yellow, to print color. Some systems also have a black cartridge for standard text, while others use the mixture of the three colors to make black. Some low-cost systems use a single cartridge with three colors. I recommend that you look for a printer that uses a separate cartridge for black and each of the primary colors.

As the head moves across the paper, the software can have any of the various colors sprayed onto the paper. The three colors blend to produce any color of the rainbow.

Cartridge Refills

The black inkjet cartridges are good for about 700 pages of text. The color cartridges yield about half this many pages. They must then be replaced or refilled. A new cartridge might cost $25 to $30. One reason for the high cost is because they usually have a built-in electronic head assembly. Regardless, it is wise to have a spare cartridge that can be dropped in when the ink in a cartridge is depleted. ACSI Bulk Inks (770-925-2616) has refill kits for black and all the colors. Signal Computing Company (800-454-2288) also has refill kits for most inkjet printers.

I have a Canon inkjet multifunction printer, copier, and fax machine. The cartridges for it have a small cap in the top that can be pried off so that they can be refilled. For some cartridges, you might have to drill a hole. The hole can then be covered with almost any kind of adhesive tape. ACSI Company sells a bellows-type syringe that can be used for refilling cartridges. Almost any type of large-bore syringes would work. See Fig. 15-1.

A sponge inside the cartridge absorbs the ink. There might be an excessive amount of ink when it is first used. It is a good idea to make a few copies or use the cartridge a few times to get rid of any excessive ink.

Transparencies for Presentations

If you do any presentations using an overhead projector, inkjets can handle transparencies very well. Color inkjet printers are ideal for creating low-cost color transparencies for presentations, graphs, schematic plotting, and drawings.

Compared to the less-than $300 inkjets, there are some inkjet printers that are rather expensive. Of course, there are several options and features on different products.

Figure 15-1
A kit for refilling an inkjet cartridge.

Many printer companies have several different models of their products. Check through the ads in computer magazines. Here are some of the color inkjet companies and their contact information:

- Canon Corporation: 800-848-4123, www.usa.canon.com
- Hewlett-Packard: 800-752-0900, www.hp.com
- Lexmark International: 800-539-6275, www.lexmark.com
- Okidata: 800-654-3282, www.okidata.com

Call the companies for brochures and specifications.

There are several inkjet and color inkjet printers that I did not mention. There are many different models, from different companies with different features, functions, and prices. Look for ads in the major computer magazines.

Inkjet Supplies

The original cost of a printer is not the end. If you do much printing, the cost of supplies might be more than the cost of the printer. Ink cartridges might cost from $30 to $35. Some cartridges only last for about 300 pages. It is possible to refill some of the cartridges.

Multifunction Inkjet Machines

Many times, in a SOHO, you need to make one or more copies or to scan something. A large office can afford to have high-end copiers, scanners, plain-paper fax machines, and printers. Each of these items is rather expensive, however, and if not used very often, the cost cannot be justified. Besides, in a SOHO, especially one like mine, there just isn't room for all of these separate machines.

Several companies have noted the fact that most of these machines have a lot in common. There are now many multifunction machines that can copy, scan, fax and print. Most of them are fairly reasonable in cost when you consider what they can do. Another big plus is that these four-in-one machines take up very little space. Figure 15-2 shows a Canon device that incorporates a color inkjet printer, fax, copier, and scanner. I use it mostly for faxing and copying.

The scan utility of most of these multifunction machines operates like the copy utility. The scan can be sent to a computer, but unlike most scanners, these do not have optical character recognition (OCR) ability. Still, they are very handy to have.

Many of the machines come with several software packages, such as document management, that can help you organize scanned data. Some of them come with business-card readers and organizers, with OCR soft-

Figure 15-2 A multifunction machine that works as a color inkjet printer, a fax machine, a scanner, and a copier.

ware, and with faxing software. Many of the multifunction machines can print color, but copy in black and white only.

Here are a few manufacturers of these machines:

- Canon Corporation: 800-828-4040, www.usa.canon.com
- Epson: 800-289-3766, www.epson.com
- Hewlett-Packard: 800-752-0900, www.hp.com
- Lexmark: 800-539-6275, www.lexmark.com
- Xerox: 800-832-6979 www.xerox.com
- The following is an example of some specifications for a Hewlett-Packard multifunction machine. Specifications from other companies would be similar.

HP OfficeJet 630

The HP OfficeJet 630 is an All-in-One product that makes it easy to complete your work. As a color printer, color copier, color scanner and plain paper fax it is fully integrated and easy to use.

PRODUCT COMES EQUIPPED WITH:

A power cord, Printer/scanner interface cable, One black print cartridge, one color print cartridge, CD-ROM disk containing the HP OfficeJet Series 600 software, Online help system and user's guide, Paper/document loading tray, HP OfficeJet Series 600 Ready*Setup*Go Card, Caere OmniPage Limited Edition Optical Character Recognition (OCR) documentation, Fax/phone connector with attached phone cord, Scan/copy sleeve (for faxing and scanning smaller-than-standard-sized documents and for protecting photos)

BONUS! SOFTWARE

Corel Print & Photo House, Select 2.0, Caere OmniPage Pro "Try-Before-You-Buy," Starfish Software Sidekick.

PHYSICAL SPECIFICATIONS

Dimensions: With tray installed: 17.0″w × 14.15″d × 10.15″h, Weight: 15 lbs.

PRINT

600 × 600 dpi black with Resolution Enhancement technology (RET), 600 × 300 dpi color with HP ColorSmart technology, Up to 5ppm black and 2ppm color, Plain paper, transparencies, glossy paper, premium inkjet paper, envelopes, labels, and card stock, 150 sheet paper tray, Letter, legal, executive size paper, Single envelope feeder, 10 envelopes in tray.

FAX

Plain paper and PC faxing, 100 speed dials, 65 page memory, 14.4 Kbps transmission speed, Fine, standard, 300 dpi and photo transmission resolutions,

Automatic document reduction, Automatic redial up to 5 times, Confirmation and activity reports, 20 page automatic document tray, Broadcasting up to 95 locations, Error correction mode, Junk fax barrier, Fax forwarding, Distinctive ring detect, Automatic fax/answering machine switching. COPY 600 × 300 dpi color ** and black/white, Sheet-fed design with adjustable feeder, Up to 99 copies from original, Digital zoom from 50% to 200%, Collation/Correct Order Output Includes digital image processing for high quality SCAN Up to 1200 dpi enhanced (300 dpi optical), 24-bit color (millions of colors), 8-bit grayscale (256 levels of gray), Caere OmniPage Ltd. Edition OCR software included, TWAIN interface. Scanning Resolution:up to 1200 dpi enhanced (300 dpi optical)

8-bit grayscale (256 levels of gray)

24-bit color (millions of colors)

OCR Software: Caere OmniPage Ltd. Ed. OCR software included

General

As an ENERGY STAR(SM) Partner, Hewlett-Packard Company has determined that this product meets ENERGY STAR(SM) guidelines for energy efficiency.

Multifunction Laser Machines

All of the machines mentioned so far use inkjet technology. Here are a few additional companies whose printers use laser technology:

- Brother International: 800-284-4357, www.brother.com
- Panasonic Company: 201-348-9090, www.panasonic.com

Laser technology provides better resolution than inkjets. Also, laser printers are much faster than inkjets. These machines are comparably priced to some of the inkjet multifunction machines.

Wide-Format Printers

Several companies make wide-format color printers that can print such things as large posters, signs, banners, point-of-sale (POS) displays, tradeshow materials, advertisements, business and presentation graphics, and billboards. Most of these printers can print on 36-inch widecut sheets or roll sheets as long as 50 feet. Usually, the paper has to be specially coated. Most of these printers use a high-resolution inkjet technology. The cost of these printers ranges from $6,000 up to $20,000.

Using standard silkscreen techniques or large four-color printers to make a large poster or banner might cost from $1000 up to $6000 or more. The same poster can be printed on a wide-format inkjet printer for $200 to $300 or less.

Another type of wide-format printer uses an electrostatic process with special cyan, magenta, yellow, and black (CYMK) toners. The special paper is electrostatically charged, and the toner adheres to the charged areas. These high-speed printers have a very high resolution that is suitable for lifesize posters, banners, or for several types of signs. The signs and posters can be used in exterior areas where they can withstand temperature changes and sun and rain. The electrostatic printers are rather expensive, at $30,000 up to $100,000.

Most wide-format printers use a raster image processor (RIP), a software controller. The RIPs act as color and ink-control managers, and handle enlargement, rotation, tiling, paneling, previewing, screening, and other tasks. RIP software is made by several different companies, so it is not all the same. Here are a few of those companies:

- CalComp: 714-821-2100, www.calcomp.com
- Hewlett-Packard: 800-367-4772, www.hp.com

Laser Printers

The Hewlett-Packard LaserJet was one of the first lasers. It was a fantastic success and became the de facto standard. There are now hundreds of laser printers on the market. Most of them emulate the LaserJet standard. Even IBM's laser printer emulates the HP standard.

Laser printers have a combination of copy machine, computer, and laser technology. They have excellent print quality, but they have lots of moving mechanical parts and are rather expensive. Laser printers use synchronized, multifaceted mirrors and sophisticated optics to write the characters or images on a photosensitive rotating drum. The drum is similar to the ones used in repro machines. The laser beam is swept across the spinning drum and is turned on and off to represent white and dark areas. As the drum is spinning, it writes one line across the drum, then rapidly returns and writes another. It is quite similar to the electron beam that sweeps across the face of a TV screen or computer monitor, one line at a time.

The spinning drum is sensitized by each point of light that hits it. The sensitized areas act like an electromagnet. As the drum rotates through the carbon toner, the sensitized areas become covered with the toner. The paper is then pressed against the drum. The toner that was picked up by the sensitized areas of the drum is left on the paper. The paper is then sent through a heating element, where the toner is heated and fused to the paper.

Except for the writing to the drum, this is the same thing that happens in a copy machine. Instead of using a laser to sensitize the drum, a copy machine takes a photograph of the image to be copied. A photographic lens focuses the image onto the rotating drum, which becomes sensitized to the light and dark areas projected onto it.

Engine

The drum and its associated mechanical attachments is called an *engine*. Canon, a Japanese company, is one of the foremost makers of engines. They manufacture them for their own laser printers and copy machines, and for dozens of other companies, such as Hewlett-Packard and Apple. Several other Japanese companies manufacture laser engines.

Low-Cost Laser Printers

Because of the large number of companies manufacturing laser printers, there is lots of competition, which is a great benefit to consumers. The competition has driven prices of both lasers and dot matrix printers down. It has also forced many new improvements.

Until recently, most laser printers had a resolution of only 300×300 dots per inch (dpi). Most lasers now have a resolution of 600×600, and some have 1200×1200 dpi. Some of these higher-resolution printers are now selling for $500 or less.

Memory

If you plan to do any graphics or desktop publishing (DTP), you will need to have at least 1 Mb of memory in the printer. Before it prints the first sheet, the printer loads the data into its memory and determines where each dot will be placed on the sheet. Of course, the more memory, the faster and better the printout.

Not all lasers use the same memory configuration. For some machines, you must buy a special plug-in board for the memory. Check the type of memory that you need before you buy. Several companies offer laser memories, including ASP (800-445-6190) and Elite (800-942-0018). Look in computer magazines for ads from other companies.

Page Description Languages

If you plan to do any complex desktop publishing, you might need a page-description language (PDL) of some kind. Text characters and graphics images are two different "species." Laser-printer controllers are somewhat similar to monitor controllers. The monitor adapters usually have all of the alphabetical and numerical characters stored in ROM. When you press the letter A from the keyboard, it dives into the ROM chip, drags out the A, and displays it in a precise block of pixels wherever the cursor happens to be. These are called *bitmapped characters.* If you wanted to display an A that was twice as large, you would have to have a complete font set of that type in the computer.

As mentioned, printers are very much like the monitors and have the same limitations. They have a library of stored discrete characters for each font that they can print. My dot-matrix Star printer has an internal font and two cartridge slots. Several different font cartridges can be plugged into these slots, but the printer is still limited to those fonts that happen to be plugged in.

With a PDL, the laser printer can take one of the stored fonts and change it, or scale it, to any size you want. These are *scalable fonts.* With a bitmapped font, you have one type face and one size. With scalable fonts, you can have one typeface with an infinite number of sizes. Most laser printers accept ROM cartridges that may have as many as 35 or more fonts. You can print almost anything you want with these fonts, if your system can scale them.

A PDL controls and tells the laser where to place the dots on the sheet. Adobe's PostScript is the best-known PDL.

Speed

Laser printers can print from four to over ten pages per minute, depending on the model and what they are printing. Some very expensive high-end printers can print over 30 pages per minute. A dot-matrix printer is concerned with a single character at a time. Laser printers compose, then print, a whole page at a time. With a PDL, many different fonts, sizes of type, and graphics can be printed. Since the laser must determine where every dot that makes up a character or image is to be placed on the paper before it is printed, the more complex the page, the more memory it will require, and the more time needed to compose the page. It might take several minutes to compose a complex graphics. Once composed, it prints out very quickly.

Resolution

Most lasers now print 600×600 dots per inch (dpi) resolution. This is very good, but it is not nearly as good as the 1200×1200 dpi used for typeset in standard publications. The LaserMaster has models that can print at 1200×1200, and some that go as high as 1800 dpi. They also have upgrade kits for the HP LaserJet III and LaserJet 4 that can increase the resolution to 1200 DPI. Call LaserMaster at 800-327-8946 for details and brochures.

Most lasers print in the $8^1/_2$-×-11-inch, or A-size, format. CalComp, a division of Lockheed (714-821-2000), has developed a 600×600 high-resolution laser that can print in the $8^1/_2$-×-17-inch B-size format. QMS, Xerox, and several other companies have also developed large-format printers.

Maintenance

Most lasers use a toner cartridge that is good for 3000 to 5000 pages. The cost of an original cartridge is about $75. Several small companies are now refilling the spent cartridges for about $30 each. It might be a good idea to keep an extra cartridge as a spare. The toner cartridge is sealed, so it will last for some time on the shelf. I had a cartridge go out on a weekend when I was working on a tight deadline. Most stores that sell cartridges were closed. Since then, I keep a spare on hand.

Most laser printers keep track of the number of sheets that have been printed. If you have an HP LaserJet, you can use the front panel buttons to run a self-test. This tells you the configuration, how much RAM is installed, what font cartridges are installed, the type of paper tray, how many pages have been printed, and runs several other tests. When the toner gets low, most lasers will display a warning message in the digital readout window. If the print is very light, the toner might be low. If you remove the toner cartridge and turn it upside-down and shake it vigorously, sometimes you can get a few more copies out of it. This might help until you can get a replacement.

Of course, there are other maintenance costs. Since these machines are very similar to copy machines, they have a lot of moving parts that can wear out and jam up. Most of the larger companies give a Mean Time Between Failures (MTBF) of 30,000 to 100,000 pages. Remember, however, that these numbers are only average figures and not a guarantee. Most lasers are expected to have an overall lifetime of about 300,000 pages. In the last seven years, I have printed out 28,520 sheets—I still have a long way to go.

Paper

There are many different types and weights of paper. Almost any paper will work in your laser, but if you use cheap paper, it could leave lint inside the machine and cause problems in print quality. Generally, any bond paper or good paper made for copiers will work fine. Colored paper made for copiers will also work fine. Some companies mark copier paper with the word *Laser* and charge more for it.

Laser printers will accept paper from 18 pounds up to 24 pounds easily. I have even used 67-pound stock for making my own business cards. It is a bit heavy for wrapping around the drums, and it jams once in a while. Some lasers use a straight-through path, so the heavier paper should not cause any problems in these machines.

Many laser printers are equipped with trays to print envelopes. Hewlett-Packard recommends envelopes with diagonal seams and gummed flaps. Make certain that the leading edge of the envelope has a sharp crease.

Labels

The Avery Company (818-858-8245) and a few other companies make address labels that can withstand the heat of the fusing mechanism of the laser. There are also other specialty supplies that can be used with your laser. The Integraphix Company (800-421-2515) carries several different items that you might find useful. Call them for a catalog.

Here are some companies who make small special printers for labels:

- Brother International: P-Touch PC, 800-284-4357
- CoStar: LabelWriter, 800-426-7827
- Seiko Instruments: Smart Label, 800-688-0817

Color Laser Printers

There are several color printers available. They cost from less than $1000 up to $15,000. Although these printers are often referred to as laser color printers, at this time, only a few actually use the laser technology. The others use a variety of thermal-transfer technologies using wax or rolls of plastic polymer. The wax or plastic is brought into contact with the paper, then heat is applied. The melted wax or plastic then adheres to the paper. Very precise points, up to 300 dots per inch, can be heated. By overlaying three or four colors, all of the colors of the rainbow can be created. The Fargo Electronics Company offers a color printer for less than $1000. Of course, it does not have all of the goodies that you would find on the high-end Tektronix Phaser or the CalComp ColorMaster.

Another type of color printer uses dye-sublimation, also called thermal dye transfer or dye diffusion. These systems use a ribbon with a continuous series of four different-color ink stripes across the ribbon. The paper that is to be printed is forced against the ink ribbon. Dots of heat are applied to the various colors, which causes the color to diffuse onto the paper. The higher the temperature, the more color that can be diffused. The dots of heat can be accurately controlled for up to 256 different shades for each color.

Dye-sublimation provides the best resolution and can provide prints that are near photographic quality. As you might suppose, however, these printers are also the most expensive. Again, the least expensive dye-sublimation printer is the Fargo.

There are several companies who now make digital cameras. The photographs taken with these cameras can be downloaded directly onto a hard disk and viewed on the monitor. But what if you wanted a copy of a photograph for an album or to sit on your desk? Fargo Electronics has developed the FotoFUN, a small color printer that uses thermal dye-sublimation technology. It can print 4×6 photos, postcards, or even use a transfer system to put a photograph on a coffee mug. These photographs are very near to the quality of film.

At present, the FotoFUN printer costs $399, but you need separate kits for print film, postcards, or the FotoMug. The print film kits cost $35.95 for 36 prints. A kit for 36 postcards costs $39.95, and a kit for four FotoMugs costs $29.95. The prices might be different by the time you read this. They are listed to give you an idea of what it costs for color printing.

Nikon Electronic has developed a dye-sublimation color photo printer they call the Coolprint. It also is limited to about 4×6 prints. It is much more expensive than the Fargo, at about $2000.

The QMS ColorScript Laser 1000 was one of the first true laser color printers. It blends four different-color toners—black, cyan, magenta, and yellow—to print out color. The drum is sensitized for each color and that color of toner is transferred to it. Once all of the colors are applied to the drum, it then prints out on ordinary paper or on transparencies. The QMS ColorScript is still rather expensive. The Hewlett-Packard LaserJet 5M was introduced a couple of years after the QMS. The technology is about the same as the QMS, but it is a bit less expensive. The Xerox Corporation also has a true laser color printer. Call them for a brochure and pricing information.

Most color printers have PostScript, or they emulate PostScript. The Tektronix Phaser CP can also use the Hewlett-Packard Graphics Language (HPGL) to emulate a plotter. These color printers can print out a page much faster than a plotter. One disadvantage of color printers is the cost. Thermal wax costs up to 45 cents per page, dye-sublimation up to $2.75 per page. Most of this cost is for the ribbons and wax rolls that are used by the color machines.

Color printers are rather slow, but the technology is improving. There will be several other color printers on the market soon. There is lots of competition, so the prices are coming down. Here are just a few of the companies who have color printers:

- CalComp Lockheed: 800-932-1212, www.calcomp.com
- Fargo Electronics: 800-258-2974, www.fargo.com
- Hewlett-Packard: 800-257-3783, www.hp.com
- QMS: 800-523-2696, www.qms.com
- Tektronix: 800-835-6100, www.tek.com
- Xerox: 800-248-6550, www.xerox.com

Plotters

Plotters can draw almost any two-dimensional shape or design under the control of a computer. The early plotters were a bit like a robot. An arm selected a pen. The pen could be moved from side to side, while at the same time the sheet of paper could be moved from top to bottom. The computer could direct the pen to any point across the paper and move the paper up or down for any point on an X-Y axis. The motors were controlled by predefined X-Y coordinates. They could move the pen and paper in very small increments, so that almost any design could be traced out. Values could be assigned of perhaps 1 to 1000 for the Y elements and the same values for the X or horizontal elements. The computer could then direct the plotter to move the pen to any point or coordinate on the sheet.

The newer plotters use inkjet technology instead of pens. This makes them much faster. The different-colored ink cartridges can be activated much quicker than moving an arm to a rack, selecting a pen, then replacing it and selecting another. Plotters are ideal for such things as printing out circuit-board designs, architectural drawings, transparencies for overhead presentations, graphs, charts, and many CAD/CAM drawings. All of this can be done in many different colors. The different colors can be very helpful if you have a complex drawing, such as a multilayered motherboard. A different color can be used for each layer.

There are several different-sized plotters. Some desktop units are limited to only A- and B-sized plots. Other large, floor-standing models can accept paper as wide as four feet and several feet long. Many of the floor models are similar to the wide-format inkjet printer/plotters.

Many good graphics and computer-aided design (CAD) programs are available that can use plotters. One of the disadvantages of the early plotters was that they were rather slow. There are now some software programs that allow laser printers to act as plotters. Of course, they are much faster than a plotter, but except for the colored printers, they are limited to black and white. Most of the laser printers are also limited to the A size, or $8^1/_2 \times 11$ inches.

Here is contact information for two plotter manufacturers:

- CalComp: 800-225-2667, www.calcomp.com
- Hewlett-Packard: 800-367-4772, www.hp.com

Visit their Web sites or call them for a product list and the latest prices.

Dot-Matrix Printers

I predicted in one of my earlier books that the dot matrix would become practically obsolete. I was very wrong. Some of the best hotels still use them to print out your bill. Thousands and thousands of businesses still depend on them for all kinds of uses. The dot matrix might be obsolete when it comes to letter-writing and fancy reports, but there is still a lot of life left in the dot matrix for many other things.

Dot matrix printers are fairly low priced, but they are limited in fonts and graphics capability. Laser-printer speed is measured by the average number of pages per minute it can print, while dot-matrix speed is measured by the characters per second (CPS) they can print. They can print much faster in the draft mode than in the Near Letter Quality (NLQ) mode. Some high-end dot matrix printers can print a whole line at a time. Some of them can print up to 1000 lines per minute. In order to get that high speed, some dot-matrix printers have four or more heads, with each head printing out a different line.

Advantages of Dot Matrix

One of the distinct advantages that dot-matrix printers have over lasers is their low cost. Some dot-matrix printers cost less than $150. However, some high-end dot-matrix printers, such as the very fast line printers, cost close to $10,000.

There are many applications where a dot matrix printer is needed to accomplish a task. Wide, continuous sheets are necessary for some spreadsheet printouts. My LaserJet can't handle anything wider than $8^1/_2$ inches. With the wide carriage on my Star dot matrix, the wide sheets are no problem.

Another advantage is the number of sheets that can be printed. Most lasers have bins that hold from 100 to 250 sheets. The dot matrix can print a whole box of 5000 fanfold, continuous sheets. (It has been my experience, though, that if you start a job that requires a lot of printed sheets, as long as you stand there and watch the printer, it will work perfectly. If you walk away and start doing something else, the printer will immediately have a paper jam or some other problem. This is probably one of Murphy's many laws. This sort of problem seldom happens with my LaserJet III.)

Many offices and businesses still use multiple-sheet forms. A laser printer can't handle these forms, but a dot matrix can easily print them. The dot matrix can also print on odd sizes, shapes, and thicknesses of paper. There are many times when I use mine to address large manila envelopes.

The U.S. Post Office has adopted a Postnet barcode that helps sort and speed up mail. If you look at some of the envelopes that you receive in the mail, you might see the Postnet bar codes below the address. Many companies that send out bulk mail use this code. Several dot-matrix printers have the Postnet barcode built in, while others offer it as an option. If you do a lot of mailing, the Post Office might give you a discount if the envelopes have the Postnet code on them.

Maintenance Costs

Maintenance costs of dot matrix are usually much less than that for lasers and inkjets. The main cost for a dot matrix is to replace the ribbon about every 3000 sheets. A dot-matrix ribbon might cost from $3 to $10. A laser toner cartridge also lasts for about 3000 sheets, and might cost from $30 to $75 to replace.

Number of Pins

There are still a few 9-pin dot-matrix printers being sold today, but most people are buying those with a 24-pin print head. The 24-pin head has much better resolution and costs only a few dollars more.

The 24-pin printer forms characters from two vertical rows of 12 pins in each row. Small electric solenoids surround each of the wire pins in the head. An electric signal causes the solenoid to push the pins forward. Dot-matrix printers are also called *impact printers* because of the pin's impact against the ribbon and paper. The solenoids press one or more of the various pins as the head moves in finite increments across the paper, so that any character can be formed.

Here is a representation of the pins if it were a 7-pin print head and how it would form the letter A:

```
1 o            o
2 o           o o
3 o          o   o
4 o         o     o
5 o        o o o o o
6 o       o         o
7 o      o           o
```

The print head moves from left to right. The numbers on the left represent the individual pins in the head before it starts moving across the paper. The first pin to be struck would be number 7, then 6, then 5, 4, 3, 5 and 2, 1, 2 and 5, 3, 4, 5, 6, then 7.

A 24-pin head would be similar to the 7-pin representation shown here, except that it would have two vertical rows of 12 pins, side by side, in each row. The pins in one row would be slightly offset and lower than the pins in the other row. Since the pins are offset, they would overlap slightly and fill in the open gaps normally found in a 9-pin system.

There is a lot of competition between the dot matrix and laser companies for your dollar. Some vendors are now selling laser printers for about the same price as some dot-matrix printers. This low cost of the lasers has forced the dot-matrix manufacturers to lower their prices. In addition to lower prices, many dot-matrix companies are also adding more features such as more memory and more fonts in order to attract buyers.

Some Disadvantages of Dot Matrix

The main disadvantage of the dot matrix is that it can't come close to the quality printing of a laser. In draft mode, if the printer has a 24-pin print head, only half of the pins will be hit. There will be noticeable spacing between the dots. For NLQ mode, all of the pins will be hit. In draft mode with a 9-pin head, all of the pins will be hit, but there will be spaces between the dots. For NLQ on a 9-pin system, the printer makes a second run with the head slightly displaced, so that the pins will hit different spots and fill in the open spaces. In draft mode the printing can be fairly fast, but has poor quality. In NLQ mode, the printer slows down considerably, but has much better quality.

Most 24-pin dot-matrix printers have a resolution of 360×360 dpi. Until recently, the standard laser was rated at 300×300 dpi. If you compared the dot-matrix output to the laser, however, you would see that the laser had a much higher resolution because it produces a much smaller dot than the dot matrix. If an A is printed out on a dot matrix, the jagged edges from the large dots are very apparent. While most lasers can use scalable type fonts, only a very few of the high-end dot-matrix printers can use them.

Most dot-matrix printers have only 8 Kb or less of memory. A few of the high-end dot-matrix printers might have as much as 64 Kb or even 128 Kb. The memory on a dot matrix can be used as a print buffer. The computer can download a file to the printer, then go about its business doing other things. Laser printers use memory a bit differently. They take the file and format the whole page in memory before they start printing. Most lasers come with a minimum of 512 Kb, and you have the option to add more. For higher speed and graphics, the laser should have a minimum of 2 Mb.

If you can get by with a dot matrix, you should be able to find one at a very good price. Look for ads in *Computer Shopper* or any of the other computer magazines.

Installing a Printer or Plotter

Most IBM-compatible computers allow for four ports, two serial and two parallel. No matter whether it is a plotter, dot matrix, or laser printer, it will require one of these ports. Most printers use the parallel port, LPT1. Most plotters use a serial port. Some printers have both serial and parallel connections.

If the serial port is used, the printer can be up to 50 feet from the computer. If the parallel port is used, normally, the cable can only be about 10 feet long. There are special devices that allow longer cables to be used. The serial printers use an RS232C connector. The parallel printers use a Centronics-type connector. When you buy your printer, buy a cable from the vendor that is configured for your printer and your computer.

Printer Sharing

Ordinarily, a printer sits idle most of the time. There are some days when I don't even turn my printer on. There are usually several computers in most large offices and businesses. Almost all of them are connected to a printer in some fashion. It would be a terrible waste of money if each computer had a separate printer that was only used occasionally. It is fairly simple to make arrangements so that a printer or plotter can be used by several computers.

Sneaker Net

One of the least-expensive methods of sharing a printer is for the person to generate the text to be printed out on one computer, record it on a floppy diskette, then walk over to a computer that is connected to a printer. If it is in a large office, an old 286 or 386 clone could be dedicated to running a high-priced laser printer. It doesn't matter whether the person carrying the floppy disk is wearing sneakers, brogans, or wing tips, "sneaker net" is still one of the least expensive methods of sharing printers.

Switch Box

If there are only two or three computers, and they are fairly close together, you can use a simple switch box to switch between the computers. If you use a switch box, and the computers use the standard parallel ports, the cables from the computers to the printer should be no more than 10 feet long. Parallel signals will begin to degrade if the cable is longer than 10 feet and could cause some loss of data. A serial cable can be as long as 50 feet.

If an office or business is fairly complex, several electronic switching devices are available. Some of them are very sophisticated and can allow a large number of different types of computers to be attached to a single printer or plotter. Many of them have built-in buffers and amplifiers that can allow cable lengths up to 250 feet or more. Belkin has several peripheral sharing devices. Check their Web site.

Printer-Sharing Sources

Here are a few companies who provide switch systems:

- Belkin Components: 310-515-7585, www.belkin.com
- Black Box Corporation: 412-746-5530, www.blackbox.com
- Digital Products: 800-243-2333, www.digprod.com

Contact them for their product specs and current price list.

Wireless Connections

Many of the Pentium class and later motherboards now have an infrared (IrDA) built-in port. The IrDA systems are similar to TV remote controls. The IrDA ports can be used to connect keyboards, notebook computers and printers. The JetEye from Extended Systems Company at 800-235-7576 is two small devices, one plugs into the parallel printer port on the computer and the other plugs into the printer connector.

The Merrit Computer Products Company at 800-627-7752 has a wireless printer sharing kit. Instead of IrDA it uses a radio frequency. The system can support up to 16 computers and four printers.

Network Printers

Almost any printer can be attached to a network and called a network printer. But several companies make fast, high end, heavy duty laser printers specifically for networks. The prices may range from less than $1000 up to more than $30,000. Many of the printers come bundled with special network printer management software and internal network interfaces. The print speed may range from 12 pages per minute (ppm) and up to 60 ppm. Some of them are capable of duplex printing or printing on both sides of the paper. The resolution may be from 300 dots per inch (dpi) up to 1200 dpi. They may come with several different page description languages (PDLs) such as PostScript, Hewlett-Packard HPGL, Intellifont or True Image. They may have a paper tray that can hold as many as 3000 sheets.

Here is a press release from Xerox about their network printers. This will give you an idea of what a network printer costs at this time. It may be different when you read this.

> ROCHESTER, N.Y.—In its latest challenge to its network printing competitors, Xerox Corporation today announced price reductions of up to 24 percent on the DocuPrint 4517 and 4517 mp, making the two network printers the most affordable models in their class.
>
> At prices up to $300 less than comparable products from Hewlett-Packard and others, the DocuPrint 4517 and 4517 mp are now the low-cost leaders in the 17-page-per-minute speed range. With expected street prices starting at $975 and running costs of about a penny per page, the 4517 offers a lower total cost of ownership than the new 17 ppm HP LaserJet 4000 printers.
>
> In addition, Xerox announced availability and shipment of its 32- and 24-ppm printers DocuPrint N32 and N24 Network Laser Printers, which have had a strong start since their late September introduction. Xerox reports thousands of customers' orders worldwide.
>
> The DocuPrint N32, with a street price starting around $2,900, is 33 percent faster and $500 less expensive than the closest comparable version of the HP LaserJet 5si. The DocuPrint N24, with a street price around $2,450, costs about 30 percent less than a similarly configured 24 ppm HP LaserJet.

Here is contact information for some other companies who manufacture network printers:

Dataproducts Corporation 800-980-0374 www.dataproducts.com
Digital Equipment Corporation 800-777-4343 www.digital.com
Hewlett-Packard 800-752-0900 www.hp.com
Kyocera Electronics 800-232-6797 www.kyocera.com
Lexmark International 800-891-0331 www.lexmark.com
QMS, Inc. 800-523-2696 www.qms.com
Xerox Corporation 800-349-3769 www.xerox.com

Visit their Web sites or call the companies for more information.

Green Printers

The entire computer industry is under pressure to produce energy-conservation products. The federal government will no longer buy computer products that do not meet Energy Star standards. Printers, especially laser printers, are notorious for being energy hogs. Hewlett-Packard and most other manufacturers are designing newer models that go into a "sleep mode" after a period of inactivity. Ordinarily, it takes from 20 to 30 seconds for a printer to warm up. Some of these models maintain a low-voltage input so that they can warm up almost instantly.

Progress

If you mention Johann Gutenberg, most people think of the first printed Bible. Actually, Gutenberg developed the movable print and started the printing of the Bible, but he ran out of money. He borrowed from Johann Fust, and when he couldn't repay the loan, Fust took over the printing press and completed printing the Bible. So, it was Fust who was first to print the Bible. There is a copy of this Bible in the British Museum.

If Gutenberg were around today, you can bet that he would be quite pleased with the progress that has been made in the printing business. We have come a long way since 1436.

CHAPTER 16

Essential Software

This chapter can save you hundreds of dollars on software. You cannot operate a computer without software. It is as necessary as hardware. Software is merely instructions that tells the hardware what to do. Computers are dumb. Computers will only do what the software tells them to do.

Off-the-Shelf and Ready-to-Use Software

There are a few basic programs that you will need. I can't possibly list all of the software that is available for the Pentium II. There is more software, already written and immediately available, than you can use in a lifetime. Software companies are constantly revising and updating their software. There are off-the-shelf programs that can do almost everything that you could ever want to do with a computer.

There are several categories of programs that you will need. Just a short time ago, the first thing you needed was a separate Disk Operating System (DOS), but Windows 95 has eliminated the need for that. Windows 95 does a lot, but you will still need word processors, databases, spreadsheets, utilities, shells, communications, and graphics. Depending on what you intend to use your computer for, there are hundreds of other programs for special needs.

List Price vs. Discount Price

I list prices several times in this chapter. Prices listed are for comparison only. They will be different by the time you read this—no doubt, lower.

Software can be more expensive than the hardware. The prices also vary from vendor to vendor. Quite often, software will have an inflated list price that is about twice the discount price. The software vendor can say, "Look at how much you are saving. We cut the price almost in half just for you." Most people are a bit wiser now, so many companies have stopped listing an unreasonable price and just list a "discount" price. If you look through the catalogs listed in this chapter, you will find that the discount price is the same, or within just a few dollars, in almost all of the catalogs. However, a few vendors have prices that are considerably lower. Order all of the catalogs and do your own comparisons.

Surplus Software

One of the best ways that I know of to save on software is to buy it from Surplus Software at 800-753-7877 or www.surplusdirect.com. Quite often, a lot of software packages have not been sold when a new version is released.

The software business is somewhat like the soap business. Both software and soap companies have to come out with a new and improved version every year. Often, the new and improved versions don't perform much better than the old ones did, or they might do things that you have no need for.

Like most people, I never use all of the capabilities of my software. If you would like to save some money and don't mind using an older software version, call Surplus Software and ask for a copy of their free catalog. They have hundreds of surplus software packages still in their original shrinkwrap. Unfortunately, they don't have space to list them all. If you don't see a package that you need, call them and ask for it.

Surplus Software also carries several low-cost hardware components, just about everything you would need to upgrade. They also have upgrade kits and offer barebone systems that can be used to build your own.

Software Upgrades

Most computer and software stores, such as Egghead and CompUSA, participate in upgrade discounts. These discounts can save you a considerable amount of money. There are two different types of upgrades: live upgrades and competitive upgrades.

Live Upgrade Discounts

You can buy Lotus SmartSuite Release 2.1 for $44.99. This package has the Lotus 1-2-3 spreadsheet, Approach database, Ami Pro word processor, Freelance Graphics presentation software, and Lotus Organizer for personal information management. You can spend $25 more and get Lotus SmartSuite 96 for $69.99 from Surplus Software. This software has everything listed in Release 2.1, but updated to the 1996 release. In addition, SmartSuite 96 has Lotus ScreenCam, screen-recording software that lets you create and distribute custom audiovisual communications.

You can probably do just about all that you could ever want to do with SmartSuite 96. If you really must have the latest, however, SmartSuite 97 is listed in a discount magazine as $439.99. But you can get SmartSuite 97 for only $137.99 a live upgrade. A *live upgrade* is a previous version of the same product. So, if you buy SmartSuite 96 from Software Surplus and trade it in, you can save $302. You can save $327 if you buy the SmartSuite Release 2.1 and trade it in.

The software packages listed here are only listed as examples. As you might imagine, their stock changes frequently as new and later version products are released. There is no guarantee that they will have the packages listed by the time you read this. Call Surplus Software and ask for their latest catalog.

Software Surplus also has an academic program that can save you a fantastic amount of money on a large number of brand-new software packages. These packages are offered to accredited K-12 schools, colleges, universities, and current-term students, faculty, and staff. To place an order, students must have a student ID, current-term class registration, or schedule. Faculty and staff must have an ID, college or university pay stub, or photocopy of a current teaching contract. Credentials can be faxed to 541-386-4227, or you can mail copies to P.O. Box 2000, Hood River, OR, 97031-2000.

Here are just a few examples of what you can save on brand-new software if you qualify:

- You can buy Corel WordPerfect Suite 7 for $36.99. A discount magazine lists it for $287.
- You can buy Office Professional 7 for $123.99. A discount magazine lists it for $499.
- You can buy Microsoft Office Pro 7.0 for $189, Microsoft Standard 7.0 for $149.99. A discount magazine lists Microsoft Office Pro for $579, while Microsoft Office Standard is $449.

Competitive Upgrade Discounts

You might get an even better deal on, say, the most recent version of Microsoft Word if you trade in an older copy of one of Word's competitors, such as WordPerfect, Ami Pro or any of several other packages. The Software Surplus catalog offers earlier versions of several packages.

Microsoft is not the only one who plays this game. You can trade in any previous version of WordPerfect or any competitor of WordPerfect. Many other companies also accept competitive trade-ins for upgrades.

Proof of Purchase for Upgrade Discount

Before you buy a major software product, call the software company and ask what would qualify for a competitive package to trade in for what you want to buy. There is usually quite a bit of latitude.

Often, they will ask for the title page from the original manual for proof of purchase. Software companies have no use for older, used copies of programs. It would just clutter up their stores. You can keep the old software and the rest of the manual. You might even be able to get a title page from a friend who has an older copy of a software package you want to buy. (This is another good reason why you should belong to a user group.)

The proof of purchase varies among the different software publishers. You might be required to provide one or more of four general types of proof of purchase or ownership:

1. The title page of the user manual
2. A copy of a sales receipt or invoice
3. The serial number of the software program
4. A photocopy of the original program disk

Most of the larger software vendors, such as Egghead and CompUSA, participate in these programs. If you are buying through mail order, you may mail or fax a copy of the required items. Call the companies and ask what their requirements are.

CD-ROM Discs and Multimedia

Surplus Software also lists hundreds of low-cost CD-ROM discs. The discs have hundreds of different kinds of software for business, graphics, education, science, games, entertainment and other subjects.

If you like beer, they even offer a CD that tells you how you can brew your own.

Shareware and Public-Domain Software

Also, remember that there are excellent free, public-domain programs that can do almost everything that the high-cost commercial programs can do. Check your local bulletin board, user group, or the ads for public-domain software in most computer magazines. There are also some excellent shareware programs that can be registered for a nominal sum.

Try Before You Buy

The Software Dispatch Company (800-289-8383) can send you a CD-ROM disc that has several software programs on it. You can look at them and try them. If you find one that you would like to buy, just give them a call. Have your credit card ready. They will give you a password that you can use to unlock that particular program and download it to your hard disk.

This CD-ROM has just about all the software that a person in a small office or home office (SOHO) would ever need.

Software Catalogs

There are several direct-mail discount software companies. If you are undecided about what you need, call the companies for a catalog, then decide. Many of the companies who send out catalogs sell both software and hardware. They usually have very good descriptions of the software and hardware along with prices. In a book like this, I just don't have the available space to describe the software and hardware like the catalogs do. The catalogs are an excellent way to get the basic facts about software.

Be aware, however, that some of these companies are not exactly discount houses. You might find better prices at your local store or in some of the computer magazines. Also, note that some of the catalogs do not have a date on them. They usually have some sort of unintelligible code near the mailing address. If you order from one of the catalogs, they will ask you for the code. They will then charge you the price listed in that particular catalog. Prices of software and hardware change almost overnight, so if you don't have the latest catalog and you order, you might not be paying the latest price.

Here are just a few of the companies who will send you their software catalogs:

- Computer Discount Warehouse (CDW), 800-330-4239
- DellWare, 800-847-4051
- Egghead, 800-344-4323
- Desktop Publishing (DTP Direct), 800-325-5811
- Elek-Tek, 800-395-1000
- Global Software & Hardware, 800-845-6225
- J&R Computer World, 800-221-8180 (mostly Macintosh)
- JDR Microdevices, 800-538-5000
- Insight CD-ROM, 800-488-0002
- MicroWarehouse, 800-367-7080
- PC Connections, 800-800-5555
- The PC Zone, 800-258-2088
- PowerUp! Direct, 800-851-2917
- Shareware Express, 800-346-2842
- Software Spectrum, 800-787-1166
- Tiger Software, 800-888-4437

Essential Software Needed

I can't possibly list all of the thousands of software packages available. The computer magazines listed in Chapter 19 often have detailed reviews of software. Of course, they usually have many advertisements for software in every issue. The following sections briefly describe some of the essential software packages that you will need.

Operating Systems

I spent a lot of time trying to learn DOS. One of the problems with DOS was that it was hard to learn. It has over 50 commands, but I hardly ever used more than 15 or 20 of them. One reason that the Macintosh was so popular was that you didn't have to remember a lot of commands. You just used the mouse to point and click.

Just about the time I was getting pretty good at using DOS, Microsoft came out with Windows 3.1. It helped a whole lot. Again, though about the time when I got pretty good at using it, Microsoft came out with Windows 95. I have been using it for two years now. There is still a lot I haven't learned about it, but I am getting pretty good. So, at the time of this writing, Microsoft is getting ready to release Windows 98. Hopefully, it will not be too different from Windows 95.

Having to start learning every new program that comes out is almost like having to learn a new language every so often. It sure would be nice if they could choose a system and stay with it. Of course, progress does not stand still. The new Windows 98 will have the Internet Explorer 4.0 browser added as part of the package. It will also have support for Accelerated Graphics Port (AGP) and Advanced Configuration and Power Interface (ACPI). The Universal Serial Bus will also be supported in Windows 98. Windows 98 should have improved support for Plug-and-Play, and several other changes and additions.

Some say that the additions and changes might not be worth the effort to upgrade, but millions of people will do it. I probably don't really need it, but I will be one of the million who will upgrade.

Word Processors

The most-used of all software is word processing. There are literally dozens of word processor packages, each one slightly different than the others. It amazes me that software publishers can find so many different ways to do the same thing.

All of the major word processors come with a spelling checker and a thesaurus. They can be very handy, but they are usually quite limited. Most of them have a spelling checker. In Microsoft Word 7.0 that comes with Office for Windows 95, if you type in a word that isn't in the dictionary, it will offer one that it thinks is what you meant. If you type in *zzzz*, Word will tell you that it isn't in the dictionary and offer the suggestion of *sex*. This was posted on the Internet, and a lot of people thought it was rather funny. I have just checked the version of Word for Windows that comes with Office 97. It still offers the same suggestion. Evidently Bill didn't see the Internet post.

Word processors usually also include several other utilities, such as a calculator, communications programs for your modem, outlines, desktop publishing, and print merging. There are several very good word processor programs. A few of the most popular are discussed here.

WordStar I use WordStar. I am almost ashamed to admit it because I am afraid that people will laugh at me behind my back. At one time, WordStar was the premier word processor; number one in its field. It has lost a lot of its luster, however, and has been displaced by others, such as WordPerfect and Microsoft Word.

I started off with WordStar 3.0 on my little CP/M Morrow with a hefty 64 Kb of memory and two 140-Kb, single-sided disk drives. It took me some time to learn it. I have been using it for so long that I can almost do it in my sleep. I have tried several other word processors and found that most of them would require almost as much time to learn as WordStar did originally. Learning to use a new word processor is almost like learning a new language. It is a proven fact that the older one gets, the more difficult it is to learn a new language. I don't have a lot of free time. WordStar does all I need. In fact, WordStar, like most other programs, has lots of utilities and functions that I have never used.

I have several other word processors that I use once in a while because I have to write about them. But when I write about them, I usually use WordStar to do it. WordStar has both DOS and Windows versions. WordStar is now as obsolete as the 360-Kb floppy drive. Alas, how the mighty have fallen.

WordPerfect WordPerfect has the ability to select fonts by a proper name, simplified printer installation, most desktop publishing functions, support for columns, graphics, and many other useful functions and utilities. WordPerfect, now part of the Corel Corporation, also has several other software products, such as WordPerfect Presentations; WordPerfect Office for e-mail, scheduling, and calendaring; DataPerfect, a database; and WordPerfect Works, an integrated software package.

Microsoft Word Microsoft Word for Windows lets you take advantage of all of the features and utilities of Windows. If you have previously learned a different word processor, such as WordPerfect, Word can let you use WordPerfect's commands. Besides an excellent word processor, Word does just about everything that is needed for such things as desktop publishing, generating reports, making charts and drawings and giving presentations. It handles columns, imports graphics, and can import data from databases, spreadsheets, and other files. It even has an automatic spelling corrector for people like me who constantly type *teh* instead of *the*. It has many more features than I would ever use, even if I could learn them all.

Lotus WordPro 96 Lotus WordPro 96 has all the tools you need to create professionally looking documents. It has several preformatted templates and intuitive tools such as revision marking, a highlighter and comments.

Database Programs

Database packages are very useful for business purposes. They allow you to manage large amounts of information. Most programs allow you to store information, search it, sort it, do calculations on it, and make up reports from it. At present, there are almost as many database programs as there are word processors. Some of them will allow the interchange of data from one program to another. The average price for the better-known database packages is almost twice that of word processors.

dBASE dBASE II was one of the first database programs for the personal computer. It has gone through several revisions and improvements. It is a very powerful program and has hundreds of features. Previous versions were highly structured and could be a bit difficult to learn. The new Windows version is very easy to use; in many cases, just point and click, or click and drag. You can create forms or design reports very quickly and easily. It has excellent built-in help and tutorials.

dBASE is downward-compatible, so the 7 million users who have databases generated by the older versions can still use their old data. It is now possible to buy Visual dBASE 5.5 and the Visual dBASE Compiler bundled together, so that you can easily create and distribute database applications.

Paradox Paradox is fairly easy to learn and use, and is fast and powerful. It is designed for both beginners and expert users. It is a powerful, full-featured, relational database that can be used on Windows 95 or Windows NT, on a single PC or on a network. Its Query By Example is very helpful for beginners and experts alike.

Paradox has a very powerful programming language, PAL. Experienced programmers can easily use it to design special applications. You can contact Borland International, which makes Paradox, at 408-438-5300.

askSam The funny-looking name is an acronym for *Access Knowledge via Stored Access Method*. It is a free-form, text-oriented database management system. It is very much like a word processor. In fact, if you can use a word processor, you will have no trouble using askSam. Data can be typed in randomly, then sorted and accessed. Data can also be entered in a structured format for greater organization.

askSam is not quite as powerful as dBASE or Paradox, but it is much easier to learn and use. It is also much less expensive. It is ideal for most business database needs. It is also great for personal recordkeeping, such as for expenses.

I have been audited twice by the IRS because of my home office. I now put all of my tax records in askSam. It will save me a lot of time and trouble the next time they audit me.

The Windows version of askSam even has a spellchecker and hyperlink. A hyperlink in a document can link up with other parts of a document, open a new document or report, and perform several other useful functions.

You can get askSam from Seaside Software (800-800-1997). They also have a discount program for students. Students can get a very good discount when they buy the program when the order is placed by an instructor. Any instructor who places an order for 10 or more copies gets a free copy. They also have a very low price to upgrade from a previous version.

High-End Database Programs There are several high-end database programs for networks and network servers, such as Oracle and Sybase SQL. Most of these databases are 32-bit programs that will suit the Pentium II very well.

Spreadsheets

Spreadsheets are primarily number-crunchers. They have a matrix of cells in which data can be entered. Data in a particular cell can be acted on by formulas and mathematical equations. If the data in the cell that is acted on affects other cells, recalculations are done automatically.

Several of the tax software programs use a simple form of spreadsheet. The income and all the deductions can be entered. If an additional deduction is discovered, it can be entered, and all the calculations will be done over automatically. In business, spreadsheets are essential for inventory, expenses, accounting purposes, forecasting, making charts, and dozens of other vital business activities.

There are many spreadsheet programs. A few of them are discussed here.

Lotus 1-2-3 Lotus 1-2-3 was one of the first spreadsheets. It is still one of the most powerful and popular. The discount price listed in several catalogs is $309.95. The upgrade price is $95.95. Any previous version of 1-2-3 can be used for a live upgrade. Competitive spreadsheets such as Excel, Quattro, Quattro Pro, or SuperCalc can qualify for a competitive upgrade. (Prices listed are for comparison only and will probably be different by the time you read this.)

Check through any of the catalogs listed earlier or call Lotus Development at 617-577-8500. Lotus is now a division of IBM.

Microsoft Excel Microsoft Excel is a very powerful spreadsheet program, with pull-down menus, windows, and dozens of features. It can even perform as a database. It has a long list of other features. Excel is one of the products that makes up Microsoft Office.

Several catalogs have a discount price for Excel of $299.95. A live upgrade is only $89.95, a competitive upgrade is $119.95.

Quattro Pro The Quattro Pro spreadsheet looks very much like Lotus 1-2-3. In fact, Lotus sued Borland, the maker of Quattro Pro, because it has the "look and feel" of 1-2-3. After dragging through the courts for several years and costing hundreds of thousands of dollars, a judge ruled against Lotus. Quattro Pro has better graphics capabilities for charts, calculates faster, has pull-down menus, can print sideways, and has several features not found in Lotus 1-2-3. It is fully compatible with Lotus 1-2-3 spreadsheet files. It is very easy to learn, with features like Object Help, Interactive Tutors, and Experts. Like most other major software packages, earlier versions of Quattro are available from Surplus Software for very low prices.

There are many other spreadsheet programs. Check the ads and reviews in computer magazines.

ACT! for Windows

ACT! for Windows from Symantec (408-253-9600) is a business-contact database program that lets you store names, addresses, phone numbers, and other information about your customers, accounts, notes, or other entities. It has a history log that automatically records all completed activities for each contact. The information and records can be easily accessed in seconds.

Suites

One of the best ways to buy software now is to buy a suite. A suite usually costs much less than buying each package separately. The suites usually have the most important items, such as a word processor, a spreadsheet, and a database. They might also have items such as presentation software, personal information manager (PIM), financial managers, groupware, e-mail, and Web tools. Software programs in the suite packages are integrated so that they will all work together. Sometimes, a whole suite of programs will cost about the same as a single program.

Some of the most popular suites are Microsoft Office 97, Lotus SmartSuite 97, and CorelWordPerfect Suite 8. Some of the new programs, such as Office 97, have so many utilities and goodies that you could easily get lost trying to find and use them all.

Microsoft Office has several different versions. Microsoft Office 97 might cause some problems for those who have upgraded from a previous version of Office. Like many other "newly improved and better" products, the improvements add quite a lot of changes. It might take a lot of time to relearn all of the new things. Quite often, the new stuff doesn't do much more than the old stuff.

Microsoft has a Web page at www.microsoft.com/office that can help in some cases. They list the latest news about Office and have a list of Frequently Asked Questions (FAQs). If you are like me, though, I never seem to be able to find an answer to my questions at a site like this. And there is almost no chance of getting to speak to a live person about your problem.

Microsoft Home and Small Business Value Pack is another version of Microsoft Office. It has Word, Excel, Publisher, and Microsoft Bookshelf.

Microsoft Works could be called a poor man's suite. It has word processing, a spreadsheet, a database, communications, charting, and drawing all in one package. It also includes Microsoft Bookshelf. A discount house is offering this software package for $73. The same discount house offers other suites for prices from $279 to $559, so you know that Microsoft Works cannot be nearly as powerful or have as many goodies as the full-featured suites. Depending on what you want to do, though, Microsoft Works might be all you need.

Utilities

Utilities are essential tools that can unerase a file, detect bad sectors on a hard disk, diagnose problems, unfragment a disk, sort, and do many other things. Norton Utilities was the first, and is still foremost, in the utility department.

Norton Utilities The Norton Utilities are constantly being upgraded, and new improved functions are added. The latest Norton Utilities is a program that everybody should have. It has several excellent utilities that can help you run Windows 95 better and save you time and money. One new feature helps to resolve software conflicts when you install a new program. The new Norton System Genie can help you customize Windows 95 to work the way you want it to. Its new SMART Sensor can alert you of potential hard-drive problems. The Norton Disk Doctor (NDD) file can automatically repair disk problems, both hard and floppy. The Norton Disk Editor lets you explore and repair sectors of a hard disk. File Fix lets you repair data files. The Unerase command is great for recovering accidentally erased files.

The latest version of Norton Utilities for Windows 95 improves many of the old, standard features and adds several new ones. It has added several new utilities that can help in diagnosing, troubleshooting, and repair. Norton can automatically check all of your hard drives for crosslinked files, fix any corrupted files, and ask if you want to make out a report. It will then make a mirror image of the FAT and store it in a second location. If the primary FAT is damaged, you will still be able to access your data from the secondary FAT.

Norton AntiVirus is a simple and easy-to-use package that detects, destroys, and prevents virus infections. It has automatic virus removal and works with files downloaded from the Internet. The no-good #$%@&^*(&^# people who write viruses are always coming up with new ones. In a family book like this, I can't tell you what I really think about people who stoop so low as to write viruses that harm others. They are sick individuals. Solitary confinement for life without any possibility of ever seeing a computer might not be punishment enough. To keep up with the new viruses being created, Norton AntiVirus has free LiveUpdates on the Internet each month. The free virus information can be obtained from the Virus Hotline at 541-9VIRUS9, the Symantec BBS, America Online, CompuServe, or the Microsoft Network.

To find out more about Norton and other Symantec products, call their faxback number at 800-554-4403. Ask for their catalog directory to determine which numbers to order, or check their Web site at www.symantec.com.

CheckIt 5.0 CheckIt version 5 for Windows 95 and CheckIt Professional Edition are 32-bit hardware troubleshooting utilities available from TouchStone Software (714-969-7746, www.touchstonesoftware.com).

CheckIt provides tools to help pinpoint and solve computer problems, backup and restore critical system files, install new hardware components, uncover hidden conflicts, and optimize system performance quickly and easily. QuickCheck tests and locates problems automatically. If a problem is detected, whether it is a hardware glitch, setup conflict, or change in performance, the program's exclusive troubleshooter guides the user to the tests and information needed to solve it quickly. These include hardware tests, extensive system information, and a fast, easy way to compare system changes.

CheckIt's Find It feature allows users to search for the specific information they need, rather than having to look through pages of system information. In all, CheckIt offers over a dozen comprehensive information displays, identifying everything users need to know about their motherboard, memory, modem, drives, video, ports, printer, and Internet connections.

System conflicts, which result from two hardware devices using the same system resources, can be very hard to find. CheckIt monitors all system resources (IRQ, DMA, and memory ranges) and the devices using them, highlights the conflicts, and guides the user to the tools needed to resolve them.

Every time a user installs new hardware or loads a new software program, subtle changes are made to critical system files. The changes are often the cause of many types of PC problems. CheckIt's System Spy keeps track of these changes by taking "snapshots" of the system's hardware, critical system files, and performance. The user can then identify the differences by comparing the latest snapshot with a previous one. CheckIt offers real hardware tests that examine the user's system from top to bottom, paying special attention to the devices used most often. At the end of each test, CheckIt produces a report showing exactly what devices have passed and failed. This information is essential for repairing or replacing a component, or for working with a technician. Tests include CheckIt Modem and CheckIt Video, as well as powerful tests for the user's motherboard, drives, memory, ports, and CD-ROM.

CheckIt automatically saves the Windows Registry and critical system files so users have a recent backup if Windows becomes corrupted.

The new CheckIt Professional Edition provides the best suite of advanced PC diagnostics available. By combining CheckIt for Windows 95, CheckIt for DOS, PC-cillin 3.0 Anti-Virus, special loopback plugs for precise port testing, and a full year of free program upgrades, CheckIt Professional Edition gives professional technicians and power users the capability to solve more in-depth and complex PC problems.

CheckIt for DOS allows users to troubleshoot PCs when Windows won't run. They can access detailed information on a system's hardware, run full diagnostic tests on all key hardware components, and restore critical system files. Users can also generate custom batch tests and configure individual test applets for burn-in testing and troubleshooting multiple PCs.

The full version of TouchStone Software's award-winning PC-cillin Anti-Virus for Windows 95 features 100 percent-guaranteed virus protection, free lifetime pattern-file updates, and exclusive MacroTrapd technology to automatically detect and remove both known and unknown strains of destructive macro viruses.

CheckIt's exclusive Active Update allows users to receive free program upgrades and enhancements for a full year, keeping their troubleshooting capabilities on the cutting edge.

Directory and Disk Management Programs

There are dozens of disk management programs that help you keep track of your files and data on hard disk, find them, rename them, view them, sort them, copy them, delete them, and perform many other useful tasks. These programs can save an enormous amount of time and make life a lot simpler.

XTree for Windows XTree was one of the first, and still one of the best, disk-management programs available. I use it to view my files, then delete unnecessary ones. I also use it to copy and back up files from one disk or directory to another. It also lets you sort files by date or alphabetically. I often look at the datestamp so I know which files are the latest. It has many other excellent features. I don't know how anyone can get along without XTree.

XTree is a part of the Symantec Companies. Symantec has a large number of excellent software products. If you have a fax machine, you can call their automated fax system at 800-554-4403 and have them fax you information about any of their products.

Turbo Browser for Windows 95 Turbo Browser is similar to Windows 95 Explorer, except that it does much more. You can drag and drop files, cut, copy, paste, delete, and rename files. You can also back up files to removable media in Zip format with built-in PKZIP, convert graphic files from one format to another, extract text from document or spreadsheet files, and much more. It is a great companion for word processor, spreadsheet, and graphic authoring tools.

For more information about Turbo Browser, contact Pacific Gold Coast at 516-759-3011 or www.turbobrowser.com, or e-mail them at 74777.3450@compuserve.com.

TurboZip TurboZip is a Zip/Unzip utility from the Pacific Gold Coast Company, who makes the Turbo Browser just discussed.

PKZIP PKZIP is one of the most used and useful tools that has been around for several years. PKZIP allows you to compress files so that they take less space on a floppy disk or hard disk. A Zip file takes much less time to download or upload to the Internet. PKZIP lets you save or archive files that are not used very often in compressed form to save hard-disk space.

PKZIP is the de facto standard for most software compression today. You can contact PKWARE at 414-354-8699, www.pkware.com.

DiskMapper DiskMapper can visually show you how much space each program is using on your hard disk. It then gives you the option to remove, compress, or archive the files. Its visual "roadmap" helps you decide where to free up space on your hard disk. It is a great utility from MicroLogic (201-342-6518, www.miclog.com).

Computer-Aided Design

Most CAD programs are high-end programs that require very good, high-resolution monitors and powerful computers. The Pentium is an ideal computer for computer-aided design.

AutoCAD

AutoCAD, from the Autodesk Company, is a high-end, high-cost design program. It is quite complex, with an abundance of capabilities and functions. It is also rather expensive, at about $3000. Autodesk is the IBM of the CAD world and has more or less established the standard for the many clones that have followed. You can contact Autodesk at 415-332-2344 or www.autodesk.com.

Generic CADD

Autodesk has several modules and other programs that cost less than the full-blown AutoCAD. One of them is Generic CADD 6.0. For more information about it, call 800-228-3601, extension 803.

Home Series

Autodesk also has a set of five low-cost programs they call the Home Series. These programs are HOME, KITCHEN, BATHROOM, DECK, and LANDSCAPE. You don't have to be an architect to design your dream home, design an up-to-date kitchen, bathroom, or deck, or plan your landscape. Each of the five programs have a list price of $59.95. The programs come with a library of professional symbols, such as doors, outlets, furniture, fixtures, and appliances, which you can import and place in your drawing. Each program tracks the materials specified in your drawing and automatically creates a shopping list.

3D PLAN

Autodesk recently added 3D PLAN, a program that lets you look at any of the plans that were created in the HOME, KITCHEN, BATHROOM,

DECK, OR LANDSCAPE programs in three dimensions. Surfaces are shaded to add a realistic appearance.

I would recommend these programs to anyone who plans to design their own home or do any remodeling on an older home. They can save you hours of time and lots of money.

DesignCAD 2D and DesignCAD 3D

The DesignCAD programs do just about everything that AutoCAD will do at a lesser cost. DesignCAD 3D allows you to make three-dimensional drawings. These two programs are available from American Small Business Computers (918-825-4844).

Several other companies offer CAD software. Check the computer magazines.

Miscellaneous Software Programs

There are many programs for things such as accounting, statistics, finance, graphics, and other specialized applications. Some are very expensive, some are very reasonable.

CorelDRAW

CorelDRAW can be used for such things as drawing, illustration, page layout, charting, animation, desktop publishing, and presentations. It has word processing, OCR, over 5000 drag-and-drop symbols and shapes, over 18,000 clipart images, over 750 fonts, and many other features and utilities. Corel has several other excellent software packages. Contact them for a brochure at 613-728-3733 or www.corel.com.

CorelSCSI

CorelSCSI is a program that has software and several SCSI drivers that work with most major SCSI host adapters, such as Always, DPT, Ultrastor, and Adaptec. It also has SitBACk, a software program for unattended backup, as well as several other programs and utilities.

Uninstaller for Windows

When a program for Windows is installed on your computer, it copies pieces and portions into several different areas. If you decide later that you don't want that application, you can use DOS to delete the program, but it will not delete all references to the program. Every time you load Windows, it might hunt for that program, then tell you that it can't find it. Even some demo programs load themselves into several areas that are difficult to clean out. Use the DOS editor and look at Win.ini sometime. You might find references there to programs that you erased months ago. These leftover bits and pieces can clutter up your disk considerably.

The Uninstaller from MicroHelp can track down all of the different parts of a Windows program and delete them. Even if you are a Windows pro, the Uninstaller can save you time. You can contact MicroHelp at 770-516-0899 or www.microhelp.com.

CleanSweep 95

CleanSweep 95 can check all of the files on your hard disks. If it finds two or more files with the same name in different directories, it will display them. It will also show the date the file was created, the number of bytes in the file, and how often it has been accessed. You then have the opportunity of backing up or archiving one or both of the files. You are also given the option of moving the file and all of its associated components to another directory or to a network, or it will let you delete one or more files and its associated components. CleanSweep 95 is from Quarterdeck (310-309-3700, www.qdeck.com).

StreetSmart

StreetSmart from Charles Schwab Company (800-334-4455) lets you use your computer and modem to trade stocks, options, mutual funds, and bonds. It lets you research Dow Jones News and Dow Jones databases, use MarketScope for the S&P database and news, stock ratings, and buy/sell recommendations, and use Company Reports to do comprehensive research on earnings and financials. You can create your own performance graphs, import and export critical financial data, and customize your portfolio reports. If you have any interest in the stock market, you should have a copy of StreetSmart.

Money Counts

Money Counts is a very inexpensive program that can be used at home or in a small business. With it, you can set up a budget, keep track of all of your expenses, balance your checkbook, and perform several other functions. It is from Parsons Technology (800-223-6925, www.parson stech.com).

It's Legal

It's Legal is software that helps you create wills, leases, promissory notes, and other legal documents. Like Money Counts, it is from Parsons Technology.

WillMaker

WillMaker from Nolo Press (510-549-1976, www.nolo.com) is a low-cost program that can help you create a will. Everyone should have a will, no matter what age you are or how much you own. Many people put it off because they don't want to take the time, or they don't want to pay a lawyer a large fee. This inexpensive software can help you easily create a will that can prevent many family problems. We don't like to think about this sort of thing, but it happens to everyone, sooner or later.

Living Trust Maker

Living Trust Maker is also from Nolo Press. It is a program that every family should have. Even if you have a will, it is possible that it could end up in probate court. You might have heard some of the horror stories about how probate can take several years to settle, and the costs can completely eat up all of a large estate. A living trust can avoid probate and its lengthy and costly processes.

Ordinarily, a living trust requires a lawyer and can be relatively expensive. With the Nolo Press Living Trust Maker, you can create your own living trust without a lawyer. The program allows you to fashion the trust to your unique needs. The software guides you through the process, but it comes with a large user guide and legal manual that can explain and answer most of your questions. Nolo Press has free technical support if you have any problems.

Nolo Press has several other books and software. Call them for a catalog, or access them online at www.nolo.com.

Familytreemaker

Many people are curious about their ancestors. The computer has made it possible to do searches and dig up all kinds of facts about our forefathers and foremothers. The Broderbund company has a Web site at www.familytreemaker.com that lets you search online for millions of people. It has records of just about everyone who has ever been issued a birth certificate, death certificate, marriage license, or any other record. Broderbund also sells software that lets you make charts and other things necessary for a family tree.

I just did a search on the Web site for *Pilgrim,* and it came back and told me that there were over 13,500 pages with the name *Pilgrim* mentioned. I have a niece who is into family-tree stuff. She made up a booklet of our immediate family. I wrote this for the cover of her booklet:

> When you search my family tree
> Please don't search too diligently
> Cause I'm afraid that you may find
> A monkey hiding in that tree.

I might also add that you might find a few cattle rustlers or other unsavory characters hanging from my tree. :-)

Software for Kids

One of the big reasons to have a home computer is for the kids. If you have children and you don't have a computer, they are being handicapped. In today's society, a child needs all the help he or she can get in order to make it as an adult. A computer is absolutely essential to help in the very important early training. Thousands of software programs—commercial, shareware, and public-domain—have been developed for children. Most of the software catalogs listed earlier in this chapter have listings for children's software.

A good example of a children's educational program is the Smithsonian Institution Dinosaur Museum from the Software Marketing Corporation (602-893-2042). Many programs such as this come on CD-ROMs. This one comes on five 1.44-Mb floppies. The program is in 3D, so a pair of plastic 3D video glasses comes with it.

KidSoft Magazine (800-354-6150) has dozens of reviews of software for kids.

Software Training

Most software manuals are very poorly written. You can usually tell how bad the manuals are by the number of books written telling you how to use the software. Microsoft is the largest software publisher in the world. They also have a very large book-publishing house, the Microsoft Press. They publish hundreds of books each year to help people learn to use the software they publish. A cynical person might suspect that Microsoft publishes poor manuals so that they can sell more books.

There are also several companies who conduct training classes and seminars for learning some of the most popular software. These seminars may cost several hundred dollars for a one- or two-day session. I can't learn enough in one or two days to justify the cost of some of the seminars. If you pay $500 or $600 dollars for a software package, you shouldn't have to spend another $500 or $600 to learn how to use it.

One of the better ways to learn software is by using videotapes. The ViaGrafix Company (800-842-4723) has about 200 different videotape courses. They have tapes on all of the most popular software, and even some that are not so popular. You should be able to find a tape for almost any program imaginable. They even have instructional tapes on networking, telecommunications, programming, and much more. You can view the tapes at your leisure and learn at your own pace. Call them for a catalog.

ViaGrafix now has several training programs on CD-ROM, which is even better than a videotape.

There is one company that takes out full page ads in local newspapers and offers a free videotape of any of several programs. They ask for a credit card number to pay a nominal sum for shipping. When you receive the tape, you will notice very small print that says they will ship additional videotapes on a regular basis for a cost of $39.95. I get a lot of mail, so I don't read everything as closely as I should. I began getting a new videotape every month. I finally read the small print. I was rather unhappy with this company and felt that this was almost fraudulent because I did not order the tapes. Now I read the invoices.

LapLink for Windows

If you do any traveling, it is almost essential that you have a laptop computer. If you work in an office, it is very convenient to copy data from a desktop PC to a laptop to bring work home. Sometimes, though, it is a problem transferring files and data from the PC to the laptop, then back to the PC.

For many years, Traveling Software (800-343-8080, www.travsoft.com) has been foremost in providing software and cables specifically for this purpose. They have now developed several new utilities that makes file transfer faster and easier. You can now use LapLink with a modem to tie into the office PC or a network so that you can work at home, or update your files or access your e-mail while traveling. The PCs are connected with the supplied cables by using the LPT1 parallel printer ports, the COM serial ports, by modem, by wireless devices, or over a network such as Novell. Using the cables and software, two computers can be tied together in a very low-cost type of network. If you own a laptop or work in an office with two or more computers, you could probably save a lot of time with LapLink for Windows.

Summary

I can't possibly mention all of the fantastic software that is available. There are thousands and thousands of ready-made software programs that will allow you to do almost anything with your computer. Look through any computer magazine for the reviews and ads. You should be able to find programs for almost any application.

CHAPTER 17

How Your Computer Can Help You

You might be a young person who has not yet made up your mind as to what career to pursue. A recent *U.S. News and World Report* article listed 20 of the hottest jobs at this time. Most of them require some knowledge of computers. Nearly all require a college degree, some experience, and quite often, a lot of luck. Even if you have a career, but you are not too happy with it, you might want to switch. Here are some of the jobs from the list:

1. Accounting, which might include Payroll Clerk, Billing Manager, Internal Auditor, CPA Consultant, Corporate Tax Manager.
2. Arts and Entertainment—Acting, Choreography, Computer Animation
3. Banking and Finance—Bank Branch Manager, Collections Specialist, Credit Analyst, Financial Analyst, Investment Banker, Loan Review Officer, Mortgage Lender
4. Communications—TV News Reporter, TV News Producer, PR Account Executive, Publicist
5. Education—Teachers for Math, Science, Computer Science, Chemistry
6. Telecommunications—Wireless Software Programmer, Telephone operator, Telephone Company Service Representative, Telephone Technician, Cable Service Representative, Cable Technician
7. Trades—Truck Driver, Painter, Welder, Carpenter, Electrician, Heavy Machine Operator
8. Travel and Hospitality—Airline Reservations Agent, Travel Agent, Restaurant Manager, Menu Consultant
9. Engineering—Computer Engineering, Mechanical Engineer, Civil Engineer, Petroleum Engineer, Chemical Engineer
10. Environment—Environmental Consultant, Sierra Club Regional Field Representative, Forest Ecology Consultant, Industry Toxicologist, Natural Resources Economist
11. Health Care—Medical Doctor, Medical Assistant, Dietitian, Speech Therapist, Registered Nurse, Nurse Practitioner, Pharmacist, Optometrist
12. Public Services—Therapeutic Recreation Specialist, Firefighter, Police Officer, Mail Carrier
13. Sales—Electronics Specialist, Software Sales, Sales Rep, Sales Account Manager

14. Social Work—Grief Specialist, Home Health Care Social Worker, Geriatric Social Worker, Marriage Counselor, Child Protective Services Social Worker
15. Management—Manager Supply Chain, Logistics, Marketing Manager, Management Consultant
16. Medicine—Cosmetic Dentist, Family Practice MD, Psychiatrist, Allergist/Immunogist, Pediatrician, Internist, Pathologist, Anesthesiologist, Ob-Gyn, Radiologist, Surgeon
17. Personal Services—Professional Organizers, Wedding Consultant, Landscaper, Pool Service, Day Care Provider
18. Human Resources—Human Resources Specialist, Human Resources Consultant, Affirmative Action Consultant, Recruitment Manager, Benefits Director
19. Internet/New Media—Data Control Technician, Webmaster, Online Content Manger, Audio Engineer
20. Law—Business Expert Attorney, IRS Attorney, Intellectual-property Attorney

There are many, many applications and ways to use your computer to advance your career, manage a business, or just provide entertainment. I can't possibly list them all, but this chapter covers a few uses.

Resumé

There are few people who can't use a good resumé. It is one of the better ways to get your foot in the door if you are looking for a job. Many large companies are now using scanners to create databases of all of the resumés that are sent to them. They can then have the computer search for whatever qualities they are looking for at the moment. To make sure your resumé gets into their computer, you should use a good printer with a standard font to create it. In order to find out what the companies are looking for, look at the want ads from major companies to see what keywords are used. List your strongest and best skills first. Don't hide them in the middle of a long list.

Several books and software programs can help you create a good resumé. Two books are *Be Your Own Headhunter Online* by Pam Dixon, published by Random House, and *Electronic Resume Revolution* by Joyce Lain, published by John Wiley & Sons.

The low-cost WinWay Resume 4.0 program from WinWay Corporation (800-4WINWAY, www.winway.com), with an estimated street price of $39.95, comes on a CD-ROM that is full of good information. It not only helps you write a good resumé, it also helps you find a job. Some of the features included in the package are automatic resumé and letter writing, contact management, interview simulation, and salary negotiation. The CD-ROM has over 12,000 job descriptions to help you tailor your resumé and cover letter. You can even use the program to link to the Internet, where it lets you send your resumé as e-mail and helps you to find jobs via the Internet. If you are looking for a job, the cost of this program might be one of the best investments you can make. They even offer a 30-day money-back guarantee.

Many of the jobs on the Internet require a degree in computer science. Most local colleges and universities now offer computer courses. There are even several colleges and universities who offer home-study courses or distance learning over the Internet. Check the courses offered by the McGraw-Hill World University at www.mhcec.com, or call 888-649-8648, extension 2621.

Some colleges and universities offer college credit courses over local TV channels, usually the Public Broadcasting channels. This type of learning can be a fantastic alternative to driving to class, trying to find a parking spot, then sitting in class at a certain time. If the class is offered on TV, you can use a VCR to record it, watch it when you have the time, or watch it several times in order to learn it. If it is on the Internet, you can usually download the lessons to your hard disk and study when you have time. It is a great way to learn and get a college or university degree.

Home Office

SOHO is a new acronym that has recently been created to stand for small office, home office. Many businesses can be operated from a home office. Several advantages in having a home office are no commuting, no high office rent, the possibility of taking care of young children at the same time, and setting own hours. More and more businesses are allowing their employees to work from home and telecommute. Some jobs can be done from home as easily as at a big office.

There is one other very important savings if you work at home: you don't have to spend a lot of money for clothes. This is especially so for women. I might get in trouble for this, but it seems that women are a lot more sensitive as to not only what they wear, but what other women wear. It is almost unthinkable for a woman to wear the same outfit more than once a week. We men are much better off. We can even wear the same shirt twice a week, if we wear a tie to hide the ring-around-the-collar.

An excellent reason for working at home is not having to sit in traffic jams for hours. The Los Angeles freeways are choked 24 hours a day. Many people have cellular phones and do business while sitting still in the middle of a 70-mile-per-hour freeway that doesn't have a stop sign for a hundred miles. Some people have even installed fax machines in their cars. And of course you know that about 60,000 people are killed each year on our highways. Telecommuting or doing business from home could save your life.

Several computer programs let you connect your home computer to an office computer. A modem and the Internet might be all you need.

You should be aware that the IRS looks very close at any deductions for a home office. I have been audited twice, and each time had to pay more because they disallowed some of my deductions. I didn't mind so much having to pay more, although I still think my deductions were legitimate. What really cost me was the large amount of time and trouble. The next time they audit me, and I am pretty sure they will, I am going to ask them how much. If it is within reason, I will just write out a check. It will be much less expensive than having to go through the hassle of trying to explain and justify my deductions.

Deducting the Cost of Your Computer

If you have a home office for a business, you might be able to deduct part of the cost of your computer from your income taxes. You might even be able to deduct a portion of your rent, telephone bills, and other legitimate business expenses.

Some IRS Rules

I can't give you all of the IRS rules for a home office, but there are several deductions available if you use a portion of your home exclusively and regularly to operate your business. These deductions might include portions of your real estate taxes, mortgage interest, operating expenses (such as home insurance premiums and utility costs), and depreciation allocated to the area used for business. You might even be able to deduct a portion of the cost of painting the outside of your house or repairing the roof.

You should be aware that the IRS looks very closely at Home Office expenses. Before you deduct these expenses, I would recommend that you buy the latest tax books and consult with the IRS or a tax expert. There are many rules and regulations, and they change frequently. For more information, call the IRS and ask for publication 587, "Business Use of Your Home." Look in your telephone directory for the local or toll-free number for the IRS.

Whether you have a home office or not, keep good records. I have been rather sloppy in keeping records in the past. After being audited twice for a home office, however, I am a changed man.

Quicken

I now use Quicken from Intuit to keep track of all my expenses. Quicken is very easy to use. The data from it can be imported into TurboTax, which can help make the onerous tax-time task a bit easier.

Be aware that the latest versions of Quicken come with the Netscape browser. I already had Netscape installed. When I installed Quicken, its Netscape conflicted with the one already installed, and I couldn't use either one. I reinstalled Quicken and when it asked if I wanted to install Netscape, I just said no, and it cured all my problems. It only took me a day and a half to find the problem.

Home Office as a Tax Preparer

Congress and the IRS change the tax rules every year. Every year they become more and more complicated. It is almost impossible for the ordinary person to be aware of, comprehend, and understand all of the rules and regulations. Some of the rules are even difficult for the IRS. If you call several IRS offices with complicated questions, about 50% of the answers you get will be completely opposite.

If a person works at a single job and has a single source of income, the forms are fairly simple. If you have several sources of income or a small business, however, preparing your taxes can be a nightmare. It is an impossible task for many people, and they must hire a tax preparer. Many tax preparers charge from $50 to over $100 dollars an hour.

Since the tax rules change so often and are so difficult for the average person to comprehend, being a tax preparer is almost like having a guaranteed income. If you have any inclination for accounting and tax preparation, you might consider taking a course to become a CPA or tax preparer. Many community colleges offer courses in accounting, but the H&R Block Company is probably the best place to learn tax preparation. They conduct several classes throughout the year in various locations. Just to give you an indication of how profitable tax preparation can be, the H&R Block Company owned CompuServe. They recently sold it to AOL for several million dollars.

It is not absolutely necessary to be an accountant in order to be a tax preparer, but it helps a whole lot. Another reason to learn accounting is that many small businesses can't afford to hire full-time accountants. Many of them hire accountants on a part-time basis to keep their books and accounts in order.

Several good software programs can be used for accounting. Computer Associates at 516-324-5224 has several good accounting programs for both small and larger businesses. Check their Web site at www.cal.com. Another low-cost accounting package is Peachtree Accounting for Windows. Check their Web site at www.peach.com. Also, Check the mail-order catalogs listed in Chapter 18 for more accounting and other software.

Tax Programs

Since you have a computer, it might not be necessary for you to pay a tax preparer to do your taxes. Several tax programs can do the job for you. Unless you have a very complicated income, it can be done quickly and easily. In many cases, the cost of the program could be less than the cost of having a tax preparer do your taxes.

Besides doing your own taxes, most of these programs allow you to set up files and do the taxes of others. Many software companies offer tax-preparation programs for professional tax businesses, but usually at a much higher price. All of the programs operate much like a spreadsheet, in that the forms, schedules, and worksheets are linked together. When you enter data at one place, other affected data is automatically updated. Most of them have a built-in calculator so that you can do calculations before entering figures. Many of them allow "what if" calculations to show what your return would look like with various inputs. Most of the companies that make these programs also have software for state income taxes. Most of them will allow you to print out IRS forms that are acceptable.

TurboTax TurboTax from the Intuit Company (www.intuit.com) is an excellent program and is fairly easy to install and learn. It starts out with a personal interview about your financial situation for the past year. It then lists forms that you might need. Based on the present year's taxes, it can estimate what your taxes will be for next year. It is constantly updated to the latest IRS rules and regulations. You can't expect a person, even CPAs and IRS employees, to remember all the rules and regulations.

People have called several IRS clerks with questions. Conflicting answers would be given about 50% of the time. If you accept the answer to a question from an IRS clerk, and it happens to be a wrong answer, guess who is at fault? Since TurboTax has the latest rules and regulations in the software, it is probably more trustworthy than the average IRS clerk. It can probably do more for you than many CPAs and is a lot less expensive.

Quicken, from TurboTax, is a financial software program that is an ideal adjunct to TurboTax. You can use Quicken to keep track of all of your financial records, then at the end of the year, the records can be directly imported into the TurboTax program.

Electronic Filing The IRS now accepts electronic filing from certain tax preparers and companies. Eventually, you should be able to complete your taxes from TurboTax or some other program, then use your modem to send it directly to the IRS. This, of course, saves you a lot of time and will save the IRS even more. Ordinarily, the IRS has to input the data from your return into their computers by hand. Can you imagine the amount of time saved if they could receive it directly into their computers? So the IRS encourages electronic filing.

Electronic filing also offers advantages to you. Here are just a few:

- Faster refund (up to three weeks faster)
- Direct deposit of the refund
- More accurate return resulting in fewer errors
- Receipt of the return acknowledged by IRS
- Reduced paperwork
- Saves IRS labor, therefore taxpayers' money

Some people have used electronic filing to file false claims for refunds. You can be sure that from now on the IRS agents will be checking to make sure that no one is filing refund claims for their cat or dog.

There are still some limitations. For more information, call 800-829-1040 and ask for the Electronic Filing Coordinator, or check with your local IRS office to see if electronic filing is possible in your area.

Other Tools of the Trade

The following items are some other tools that can go very well with your computer in business uses.

Smart Cards

Smart Cards are similar to standard credit cards. One major difference is that they are programmed or loaded with a certain amount of cash from your account. Each time you use the card to pay for an item, a Smart Card reader deducts the amount of cash from the card. This system has been used for some time in Europe and has recently been approved for use in China. It has been a bit slow to catch on here, but it is expected to be very popular within the next few years.

Besides storing the equivalent of cash on the card, there is room for several other things, such as one's health history and a large assortment of other critical data.

Point-of-Sale Terminals

Point-of-sale (POS) terminals are usually a combination of a cash drawer, a computer, and special software. A POS system provides a fast customer checkout, credit-card handling, auditing, security, reduces paperwork, and provides efficient accounting. By keying in codes for various items, the computer can keep a running inventory of everything that is sold. The store owner can immediately know when to reorder certain goods. A POS system can provide instant sales analysis data as to which items sell best, buying trends, and of course, the cost and profit or loss.

There are several POS systems. A simple cash drawer with a built-in 40-column receipt printer might cost as little as $500. More complex systems cost $1500 and more. Software might cost from $175 up to $1000, but it can replace a bookkeeper and an accountant. In most successful businesses that sells goods, a POS system can easily pay for itself.

Here are a few of the POS hardware and software companies:

- Alpha Data Systems, 404-499-9247
- CA Retail, 800-668-3767
- Computer Time, 800-456-1159
- CompuRegister, 314-365-2050
- Datacap Systems, 215-699-7051
- Indiana Cash Drawer, 317-398-6643
- Merit Digital Systems, 604-985-1391
- NCR Corporation, 800-544-3333
- Printer Products, 617-254-1200
- Synchronics, 901-761-1166

Bar Codes

Bar codes are a system of black and white lines that are arranged much like the Morse code of dots and dashes. By using combinations of wide and narrow bars and wide and narrow spaces, any numeral or letter of the alphabet can be represented.

Bar codes were first adopted by the grocery industry. They set up a central office that assigned a unique number, a Universal Product Code (UPC), for just about every manufactured and prepackaged product sold in grocery stores. Different sizes of the same product have different and unique numbers assigned to them. The same type of products from different manufacturers will also have unique numbers. Most large grocery stores now sell everything from automobile parts and accessories to drugs and medicines. Each item has its own bar-code number.

When the clerk runs an item across the scanner, the dark bars absorb light and the white bars reflect light. The scanner decodes this number and sends it to the main computer. The computer then matches the input number to the number stored on its hard disk. Linked to the number on the hard disk is the price of the item, the description, the amount in inventory, and several other pieces of information. The computer sends back the price and the description of the item to the cash register, where it is printed out. The computer then deducts that item from the overall inventory and adds the price to the overall cash received for the day.

A store might have several thousand items with different sizes and prices. Without a bar-code system, the clerk must know most of the prices, then enter them in the cash register by hand. Many errors are committed. With bar codes, the human factor is eliminated. The transactions are performed much faster and with almost total accuracy.

At the end of the day, the manager can look at the computer output and immediately know such things as how much business was done, what inventories need to be replenished, and what items were the biggest sellers. With the push of a button on the computer, he or she can change any or all of the prices of the items in the store.

Bar codes can be used in many other ways to increase productivity. They can keep track of time charged to a particular job, track inventory, and provide many other benefits. There are very few businesses, large or small, that cannot benefit from the use of bar codes.

There are several different types of bar-code readers or scanners. Some are actually small portable computers that can store data, then be downloaded into a larger computer. Some systems require their own interface card, which must be plugged into one of the slots on the computer motherboard. Some companies have devised systems that can be inserted in series with the keyboard, so that no slot or other interface is needed.

KeyTronic has a keyboard with a bar-code reader as an integral part of the keyboard. If you are interested in the bar code and automatic identification technology, there are two magazines that are sent free to qualified subscribers:

ID Systems
174 Concord Street
Peterborough, NH 03458
603-924-9631

Automatic I.D. News
P.O. Box 6158
Duluth, MN 55806-9858

Call or write for subscription qualification forms. Almost everyone who has any business connections can qualify.

Special printers have been designed for printing bar-code labels. Labels can also be printed on the better dot-matrix and laser printers. There are several companies who specialize in printing labels to your specifications. See Chap. 16 for more information.

Networks

If you have a SOHO with two or more computers, you probably need to connect them in a network. You might think that hooking up a network would be very complicated. Some systems are, but hooking up two to four computers can be very simple.

Windows 95 helps make it simple. It has built-in software to recognize a network card and configure the system. All you need is a network interface card (NIC) for each unit, a length of coaxial cable to connect the computers, and BNC connectors. The BNC connectors on the end of the line should have terminating resistors.

Instead of BNC connectors, some NICs are designed for RJ-45 connectors. These NICs do not need the terminating resistors.

Types of Networks

The term *network* can cover a lot of territory. Some networks are worldwide. The telephone system is a good example of a worldwide network. Some computer networks connect only two or three computers, others have thousands tied together. Networks are made up of two major components: hardware and software. The hardware may consist of boards, cables, hubs, routers, and bridges. Several different companies supply network operating software (NOS). The main ones are Novell, Microsoft, and IBM.

There are a few standards so that the hardware and software from the major companies are compatible. For instance, software from either Novell or Microsoft will work on boards and systems from several different vendors and manufacturers.

There are several different types of networks, such as zero-slot types, proprietary systems, peer-to-peer types, local area networks (LANs), and wide area networks (WANs). A LAN is usually a system within a single building, plant, or campus. A LAN may include several different types of systems.

A *zero-slot* network is usually two computers tied together with a cable through their serial or parallel ports. Special software allows access to the hard disk of each unit. Files can be viewed, copied, and transferred between computers. It is a very inexpensive way to share resources. A disadvantage is that it might be limited to a maximum of 115,000 bits per second, which is relatively slow. Another disadvantage is that the distance between the two computers might be limited to about 50 feet.

LapLink from Traveling Software (800-527-5465, www.travsoft.com) is very good if you need to tie a couple of computers together in a small office. Some companies have proprietary systems for small networks and peer-to-peer systems. Moses Computer (408-358-1550) has several systems that are ideal for small networks. I have a MosesALL! IV! Computer network system in my office. For small businesses or small groups, a proprietary system might be all that you need. They are usually inexpensive, yet can have many of the utilities and functions of the large systems.

I also have two other types of network interface cards (NICs) in my office. They are both Ethernet boards. I have several software programs that these boards will work under, such as Microsoft LAN Manager, Novell's NetWare Lite, Windows for Workgroups, Windows 95, and Windows NT. A disadvantage with using the proprietary systems is that they have their own nonstandard software and hardware. These proprietary systems might not work with standard network operating software and hardware.

A *peer-to-peer* network can be rather sophisticated. It requires a network card in each computer and special software. Depending on the type of system, it might operate from 1 MHz up to 10 MHz or more. A peer-to-peer network is distinguished from a client-server network in that the computers communicate with each other, rather than with a large file server. They can share and transfer files, and utilize the resources of all the computers on the network. Figure 17-1 shows an NIC and cabling for a peer-to-peer network.

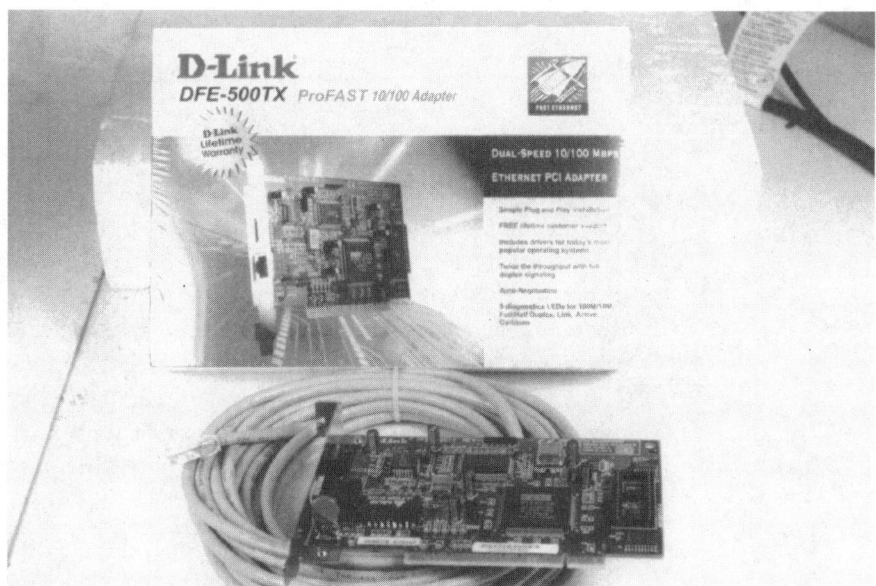

Figure 17-1 A network interface card (NIC) and cabling.

In a *client-server* network, one computer is usually dedicated as the server. A Pentium II computer is ideal as a file server. It can have a very large hard disk that contains all of the company's files and records. The individual computers attached to the server are called *workstations*. The workstations can access the files and records, and change or alter them as necessary. This kind of file-server network offers several advantages to the company. You only have to buy software for one machine. You do have to pay for a license for each of the networked computers, but it costs much less than having to buy software for each machine.

A network can keep all of your records and data in one place. This can allow close control of the updating and revisions of the data. A network allows communication between each of the networked computers, and might also allow the users to share a single printer, fax, modem, or other peripheral.

RAID

One disadvantage with a network server is that if the main server goes down, the whole system is down. The data and records must also be routinely backed up. For critical data, it might be necessary to have a RAID (Redundant Array of Inexpensive Disks) system that automatically makes two or more copies of all data. A less-expensive type system involves using a couple of large IDE hard disks and a couple of SCSI hard disks. Since they use different interface controllers, there is less chance that both of them would fail.

UPS

For critical data, it is also necessary that the server be supplied with a UPS (Uninterruptible Power Supply). A UPS is essential in areas where there is frequent lightning and electrical storms. It is also necessary in areas where there are wide variations in the electrical supply, or where there might be "brownouts." American Power Conversion (APC) at 800-800-4272, www.apcc.com, has some excellent UPS systems. They can supply you with a system for a single user or for a fairly large network.

In some older houses and even in businesses, there can be wiring faults. When an outlet is wired, if it is a two-wire outlet, it should have a long slot and a shorter slot. If you remove the outlet and look at how it is wired, it should have a white wire going to the longer slot and a black or other colored wire attached to the shorter slot. The white wire is ground and should be attached to a water pipe or some other ground at the fuse box. If it is a three-wire outlet, which should be standard for all newer installations, the long slot should have the white ground wire and the short one should have the hot black or other color wire. The *U* part of the outlet might have a single bare copper wire that is also attached to ground at the fuse box. Of course, if the outlet is miswired, it can be dangerous or even deadly. A miswired outlet can also cause grounding problems among your systems.

NOS

Of course, a network will need network operating software (NOS). Novell is the leader in both network software and NICs. Windows NT can also be used as an NOS. Several companies provide NOS and NICs for small networks. Lantastic from the Artisoft Company (602-670-7326) is one of the better-known suppliers. Novell also has Novell Lite for small networks. Microsoft Windows 95 can also be used for small networks.

There are three main methods, or topologies, of tying computers together: Ethernet, Token Ring, and Star. Each system has some advantages and disadvantages. The Ethernet system is the most popular.

Desktop Publishing

Depend on outside printing for a company's brochures, manuals, and documents can be quite expensive. Desktop publishing (DTP) might save the company a lot of money. A high-end DTP software program such as PageMaker and CorelDRAW Ventura is necessary if you expect to do a lot of DTP. For many projects, however, Word for Windows 95, WordPerfect for Windows, or any other good word processing program might be all you need.

Ipublish is a good, low-cost software program that can be used to publish on paper, on the Web, or for presentations. It is a good program for a small business or for a SOHO. It is very easy to use, even for building Web pages in HTML. Check their Web site at www.design.intelligence.com for the latest information. They even offer a 30-day free trial. Microsoft Publisher 97 is also a good program for the SOHO. Check the Microsoft Web site at www.microsoft.com.

One of the better high-end packages is CorelDRAW Ventura from Corel (www.corel.com). Corel has several good graphic and drawing packages. They have clip art and just about everything else that is needed for DTP. Corel now has WordPerfect which, among other things, is also a very good low-cost desktop publishing program.

You might also need a good laser printer and scanner for DTP. If you plan to do any color work, you will need a color printer and scanner. DTP Direct (800-395-7778 or 800-325-5811) is a desktop publishing catalog that lists several DTP software packages as well as hardware and other DTP products. The ads in many of the computer magazines don't have much information about DTP because space is expensive, but catalogs like DTP Direct have a fairly good summary of the various features of the products. Call them for a copy of their catalog.

There are several good books on DTP. McGraw-Hill publishes several. Check the online McGraw-Hill bookstore at www.mhcec.com. There are also several magazines that are devoted to DTP. Almost every computer magazine regularly carries DTP articles.

Presentations

The word *presentation*, as used in this chapter, has several meanings. A presentation can be used for sales and promotions, for training employees, and for informing employees and other persons of policies, benefits, events, changes, updates, news, and many other messages. Presentations are not only for businesses. Almost any communication is a presentation. Even a discussion with your spouse about upgrading your computer is a presentation. Every time you have a conversation with a person, you are usually presenting ideas that you want the other person to "buy." There might be no monetary reward if a person buys your ideas, but there might be a substantial reward and sense of satisfaction to your ego.

Whether we realize it or not, most of us are nearly always presenting and selling our ideas. Usually, for this type of presentation, we don't need a lot of software and hardware. For an old-fashioned type of presentation, however, where a person stands up before a group with a projector and pointer, you might need software and hardware for text, graphics, sound, and video. A few years ago, software and hardware to accomplish all of this would have required large studios full of equipment and would have cost many thousands of dollars. Today, it can be done relatively inexpensively with a desktop multimedia PC.

The Need for Presentations

Presentations are very important business tools for sales, contract proposals, and all of the other things listed earlier. Business presentations are also used for reports. Businesses spend billions of dollars each year on presentations trying to get their messages out.

A poor presentation can be a terrible waste of a company's valuable resources. Quite often, it is not the message that is at fault, but the messenger.

Designing a Good Presentation

It is not always the presenter's fault for giving a bad presentation. He or she might not have the proper tools to make a good presentation. There are several new electronic tools, but one of the most important tools is proper training. A few people are born with the charisma that makes them perfect, silver-tongued orators. They don't need to be trained. If you are like most of us, though, you might need to learn a few basic rules to become a better presenter.

The AskMe Multimedia Center (612-531-0603) has an excellent software package, Super Show & Tell, for developing presentations. Michael O'Donnel, the company president, has written a booklet called "Making Great Presentations Using Your PC." The AskMe Company has also produced "A Guide to Multimedia on the PC," a 52-page spiral-bound booklet that has a wealth of information. Call them for copies of these very helpful publications.

Presentations are so important that there is a magazine devoted solely to them. It is free to those who qualify. Almost anyone in business can qualify. For a qualification form, write to:

Presentations
Lakewood Building
50 South Ninth Street
Minneapolis, MN 55402-9973.

Whether you ever expect to do any professional type presentations or not, you should know how to give them. You should know the basic principles of public speaking. One of the best and least expensive ways to learn is through a Toastmasters group. There are usually chapters in most cities. Look in the phone book.

We are all presenters and salespersons in almost everything we do. We can be much better salespersons if we communicate better.

Intel has a business guide with several good suggestions at their site, http://www.intel.com/businesscomputing/. They offer some business solutions for business users. Of course, they want you to use their technology, but they have some suggestions for reducing the total cost of PC ownership, network management, and business videoconferencing products.

Electronic Notes

If you are giving a talk and need notes, put them on a laptop computer. Use a large type. Have the notes arranged so that each time you press the PgDn key, new notes would roll up. Pressing PgUp should let you easily go back and review.

Set the computer on the podium, then glance down now and then at your notes. Laptops have now become very inexpensive, unless you are looking for one with a color active-matrix display. If you do much public speaking, notes on a laptop are much better than handwritten notes.

Displaying the Presentation

The slide and the overhead projector are still the most popular and most used display tools. Of course, there is no sound or motion on these systems.

With an LCD panel, any image that appears on a computer screen can be projected onto a wall or a large theater type screen. The output of a computer is plugged into the LCD panel, which is then placed on the bed of an overhead-projector system. Whatever appears on the computer screen appears on the LCD panel, which is then projected onto the screen. If the computer has a soundboard and speakers, a complete presentation with color, sound, and motion is possible.

Some LCD panels can be connected to a TV, VCR, or camcorder and project the output onto a large screen. Some LCD panel systems are rather expensive. They have an active-matrix type screen, the same type of screen used in the more expensive notebook computers. The active-matrix screen means that they require a separate transistor for every pixel in the panel, which might be several hundred thousand. One reason active-matrix panels are so expensive is that a single defective transistor makes the whole display panel defective.

There are some less expensive LCD panels that are monochrome, but can display several shades of gray. The list price for these LCD panels starts at about $1000, but the color active-matrix may cost from $4000 up to $10,000 or more.

Here are a few companies who manufacture LCD panels:

- In Focus Systems, 800-327-7231
- nViwew Corporation, 800-736-6439
- Proxima Corporation, 800-447-7694
- Sayett Technology, 800-678-7469
- Sharp Electronics, 201-529-9636
- 3M Corporation, 800-328-1371

Projection Monitors

The NEC corporation (800-632-4636) makes a couple of MultiSync projection monitors. This system takes the output from a computer, VCR, or other video source and projects it onto a large screen. The system uses red, green, and blue projection lamps, such as those used on very-large-screen television sets. Several other companies make similar projection monitors.

Large-Screen TVs

Several companies have developed small devices that allow the output of a computer to be plugged into a large screen TV. Advanced Digital Systems (310-865-1432) has the VGA to TV Elite. Panasonic has developed a 36-inch television screen that is also an SVGA computer monitor with a resolution of 800×600 pixels. Call W. Pritchard at Panasonic (201-348-7182, e-mail pritchardw@panasonic.com or www.panasonic.com).

Consumer Technology (800-356-3983) has The Presenter and The Presenter Plus, pocket-sized devices that can connect a computer output to a TV. These devices can be used with a desktop PC or a small laptop. You can carry your presentation with you on a laptop, and display it on a large television. The devices work with standard TVs or with the S-Video TVs. The Comedge Company (818-855-2784) has the Audio/Video Key, another similar device. It can be used to connect a computer to a TV, VCR, or camcorder. It has both standard video and S-VHS outputs.

Ordinarily, there is a lot of loss and degradation when a video signal is copied. If you have ever seen a videotape copy of a copy, you can see just how much is lost. Many of the newer VCRs and television sets are now equipped with the S-VHS or Super-video option. This option separates the chrominance signals from the luminance signals of composite video. The resulting signals are much cleaner, with a lot less signal loss. If you are thinking of buying a new TV or VCR, look for the S-VHS input and output types.

Camcorder Presentations

All three of the devices just mentioned can also be used to record a presentation from the computer to a VCR or camcorder. If you record your presentation on an 8mm tape recorder, you can easily take it with you. The palm-sized camcorders are small, relatively inexpensive, and can be connected to any TV. The 8mm tape cartridges can hold up to two hours of text, graphics, speech, or music. The cartridges are small enough to fit several in a coat pocket. The camcorders can run off a small battery so they don't have to have an external power source.

The Gold Disk Company (800-465-3375) offers VideoDirector. This software comes with cables that plug into your computer and camcorder. You can use the software and cables to edit and record clips of your tapes. It works under Windows, so it is very easy to use. VideoDirector is ideal for editing home videotapes or for professional editing of presentations. It also comes in a Macintosh version.

A camcorder can be an excellent presentation tool. Sony and several other companies are now manufacturing digital camcorders. The Snappy is a small device that lets you capture a single photo from a camcorder, VCR, or TV. Once the single frame is captured on disk, it can be edited, or changed or morphed. For a free demo disk and more information, call Snappy at 800-306-7529.

Digital Cameras

Several companies are now making digital camcorders and still cameras. Some of the digital camcorders, such as the Canon Optura, let you capture and download single frames or photos. They have all the utilities and benefits of a movie camera plus a still camera.

There are lots of opportunities for business use of this type of camera. Photos taken with a still camera can be downloaded directly to a hard disk. The photos can then be printed out with a color printer. For some applications, even a low-cost color inkjet printer would do.

Several realty companies in my area take color photos of houses that they have listed. They then have four-color brochures printed up, and mail them to potential buyers. Four-color printing can be very expensive. Besides, by the time the brochures are printed, the house might have already been sold. It would be a lot less expensive and take a lot less time to use a digital camera to take photos of the houses for sale, then use an inkjet printer to print up color brochures. Rather than using an inkjet printer, you might want to use one of the more expensive dye-sublimation or color laser printers. Better yet, use the digital cameras to take photos and download them into a computer for viewing.

Some digital cameras and printing systems are now film quality. The one-hour photo shops are not yet shaking in their booths, but eventually, the convenience and lower cost of digital cameras will have an impact on the film business. Many photo shops have started to recognize this fact. Many of them now have printers that can print out your digital photos or put your photos on a CD-ROM for you.

There are many other business uses for digital cameras. At this time, they are a bit expensive, but they will be coming down in price very soon. Here are a few fairly inexpensive digital cameras that cost from $500 to $1000 at this time:

- Apple QuickTake (800-538-9696)
- Casio QV-10 (800-962-2746)
- Chinon ES-3000 (800-441-0222)
- Kodak DC40 (800-235-6325)
- Logitech FotoMan Pixtura (800-231-7717)
- Dycam DC-10 (800-883-9226)

The companies mentioned here have several different models. There are also other companies who manufacture very expensive, professional digital cameras that cost from $3000 up to $40,000. Here are just a few of these products:

- Dicomed Digital Camera (800-888-7979)
- Kodak DCS 420 and DCS 200 (800-344-0006)
- Leaf Lumina and DCB II (508-836-5500)
- Nikon E2 (800-526-4566)

For the Kids

One of the better reasons to have a home computer is for your children. If you don't have a computer for the kids, then you should be ashamed of yourself. You are depriving them of one of the greatest learning tools of all time. There are lots of software packages for the kids. One of the better magazines that offers and reviews this type of software is *KidSoft*, at 800-354-6150. Check other computer magazines for ads.

Several encyclopedias on CD-ROM are good not only for kids, but also for serious business references. Grolier (www.grolier.com) has an online encyclopedia that is constantly updated. Unlike the old print encyclopedias, you would never have to worry about getting a new volume yearly. The new Collier's Encyclopedia (800-757-7707) has three CD-ROMs full of very comprehensive information. See Fig. 17-2.

Summary

There are thousands of different applications for your computer. I can't possibly list them all. Your computer is a most versatile and fantastic tool.

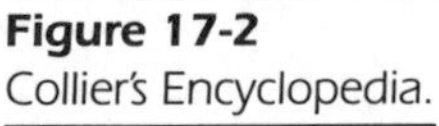

Figure 17-2
Collier's Encyclopedia.

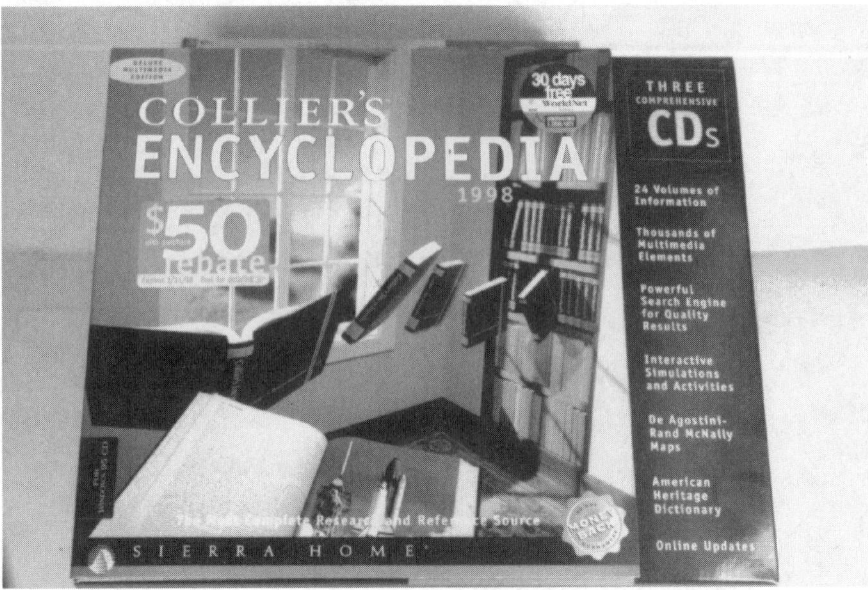

CHAPTER 18

Computer Sound of Music

Sound can be an important part of your computer system. You can run your computer without a sound board and speakers, but you will be missing out on a lot of good stuff. Sound can add fun, function, and utility to your computer.

Some Windows applications make great use of sound. The Windows Sound Recorder is an included utility that lets you record, edit, insert, mix, and play sound files that are in .WAV format. You can add sound annotations to documents such as spreadsheets, or to programs that support object linking and embedding (OLE). It is possible to run applications with sound with most any 386 or later computer, but sound works best if you have a Pentium-class computer.

What Sound Board Should You Buy?

The sound board you should choose depends on what you want to do and how much you want to spend. If you can afford it, buy the best. Creative Labs is the IBM of the sound world. Almost all sound cards adhere to the Soundblaster standards they created. Most new sound boards also adhere to the Windows 95 Plug-and-Play (PnP) standard.

Before PnP, it was sometimes very difficult to install a sound card. Often, jumpers and switches had to be set so that the board would not interfere with other installed devices. I have spent many frustrating hours in the past trying to set up sound boards. It is now fairly easy to install them if they are manufactured to the PnP specifications. Windows will configure and install properly.

There are still some low-cost boards that do not adhere to the Soundblaster standard or to Plug-and-Play. Before you buy a board, make sure that it is Soundblaster-compatible and adheres to the PnP standard. For sources, look in any computer magazine, such as *Computer Shopper, New Media Magazine, PC World, PC Computing*, or *PC Magazine*. See Chapter 19 for contact information.

A good audio board should be able to digitally record narration, sound, or music and store it as .WAV files. You should have the option of recording in mono or stereo, and be able to control the sampling rate. The board should have chips to convert the stored digital signals for analog conversion. The chips are called *Digital to Analog Converters* (*DACs*). It should also have chips to convert analog sound to digital signals. These chips are called *Analog to Digital Converters* (*ADCs*).

A good board will also have a *Musical Instrument Digital Interface* (*MIDI*). With MIDI capabilities, you can use the board with MIDI instruments, such as piano keyboards, synthesizers, and sound modules. The board should have an FM synthesis chipset that duplicates the 128 different MIDI voices and 46 percussion instruments. Instead of synthesized sound, some of the more expensive cards might have samples of actual instruments and use a wavetable for synthesis.

The board should have an audio-mixer function that allows you to control the source and level of the audio signals. Better boards will have tone controls for the bass and treble ranges. The board should also have a joystick port connector, a microphone input, and a speaker output jack.

Figure 18-1 shows a Creative Labs Blaster Awe64. It comes with microphone and several excellent software bundles.

Speakers

Most sound cards have an output of about 4 watts. That isn't very much, but you're not going to be trying to fill a concert hall. You really don't need much for your computer. You can attach any small speaker, but several companies manufacture small speakers with built-in amplifiers. The speakers are powered by batteries or by power supplied from a wall

Figure 18-1
A SoundBlaster Awe64 sound card.

outlet. They cost from $10 up to $100 for the larger ones. There are also some high-end high-fidelity systems available. Of course, high fidelity usually means high cost. Figure 18-2 shows a low-cost 60-watt system that is fine for office use. This pair cost $15 at a swap meet.

Just a few of the many companies who offer small computer speakers are Labtec, Media Vision, Koss, and Roland. Look through computer magazines for others. If you use good sound boards and speakers, your computer can be a major component in an excellent high fidelity system.

Microphones

Many sound boards come with a microphone. The type needed for voice annotations can be very inexpensive, such as those available from Radio Shack for about $5. If you expect to do any kind of high-fidelity recording, though, you definitely need a good microphone. A sound system is only as good as its weakest link. A good microphone costs from $35 to $500 or more.

There are two basic types of microphones (mics). The *dynamic* type uses a diaphragm and a coil of wire that moves back and forth in a magnetic field. The other type is the *condenser,* or *capacitor,* microphone. A capacitor is made up of two flat plates. When voltage is applied to the plates, a charged field, or capacitance, will exist between the plates. The

Figure 18-2
A pair of low-cost speakers.

capacitance depends on the voltage, the size of the plates, and the distance between the plates. If the plates are moved toward or away from each other, the capacity will change.

In a capacitor microphone, one plate is fixed and the other is a flat diaphragm. Sound pressure on the flexible diaphragm moves the one charged plate in and out, which causes a change in the capacity. Capacitor mics can be made very small, such as the lapel mics. Many professional-type microphones sold today are the wireless kind. They have a small transmitter built into the microphone, which feeds the sound to a small receiver connected to an amplifier or recorder.

Microphones may also be classified as to their pickup directionality. An *omnidirectional* mic picks up sound from all directions. A *bidirectional* mic picks up sound from opposite sides of the mic. The *cardiod* mic picks up sound in a heart-shaped unidirectional pattern (*cardi* is a prefix meaning heart). The *unidirectional supercardiod* mic picks up sound on a very narrow, straight in path.

Unlike what you might see rock stars do to a microphone, you don't have to stick a microphone in your mouth to have it pick up your voice.

Music

Computers have made enormous contributions to the creation and playing of music. It has been said that music is the universal language. Everybody likes music of one kind or another. There are many different kinds of music, and it can be used in many different ways. Music can be used to express just about every emotion known to humanity. There is music that makes you happy, elated, excited, and exhilarated. There is patriotic and marching music that can make you want to stand up and salute. There is passionate music that can arouse you and make you feel amorous. There is music that can make you feel joyful, merry, and cheerful. There is music that is touching, sad, and sorrowful. There is music that makes you feel sentimental and reminiscent. There is heartbreaking music of unrequited love that can make you feel sad and forlorn. There is serious music that is solemn, sedate, dignified. And then there is rock and roll and heavy-metal music. All of this music can be played on your computer.

Not only can you play music through your computer, you can use your computer to compose and create music, even if you know nothing at all about music. A computer is very good at converting text and graphics into digital data. Music can also be represented as digital data just as easily. Once music is digitized, you can edit it, rearrange it, add new sounds to it, remove certain sounds from it, or change it in hundreds of different ways.

A Pentium-class computer, along with the proper software, is an excellent tool for this purpose. Music software is available from most software discount companies. Egghead (800-344-4323) has several music software packages. The Rhapsody package, for example, lets you compose, edit, and print your musical score. The low-cost Concertware lets you enter music, play it back, and edit it. They also have instruction software for the piano and for guitar.

American Music Supply (800-458-4076) has Cakewalk Professional, which is one of the most complete programs for music. They have several versions of Cakewalk. It can let you record up to 16 tracks. It lets you create music, edit it, print it, and control it in MIDI sequences. American Music also has several other software programs, such as Band in A Box, Sound Forge, Steinberg Cubase Score, and Music Ace. American Music Supply also has just about every kind of musical instrument known. Call them for a catalog.

There are lots of articles and ads for music software in the music magazines and catalogs listed near the end of this chapter.

Internet Telephone and Video

It can cost up to 35 cents or more per minute to make a local telephone call. If it is long-distance, or to another country, it might cost a small fortune. I can use my computer to send a message over the Internet to anyplace in the world for the cost of a local call. That message is being sent using the telephone system. Several companies have developed hardware and software that lets you use the Internet for telephone calls. In some cases, Internet Service Providers (ISPs) might have to provide extra hardware at their server. In this case, they might charge extra for phone use, but even then it will be much less expensive than the telephone company's charges.

Some companies have developed low-cost video cameras and other hardware to let you send video over the Internet. Diamond Multimedia (www.diamondmm.com) has a low-cost kit for voice and video over the Internet. They claim that it can be used without having to pay a surcharge because the ISP will not have to install any special equipment.

To use the telephone or video on the Internet, you will need a sound board, a microphone, and speakers.

Teleconferencing

One important reason to have a sound board and speakers in your computer is for voice and data conferencing. Two computers can be linked together on a network in an office, a large campus, or by modem anywhere in the world. Several modems and faxes are now capable of sending and receiving voice and data. A couple are WinFax Pro 7.0 from Delrina (800-268-6082 and Fax Center PC Server from SoftLinx (800-899-7724).

My 28.8 Kb Sportster Vi Fax/Modem from U.S. Robotics with voice mail lets me play and record voice messages. Here are a few other products that do about the same thing:

- Aztech Labs' Aztech Audio Telephony 2000 (800-886-8859)
- Best Data's ACE 5000 (800-632-2378)
- Boca Research's Sound Expression (407-997-6227)
- Creative Labs' Phone Blaster (800-998-5227)
- Diamond Multimedia's TeleCommander 2500XL (800-468-5846)
- IBM PC Options' Multimedia Modem (800-426-2968)
- Prometheus Products' CyberStereo (800-477-3473)
- Reveal Computer's Decathlon XL (800-738-3251)
- U.S. Robotics' Sportster (800-342-5877)

The OfficeF/X from Spectrum Signal Processing (800-667-0018) includes a modem/fax, Sound Blaster-compatible sound card, voice mail, and speakerphone. It can distinguish between incoming voice, modem, or fax calls and route the call appropriately.

Microsoft has developed MS Phone, a telephony application for Windows 95 that functions as a telephone, speakerphone, answering machine, PBX, interactive voice response (IVR), and personal assistant. With this application, you will be able to use voice commands to operate your computer. The AT&T Computer Telephone 8130 connects to a serial port on the computer and provides several functions, such as contact management, logging of incoming and outgoing calls, and caller ID.

Sound, Microphones, and Speakers

Sound is made by the pressure on air created by a vibrating object. The pressure of the vibrations causes the air to move back and forth, creating sound. If a microphone is placed in the vicinity of the sound, it can capture an image of the sound and turn it into electrical impulses. There are several different types of microphones. One basic type has a diaphragm that vibrates due to the pressure of the sound waves. The diaphragm is attached to a coil of wire that moves in and out of the field of a permanent magnet. The movement of the coil of wire in the magnetic field produces an analog voltage that varies according to the vibration of the sound. You can record the electrical pulses, then use electronics to amplify the small signals, causing a loudspeaker to reproduce the original sound.

Basically, a loudspeaker is quite similar to the microphone. The speaker has a coil of wire that is attached to the speaker cone. The coil of wire is surrounded by a strong permanent magnet. Moving a coil of wire through a magnetic field produces a voltage; passing voltage through a coil of wire produces a magnetic field. The polarity of the magnetic field thus created varies from plus to minus depending on the polarity of the voltage. As the positive and negative pulses of voltage are passed through the coil of wire, it alternately attracts and pulls the coil into the magnet, or repels it, pushing the coil and cone outward. The movement of the speaker cone produces pressure waves that are a replica of the original sound.

Digital Sampling

Some large, mainframe network computers operate by giving each person on a network a small slice of time. This is called *timesharing*. If the time was divided into millionths of second, a person might receive a couple of slices, then the next person would get a few slices, then a few millionths of a second later, the first person would get a few more slices of data. It would be done so fast, that a user would not realize that the data was being received only part of the time. Hundreds, or even thousands, of people could be on a single line, all receiving different data, at the same time.

Digitizing an analog voltage is somewhat similar to timesharing. Digital samples, or slices, are taken of the analog waves. If the number of digital samples per second is rather low, then there can be a lot of unrecorded space between each slice. When played back, the unrecorded space can usually be electronically reconstructed to some degree. If the sample rate is fairly low, however, with wide spaces between each sample, the output sound will be somewhat less than high fidelity.

The higher the frequency of the sample rate, the more closely the output sound will match the original. Then why not take higher-frequency samples? Because the higher the frequency of the digital sample rate, the more space is required to store or record it. High-fidelity digital sound requires a tremendous amount of disk space.

Sampling Rates and Bits

Sound can be digitized using 8-bit samples or 16-bit samples. An 8-bit system can chop a wave form into a maximum of 256 steps, or 2^8. A 16-bit system (2^{16}) can save up to 65,000 pieces of information about the same wave form. As you can imagine, the 16-bit system offers much higher fidelity, but at a greater need for storage space.

Using an 8-bit mode with a sample rate of 11 KHz, you will be recording 11,000 bytes of data each second, or 661 Kb per minute. If you were recording in 8-bit stereo at the same rate, the storage requirement would double, or 1.6 Mb for one minute. To record in 16 bits at 11 KHz, it would be twice the bits per second of 8-bit mode at the same rate: or 22,000 bytes per second, or 1.6 Mb per minute.

Most speech has a frequency range from about 300 Hz up to about 6 KHz. Sampling at 11 KHz and 8 bits is good enough for speech, but it would not be very good for high-fidelity music. Most systems are capable of sampling at 22 KHz and 44.1 KHz in both monaural and stereo modes. A sample rate for 44.1 KHz in monaural would be 82.2 Kb per second, 5.292 Mb per minute. In stereo, it would be doubled, to 10.5 Mb per minute. One hour of recording at this sample rate would require over 630 Mb. Most audio CDs have about 630 Mb of storage space and can play for about one hour.

Standard digital sampling rates in the audio industry are 5.0125, 11.025, 22.05, and 44.1 KHz.

Why the 44.1-KHz Sample Rate?

If we had perfect hearing, we could hear sounds from 20 Hz, or cycles per second, up to 20 KHz. Most of us, especially older people, have a much narrower hearing range. So why should we worry about a 44.1-KHz sample rate? This is more than twice the frequency that we could hear, even if we had perfect hearing.

Many instruments and other sounds have unique resonances and harmonics that go beyond the basic sounds they produce. These resonances and harmonics are what makes a middle-C note on a piano sound differently than the same note on a violin or trumpet. Many of the harmonics and overtones of sound are in the higher frequencies. In digital recording, the upper frequency must be at least twice what you can expect when it is converted to analog. So, a 44.1-KHz digital signal will produce a 22-KHz analog signal.

Resolution

We often speak of the resolution of our monitors. The more pixels displayed, the sharper the image, and the higher the resolution. We also use the term *resolution* to describe digitized sound. The higher the sampling rate and the more bits of information about each sound wave, the higher the resolution and the better the fidelity.

There is a limit to the resolution of an 8-bit system, no matter how fast the sample rate. The maximum samples of a waveform that can be captured by an 8-bit system is 2^8, or 256. You might think that the 16-bit system would only provide twice the resolution of an 8-bit system. Actually, however, a 16-bit system can provide 256 times more resolution, 2^{16}, or 65,536. It is apparent that a 16-bit system can give much better resolution and fidelity than an 8-bit system.

Signal-to-Noise Ratio (SNR)

Analog audio is made up of voltage sine waves that vary up and down continuously. Noise and static are also made up of similar sine waves. Noise and static are everywhere. They are in the air, especially during electrical storms. They are in our electrical lines and in almost all electronic equipment. They are very difficult to avoid it.

The signal-to-noise (SNR) ratio is the ratio between the amplitude of the audio or video signal and the noise component. SNR is measured in decibels (dB), usually a minus dB. The larger the negative number, the better. Most sound boards, CD-ROMs drives, and other sound systems list the SNR on their specifications. Most of the better systems will have at least a −90 dB SNR. Since noise is analog voltage, a good digital system will usually have less noise than the analog systems.

Digital Signal Processors (DSP)

One of the things that helps make it possible to get so much music from the sound board is a digital signal processor (DSP). It can be a very large task just to assemble and determine which notes to output from a single instrument. It can be mind-boggling to try to do it for several instruments.

As you know, the CPU is the brains of your computer. Ordinarily, almost everything that transpires in your computer has to go through the CPU. However, certain things, such as intensive number-crunching, can be speeded up with a coprocessor. DSP chips are quite similar in function to math coprocessors. A DSP can take over and relieve the CPU of much of its burdens. DSP chips can be configured and programmed for several specific tasks, such as high-quality audio or complex graphics and video. The DSP can be used for musical synthesis and many special digital effects.

At one time, DSP chips were rather expensive, but now the chips are quite reasonable. Since they add very little to the cost, more and more manufacturers are adding DSP chips to their sound boards. Before you buy a sound board, check the specifications. Turtle Beach Systems was one of the first to design and implement DSP technology on their Multi-Sound boards. Creative Labs followed soon after, with their Sound Blaster 16 ASP. Figure 18-1 shows their latest, the Awe64.

Several other companies are now manufacturing boards with superior DSP technology. These chips add so much function and utility to the sound board that eventually every manufacturer will be using them.

Installing a Sound Board

The CPU of your computer is always busy and can only be interrupted by certain devices that need its attention. The obvious reason for this is to keep order. If all of the devices tried to act at the same time, there would be total confusion. So, computers have 16 interrupts, or IRQ lines, and each device is assigned a unique number. The devices are given priority according to their ranking number. For instance, if the CPU received an interrupt request from the keyboard, which is IRQ 1, and a request from a mouse, on IRQ 4, the keyboard request would be answered first.

If two devices are set for the same IRQ, it will cause a conflict. You might have to set one or more jumpers or switches on your board before you install it. If it has been designed and manufactured to the Plug-and-Play (PnP) specifications, you might not have to worry about setting switches and jumpers.

Just as your house has a unique address, areas of RAM have distinct addresses. Certain devices use certain portions of RAM to perform some of their processing. Therefore, you might have to set jumpers or switches for the input/output (I/O) address of your sound card. The default address, the one set by the factory, will probably be 220. This is the Sound Blaster standard, and it is used by many others.

There might also be a set of jumpers to set the Direct Memory Access (DMA) channel. On most PCs, there are three or more DMAs, and they don't usually cause a conflict if two or more devices are set to the same channel.

Most of the newer audio boards meet the PnP Specification. If so, your computer BIOS will recognize these boards and automatically configure them. Many older boards have built-in diagnostics that can detect a conflict with the IRQ or I/O settings. Still, you might have trouble determining which other device is causing the conflict. To see what devices are being used by the 16 IRQs in Windows 95, you can double-click on My Computer, then Control Panel, then System, Device Manager, and Computer. It can show all of the IRQs and which components are using them.

One of the benefits of CD-ROM drives is that they can play sound and music along with text, graphics, and motion. You can play CD audio discs on most CD-ROM drives. Most CD-ROM drives have a small audio connector on the back panel. A special cable is used to connect to the sound board. Unfortunately, there are no standards for the audio connector for the CD-ROM; it might be different on sound boards from different companies. Because there are so many variations, the audio cable is often not included with the sound board or with the CD-ROM drive. You might have to special-order it. They cost about $5. The audio cable plugs into a miniature connector on the back of the CD-ROM drive. The other end plugs into a small connector on the sound board.

Musical Instrument Digital Interface (MIDI)

Electronic circuits can be designed to oscillate at almost any frequency. The output of the oscillating circuit is a voltage that can be amplified and routed through a loudspeaker to reproduce various sounds. In the early 1970s, Robert Moog used voltage-controlled oscillators (VCOs) to develop the Moog synthesizer. With a synthesizer, you can create synthetic musical sounds that imitate different instruments. The sounds from the early systems didn't sound much like real musical instruments.

Also in the early 1970s, John Chowning of Stanford University developed digital FM synthesis. The Yamaha Corporation licensed the technology from Stanford and introduced the first FM digital synthesizer in 1982. Since that time, there have been some tremendous technological advances. Today, a person might not be able to discern whether a sound was synthesized or came from a real instrument.

In some instances, the music from a sound board does come from real instruments. Sample notes are recorded from instruments. Under computer control, any of the stored samples can be joined and played back. The notes can be held for a half note, or shortened to a quarter note, or for whatever the music requires. Samples from several instruments can all be played at the same time. The music can sound as if it were produced by a live, hundred-piece orchestra. And it all comes from a chip that is about 1 inch square. It is absolutely amazing.

The early VCOs were rather crude. The electronic industry was still in its infancy. There were no integrated circuits. As the electronic industry and technology evolved, newer and better VCOs developed and were incorporated into musical instruments.

The MIDI Standard

Originally, there were no standards for the VCOs and new musical instruments. As usual, each vendor's product was a bit different than all others. In 1983, a group of companies got together and adopted a set of standards that they called the Musical Instrument Digital Interface. This was truly a historic agreement for the music industry.

MIDI and the advances in electronic technology have made it possible to generate more new music in the last ten years than was generated in the last 100 years. Synthesized music is not only used for rock and roll, but for television commercials, movies, and all types of music.

How MIDI Operates

MIDI itself does not produce music. It is only an interface, or controller, that tells other devices such as a synthesizer or a sampler which particular sound to produce. In some respects, MIDI is similar to the old-style player pianos that used a punched roll of paper to play. Briefly, the MIDI specification says that a MIDI device must have at least two MIDI connectors, an input and an output. (These are DIN connectors, the same type as used for the computer keyboard connector on the motherboard.) A MIDI device may include adapter cards, synthesizers, piano-type keyboards, various types of instrument pickups, digital signal processors, and MIDI-controlled audio mixers.

One of the great advantages of MIDI is that it allows many different electronic instruments to communicate with each other. When two MIDI instruments are connected, the devices exchange information about the elements of the performance, such as the notes played and how loud they are played. A master keyboard can be connected to two or more MIDI electronic keyboards or other MIDI devices. Any note played on the master can be also played on the connected MIDI "slaves." The electronic keyboards can emulate several different instruments. One person playing the master can use the slaves to make it sound as though a very large orchestra were playing. There are many options available, such as allowing you to record the notes played, then play them back or edit and change them.

General MIDI Signals

There are 128 common instrument sound signals for MIDI control. Each signal is numbered, 1 to 128. (You might also see them numbered 0 to 127). The standard was originated by the Roland Corporation and is now coordinated by the MIDI Manufacturers Association (MMA). If the MIDI receives a signal and it is connected to a synthesizer, keyboard, or any MIDI instrument, it will trigger the device to play a note corresponding to the signal number. For instance, a signal on number 3 would cause a honky-tonk piano sound; number 40 would be a violin.

Note that there are 16 different instrument classifications. Every eight numbers represent sounds from a basic class of instrument. For instance, the first eight sounds are made by piano-type instruments, the next eight are made by chromatic percussion instruments, then organs, etc. There are an additional 46 MIDI note numbers for nonmelodic percussion instruments. These numbers include such things as drums, a cowbell, wooden blocks, triangles, and cymbals.

Synthesizers

The MIDI specification was primarily designed as a standard for controlling synthesizers. It did not specify how a synthesizer should create a sound or what sounds should be created.

The word *synthesize* means to combine or put together. Synthesizers can combine two or more wave forms to form new sounds. There are several types of sound waves or oscillations. Each musical note has a basic oscillation frequency. For instance, A2 has a frequency of 220 oscillations per second, or 220 Hz. The note E3 vibrates at 330 Hz, A4 at 440 Hz, and E6 at 660 Hz. You could generate pure, single-frequency sine waves of each of these notes, but they would be rather dull and uninteresting. The actual notes are a combination of oscillation frequencies.

Even though it has the same basic frequency, if a note is played on different instruments, there will be distinct differences in the sounds. The note A4 played on a trombone sounds quite different than A4 played on a guitar. They sound differently because they are not pure, single-sine-wave frequencies. The vibrations of a basic note cause other vibrations in the metal of a trombone or the wood of a guitar. These extra vibrations are the timbre that adds tone color to a sound and distinguishes it from a note played on another instrument.

Harmonics

An important cause for differences in sounds is the harmonics created. A guitar string plucked to play A4 will vibrate at 440 Hz. If you photographed the vibrating string with a high-speed movie camera, then slowed it down, you would see a primary node of vibrations, but there would also be several smaller nodes on the string. These smaller nodes would be vibrating at twice the frequency of the primary node, and some would even be vibrating at four times the primary frequency. The sounds made at the higher frequencies blend with the primary sound to give it tone and color.

These higher frequencies are called *harmonics*. Harmonics are even multiples of the fundamental oscillation of a note or its basic pitch.

Envelope Generator

Bob Moog determined that there are four main criteria in each sound. He identified them as attack, decay, sustain, and release (ADSR). The *attack* determines how fast the initial sound rises. It might hold at the initial height for a while, then start to *decay*. *Sustain* determines how long the sound is audible while a key is held down. *Release* is the rate at which the sound intensity decreases to zero after the key is released. The ADSR electronic envelope is used in synthesizers to describe almost any sound.

Wave Tables

FM synthesized sounds are usually not as good as the sound generated from an actual instrument. The more expensive sound cards and many of the better MIDI instruments use digital samples of real sounds. This requires some memory to store the samples, but actually not as much as you might think. For instance, a piano has 88 notes or keys, but it is only necessary to sample a few notes. Since they are all piano notes, the main difference is the pitch.

Middle A, or A4, has a frequency of 440 Hz, while A2 has a frequency of 220 Hz. A sample of a single A can be electronically altered to make it sound like any A on the piano keyboard, so you only need a sample of an A, B, C, D, E, F, and G. With a small sample of each of these notes, any note of the 88 on the piano can be created.

It also would not matter whether the note was a quarter note, half note, or whole note. Once the note is simulated, it can be held for as long or as short a time as necessary. The same type of system would be used to sample notes from other instruments. It would be a little simpler to store notes from other instruments because most of them don't have as many notes as a piano. A piano is one of the few instruments that allows more than one note to be played at the same time.

The samples are stored in ROM. When a note is called for, the sample is read from ROM, placed in RAM, electronically adjusted for whatever note is needed, then sent to an amplifier and loudspeaker. The more instruments sampled and the more samples stored, the more memory is required, both ROM and RAM. Some high-end keyboards might have 10 Mb or more of ROM and about 4 Mb of RAM.

Sequencers

Sequencers are a type of recorder that uses computer memory to store information about a performance. Like the MIDI, it does not record the sound itself, just the information about the sound. Even if you know nothing at all about music, you can write and compose music with a sequencer connected to a synthesizer or other electronic instrument. If you know a little bit about music, you can become an expert composer with a sequencer.

Most sequencers are software programs that allow you to create, edit, record, and playback musical compositions on a hard disk in the MIDI message format. A sequencer memorizes anything you play and can play it back at any time. Sequencers are similar to multitrack recorders, except that they are much faster, since the tracks are on a computer. The computer also lets you do hundreds of things better, quicker, and easier than a tape recorder. A sequencer lets you edit music in thousands of ways that are not possible with a tape machine. With a single MIDI instrument, an entire album could be recorded.

A sequence can be part of a song, a single track of a song, or the whole song. The sequences are laid down in tracks. Several tracks of different instruments can be laid down separately, then all played back together. A single track can be played back, and edited or changed. Tracks can be recorded at different times, then blended together. A song or an album can be created by a group even though one member might be in New York, one in Los Angeles, or others scattered all over the country. Each member of the group could record their part on a disk, then ship it to a studio, where all of the tracks could be edited and blended together.

Some sequencers allow you to record channels while playing back existing channels. Tracks can be laid down over other tracks without erasing what is already there. Portions of a track can be erased and new material inserted. The editing capabilities are almost unlimited.

Some synthesizers and keyboards have a built-in hardware sequencer. The hardware sequencer allows you to do many of the same things that sequencer software allows, but a hardware sequencer does not have the capabilities of a computer.

Sequencer software such as Cakewalk lets you record in real-time as an instrument is being played. You can also use the step-entry mode and enter one note at a time. The notes can be entered from a computer keyboard or a piano-type MIDI keyboard that is connected to the computer. The software is intelligent enough to take step-entry notes, and combine them with the proper staff notation and timing. Some software will even add the proper chords to the step entry.

Other Windows sequencer software programs are Cadenza, Master Tracks Pro, and Midisoft for Windows. Many of the music software programs will also print out music scores.

When you consider the modern technology that allows the editing and re-editing of a song until the cut is perfect, you have to admire the works of some of the early recording artists. They usually didn't get the opportunity to go back and change a mistake or to improve a lick here and there.

Piano Keyboards

It is possible to use a computer keyboard to edit or create music, but it is a lot easier to work with an electronic piano keyboard. Many electronic keyboards have built-in synthesizers and MIDI connections. If you are interested in music, one of the magazines that you should subscribe to is *Electronic Musician* (800-843-4086). It has excellent articles about music and new devices, and is of interest to professional musicians as well as amateurs and anyone who enjoys music. They also publish an annual *Digital Piano Buyer's Guide* available from Mix Bookshelf (800-233-9604). Mix Bookshelf specializes in books for musicians. Another book that they carry is *The Musical PC*. It is an excellent book for anyone who wants to learn more about music and computers. Another book they carry is *Making Music with Your Computer*. It would be very helpful to anyone just getting into music. There are also articles in the book that would be of interest to an old pro.

Another magazine for musicians and anyone interested in music is called *Musician* (800-347-6969). It is published primarily for the professional musician, but is of interest to anyone who enjoys music and wants to keep up with what is happening in the music and entertainment field.

Music Software and Hardware

There are several software packages that you can use with your computer to make music. Listed here are just a few:

- The Cakewalk Company (800-234-1171) has some of the most comprehensive music software in the business. They also have Cakewalk Pro Audio, which is a MIDI sequencer. Call them for information and a Demo Pack.
- The Kurzweil Company (800-421-9846) has an extensive line of music products.
- Pro Tools III from Digidesign (800-333-2137) lets you record, edit, process, mix, and master your music.
- Jammer from Soundtrek (800-778-6859) allows you to enter a few chords then choose from over 200 band styles to create professional-sounding songs.
- The EMAGIC Company (916-477-1051) has several software packages. Call them for a brochure.
- The Free Play Company (310-459-8614) sells World Music Menu, which can help you create music similar to that of countries from around the world.
- The PG Music Company (800-268-6272) has Band-In-A-Box, in which you type in a few chords and it supplies the rest. It automatically generates professional-quality accompaniment instruments. PG Music also offers several other music software programs.

Many other companies offer software that can let you make beautiful music with your computer. To find out more about these companies, subscribe to *Electronic Musician* and the other music magazines and catalogs listed in this chapter.

Catalogs

You will need music software for your PC. The Soundware catalog at 800-333-4554 lists hundreds of music software programs. They have a comprehensive and detailed description of each program listed. Even if you don't intend to order a program, the descriptions in the catalog can give you a good idea of what is available. Call them for a catalog.

The Musician's Friend catalog (800-776-5173), the American Musical Supply catalog (800-458-4076), and Manny's Mailbox Music (800-448-8478) all have hundreds of musical instruments, supplies, videotapes for training, and books. Call them for catalogs.

Trade Shows

Partly due to the success of the COMDEX shows, there are now lots and lots of trade shows. There are several music-related ones that you might be interested in.

The National Association of Music Merchants (NAMM) has two large shows each year, usually one near Los Angeles in the winter and one in Nashville during the summer. There are usually hundreds of exhibitors at these shows. You will find just about every imaginable musical product at them. They have dozens of rooms where amplifiers and loudspeakers are demonstrated. There are hundreds of electronic keyboards on the floor, everything from the small toys up to the very expensive grand pianos. They also have several old-fashioned nonelectronic pianos, all the way from the spinet up to the concert grand. If you are at all interested in music, this is the place to see all that is available. To find out when and where the next NAMM show will be held, you can call 619-438-8001.

The Consumer Electronics Show (CES) also presents two large shows each year, a winter show held in Las Vegas during the first week in January and a summer show held in Chicago during the first week in June. This show also has several music and musical instrument exhibitors. To find out more about this show, call 202-457-8700.

If you are interested in multimedia, you can order my book, *Build Your Own Multimedia System and Save a Bundle,* from McGraw-Hill at 800-262-4729. It is also available at most bookstores.

CHAPTER 19

Component Sources

How much you save by assembling your own computer will depend on what components you buy and whom you buy them from. You will have to shop wisely and be fairly knowledgeable about the components in order to take advantage of good bargains. It is very difficult to keep up and know what is going on in this ever-changing industry. One of the best ways to do this is to subscribe to some of the many computer magazines. You can look through the magazines and do price comparisons of the various components and systems.

Most computer magazines now have Web sites. You might not even have to subscribe to get all the information you need. Most of the magazine Web sites are updated frequently. The way the computer industry changes, some of the articles in the monthly magazine might be obsolete by the time you get it. Another good way to keep up is to attend the many computer shows and swap meets.

Computer Shows and Swap Meets

I have done a lot of my buying at computer shows and swap meets. There is a computer show or swap meet almost every weekend in the larger cities. Sometimes, there are two or three in the Los Angeles area on the weekends. If you live in or near a large city, check your newspaper for ads. To set up a computer swap, an organizer will usually rent a large building, such as a convention center or a large hall. Booth spaces are then rented out to the various local vendors. Most of the booths will have good, reputable, local business people. Most of the shows have a circus like atmosphere about them and I often go just because of this.

One of the best features of the swap meets is that almost all of the components that you will need are there in one place on display. Several different booths will have similar components for sale. I usually take a pencil and pad with me to the shows. I walk around and write down the prices of the items that I want to buy, and compare prices at the various booths. There can be quite a wide variation in the prices. You can also haggle with most of the dealers at the shows, especially when it gets near closing time. Rather than pack up the material and lug it back to their stores, many will sell it for a lower price.

The Lure of Las Vegas

The Softbank Company (617-433-1500) sponsors the Computer Dealers Exposition (COMDEX). They put on two of the largest annual computer shows in the country. Spring COMDEX is usually held in Atlanta, or sometimes in Chicago. A much bigger fall COMDEX is held during November in Las Vegas. The attendance goes up every year. When I first started attending in 1984, they only had about 60,000 people at Las Vegas. The fall 1997 show in Las Vegas attracted almost a quarter-million people for the five days. Every hotel room in Las Vegas is usually sold out six months before the show. If you can find a room, you can expect to pay two or three times what the room would ordinarily cost. They also demand a minimum three-night stay.

COMDEX is the most popular show of its kind in the nation. A cynical person might say that the large number of people who attend the Las Vegas show are not there strictly for business. Some might think that some of these people are there because of the other shows and attractions in Las Vegas. I am sure, however, that the fact that they can write the whole thing off as a business expense never enters their head. In addition to the Spring COMDEX, Softbank has now started a New Media Expo, which will be held in Los Angeles in the Spring. Since Atlanta and Los Angeles do not have the extra attractions that Las Vegas has, however, the attendance is usually less than one-fourth that of the Las Vegas show. The Softbank Company also puts on international shows in several foreign countries.

Your Local Store

Most of the vendors at the swaps are local business people. They want your business and will not risk losing you as a customer. There might be a few vendors from other parts of the country, however. If you buy something from a vendor who does not have a local store, be sure to get a name and address. Most components are reliable, but there is always a chance that something might not work. You might need to exchange it or get it repaired, or you might need to ask some questions or get some support to get it working.

Again, computers are very easy to assemble. Once you have bought all of the components, it takes less than an hour to assemble your computer. It is possible to make a mistake, however. Most components are now fairly reliable, but there is a possibility that a new part could be defective. Most dealers will give you a warranty of some kind and will replace defective parts.

If there is something in the system that prevents it from operating, you might not be able to determine just which component is defective. Besides that, it can sometimes take a considerable amount of time to remove a component like a motherboard and return it to someone across town—or even worse, someone across the country. If at all possible, therefore, try to deal with a knowledgeable vendor who will support you and help you if you have any problems.

Magazines and Mail-Order

Every computer magazine carries pages and pages of ads for compatible components and systems that can be sent to you through the mail. If you live in an area where there are no computer stores or shows, you can buy by mail.

One of the biggest magazines in size and circulation is *Computer Shopper.* It usually has over 1000 tabloid-sized pages. About 90% of the magazine is made up of full-page ads for computer components and systems. They do manage to get a few articles in among the ads. For subscription information, call 800-274-6384 or visit their Web site, www.cshopper.com. *Computer Shopper,* and some of the other magazines, have a categorized list of all the products advertised in the magazine and what page the product is on. A recent issue of *Computer Shopper* had a compilation of 14,000 products, listed in 170 different categories. Their "Product Index" makes it very easy to find what you are looking for. Sometimes, they will have several vendors offering the same product. This makes it easy to determine which one offers the better price.

Another reason to use mail-order is because it might be less expensive than the local vendors. Local vendors usually have their stores in a fairly high-rent district; a mail-order company might be working out of a back bedroom. Most local vendors have to buy their stock from a distributor. The distributor usually buys it from the manufacturer or a wholesaler. By the time you get the product, it might have passed through several companies who each have made some profit. Most direct marketers who advertise by mail have cut out the middlemen and passed their profit on to you.

Still another reason why I do a lot shopping by mail is because of state taxes. In California, the state sales tax is as much as 8.50%. If I buy a computer system in California for $1000, it will cost me about $85 just for sales taxes. Even if I have to pay shipping charges for mail-order, it is usually much less than the sales tax.

The states have tried several times to eliminate this loophole and make you pay taxes no matter where you buy, but so far they have been unsuccessful. According to a recent news article, the larger states are again trying to force mail-order companies to collect sales taxes. If they are successful, a lot of people might stop ordering by mail. Considering the advantages of mail order, however, it might still be worth it, even if you have to pay the taxes. You can order from home, which means you don't have to spend half a day fighting traffic to get to the store, then looking for a parking space. You can have mail-order delivered directly to your door. If you are in a hurry and don't mind paying a bit more, you can have it delivered the next day.

Without computer magazines, there would be no mail-order, and without mail-order, there would be no computer magazines. Ads are the lifeblood of magazines. The subscription price of a magazine doesn't even come close to paying for the mailing costs, so they must have ads to exist.

I don't mind ads. I look at most of them and learn what is available. However, most of the magazines have become greedy in trying to see how many ads they can get into the magazine. Almost all of them now double the front and back cover and use them for ads. They also place several pages of ads before they list the table of contents. Sometimes, it is very difficult to find the contents.

One company started buying several pages of heavy stock paper and ran photos of cows and other things that have nothing to do with computers. I have no idea at all why it worked, but it is now one of the largest direct-mail companies. Other companies have noted the success and emulated this company's ads. Whenever something is successful, other companies jump on the bandwagon and do the same. Many of them buy very stiff pages for their ads. And of course, there are always lots of business-reply cards.

The whole idea of the stiff pages is to get you to notice their ads, make them stand out. These ads might stand out, but it becomes very difficult to leaf through a magazine with all the business-reply cards and slick ads about cows. Sorry advertisers, but the first thing I do when I pick up a magazine with all this stuff is to tear the ads out and throw them away. They don't make me want to buy their product, they just irritate me.

Honest Ads

Most mail-order vendors are honest, but a few bad advertisers can ruin a magazine. *PC World* has a regular "Consumer Watch" column. If you have a problem with a mail-order vendor that you can't resolve, write to them. They can usually get it resolved. For *PC World* subscription information, call 800-234-3498. Several computer magazines have formed the Microcomputer Marketing Council (MMC). It is part of the Direct Marketing Association (6 East 43rd Street, New York, NY 10017). They have an action line at 212-297-1393. They police the advertisers fairly closely.

You should be sure of what you need and what you are ordering. Some of the ads aren't written very well and might not tell the whole story. Ads are expensive so they might abbreviate or leave out a lot of important information. If possible, call the advertiser up and verify what is written. Also ask what their return policy is for defective merchandise and how long it takes before the item will be shipped.

Don't forget to ask for the current price. The ads are usually placed about two months before the magazines are delivered or hit the stands. The way prices are coming down, there could be quite a change in cost at the time you place your order. Of course, if you send them the advertised price, I am sure that they will not refuse it. A $2 or $3 phone call could save you a lot of time, trouble, and grief, and maybe even some money.

Ten Rules for Ordering by Mail

Here are some brief rules that you should follow when ordering by mail:

1. *Look for a street address.* Make sure the advertiser has a street address. In some ads, they give only a phone number. If you decide to buy from this vendor, call and verify that there is a live person on the other end with a street number. Before you send any money, though, do a bit more investigation. If possible, look through past issues of the same magazine for previous ads. If a vendor has been advertising for several months, then it is probably okay.
2. *Compare other vendors' prices.* Check through the magazines for other vendors' prices for this product. The prices should be fairly close. If it appears to be a bargain that is too good to be true, then...you know the rest.
3. *Buy from MMC members.* Buy from a vendor who is a member of the Microcomputer Marketing Council (MMC) of the Direct Marketing Association (DMA), or other recognized association. There are now about 10,000 members who belong to marketing associations. They have agreed to abide by the ethical guidelines and rules of the associations.

Except for friendly persuasion and the threat of expulsion, the associations have little power over the members. Most of them realize what is at stake, however, and put a great value on their membership. Most who advertise in the major computer magazines are members.

The Post Office, the Federal Trade Commission, the magazines and the legitimate businessmen who advertise have taken steps to try to stop the fraud and scams.

4. *Do your homework.* Read the ads carefully. Advertising space is very expensive, so many ads use abbreviations. Many ads might not be entirely clear. If in doubt, call and ask. Know exactly what you want, state precisely the model, make, size, component, and any other pertinent information. Tell them which ad you are ordering from, ask them if the price is the same, if the item is in stock, and when you can expect delivery. If the item is not in stock, indicate whether you will accept a substitute or want your money refunded. Ask for an invoice or order number. Ask the person's name. Write down all of the information, the time, the date, the company's address and phone number, the description of the item, and the promised delivery date. Write down and save any telephone conversations, the time, date, and the person's name. Save any and all correspondence.
5. *Ask questions.* Ask if the advertised item comes with all the necessary cables, parts, accessories, software, etc. Ask what the warranties are. Ask about the seller's return policies and refund policies. Find out with whom you should correspond if there is a problem.
6. *Don't send cash.* You will have no record of cash. If possible, use a credit card. If you have a problem, you can possibly have the bank refuse to pay the amount. A personal check might cause a delay of three to four weeks while the vendor waits for it to clear. A money order or credit card order should be filled and shipped immediately. Keep a copy of the money order.
7. *Ask for a delivery date.* If you have not received your order by the promised delivery date, notify the seller.
8. *Try the item out as soon as you receive it.* If you have a problem, notify the seller immediately by phone, then in writing. Give all details. Don't return the merchandise unless the dealer gives you a Return Material Authorization (RMA). Make sure to keep a copy of the shipper's receipt or packing slip, or some evidence that the material was returned.

9. *Know what to do if it is defective.* If you believe the product is defective or you have a problem, reread your warranties and guarantees. Reread the manual and any documentation. It is very easy to make an error or misunderstand how an item operates if you are unfamiliar with it. Before you go to a lot of trouble, try to get help from someone else. At least get someone to verify that you do have a problem. There are many times when a problem will disappear, and the vendor will not be able to duplicate it. If possible, when you call, try to have the item in your computer and be at the computer so you can describe the problem as it happens.
10. *Try to work out your problem with the vendor.* If you cannot resolve the problem with the vendor, then write to the consumer complaint agency in the seller's state. You should also write to the magazine where you saw the ad and to the DMA at 6 East 43rd Street, New York, NY 10017.

Federal Trade Commission Rules

Here is a brief summary of the FTC rules:

1. *Must ship within 30 days.* The seller must ship your order within 30 days unless the ad clearly states that it will take longer.
2. *Right to cancel.* If it appears that the seller cannot ship when promised, you must be notified and given a new date. The seller must give you the opportunity to cancel the order, and refund your money if you desire.
3. *Must notify if order can't be filled.* If the seller notifies you that your order cannot be filled on time, a stamped self-addressed envelope or card must be included so that you can respond to this notice. If you do not respond, the seller may assume that you agree to the delay. It still must ship within 30 days of the end of the original 30 days, or cancel your order and refund your money.
4. *Right to cancel if delayed.* Even if you consent to a delay, you still have the right to cancel at any time.
5. *Must refund money if canceled.* If you cancel an order that has been paid for by check or money order, the seller must refund the money. If you paid by credit card, your account must be credited within one billing cycle. Store credits or vouchers in place of a refund are not acceptable.

6. *No substitutions.* If the item you ordered is not available, the seller may not send you a substitute without your express consent.

Sources of Knowledge

There are several good magazines that can help you gain the knowledge needed to make sensible purchases and learn more about computers. These magazines usually carry interesting, timely, and informative articles and reviews of software and hardware. They also have many ads for computers, components, and software. Some of the better magazines that you should subscribe to are *Computer Shopper, Byte, PC Computing, PC World,* and *PC Magazine.* Most of these magazines are available on local magazine racks, but you will save money with a yearly subscription. Besides, they will be delivered to your door.

If you need a source of components, you only have to look in any of these magazines to find hundreds of them. If you live near a large city, there will no doubt be several vendors who advertise in your local paper. Another source of computer information can be found in the several good computer books published by McGraw-Hill. There are hundreds of computer-related books and magazines. If you read every one of them, you still will not be able to keep up with the flood of computer information.

Recommended Computer Magazines

Here are just a few of the magazines that will help you keep abreast to some degree:

AUDIO-FORUM
96 Broad Street
Guilford, CT 06437

Byte Magazine
P.O. Box 558
Hightstown, N.J. 08520

CD-ROM Multimedia
P.O. Box 2946
Plattsburgh, NY 12901-9863
800-565-4623

CD-ROM Today
Subscription Department
P.O. Box 51478
Boulder, CO 80322-1478

Computer Currents
5720 Hollis Street
Emeryville, CA 94608

Computer Graphics World
P.O. Box 122
Tulsa, OK 74101-9966

Computer Life
P.O. Box 55880
Boulder, CO 80323-5880

Computer Shopper
P.O. Box 51020
Boulder, CO 80321-1020

Computer World
P.O. Box 2044
Marion, OH 43306-2144

Desktop Video World
P.O. Box 594
Mt. Morris, IL 61054-7902

Digital Imaging
Micro Publishing
21150 Hawthorne Boulevard #104
Torrance, CA 90503

Digital Video
P.O. Box 594
Mt. Morris, IL 61054-7902

Electronic Musician
P.O. Box 41525
Nashville, TN 37204-9829

EMedia Professional
462 Danbury Road
Wilton, CT 06897-2126
800-806-7795
emediasub@onlineinc.com

Home Office Computing
P.O. Box 51344
Boulder, CO 80321-1344

Imaging Magazine
1265 Industrial Highway
Southampton, PA 18966
800-677-3435

Internet
P.O. Box 713
Mt. Morris, IL 61054-9965

KidSoft Magazine
718 University Avenue #112
Los Gatos, CA 95030-9958
800-354-6150

LAN Magazine
P.O. Box 50047
Boulder, CO 80321-0047

MicroTimes
5951 Canning Street
Oakland, CA 94609

MUSICIAN'S Friend
P.O. Box 4520
Medford, OR 97501

National Association of Desktop Publishers
P.O. Box 11668
Riverton, NJ 08076-7268

Nuts & Volts
430 Princeland Court
Corona, CA 91719-1343

PC Computing
P.O. Box 50253
Boulder, CO 80321-0253

PC Magazine
P.O. Box 51524
Boulder, CO 80321-1524

PC Novice
P.O. Box 85380
Lincoln, NE 68501-9807

PC Today
P.O. Box 85380
Lincoln, NE 68501-5380

PC World
P.O. Box 51833
Boulder, CO 80321-1833

PRE
8340 Mission Road #106
Prairie Village, KS 66206

Publish!
P.O. Box 51966
Boulder, CO 80321-1966

Repair, Service & Remarketing News
P.O. Box 670
Joplin, MO 64802-0670
417-781-9317
Fax 417-781-0427

Video Magazine
P.O. Box 56293
Boulder, CO 80322-6293
800-365-1008

Videomaker Magazine
P.O. Box 469026
Escondido, CA 92046
800-334-8152

Virtual City
P.O. Box 3007
Livingston, NJ 07039-9922

Virtual Reality
P.O. Box 7703
San Francisco, CA 94120
415-905-2563

Voice Processing Magazine
P.O. Box 6016
Duluth, MN 55806-9797

Windows Magazine
P.O. Box 58649
Boulder, CO 80322-8649

Free Magazines to Qualified Subscribers

The magazines listed in this section as free are sent only to qualified subscribers. The subscription price of a magazine usually does not come anywhere near covering the costs of publication, mailing, distribution, and other costs. Most magazines depend almost entirely on advertisers for their existence. The more subscribers a magazine has, the more it can charge for its ads. Naturally, they can attract a lot more subscribers if the magazine is free.

PC Week and *InfoWorld* are excellent magazines. They are so popular that the publishers have to limit the number of subscribers. They cannot possibly accommodate all the people who apply. They have set standards that must be met in order to qualify. They do not publish the standards, so even if you answer all of the questions on the application, you still might not qualify.

To get a free subscription, you must write to the magazine for a qualifying application form. If you attend one of the larger computer shows such as COMDEX, they will have free samples and qualifying forms. The form asks several questions, such as how you are involved with computers, the company you work for, whether you have any influence in purchasing the computer products listed in the magazine, and several other questions that gives them a very good profile of their readers.

I wouldn't tell you to lie, but it might help you qualify if you exaggerate just a bit here and there. Especially when it asks what your responsibilities are for the purchasing of computer equipment. I am pretty sure that they will not send the FBI out to verify your answers. One way to qualify for most of these free magazines is to become a consultant. There are very few rules and regulations as to who can call themselves a consultant. (You should be particularly aware of this fact if you decide to hire a consultant.)

The list of magazines here is not nearly complete. There are hundreds of trade magazines that are sent free to qualified subscribers. The Cahners Company alone publishes 32 different trade magazines. Many of the trade magazines are highly technical and narrowly specialized.

Advanced Imaging
445 Broad Hollow Road
Melville, NY 11747-4722

Automatic ID News
P.O. Box 6158
Duluth, MN 55806-9870

AV Video Production & Presentation Techniques
701 Westchester Avenue
White Plains, NY 10604
914-328-9157

Beyond Computing
1133 Westchester Avenue
White Plains, NY 10604

California Business
P.O. Box 70735
Pasadena, CA 91117-9947

CD-ROM News Extra
462 Danbury Road
Wilton, CT 06897-2126

Client/Server Computing
Sentry Publishing Company
1900 West Park Drive
Westborough, MA 01581-3907

Communications News
2504 Tamiami Trail North
Nokomis, FL 34275
813-966-9521

Communications Week
P.O. Box 2070
Manhasset, NY 11030

Computer Design
P.O. Box 3466
Tulsa, OK 74101-3466

Computer Products
P.O. Box 14000
Dover, NJ 07801-9990

Computer Reseller News
P.O. Box 2040
Manhasset, NY 11030

Computer Systems News
600 Community Drive
Manhasset, NY 11030

Computer Technical Review
924 Westwood Boulevard #65
Los Angeles, CA 90024

Computer Telephony
P.O. Box 40706
Nashville, TN 37204-9919
800-677-3435

Data Communications
P.O. Box 477
Hightstown, NJ 08520-9362

Datamation
P.O. Box 7530
Highlands Ranch, CO 80163-9130

Designfax
P.O. Box 1151
Skokie, IL 60076-9917

Document Management & Windows Imaging
8711 East Pinnacle Peak Road, #249
Scottsdale, Arizona 85255

ec.com
14407 Big Basin Way
Saratoga, CA 95070-9905
847-291-5212

EE Product News
P.O. Box 12982
Overland Park, KS 66212

Electronic Design
P.O. Box 985007
Cleveland, OH 44198-5007

Electronic Manufacturing
P.O. Box 159
Libertyville, IL 60048

Electronic Publish & Print
650 South Clark Street
Chicago, IL 60605-9960

Electronic Publishing
P.O. Box 3493
Tulsa, OK 74101-9640

Electronics
P.O. Box 985061
Cleveland, OH 44198

Enterprise Systems Journal
P.O. Box 3051
Northbrook, IL 60065-3051

Federal Computer Week
P.O. Box 602
Winchester, MA 01890

ID Systems
P.O. Box 874
Peterborough, NH 03458

Identification Journal
2640 North Halsted Street
Chicago, IL 60614-9962

Imaging Business
P.O. Box 5360
Pittsfield, MA 01203-9788

InfoText
Advanstar Communications
P.O. Box 6490
Duluth, MN 55806-6490

InfoWorld
P.O. Box 1172
Skokie, IL 60076

InterActivity Media Magazine
P.O. Box 1174
Skokie, IL 60076-8174

LAN Times
122 East 1700
South Provo, UT 84606

Lasers & Optronics
301 Gibraltar Drive
Morris Plains, NJ 07950

Machine Design
P.O. Box 985015
Cleveland, OH 44198-5015

Managing Office Technology
1100 Superior Avenue
Cleveland, OH 44197-8092

Manufacturing Systems
P.O. Box 3008
Wheaton, IL 60189-9972

Medical Equipment Designer
29100 Aurora Road, #200
Cleveland, OH 44139

Micro Publishing News
21150 Hawthorne Boulevard #104
Torrance, CA 90503

Mini-Micro Systems
P.O. Box 5051
Denver, CO 80217-9872

Mobile Office
Subscription Department
P.O. Box 57268
Boulder, CO 80323-7268

Modern Office Technology
1100 Superior Avenue
Cleveland, OH 44197-8032

MrCDRom
Maxmedia Distributing, Inc.
P.O. Box 1087
Winter Garden, FL 34787

Multimedia Merchandising
P.O. Box 99400
Collingswood, NJ 08108-9972
Fax 609-488-6188

Network Computing
P.O. Box 1095
Skokie, IL 60076-9662

Network Journal
600 Harrison Street
San Francisco, CA 94107
800-950-0523

Network World
161 Worcester Road
Framingham, MA 01701
508-875-6400

NewMedia
P.O. Box 10639
Riverton, NJ 08076-0639
415-573-5170

Office Systems
P.O. Box 3116
Woburn, MA 01888-9878

PC Week
P.O. Box 1770
Riverton, NJ 08077-7370

Photo Business
1515 Broadway
New York, NY 10036

Photo Lab Management
P.O. Box 1700
Santa Monica, CA 90406-1700

The Programmer's Shop
5 Pond Park Road
Hingham, MA 02043-9845

Quality
P.O. Box 3002
Wheaton, IL 60189-9929

Reseller Management
P.O. Box 601
Morris Plains, NJ 07950

Robotics World
6255 Barfield Road
Atlanta, GA 30328-9988

Scientific Computing
301 Gibraltar Drive
Morris Plains, NJ 07950

Software Magazine
Westborough Office Park
1900 West Park Drive
Westborough, MA 01581-3907

Speech Technology Magazine
CI Publishing
43 Danbury Road
Wilton, CT 06897-9729
203-834-1430

STACKS
P.O. Box 5031
Brentwood, TN 37024-5031

Sun Expert
P.O. Box 5274
Pittsfield, MA 01203-9479

Surface Mount Technology
P.O. Box 159
Libertyville, IL 60048

Telecommunications
P.O. Box 850949
Braintree, MA 02185

Component and Software Catalogs

Several companies publish special catalogs for components and software through direct mail. Even IBM has got into the act. You should be aware that most of these companies charge a bit more than those who advertise in the major magazines. Ads cost a lot of money, however, so there usually isn't too much information about an advertised product in the major magazines. The direct-mail companies usually have room in their catalogs to give a fairly good description and lots of information about the product. The catalogs are free.

Here are just a few:

Arlington Computer Products,
800-548-5105

Black Box Corporation
P.O. Box 12800
Pittsburgh, PA 15241

Bull Express, 800-343-6665

CompuClassics
P.O. Box 10598
Canoga Park, CA 91309

Compute Ability
P.O. Box 17882
Milwaukee, WI 53217

Computers & Music
647 Mission Street
San Francisco, CA 94105

DAMARK, 800-729-9000

Data Cal Corporation, 800-842-2835

Data Comm Warehouse, 800-328-2261

DataCom Mall, 800-898-3282

Dell Network & Communications,
800-509-3355

DellWare, 800-449-3355

Digi-key Corporation
701 Brooks Avenue South
P.O. Box 677
Thief River Falls, MN 56701-0677

Digital PCs Catalog,
800-642-4532

DTP Direct, 800-890-9030

Edmund Scientific Company
101 East Gloucester Pike
Barrington, NJ 08007-1380

Edutainment Catalog (mostly kid's software), 800-338-3844

Egghead Software, 800-344-4323

ELEK-TEK, 800-395-1000

Global Computer Supplies
2318 East Del Amo Boulevard,
Department 64
Compton, CA 90220
800-845-6225

Global DataCom, 800-440-4832

Global Industrial Equipment, 800-645-1232

Hello Direct (telephone products), 800-444-3556

IBM PC Direct, 800-426-2968

Image Club Graphics, 800-387-9193

JDR Microdevices
2233 Samaritan Drive
San Jose, CA 95124

KidSoft Software Catalog, 800-354-6150

MAILER'S Software
970 Calle Negocio
San Clemente, CA 92673

MEI/Micro Center, 800-634-3478

MicroWarehouse
1720 Oak Street
P.O. Box 3014
Lakewood NJ 08701-3014

Momentum Graphics, Inc.
16290 Shoemaker
Cerritos, CA 90701-2243

Mr. CD-ROM, 800-444-6723

Multimedia World
P.O. Box 58690
Boulder, CO 80323-8690

One Network Place
4711 Golf Road
Skokie, IL 60076

Paper Catalog
205 Chubb Avenue
Lyndhurst, NJ 07071

Pasternack Enterprises
P.O. 16759
Irvine, CA 92713

PC Connection
6 Mill Street
Marlow, NH 03456

PC Mall, 800-555-6255

PCs Compleat, 800-385-4522

Personal Computing Tools
90 Industrial Park Road
Hingham, MA 02043

Power Up!, 800-851-2917

PrePress
11 Mt. Pleasant Avenue
East Hanover, NJ 07936-9925

Presentations
Lakewood Building
50 South Ninth Street
Minneapolis MN 55402-9973

Processor, 800-334-7443

PROJECTIONS
Business Park Drive
Branford, CT 06405

QUEBLO
1000 Florida Avenue
Hagerstown, Maryland 21741

Software Labs
100 Corporate Pointe #195
Culver City, CA 90230-7616

Software Spectrum, 800-787-1166

Soundware
200 Menlo Oaks Drive
Menlo Park, CA 94025

South Hills DATACOMM
760 Beechnut Drive
Pittsburgh, Pennsylvania 15205

System ID Warehouse (barcode catalog), 800-397-9783

T2 Tech Squared, 800-890-9375

TENEX Computer Express
56800 Magnetic Drive
Mishawaka, IN 46545

TigerSoftware,
800-888-4437

Tools for Exploration
4460 Redwood Highway, Suite 2
San Rafael, CA 49043

United Video & Computer,
800-448-3738

UNIXREVIEW
P.O. Box 420035
Palm Coast, FL 32142-0035

Public-Domain and Shareware Software

There are several companies who provide public-domain, shareware, and low-cost software. They also publish catalogs listing their software. Some might charge a small fee for the catalog.

Here are a few:

Computer Discount Warehouse,
800-330-4CDW

Computers International,
619-630-0055

The Computer Room,
703-832-334

IIndustrial Computer Source,
800-523-2320

Industrial Software Library,
800-523-2320

International Software Library,
800-992-1992

J&R Computer World,
800-221-8180

Jameco Electonic Components,
415-592-8097

Micro Star,
800-443-6103

MicroCom Systems,
408-737-9000

MMI Corporation,
800-221-4283

National PD Library,
619-941-0925

Numeridex,
800-323-7737

PC Plus Consulting,
818-891-7930

PC Zone,
800-258-2088

PC-Sig 1030D,
800-245-6717

PrePress Direct, 800-443-6600

PsL News, 800-242-4775 (costs $24 year)

Public Brand Software, 800-426-3475

Selective Software, 800-423-3556

Shareware Express, 800-346-2842

Software Express/Direct, 800-331-8192

Softwarehouse, 408-748-0461

Zenith Data Systems, 800-952-3099

Computer Books

There are several companies who publish computer books. One of the larger companies, of course, is McGraw-Hill (800-262-4729). In addition to mail-order, McGraw-Hill also has an online bookstore at www.mcgraw-hill.com/books.html. They have over 9000 titles available in many different categories. It is easy to search for any title or type of book. Computer books from Osborne/McGraw-Hill are also listed there, or you can call them 800-227-0900. Call them for a current catalog listing of the many books that they publish.

I admit that I am a bit prejudiced when it comes to McGraw-Hill books, but I recommend them highly. You can also access and search the thousands of books at the Amazon online bookstore at www.amazon.com. They claim to be the world's largest online bookstore. They carry all of my books—just do an author search on *Aubrey Pilgrim*.

CHAPTER 20

Troubleshooting and Repairing Your PC

This is one of the longest chapters in this book, but I must tell you that you might not be able to find the answer to your problems in this chapter. There are a thousand and one things that can go wrong in a computer, in both hardware and software. This chapter could be ten times as long and still not cover every possible problem. However, this chapter does cover most of the major problems that you might experience.

When speaking of troubleshooting, most people think of hardware problems. I have had far more trouble with software problems than with hardware, however. Software problems might be even more difficult to solve than hardware problems.

Windows 95 can help solve some problems. When I built my 200-MHz Pentium Pro, rather than buy all new components, I just upgraded my old 60-MHz Pentium. I had two hard disks in the unit, a Maxtor 540-Mb IDE and a 1.05-Gb Seagate SCSI. When I attached all of the components to the Pentium Pro motherboard on the benchtop, they worked perfectly. When I installed the components in the case and tried to boot up, however, the Windows 95 screen came up and froze.

I rechecked all of my cable connections, made sure that the boards were seated, then tried again to boot up. Again, it got as far as the Windows 95 screen, then froze. I turned off the power, and this time pressed F8 as it was booting up. Out of the options that came up, I chose number 5, "Step-by-step confirmation." This displays each line of the Config.sys file and asks whether you want to load it or not.

When it got to the line that loaded my SCSI driver, the system hung up again, so I knew that it must be either my Toshiba CD-ROM or my Seagate hard drive. I disconnected them both, and the system booted perfectly. I then reconnected the CD-ROM, and it booted perfectly. I then switched the connector from the CD-ROM to the hard disk, and it hung again.

Evidently, something happened to the hard disk during the time I disconnected it on the bench and installed it in the case. Of course, I was disappointed. I had paid over $700 for this SCSI drive a couple of years ago. I wasn't too concerned about the data on the drive because I had it all backed up on the Maxtor IDE drive. That is the beauty of having at least two large hard drives.

I called the Seagate customer service center at 800-468-3472 and was pleasantly surprised to learn that I had a five-year guarantee on this drive. All I had to do was send it in, and they would either repair or replace it. A couple of weeks later, they sent me a new drive. Of course, since it was a different drive, none of my data was on it. There was no note or indication as to what the problem had been.

The F8 utility of Windows 95 is an excellent tool. Without it, I might not have been able to figure out what was wrong. There are other times when one of my computers will not boot up, but it will usually boot if I use the F8 key and load each item in my Config.sys and Autoexec.bat files individually. I usually expect to see it hang on one of the files or device drivers, but it doesn't. There is probably a good reason why it won't boot normally, but even after 30 years in electronics, I have to admit that there is a whole lot that I do not know.

Finding the cause of the problem is the first step in fixing it. There are several hardware and software diagnostic tools available that can help you find and fix the problems. A few of them are discussed in this chapter.

Computer Basics

Troubleshooting will be a little easier if you know just a little of the electronic basics. Computers are possible because of electricity. Under the control of software and hardware, small electric on/off signal voltages are formed when you type from the keyboard or when data is read from a disk or other means of input. This voltage is used to turn transistors on and off to perform various tasks.

An electric charge is formed when there is an imbalance or an excess amount of electrons at one pole. The excess electrons will flow through whatever path they can find to get to the other pole, much like water flowing downhill to find its level. Most electric or electronic paths have varying amounts of resistance, so that work or heat is created when the electrons pass through them. For instance, if a flashlight is turned on, electrons will pass through the bulb, which has a resistive filament. The heat generated by the electrons passing through the bulb causes the filament to glow red-hot and create light. If the light is left on for a period of time, the excess electrons from the negative pole of the battery will pass through the bulb to the positive pole of the battery. Electrons will continue to flow until the amount of electrons at the negative and positive poles are equal. At this time, there will be a perfect balance and the battery will be dead.

A computer is made up of circuits and boards that have resistors, capacitors, inductors, transistors, motors, and many other components. These components perform a useful function when electricity passes through them. The circuits are designed so that the paths of the electric currents are divided, controlled, and shunted to do the work that you want done. The transistors and other components can force the electrons to go to memory, to a disk drive, to the printer, or wherever the software and hardware directs it to go.

If an electronic circuit is designed properly, it should last several lifetimes. Unlike an electron tube, which has filaments that burn out, there is nothing in a semiconductor or transistor to wear out. Occasionally, however, too many electrons might find their way through a weakened component and cause it to heat up and burn out. Or, for some reason, the electrons might be shunted through a path or component where it shouldn't go. This can cause an intermittent, partial, or complete failure.

Electrostatic Voltage

Before you touch any electronic component or handle them, you should ground yourself and discharge any electrostatic voltage that might have built up on your body. It is possible for a person to build up a charge of 4000 volts or more of electrostatic voltage. If you walk across a carpet and then touch a brass doorknob, you might see a spark fly and get a painful shock. If you should touch a fragile electronic component, this high voltage can be discharged through the component. It might weaken the component or possibly ruin it.

Most electronic assembly lines have the workers wear a ground strap whenever they are working with any electrostatic-discharge sensitive components. You can discharge yourself by touching an unpainted metal part of the case of a computer or other device that is plugged into a wall socket. The computer or other grounding device does not have to be turned on in order to discharge yourself.

Document the Problem, Write It Down

The chances are, if a computer is going to break down, it will do it so at the most inopportune time. This is one of the basic tenets of Murphy's immutable and inflexible laws. If it breaks down, try not to panic. Ranting, cussing, and crying might make you feel better, but it won't solve the problem. Instead, get out a pad and pencil and write down everything as it happens. It is very easy to forget. Write down all the particulars, how the cables were plugged in, the software that was running, and anything that might be pertinent. You might get error messages on your screen. Use the PrtSc (Print Screen) key to print out the messages, if possible.

If you can't solve the problem, you might have to call someone or your vendor for help. If you have all the written information before you, it will help. Try to call from your computer, if possible as it is acting up. If it is a software problem, have your serial number handy. Most organizations ask for that before anything else.

Instruments and Tools

For high levels of troubleshooting, you would need some sophisticated tools and expensive instruments to do a thorough analysis of a system. You would need a good, high-frequency oscilloscope, a digital analyzer, a logic probe, and several other expensive pieces of gear. You would also need a test bench with a spare power supply, spare disk drives, and plug-in boards. It would be very helpful to have a diagnostic card such as the POST-PROBE or the Ultra-X and several of the diagnostic and utility software programs discussed later in this chapter.

It would also be helpful to have a known-good computer with some empty slots so that you could plug in suspect boards and test them. You would also need a voltohmmeter, some clip leads, a pair of side cutter dikes, a pair of long-nose pliers, various screwdrivers, nutdrivers, a soldering iron, and solder. You would need a good workbench with plenty of light over the bench and a flashlight or other small light to light up the dark places in the computer case.

Besides the expensive tools and instruments needed for high-level troubleshooting and repair, you would need quite a lot of training and experience. Fortunately, you don't need the expensive and sophisticated tools and instruments for most computer problems. Just a few simple tools and a little common sense are all that is needed for the majority of the problems.

Here are some tools that you should have around. It is good to have these tools, even if you never have any computer problems:

1. You should have a pad and pen near your computer so that you can write down all of the things that happen if you have a problem.

2. You should have several sizes and types of screwdrivers. A couple of them should be magnetic for picking up and starting small screws. You can buy magnetic screwdrivers, or you can make one yourself. Just take a strong magnet and rub it on the blade of the screwdriver a few times. The magnets on cabinet doors will do, or the voice-coil magnet of a loudspeaker. Be very careful with any magnet around your floppy diskettes. It can erase them.
3. You should also have a small screwdriver with a bent tip that can be used to pry up ICs. Some of the larger ICs are very difficult to remove. One of the blank fillers for the slots on the back panel of the computer also makes a good prying tool.
4. You should have a couple pairs of pliers. You should have at least one pair of long-nose pliers.
5. You should have a set of nutdrivers. Many of the screws have slotted heads for screwdrivers as well as hexagonal heads for nutdrivers. A nutdriver is usually much easier to use than a screwdriver.
6. You might need a pair of side cutter dikes for clipping leads of components and cutting wire. You might buy a pair of cutters that also have wire strippers.
7. By all means, buy a voltohmmeter. There are dozens of uses for a voltohmmeter. They can be used to check for the wiring continuity in your cables, phone lines, switches, etc. You can also use a voltohmmeter to check for the proper voltages in your computer. There are only two voltages to check for, 12 volts and 5 volts. The DX4 and Pentium 90, 100, and 120-MHz CPUs require 3.3 volts, but usually a voltage regulator on the motherboard or on the CPU socket reduces the 5-volt supply to the required 3.3 volts. You can buy a relatively inexpensive voltohmmeter at any Radio Shack store or an electronic store.
8. You will need a soldering iron and some solder. You shouldn't have to do much soldering. but you never know when you might need to repair a cable or do some other minor soldering job.
9. You should also have several clip leads. Clip leads are insulated wires with alligator clips on each end. You can use them to extend a cable, short out two pins, or for hundreds of other uses. You can buy them at your local Radio Shack or electronic store.
10. You need a flashlight for looking into the dark places inside the computer or at the cable connections behind the computer.

The chances are very slim that you will ever need all of these tools unless you are in the repair business. Even then, there will be very few times when you will have to use some of them, especially if you are working on a Pentium Pro system. Still, it is nice to have them available if you ever do need them.

Solving Common Problems

For many of the common problems, you won't need a lot of test gear. Often, a problem can be solved by using your five senses: sight, hearing, smell, touch, and taste. (Actually, you won't be using taste very often.)

- Eyes—If you look closely, you can see a cable that is not plugged in properly, a board that is not completely seated, a switch or jumper that is not set properly, and many other obvious things, such as smoke.
- Ears—Listen for any unusual sounds. Ordinarily, those little electrons don't make any noise as they move through your computer at about two-thirds of the speed of light. The only sound from your computer should be the noise of your drive motors and the fan in the power supply.
- Nose—If you have ever smelled a burned resistor or a capacitor, you will never forget it. If you smell something very unusual, try to locate where it is coming from.
- Touch—If you touch the components and some seem to be unusually hot, it could be the cause of your problem. Except for the insides of your power supply, there should not be any voltage above 12 volts in your computer, so it should be safe to touch the components, even when the power is on. Before touching a component, be sure that you have discharged yourself of any electrostatic voltage.

The Number-One Cause of Problems

If you have added something to your computer or done some sort of repair and the computer doesn't work, something might not have been plugged in correctly, or you might have made some minor error in the installation. If you have added a component, remove it to see if the computer works without it. Never install more than one item at a time. Install an item, then check to see if it works, then install the next one.

By far the greatest problem in assembling a unit, adding something to a computer, or installing software is not following the instructions. Quite often, it is not necessarily the fault of the person trying to follow the instructions. I am a member of Mensa, and have worked in the electronic industry for over 30 years, but sometimes I have great difficulty trying to decipher and follow the instructions in some manuals. Sometimes, a very critical instruction or piece of information is inconspicuously buried in the middle of a 500-page manual.

The Importance of Documentation

You should have some sort of documentation or manuals for all of your computer components and peripherals. You should have a written record of the switch and jumper settings of each of your boards. It is also very important that you have the drive type and the CMOS information of your hard drives written down with your records or on a special floppy disk. If for some reason your system fails, you might not be able to access your hard drive and its data if you don't know the drive type listed in your CMOS configuration.

You should know what components are inside your computer how they are configured. The Plug-and-Play components now make it a lot easier, but there are still items that do not conform to the PnP specifications.

Norton Utilities lets you make a rescue disk that has a copy of your CMOS, boot record, partition tables, and Autoexec.bat and Config.sys files. This disk is bootable, so it can be used any time if you lose your CMOS or any of the other vital information. PC Tools also lets you make an emergency disk similar to the Norton rescue disk.

What to Do If It Is Completely Dead

There are several software diagnostic programs that are great in many cases, but if the computer is completely dead, the software won't do you any good. If it is completely dead, the first thing to do is check the power outlet. If you don't have a voltmeter, plug a lamp into the same socket and see if it lights. Check your power cord. Check the switch on the computer. Check the fan in the power supply. Is it turning? The power supply is one of the major components that frequently becomes defective. If the fan is not turning, the power supply might be defective. However, the fan might be operating, even though the power supply is defective.

Do any of the panel lights come on when you try to boot up? Does the hard-disk motor spin up? If there is a short anywhere in the system, the power supply will not come on. The fan won't turn, and none of the drives will come on. The power supply has built-in short-circuit protection that shuts everything down when the output is shorted. The power supply has four or more cables for the various drives. Unplug the drives one at a time and try the system. If the system works after a drive is unplugged, then you have found the problem. (I hate to say this, but I am pretty sure that one of Murphy's laws dictates that a problem will never be this easy to solve.)

Memory Problems

SIMM chips are very easy to install. Just drop them in on a slant and lift them slightly until they lock in. It is possible to have a module that is not seated properly, however. If this happens, the computer might not boot up. The screen might be completely blank with no error messages or any indication of the problem.

I had a lot of problems when I tried to replace my old Cyrix 100 MHz with the Tyan motherboard and the AMD 233-MHz CPU. I had four 8×2 chips for a total of 32 Mb on my old board. It seemed to work fine. The memory check was okay each time I booted up, but I had a blank screen when I tried to boot up with the new motherboard and CPU. I checked the SIMMs to make sure they were seated properly. Then I tried and tried again. Sometimes it would boot up, but then it would tell me that it had a fatal error and would shut down.

I reinstalled everything back in my old Cyrix motherboard and it worked fine. I reinstalled it in my new motherboard, and it booted up once in a while, but then would drop out. Once, when I turned it on, I got the blank screen. I checked the SIMMs again, but thought that maybe my monitor adapter was bad. I replaced it with a spare, but I still had a blank screen. I then removed two of the SIMMs, or one bank of memory, and everything worked fine. I then replaced one of the SIMMs with one of the two that I had removed, and sure enough, I had a blank screen. Evidently, one of the contacts on the chip was bad, or the chip itself had an intermittent defect. It took me half a day of frustration to find it.

Cables

You can check any of the cables from the power supply with a voltohmmeter. The power supply will not work unless it has a load, so have at least one disk drive plugged in. There should be +12 V between the yellow and black wires and +5 V between the red and black. If there is no voltage, then you probably have a defective power supply.

If you hear the fan motor and panel lights come on, but the monitor is dark, check the monitor's power cord, the adapter cable, and the adapter. The monitor also has fuses, but they are usually inside the monitor case. Check the documentation that came with your monitor. You should also check the monitor's brightness and contrast controls. If you have just installed the monitor, check the motherboard or adapter for any switches or jumpers that should be set. Check the documentation of your adapter board. You should also check your CMOS setup to make sure that the BIOS knows what type of monitor you have.

Remove all of the boards except for the monitor adapter and disk controller. Also disconnect all peripherals. If the system works, then add the boards back until it stops. Be sure to turn off the power each time you add or remove a board or any cable. If you have spare boards, swap them out with suspected boards in your system.

Config.sys and Autoexec.bat

In the DOS era, you could see your Autoexec.bat working during bootup. In Windows 95 it is now usually hidden, but it is still working just as it did before. If you have just added a new piece of software and your system doesn't work, or it doesn't work the way it should, check your Autoexec.bat and Config.sys files. Many programs change these files as they are being installed. These files might have commands and statements that conflict with your new software or system.

I try out a lot of different software and systems. I have had problems where a statement or command was left in the Autoexec.bat or Config.sys file from a system no longer being used. It might ask the computer to perform a command that is not there, causing the computer to go off in never-never land and keep trying to find the command or file. You will usually have to reboot to get out. You might get an error message that says, "Unrecognized command in Config.sys." It might then have an additional message: "Bad or missing file, driver or path."

You could have a misspelled word in the Config.sys file, or you might have left out a backslash or forward slash. It is quite easy to type in the wrong slash, such as a / instead of a \. The structure of Config.sys is rather strict and doesn't provide much room for error. You can use the EDIT command to change, add to, or delete portions of your Autoexec.bat or Config.sys files. Whenever you make a change to them, always keep the old one as a backup. You can rename them with the DOS REN command. You can call the old files Config.old, Autoexec.1, or whatever. If your new Autoexec.bat or Config.Sys doesn't work, you can always go back and rename the old files back to their original names.

If you have a long Autoexec.bat file that doesn't work, you might try editing out parts of it, then reboot and retry it. (Use the DOS EDIT command, which uses ASCII text. Don't use a word processor because it adds symbols and characters that will confuse the system.) You can temporarily change lines in your Autoexec.bat or Config.sys files by adding a REM (for *remark*) at the beginning of a line that you don't want to be executed.

In Windows 95, you can also edit your Autoexec.bat, Config.sys, or Win.ini files by clicking on Start, then Run, then type in sysedit. All of the systems files will be displayed in tiled fashion. Just click on any one in order to edit it.

Pressing F8 while booting up Windows 95 lets you look at each line of the Autoexec.bat and Config.sys file and prompts you for whether or not to load it. If you say no to a certain line, and the system then works, you have found the problem. You can then use the EDIT command and put a REM in front of the offending line in your Autoexec.bat or Config.sys file, and then see if it works. If so, you can delete the line or just leave it as a REM, in case you might need it later.

You should always have a "clean" boot disk that has a very lean Autoexec.bat and Config.sys on it. There might be times when you don't want any TSRs or anything in your 640 Kb of base memory in order to run a special program. If you have a lot of TSRs or other things in your 640 Kb of memory, you might not be able to run some programs.

Clearing TSRs from Memory

Windows 95 often loads lots of things in memory, and you might not even know it. Quite often, when you install a new program, it will set itself so that it will be loaded automatically in memory. Sometimes the name of the program or its icon is displayed on the bar at the bottom of the screen. To see what programs are loaded in your memory, press the

Ctrl, Alt, and Del keys at the same time. A list of anything loaded in memory will be displayed.

Use the arrow keys or mouse to highlight anything that you don't want to be loaded, then press the Enter or Return key, and it will be deleted from memory. Microsoft Explorer will always be loaded. You cannot delete it; if you do, the system will shut down.

Windows Start

I recently installed a new, larger hard drive with more partitions. In copying the files from the old disk to the new one, some of the files got copied to a different partition. When I booted up my system, I got a message that there was a problem with a shortcut. All I had to do was click OK, and the system would continue to boot up, but it was a bother.

I didn't use that program very often, so I just uninstalled it from my hard disk. Uninstalling the program did not uninstall the shortcut, however. I finally clicked on the Start button and then clicked on Settings, on Taskbar, Start Menu Programs, Advanced, and Start Menu. Then I highlighted the offending shortcut and deleted it.

Drive C:

Every program that you install on your computer wants to be loaded on drive C:. That is the default built into most software. Often, you are given the option to install the program on another drive, but a newbie might not realize this. (A *newbie* is someone new to computers, the Internet, or almost anything new. It is not meant as a putdown.) If you allow the programs to be loaded on C:, it will soon be completely filled. If you install Windows 95 on your C: drive, it takes up about 80 Mb, but it doesn't stop there. Every time you load a new program, even on another drive or in another directory, a large amount of Windows control data is added to the Windows 95 directory.

It is much like the old story about the Arab and his camel. It was a cold night on the desert, but the Arab was nice and warm in his tent. The camel asked his master if he could just put his nose in the tent. The master agreed. Then the camel complained that his head was cold, and could he please put his head in the tent. Again, the master agreed. The camel kept it up, and soon his entire body was in the tent, and the master was outside.

I have a scan program that will not run unless I have at least 10 Mb of free space on my C: drive. There are times when Netscape will not let me access some Web sites because I do not have enough free space on one of my computer's C: drive. When you set up and format a new drive, make sure that you have a large C: drive. If you have a hard drive of 1 Gb or more, I would recommend a C: drive of at least 500 Mb.

If your system is already set up, and you are running out of free space, you can try to copy some of the programs to another drive or directory. It will work best if you are able to uninstall the program and reinstall it. Many of the later programs now come with an uninstall feature that clears out all of the hidden portions of the program that are intertwined with Windows 95. Not many of the older programs had the uninstall feature.

Beep Error Codes

Every time a computer is turned on or booted up, it does a Power On Self Test (POST). It checks the RAM, floppy drives, hard-disk drives, monitor, printer, keyboard, and other peripherals that you have installed. If everything is okay, it gives a short beep, then boots up.

If it does not find a unit, or if the unit is not functioning correctly, it will beep and display an error code. It might beep two or more times, depending on the error. If the power supply, motherboard, CPU, or possibly some other critical IC is defective, it might not beep at all.

You can check the beep system by holding a key down while the system is booting up. You might hear a continuous beep. After the boot is complete, the system might give two short beeps and display the message, "Keyboard error. Press F1 to continue."

Several other beep error codes are in the system BIOS. Each BIOS manufacturer might use slightly different codes for some of the errors it finds. Some of the beep codes are for fatal errors, which cause the system to hang up completely. Suppose the beeps are arranged so that you get a beep, a pause, another beep, then three beeps close together, or 1-1-3. This code indicates that there was a failure in the CMOS setup system. One long and two short beeps, accompanied by a POST code of 400, 500, 2400, or 7400, could mean that there is an error in the CMOS RAM, a motherboard switch setting, or a defective video card. A 1-1-4 beep would indicate that there was an error in the BIOS itself. A continuous beep or repeating short beeps could indicate that the power supply or the motherboard had a fault.

Here are some of the AMI BIOS fatal-error beep POST codes:

- 1 short: DRAM refresh failure
- 2 short: Parity circuit failure
- 3 short: Base 64 Kb RAM failure
- 4 short: System timer failure
- 5 short: Processor failure
- 6 short: Keyboard controller gate A20 error
- 7 short: Virtual mode exception error
- 8 short: Display memory read/write test failure
- 9 short: ROM BIOS checksum failure
- 10 short: CMOS shutdown read/write error
- 11 short: Cache memory error

Here are a couple of nonfatal Error beep POST Codes:

- 1 long, 3 short: Conventional or extended memory failure
- 1 long, 8 short: Display/retrace test failed

Displayed POST Codes

Besides the beep POST codes, hundreds of POST codes may be displayed. The POST codes start with 100 and may go up to as high as 200,000. This does not mean that there are actually 200,000 separate codes. Most BIOS designers arrange the codes in blocks. For instance, the 100s have to do with the motherboard errors, 200s with RAM errors, 300s with keyboard errors, and 600s with floppy-drive errors. Many of the code numbers were designed for systems that are now obsolete, such as the 286 and PS/2.

Ordinarily, the codes will not be displayed if there is no problem. If there is a problem, the last two digits of the code will be something other than zeros. Each BIOS manufacturer develops their own codes, so there are some slight differences, but most of them are similar to the following:

- 101: Motherboard failure
- 109: Direct Memory Access test error
- 121: Unexpected hardware interrupt occurred
- 163: Time and date not set
- 199: User indicated configuration not correct

- 201: Memory test failure
- 301: Keyboard test failure or a stuck key
- 401: Monochrome display and/or adapter test failure
- 432: Parallel printer not turned on
- 501: Color graphics display and/or adapter test failure
- 601: Diskette drives and/or adapter test failure
- 701: Math coprocessor test error
- 901: Parallel printer adapter test failure
- 1101: Asynchronous communications adapter test failure
- 1301: Game control adapter test failure
- 1302: Joystick test failure
- 1401: Printer test failure
- 1701: Fixed disk drive and/or adapter test failure
- 2401: Enhanced graphics display and/or adapter test failure
- 2501: Enhanced graphics display and/or adapter test failure

POST Cards

Several companies have developed diagnostic cards or boards that can be plugged into a slot on the motherboard to display the POST codes. If there is a failure in the system, it can tell you immediately what is wrong. If you have eliminated the possibility of a defective plug-in board or a peripheral, then the problem is probably in your motherboard.

If the power supply is okay, you could use a diagnostic card such as the POST-PROBE from Micro 2000 (818-547-0125), the R.A.C.E.R. II from Ultra-X (800-722-3789), or the RACER II from Microdata (800-539-0123). These three cards are quite similar in the tests that they perform. They can be plugged into a computer that is completely dead except for the power supply, and they will check every chip and component on the motherboard. Each card has a small digital display that lights up a code for the condition of each component. These cards will work on any ISA or EISA machine, XT, 286, 386, 486 or Pentium. R.A.C.E.R. is an acronym for Real-time AT/XT Computer Equipment Repair.

There are several other POST cards on the market, but some of them are not very sophisticated. The Ultra-X R.A.C.E.R. II has several ROMs that can run over 70 diagnostic tests. Besides displaying the test codes on the plug-in board, the progress of the tests can be displayed on a monitor. If there is a failure in one of the tests, a fault tree will be displayed, which lists in order which chips might be at fault. In a computer where several chips interact, it is often difficult to determine exactly which chip might be at fault. The Ultra-X can narrow it down to a very few. At the end of the test, a report can be printed out.

Businesses can lose a lot of money when a computer is down. These diagnostic cards are tools that every professional repair shop and every computer maintenance department should have. It might also be well worth the money for an individual to buy one. If you have to take your computer to a repair shop, at $50 to $100 an hour, the repair could be rather expensive. You will also have to give up some of your time just to take the computer in to the shop. If the shop is busy, it might be some time before you get your computer back.

Diagnostic and Utility Software

There are several excellent diagnostic software programs available. Some of the utilities and tests are quite similar in each program. Most of them test and report on your system configuration and your system memory. Many of them do a test on your hard drives. Some of them, such as SpinRite and Disk Technician, are primarily designed for hard-disk tests and preventive maintenance.

Most BIOS chips have many diagnostic routines and other utilities built-in. These routines allow you to set the time and date, tell the computer what type of hard drive and floppies are installed, the amount of memory, the wait states, and several other functions. The AMI and DTK BIOS chips have a very comprehensive set of built in diagnostics. They can allow hard and floppy disk formatting, check the speed of rotation of the disk drives, do performance testing of hard drives, and perform several other tests.

The MSD Command

If you own a copy of MS-DOS 6.0 or later, you have an MSD (Microsoft Diagnostics) command. This utility can be used to search for files or subjects. It also gives you a wealth of information about your computer. It can show you the IRQs, the memory usage, your Autoexec.bat and Config.sys files, and many other useful bits of information. You can view the information or have it printed out.

Depending on what you have in your computer, it might take up to 20 pages to print it all out.

Norton Utilities

Norton Utilities, from Symantec Corporation (408-253-9600, www.symantec.com), includes several diagnostic and test programs and essential utilities. One of the programs is Norton Diagnostics (NDIAGS). This program tests the memory, CPU, DMA controllers, realtime clock, CMOS, and the serial and parallel ports.

Software cannot recognize and test the serial and parallel ports unless you have a loopback plug installed. These are 9- and 25-pin connectors that plug into the serial and parallel sockets. Some of the pins in these connectors are shorted out so that the software can recognize them.

Of course, Norton Utilities has all of the standard utilities, most of which are periodically updated and improved with new releases. Some of the standard utilities are Unerase, Disk Doctor, Disk Test, Format Recover, Directory Sort, and System Information.

MicroScope

MicroScope, from Micro 2000 (818-547-0125, www.micro2000.com), is an excellent diagnostic software tool. It can test the CPU, IRQs, DMAs, memory, hard-disk drives, floppy drives, video adapters, and much more. It can search for a network card and display its I/O and node address. It shows IRQ and I/O address. It tests memory and displays available memory space. It displays CMOS contents and will let you run CMOS setup. It can run video tests for memory and character sets. It can do a read, write, and random-seek test of the hard drives. It even allows you to edit sectors of the hard drive.

It can be set up to run any or all of these tests continuously. It can also be set to halt on an error or to log the error and continue. Figure 20-1 shows the Micro 2000 diagnostic software and hardware.

QAPlus/FE

QAPlus/FE from DiagSoft (408-438-8247, www.diagsoft.com), is a very sophisticated software program. Among its many functions is the ability to diagnose problems on the disk systems, memory, video, IDE and SCSI

Figure 20-1 MicroScope and POST-Probe diagnostic software and hardware from Micro 2000.

drives and interfaces, interrupts, BIOS, and serial and parallel ports. In order to test the serial and parallel ports, you need loopback plugs. The loopback plugs come free with QAPlus/FE diagnostic software.

If a semiconductor or system is going to fail, it will usually do so within the first 72 hours of use. Many vendors do a burn-in on their products to find any such systems before they are shipped, but many vendors might not have the time nor the software to properly exercise the units. QAPlus/FE can perform rigorous and continuous tests on systems for burn-in. If you buy an expensive system or component, it might be well worth the cost of buying a copy of QAPlus/FE just for the burn-in capability. If you find a defective component early, it can usually be sent back to the dealer or replaced at no cost.

CheckIt

CheckIt from TouchStone (714-969-7746, fax 714-969-1555) has long been one of the better diagnostic tools. They have recently revised and improved the programs. Here is some information from their Web site at www.touchstonesoftware.com:

> CheckIt version 5 for Windows 95 and CheckIt Professional Edition, the first ever 32-bit hardware troubleshooting utilities are designed to meet the emerging needs of today's computer users and professional technicians.

CheckIt empowers users of all levels by providing powerful tools to help pinpoint and solve computer problems, backup and restore critical system files, install new hardware components, uncover hidden conflicts, and optimize system performance quickly and easily. CheckIt version 5 features a new approach to troubleshooting that finds problems, and leads the user directly to the tools that can provide the solution. First, QuickCheck tests and locates problems automatically. If a problem is detected whether it is a hardware glitch, setup conflict or change in performance the program's exclusive Troubleshooter guides the user to the tests and information needed to solve it quickly. These include powerful hardware tests, extensive system information and a fast, easy way to compare system changes.

CheckIt's Find It feature allows users to search for the specific information they need, rather than having to look through pages of system information. In all, CheckIt offers over a dozen comprehensive information displays identifying everything users need to know about their motherboard, memory, modem, drives, video, ports, printer and Internet connections. System conflicts, which result from two hardware devices using the same system resources, can be very hard to find. CheckIt monitors all system resources (IRQ, DMA, memory ranges) and the devices using them, highlights the conflicts, and guides the user to the tools needed to resolve them.

Every time a user installs new hardware or loads a new software program, subtle changes are made to critical system files. The changes are often the cause of many types of PC problems. CheckIt's System Spy keeps track of these changes by taking "snapshots" of the system's hardware, critical system files and performance. The user can then identify the differences by comparing the latest snapshot with a previous one. CheckIt offers real hardware tests that examine the user's system from top to bottom, paying special attention to the devices used most often. At the end of each test, CheckIt produces a report showing exactly what devices have passed and failed. This information is essential for repairing or replacing a component, or for working with a technician. Tests include CheckIt Modem and CheckIt Video, as well as powerful tests for the user's motherboard, drives, memory, ports and CD-ROM.

CheckIt automatically saves Windows Registry and critical system files so users have a recent backup if Windows becomes corrupted.

The new CheckIt Professional Edition provides the best suite of advanced PC diagnostics available. By combining CheckIt for Windows 95, CheckIt for DOS, PC-cillin 3.0 Anti-Virus, special loopback plugs for precise port testing and a full year of free program upgrades, CheckIt Professional Edition gives professional technicians and power users the capability to solve more in-depth and complex PC problems.

CheckIt for DOS allows users to troubleshoot PCs when Windows won't run. They can access detailed information on a system's hardware, run full diagnostic tests on all key hardware components, and restore critical system files. Users can also generate custom batch tests, and configure the individual test applets for burn-in testing and troubleshooting multiple PCs.

The full version of TouchStone Software's award-winning PC-cillin Anti-Virus for Windows 95 features 100% guaranteed virus protection, free lifetime pattern file updates, and exclusive MacroTrapd technology to automatically detect and remove both known and unknown strains of destructive macro viruses.

CheckIt's Active Update feature allows users to receive free program upgrades and enhancements for a year. Figure 20-2 shows the CheckIt and PC-cillin software.

WINProbe

WINProbe is now a part of the Quarterdeck Company (800-683-6696, www.qdeck.com). The PC Certify program that comes with WINProbe can save a lot of time and trouble. PC Certify can be used to test all types of hard drives, floppy drives, and controllers.

Besides the drives, PC Certify does complete diagnostic tests on the whole computer. It tests the memory, serial and parallel ports, BIOS, video adapter, monitor, keyboard, and printer. The tests can be run continuously for as many times as you desire. These tests are ideal for burning in a computer. PC Certify will even print out a form for a technician to fill out. The form shows what tests were run and has a space for the technician to verify and sign.

The WINProbe portion also has the following diagnostic utilities:

- Audio for sound tests
- Communications for serial ports
- Floppy-drive RPM test
- Floppy-drive surface analysis
- Hard-drive surface analysis
- Keyboard tests
- Math Coprocessor and motherboard CPU function tests

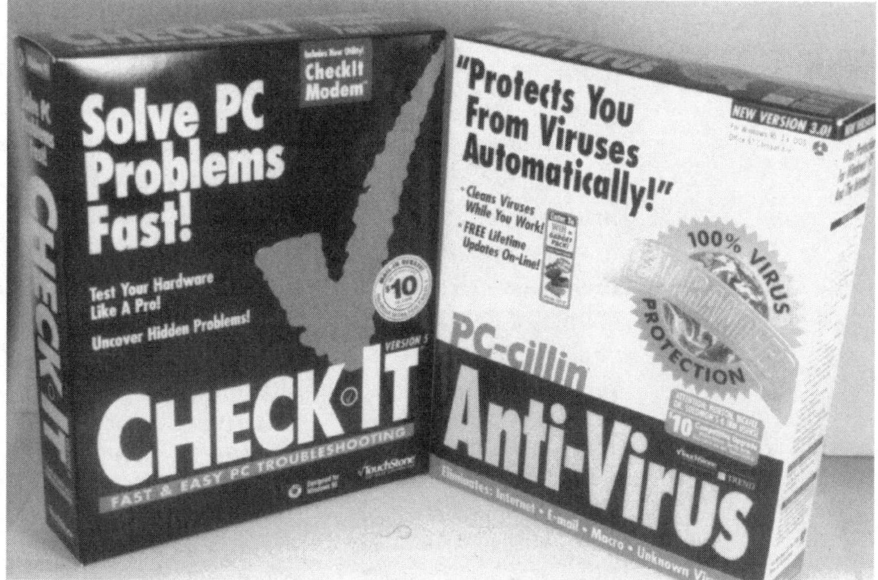

Figure 20-2 CheckIt diagnostic software and PC-cillin anti-virus software from TouchStone.

- Mouse driver tests
- Printer cable test
- RAM chip test
- Video mode tests

FIXIT is another diagnostic and repair tool from Quarterdeck. It detects and repairs potential conflicts before you install new software. It also has a list of over 1700 hardware and software companies, including phone numbers and URL addresses. If you can't fix it yourself, maybe you can find someone who can.

Quarterdeck has several excellent utilities. Visit their Web site for the latest information.

First Aid for Windows Users and PC 911

First Aid for Windows Users, from CyberMedia (800-721-7824), is a low-cost program that can spot problems, diagnose them, and then fix most of them automatically. For those it can't fix automatically, it can help you fix them manually. It fixes problems with printing, multimedia, bad INI files, path problems, missing application components, networks, and many others. The software is optimized for several of the well-known brand-name programs, such as Microsoft Office, Corel Draw, Quicken, and Paradox. In addition, CyberMedia offers free upgrades to the program that can be downloaded from CompuServe.

PC 911 is a low-cost companion program to First Aid for Windows from CyberMedia. PC 911 keeps track of all changes made to your PC's setup files. Several times in the past, I have installed programs that automatically changed my Autoexec.bat and Config.sys files to the point that my system would no longer operate. Recently, a program changed my files so that I was not able to use my word processors. It took me a couple of hours to find the problem. PC 911 could have saved me that time. PC 911 can also help you with conflicts in IRQs, DMAs, and other problems when installing multimedia and other cards.

First Aid and PC 911 can be bought separately, or you can save about one-third by buying them as a bundle. CyberMedia has several other good diagnostic programs and offers frequent upgrades. Call them for the latest.

Which One Should You Buy?

If I could only afford one program, I would be hard-pressed to choose one. All of them are good tools. Many of them have a few similar utilities, but there are also different utility features in every one of them. I can't possibly list all of the features of the products here. I suggest that you call each company and ask for literature on their products. I can't even list all of the diagnostic products that are available. New ones are being developed daily. Check computer magazines for ads and reviews.

Spares

One of the easiest ways to check a part is to have a good spare handy. If you suspect a board, it is very easy to plug in a known good one. If your computer is critical to your business and you cannot afford any downtime, then you should have a few spares handy. I would suggest that you have a spare floppy-disk drive, monitor adapter, and keyboard. These items are all fairly inexpensive.

Depending on how critical your business is and how important your computer is to it, you might even want to have spares of all your components, such as a motherboard, power supply, and all of your plug-in boards. You might have some very expensive video adapters,

PCI bus interfaces, or other boards that cost hundreds of dollars, but there are usually some equivalent, inexpensive boards for all of the boards in your system. A good PCI graphics high-resolution monitor adapter might cost as much as $300, but you can buy an ISA adapter that doesn't have all of the goodies for about $20. A low-cost board can help pinpoint the problem. If your monitor doesn't light up, but it works with a replacement adapter, then you know the probable cause of the problem.

DOS Error Messages

Even with Windows 95, you still have DOS running in the background for many programs. DOS has several error messages if you try to make the computer do something it can't do. Many of the messages are not very clear, however. Don't bother looking in the DOS manual for error messages; they are not there. If you are using IBM PC-DOS and you get an error message, just type

help *n*, where *n* is the first letter of the error message, and an explanation will pop up.

I have dozens of books on DOS, but few of them make any reference to the DOS error messages. One of the better books I have is *DOS, The New Complete Reference* by Kris Jamsa, published by Osborne-McGraw-Hill (800-227-0900). Another of his books, *DOS Secrets, Solutions, and Shortcuts,* explains DOS commands and DOS error messages in great detail, and what to do about them. These reference books should be in your library.

The following are some common DOS error messages:

Access Denied—You might have tried to write on or erase a file that was protected. The file might have been hidden or protected by an ATTRIBUTE command. Use the ATTRIBUTE command to change it.

Bad command or file name or *File not found*—You might have made a mistake in typing in the command, or the command or file does not reside in the current directory.

CHKDSK errors—You should run CHKDSK often. Some people put CHKDSK/F in their Autoexec.bat file so that it is run every time the system is booted up. (Disk Technician can do it for you.) CHKDSK might give you an error that says *nnn lost clusters found in n chains. Convert lost chains to files*

Y/N. Reinvoke CHKDSK with the /F switch (for fix), and the lost clusters will be converted to the file File000n.chk. These are usually incomplete files. When you delete a file, sometimes portions of it might be left in a sector. Or something might have caused an error in the FAT and caused portions of two different files to be written in a single sector or cluster. The files created by CHKDSK/F are usually incomplete. In most cases, they can be deleted. MS-DOS 6.22 and Windows 95 still have CHKDSK, but they also have ScanDisk, which does a better job than CHKDSK.

General failure reading or writing drive n:, Abort, Retry, Fail—The disk might not be formatted. It is also possible that track 0 on the disk, which stores the FAT, has become defective. It might be possible to restore the disk by using Norton's Disk Doctor (NDD) on it.

Invalid Directory—If you do execute a CD (Change Directory) command from the root directory, all you have to type is *CD NORTON*, or any directory you want to change to, and it will change immediately. If you happen to be in the WordPerfect directory, and you type *CD NORTON*, it will say that it is an invalid directory. If you are in any directory except the root directory, you have to type *CD \NORTON*, or whatever directory. If you type *CD /NORTON*, using the forward slash instead of the backslash, you will get the same error message.

Nonsystem disk or disk error. Replace and strike any key when ready—You had a nonbootable disk in drive A:.

Not ready error reading drive A. Abort, Retry, Fail—You might have asked the computer to go to drive A: and it was not ready, or there was no disk in the drive.

Most software packages have their own error messages. In many cases, the manual will not tell you what the error message means. You will probably have to call the software company to get an answer.

Glitches

There are times when something goes wrong for no apparent reason, and the computer might hang up. Glitches can happen when you are running almost any kind of program. Sometimes, you can get out of them with a warm boot (pressing the Ctrl, Alt, and Del keys). Other times, you might have to turn off the computer, wait a few seconds, then turn it back on. Remember that anything that you are working on is in memory. If you are working on a file that is on your disk, then you still have a copy on the disk, but if it is something that you have just typed in, when you turn off the computer or reboot, anything in memory is gone forever.

It is a good idea to save your data to disk every so often while you are working on it. By all means, try to save your work before rebooting, but quite often, if the computer hangs up, there is nothing you can do except grit your teeth and reboot.

Power Supply

The power supply is one of the most frequent causes of problems. Most of the components in your computer are fairly low power and low voltage. The only high voltage in your system is in the power supply, and it is pretty well enclosed, so there is no danger of shock if you open your computer and put your hand inside it. However, you should **never, ever** connect or disconnect a board or cable while the power is on. Fragile semiconductors might be destroyed if you do so. Semiconductors have no moving parts. If the circuits were designed properly, the semiconductors should last indefinitely.

Heat is an enemy and can cause semiconductor failure. The fan in the power supply should provide adequate cooling. All of the openings on the back panel that correspond to the slots on the motherboard should have blank fillers. Even the holes on the bottom of the chassis should be covered with tape. This forces the fan to draw air in from the front of the computer, pull it over the boards and exhaust it through the opening in the power supply case. Nothing should be placed in front of or behind the computer that would restrict air flow. If you don't hear the fan when you turn on a computer, or if the fan isn't running, then the power supply could be defective. Table 20-1 gives the pin connections and wire colors from the power supply.

TABLE 20-1

Power Supply Connections

Disk Drive Power-Supply Connections

Pin	Color	Function
1	Yellow	+12 VDC
2	Black	Ground
3	Black	Ground
4	Red	+5 VDC

TABLE 20-1 (continued) Power-Supply Connections to the Motherboard

P8 Pin	Color	Function
1	White	Power Good
2	No connection	
3	Yellow	+12 VDC
4	Brown	—12 VDC
5	Black	Ground
6	Black	Ground

P9 Pin	Color	Function
1	Black	Ground
2	Black	Ground
3	Blue	—5 VDC
4	Red	+5 VDC
5	Red	+5 VDC
6	Red	+5 VDC

The 8-bit slotted connectors on the motherboard have 62 contacts, 31 on the A side and 31 on the B side. The black ground wires connect to B1 of each of the eight slots. B3 and B29 have +5 VDC, B5 has −5 VDC, B7 has −12 VDC, and B9 has −12 VDC. These voltages go to the listed pins on each of the eight plug-in slots. Most of the other contacts on the plug-in slots are for address lines and data input/output lines. They are not often involved in problems.

Intermittent Problems

Intermittent problems can be most frustrating and maddening. They can be very difficult to find. If you suspect a cable or a connector, try wiggling it to see if the problem goes away or gets worse. I once spent several hours trying to find the cause of a floppy-disk problem. It turned out to be a loose wire in the connector. It was just barely touching the contact. A slight vibration could cause the disk drive to become erratic. A wire or cable can be broken and still make contact until it is moved. You might also try unplugging a cable or a board and plugging it back in. Sometimes, the pins might be slightly corroded or not seated properly. The copper contacts on a plug-in board can become corroded. You can clean them with an ordinary pencil eraser. Sometimes, just unplugging and plugging a board or connector back in several times can wipe away the corrosion.

Before unplugging a cable, put a stripe on the connector and cable with a marking pen or nail polish so that you can easily see how they should be plugged back in. You might even have a problem in the contacts of a DIP switch. You might try turning it on and off a few times.

Caution! Again, always write down the positions before touching any switch. Make a diagram of the wires, cables, and switch settings before you disturb them. It is easy to forget how they were plugged in or set before you moved them. You could end up making things worse. Make a mark before turning a knob or variable coil or capacitor, so that it can be returned to the same setting when you find out that it didn't help. Never mark on a circuit board with a pencil. Pencil lead is made from carbon graphite, which makes a good conductor of electricity.

Better yet, resist the temptation to reset these types of components. Most were set up using highly sophisticated instruments. They don't usually change enough to cause a problem. If too much current flows through a chip, it can get hot and fail. It might only fail at certain times when you are running a particular program. If you suspect a chip and it seems to be warmer than it should be, you might try using a hair dryer to heat it up. If it fails due to the extra heat, then you have found the problem. Be careful, though, that you do not heat up a good chip and cause it to fail.

If a component seemed to be too hot, at one time, we could spray a coolant on it, such as Freon. Because of environmental concerns, you might no longer be able to buy Freon. You might try using ice water in a plastic baggie. This will cool it. If the component then works properly, you have found your defect.

Some diagnostic software will run a system in an endless loop to try to force the system to fail.

Serial Ports

Conflicts in setting up serial-port devices can cause a lot of problems. Like the parallel ports, pins for the serial ports are available on any of the bus plug-in slots. Serial ports may be available as a group of ten pins on the motherboard, or on a multifunction plug-in board. The serial port might be a male DB25 connector with pins or a male DB9 connector. The original RS232 specification called for 25 lines, but most systems only use four or five lines, so the DB9 connector with nine pins is more than sufficient. Many of the mice sold today have the DB9 connector.

Serial ports are most often used for a mouse or other pointing device, modems, fax boards, plotters, scanners, and other similar devices. DOS supports four serial ports, COM1, COM2, COM3, and COM4. However, DOS only has two interrupt request (IRQ) lines for the serial ports, IRQ4 for COM1, and IRQ3 for COM2, so COM3 and COM4 must share the IRQ lines with COM1 and COM2. You will need special software in order to permit sharing. Devices can share because it is not likely that all four serial ports would be used at the same time.

If two devices are set for the same COM port, it will cause a serious conflict. Neither device will operate properly. When installing a mouse, modem, or FAX board, the interface plug-in boards must be configured so that none of the devices use the same port. If you have devices already installed on your system, you might not know which port they are set for.

Several programs can help you determine which ports are being used. One of the better ones is a low-cost shareware program called Port Finder. It is available from James McDaniel of mcTRONic Systems (713-462-7687). Windows 95 does a fairly good job of recognizing some Plug-and-Play hardware and setting it up, but it is not perfect. I have still had problems with conflicting hardware.

In Windows 95, to see which IRQs are being used, go to Control Panel from either the My Computer icon or the Start button on the task bar. From there, choose Systems, then on Device Manager, then double-click on Computer. It will show you all the IRQs that are being used.

Software Problems

I have had lots of problems with software. Quite often, it is my fault for not taking the time to completely read the manuals and instructions, but I don't usually have the time to read and study every page in the manual when I install a program. Many of the programs are getting easier to run. Plug-and-Play eliminates a lot of problems, but you will probably still run into lots of software problems. Many vendors have support programs for their hardware and software. If something goes wrong, you can call them. Some companies charge for their support. Some have installed 900 telephone numbers. You are charged a certain fee for the amount of time on the phone. It can cost a lot of money to maintain a support staff.

If you have a hardware or software problem, document it by writing down everything that happens. Before you call, try to duplicate the problem, or make it happen again. Carefully read the manual. When you call, it is best to be in front of your computer, with it turned on and with the problem on the screen, if possible. Before you call, have the serial number of your program handy. One of the first things they will probably ask is for your name and serial number. If you have bought and registered the program, it will be in their computer.

Many companies have set up Web sites with answers to frequently asked questions (FAQ). I have never been fortunate enough to find an answer to whatever question I have at the time on a FAQ list. Many of them have also set up faxback systems. You call a number, get a list of documents available, and they will automatically fax them to you. Again, I have had very little success in getting an answer to any of my problems, but it is a good way to get documentation and answers to the most FAQs.

It seems that everybody in business has now gone to automatic telephone-answering machines. When you call, usually long distance, you will be given several options. It might take several minutes to list them all. You press button 1 if you want one service, 2 for another, 3 for another, then when you get to that number, there will be another five or six options. You might stay on the phone for half an hour and never get to speak to a live person, or you will be put on hold to wait for the next available person. It can be very frustrating. One of the best investments I have ever made was buying a speaker phone. I can call a number, then push the speaker button and go about my other business while I am on hold.

Most software programs are reasonably bug-free, but lots of things can go wrong if the exact instructions and procedures are not followed. In many cases, the exact instructions and procedures are not very explicit. It seems that most software manuals are written by people who know the software very well. They seem to forget that the person using it for the first time does not know it.

Software companies could save millions of dollars if they produced manuals that were better written to make installation and usage easier. For every major program, there are dozens of books written to help you learn how to use it. Many training programs have been developed to teach people how to use "user-friendly" software. If you spend a lot of money on a program, you shouldn't have to spend a lot more time and money to learn how to use it. Windows 95 is a step in the ight direction in being fairly easy to use, but it is a very complex program and takes some study, training, and time to learn all of its advantages and benefits.

User Groups

There is no way to list all of the possible software or hardware problems. Computers are dumb and very unforgiving. It is very easy to plug a cable in backwards or forget to set a switch. There are thousands of things that can go wrong. Sometimes, it can be a combination of both software and hardware. Often, there is only one way to do something the right way, but ten thousand ways to do it wrong. Sometimes, it is difficult to determine if it is a hardware problem caused by software, or vice versa. There is no way that every problem can be addressed here.

One of the best ways to find answers is to ask someone who has had the same problem. One of the best places to find those people is at a users group. If at all possible, join one and become friendly with all of the members. They can be one of your best sources of troubleshooting. Most of them have had similar problems and are glad to help. Many local computer magazines list user groups in their area. The nationally distributed *Computer Shopper* magazine alternates with a listing of bulletin boards one month, and user groups the next.

Thank you for buying my book. I wish you all the best. I hope all your problems are easy ones.

GLOSSARY

ACPI An acronym for *Advanced Configuration and Power Interface,* a utility found on some newer motherboards.

active matrix LCD A system used for high-resolution liquid crystal diode (LCD) display panels, used on color laptop and portable computers. This type of display is fairly expensive, since it requires an individual transistor for each pixel. *See* passive matrix LCD.

adapter card A printed wiring board with digital circuitry that plugs into connectors on the motherboard of a personal computer, usually performing input/output functions.

ADC An abbreviation for *Analog-to-Digital Converter,* the electronic device used for converting conventional analog audio and video signals to digital form. The digital form can be processed by computer and stored as data on a computer's hard disk drive.

address The numerical value, usually in hexadecimal format, of a particular location in a computer's RAM.

ADPCM An abbreviation for *Adaptive Differential Pulse Code Modulation,* a method of digital waveform sampling encoding the difference between successive samples rather than encoding their actual values (DPCM). The differences are assigned different values based on the content of the sample. ADPCM is the storage format used by CD-ROM XA and CD-1 discs.

ADSL (Asymmetric Digital Subscriber Line) A digital phone line technology that supports high-speed connections using ordinary phone lines. ADSL is asymmetric because the uplink speeds at about 64 Kb are much less than the download speeds of up to 6 Mbps.

AGP (Accelerated Graphics Port) A new utility that makes graphics much faster. The port may be a slot on the motherboard, or it may be built into the motherboard.

algorithm 1) A digital set of instructions for solving a problem. 2) The configuration of operators in an FM synthesizer.

amplitude The strength or intensity of sound or signal; the measure of a current's deviation from its zero value.

amplitude modulation A term describing the interaction of two signals, a carrier and a modulator. The modulation signal varies the amplitude (intensity) of the carrier. In AM radio transmission, the carrier is a medium-frequency signal (550 to 1550 KHz), and the modulator is the sound signal. In sound synthesis, a low-frequency oscillator modulates a carrier that is the sound's fundamental frequency.

analog 1) A term describing a circuit, device, or system that responds to continuously variable parameters. 2) Generated by hardware rather than by software.

analog-to-digital converter A circuit that periodically samples a continuously variable voltage and generates a digital representation of its value, also called an ADC, A-to-D, or A/D converter.

ANI Automatic number identification, or caller ID.

ANSI an abbreviation for the *American National Standards Institute.* ANSI, in the Windows context, refers to the ANSI character set that Microsoft uses for Windows.

API An abbreviation for *Application Programming Interface.* Generically, a method of accessing or modifying the operating system for a program. In Windows, API refers to the functions provided by Windows, allowing applications to open and close windows, read the keyboard, interpret mouse movements, and so on. Programmers call these functions *hooks* to the operating systems.

APM and SMM An abbreviation for *Advanced Power Management* from Intel and Microsoft. It allows certain programs and operating systems to slow down various hardware components, thereby saving power. SMM stands for *System Management Mode,* a group of instructions built into the CPU.

artifact An extraneous sound or affect on an image not present in the source signal and introduced by one of the components in the recording or reproduction chain.

ASCII An acronym, pronounced *ask-ee,* for *American Standard Code for Information Interchange,* the digital code for displaying alphanumeric characters. It originally consisted 128 codes, but later it was extended to 254 characters. Some of the characters are smiley faces, playing cards, or music notes. You can see what some of them look like by using the TYPE command to view almost any .EXE or .COM file. Most word processors add control characters so that they display bold, underline, page formats, or other characteristics. Text generated on one word processor is usually quite different than that of another. It is almost like a foreign language. Most computers and word processors can handle pure ASCII characters, however. The control characters can be stripped off so that only ASCII characters are left.

aspect ratio An image's ratio of width to height. Aspect ratio is usually expressed as W:H, with W being the width and H being the height of the image. The aspect ratio of digital images is expressed as the ratio of the number of pixels in each dimension (640:480 for VGA images).

ASPI An acronym for *Advanced SCSI Programming Interface,* the industry standard for SCSI interface cards. If the card conforms to this standard, then several different peripherals from different manufacturers can be used with the card. The Adaptec Company was the original creator of this standard. *See* CAM.

ATM 1) An abbreviation for *Asynchronous Transfer Mode,* a wide-band, high-frequency protocol for data transmission. 2) An abbreviation for *Adobe Type Manager,* Adobe's system for managing TrueType fonts. 3) An abbreviation for *Automated Teller Machine,* where you can get money if you play your cards right.

AVI An abbreviation for *Audio Video Interleaved,* the Microsoft Application Programming Interface (API) designed to compete with Apple's QuickTime methodology. AVI techniques provide a software synchronization and compression standard for audio and video signals competing with DVI.

BitBlt An abbreviation for *Bit Block Transfer,* an assembly-level function used for copying graphic images in Windows applications from a source to a destination graphic context.

buffer A section of RAM where data is stored temporarily, usually containing data to be edited or inserted.

CAM An acronym for *Common Access Method,* a standard that was developed for SCSI devices. It is similar to the ASPI standard except that the interface cards have their own BIOS onboard.

camcorder A contraction of *camera* and *recorder.* The term describes a video camera and videocassette recorder combined into a single, handheld unit.

Carpal Tunnel Syndrome (CTS) Pain and numbness in the hand, wrist, and arm along the path of the medial nerve. CTS is often caused by the repetitive action of typing on a computer keyboard. *See* Repetitive Strain Injury (RSI).

CAV An abbreviation for *Constant Angular Velocity* devices, such as computer hard disks and CAV video laserdiscs, depending on the distance of the read-write head from the drive spindle.

CCD An abbreviation for *Charge-Coupled Device,* an integrated circuit consisting of a linear array of semiconductor photoreceptor elements. CCDs are used to create a bitmapped image. Each photoreceptor creates an electrical signal representing the luminance of one pixel. CCDs are primarily used in scanners, color xerographic printers, and video cameras.

CCITT An abbreviation for the *Consultative Committee International for Telephone and Telegraph* communication. CCITT establishes standards for telephone interchange and modems in Europe. Several CCITT standards for communication between modems over telephone networks have been adopted in the United States. The CCITT has been renamed the International Telecommunications Union (ITU).

CD An abbreviation for *Compact Disc.* CDs are the original format for distributing compact optical disks for audio reproduction (CD audio). This early format was jointly developed by Phillips N.V. and Sony Corporation and is described in Phillips N.V.'s Yellow Book. Control of Yellow Book CD-ROMs, such as starting and stopping the drive and file selection with your computer, requires Microsoft's MSCDEX.DRV driver.

CD-DA An abbreviation for *Compact Disk—Digital Audio,* also called "Red Book" audio. CD-DA requires compatibility with MPC specification 1.0. It enables interleaving of audio with other types of data, so recorded sound can accompany images. It is usually supplied with the CD-ROM drive when purchased as a component of an MPC upgrade kit. The CD-DA format is defined in the International Electrotechnical Commissions' (IEC) Standard BNNI-5-83-095.

CD +Graphics A format in which the subchannel (s) of an audio CD contains graphic images that may be displayed on a computer or a television set.

CD-I An abbreviation for *Compact Disk-Interactive.* CD-I refers to a class of CDs primarily designed to be viewed on conventional television sets by means of a CD-I player. CD-I players incorporate at least 1 Mb of memory (RAM), special pointing devices, and remote-control systems. CD-I players also can be used for training and other commercial and industrial applications. CD-I formats are covered by Phillips N.V.'s Green Book specification.

CD+MIDI A format in which the subchannel (s) of an audio CD contains data in standard MIDI format that can be routed to a MIDI OUT connector and played on external MIDI synthesizers or internally by audio-adapter cards.

CD-MO An abbreviation for *Compact-Disk Magneto-Optical.* Magneto-optical CDs and CD-ROMs are capable of multiple use because they can be erased and re-recorded. The standards for CD-MOs are incorporated in Phillips N.V.'s "Orange Book 1" specification. CD-MO technology is used for high-capacity, $3^1/_2$-inch "floptical" floppy disks.

CD-ROM An acronym for *Compact Disk Read-Only Memory.* CD-ROM discs can incorporate both audio and graphic images, as well as text files. Phillips N.V.'s documentation for this standard has a yellow binding, hence the term "Yellow Book" audio. MPC specification 1.0 requires multimedia PCs to include a CD-ROM.

CD-ROM XA An abbreviation for *CD-ROM eXtended Architecture,* jointly developed by Philips N.V., Sony Corporation, and Microsoft Corporation in 1989. CD-ROM XA provides storage for audio and other types of data interleaved on a CD-ROM, enabling access simultaneously.

channel message A MIDI command or data that is sent over a specific MIDI channel.

chrominance A term used in television broadcasting to describe the signal (a subcarrier of the basic black-and-white signal) containing the color information in a composite video signal. Chrominance has two components: hue (tint) and saturation (the degree to which the color is diluted by white light). Chrominance is also called chroma and is abbreviated as C.

CHRP An acronym for *Common Hardware Reference Platform,* a set of standards agreed to by Motorola, IBM, and Apple for the Power PC.

clipping Audible distortion of an audio signal, usually caused by overloading a circuit or transducer.

clock An electronic circuit that generates the pulses used to synchronize bits of information.

CLV An abbreviation for *Constant Linear Velocity,* the recording technique used with CD-ROMs (and other CD devices) specifying that the velocity of the media at the point of reading or writing remain constant, regardless of the distance from the spindle. CLV devices have a constant data transfer rate. To achieve CLV, the rotational speed of the spindle motor must be inversely proportional to the distance of the read or write point on the media from the spindle Video. Laser disc drives are produced in CLV and CAV models.

codec An acronym for *compression-decompression* for video data.

cookie A piece of information sent by a Web server to a Web browser. If you access certain sites, a cookie will generate a bit of information about you and save it. The next time you access the site, the cookie will remember you and make it easier to access the same information. Some people worry that the information gathered by cookies could be misused and abused.

CP/M An abbreviation for *Control Program for Microprocessors.* CP/M was the first operating system for personal computers. It was written by Gary Kildall in 1973. It was used by all of the early PCs, such as Osborne, Kaypro, Morrow and others. In 1980, IBM approached Gary to develop a system for the first IBM PC. IBM later went to Bill Gates...and you know the rest of the story.

CPS 1) An abbreviation fro *Cycles Per Second,* such as the frequency of an electronic circuit. 2) In speaking of printers, an abbreviation for *Characters Per Second,* referring to the speed that the printer can produce.

CTI An abbreviation for *Computer Telephony Integration,* connecting a computer to a telephone switch.

cycle A single, complete wave; the basic unit of oscillation.

DAC An abbreviation for *Digital-to-Analog Convertor.* DAC is the electronic device used to convert digital audio and video signals stored on CD-ROMs, DAT, or in computer files to analog signals that can be reproduced by conventional stereo and television components.

daisy chain The connection of several devices on a SCSI. Also, a network in which data flows from one receiving device's MIDI THRU port to another receiving device's MIDI IN port.

DAT An acronym for *Digital Audio Tape.* DAT is a process of recording sound in helical bands on a tape cartridge. This process is similar to recording video signals.

default A parameter value that exists when hardware is turned on or an application is run.

Dhrystones A benchmark that measures millions of instructions per second (MIPS).

digital-to-analog converter A circuit that generates a digital representation of a continuously variable signal, also called a DAC or D/A converter.

DIN An acronym for *Deutches Institute fur Normalization.* DIN is an organization similar to ANSI that establishes and coordinates standards for Germany. It has become the de facto standards bureau for Europe.

DLL An abbreviation for *Dynamic Link Library*. DLL is a file containing a collection of Windows functions designed to perform a specific class of operations. Functions within DLLs are called (invoked) as necessary by applications to perform the desired operations.

DNS The *Domain Naming System*, the Internet system for assigning Internet addresses.

domain name The unique name of a Web site.

drag-and-drop A Windows process whereby an icon representing an object, such as a file, can be moved (dragged) by the mouse to another location, such as a different directory, and placed (dropped) in that location. Visual Basic provides drag-and-drop capabilities for control objects.

DSP An abbreviation for *Digital Signal Processing*. Although all synthesized sound involves DSP, the term is usually applied to the creation of electronic, acoustic effects such as reverberation, chorusing, flanging, and panning.

DTV The abbreviation for *Desktop Video*, the term describing the production of videotape presentations using the multimedia capabilities of personal computers. DTV implies the capability to edit videotapes by using the playback and record functions of VCRs that can be remotely controlled by a computer.

DVI An abbreviation for Intel's *Digital-Video Interactive* standard. DVI simultaneously displays compressed video images and sound files. IBM has adopted the DVI standard for its Ultimedia product line. Microsoft adds DVI capability through its DVMCI extensions.

EISA An abbreviation for *Extended Industry Standard Architecture*, a bus specification used to interconnect adapter cards employing 32-bit memory addresses or providing multiprocessor capabilities. The EISA standard is now obsolete, although there are several systems still in existence.

Energy Star The EPA's requirement that PCs implement automatic sleep modes when the item is not being used to save energy. Many laptop computers have used similar systems for some time. Newer CPUs have a variety of power-saving options.

EPROM An acronym for *Erasable Programmable Read-Only Memory*, the type of chips usually used for ROM BIOS.

Error Correction Code (ECC) A coding system that, in conjunction with an Error Detection Coding scheme, can reconstruct erroneous data to its original value.

Error Detection Code (EDC) A coding system that detects errors in a single byte or in blocks of data. Single-byte errors are caught by parity checkers such as the ones employed in the PC's memory system. Errors in blocks of data are commonly determined by using techniques such as the Cyclic Redundancy Codes (CRC) used for data transfer by modem. More sophisticated EDC methods are employed when error correction is required, such as with CD-ROMs.

FAQ An acronym for *Frequently Asked Questions.* Many technical support systems and online services list the FAQs. Hopefully, you might find an answer to your question or problem without having to call on the telephone and switch through all the many options.

field In video terminology, half of a television image. A field consists of either the even or odd lines of a frame. When used in conjunction with computer databases, a field is a single, distinct element of a complete database record.

filter A circuit or function that alters a signal's frequency spectrum by attenuating or accenting certain portions.

firewall Hardware or software that protects a LAN or site from unauthorized access.

Firewire Apple Computer's proprietary implementation of IEEE-1394. IEEE-1394 is somewhat like the Universal Serial Bus (USB). It is a high-speed bus that can accommodate several devices.

firmware Software that is embedded in the computer's ROMs or elsewhere in the computer circuitry. You cannot ordinarily change or modify firmware.

FM synthesis A method of generating complex waveforms by modulating the frequency of audio waveforms (carriers) with other waveforms (modulators); frequency modulation.

frame rate In film or video, the frequency at which single frames are shown, usually equal to 24, 25, or 30 frames per second.

frequency The rate of oscillation, which determines pitch, measured in cycles per second, or Hertz.

FTP An abbreviation for *File Transfer Protocol,* a TCP/IP protocol for transferring files from one machine to another or from sites on the Internet.

fundamental frequency A sound's primary frequency; the first harmonic.

genlock A process for synchronizing the video display of a computer to the frame synchronization signal of NTSC, PAL, or SECAM video. This process allows a computer-generated graphics to be viewed on a television set or recorded with a VCR. Genlock capability is required to add computer-generated titling to video productions.

GIF An acronym for *Graphic Interchange Format*. GIF is the file format (and extension) used to store most graphic images in the CompuServe forum libraries, and on the Internet in general.

global Pertaining to a computer program as a whole. Global variables and constants are accessible to, and may be modified by, program code at the module and procedure level.

grayscale A description for monochrome (black and white) images displayed in various intensities of black. The most common format is an 8-bit grayscale, providing 256 shades of gray. Four-bit grayscale images with 64 shades are also used.

harmonic A simple component of a complex waveform that is a whole-number multiple of the fundamental frequency.

HDTV An abbreviation for *High-Definition Television*, a form of television transmission that results in clearer images, especially on large-screen sets. Our present standard is 525 lines swept across the screen from top to bottom. HDTV would increase the number and give much better resolution.

Hi8 An abbreviation for *High Band 8mm*, a format developed by Sony Corporation for camcorder videotapes. Hi8 provides the capability of recording PCM digital audio and time-code tracks in addition to conventional analog audio and enhanced-quality video information.

High Sierra format A name assigned to the predecessor of ISO standard 9660 defining the table of content and directory structure of CD-ROMs for computer applications. Microsoft's MSCDEX.DRV driver reads the table of content and directory structure and converts the latter to the structure used by DOS. This function enables you to treat CD-ROM files as if they were located on a conventional hard disk drive.

HMS time Time expressed in hours, minutes, and seconds, usually separated by colons.

HTML An abbreviation for *Hypertext Markup Language*, a special language used to create Web pages.

http An abbreviation for *Hypertext Transfer Protocol,* the World Wide Web text-based protocol.

Hz An abbreviation for Hertz, the fundamental unit of frequency of audio and radio waves. Hertz was previously called cycles per second (cps). Most people can discern sounds that range in frequency from about 20 to 18,000 Hz.

icon In Windows, a 32 × 32-pixel graphic image, usually in color. An icon identifies the application in the Program Manager window when the application is minimized and in other locations in the application chosen by the programmer.

interlaced The method of displaying television signals on conventional TV sets and computer monitors. Alternative fields of images, consisting of the even or odd horizontal lines comprising the image, are displayed in succession.

interleaved A method for containing sound and video information in a single file but in separate chunks, so digital images and audio signals may be transferred from a file to the computer's memory without delays incurred by CD-ROM seek operations.

IP An abbreviation for *Internet Protocol,* a protocol used to send packets of data over the Internet.

ITU The International Telecommunications Union, formerly called the CCITT, a United Nations committee that tries to convince nations and companies to standardize telecommunications devices and protocols. *See* CCITT.

ISA An abbreviation for *Industry Standard Architecture,* the specification of the connections to plug-in adapter cards with 16-bit memory addressing capability. ISA is the bus structure used in conventional IBM-compatible computers using the 8088, 80286, 80386, and 80486 CPU chips.

ISDN An abbreviation for *Integrated Services Digital Network,* a digital telephone network that allows much faster communications.

ISO An abbreviation for the *International Standards Organization.* The ISO is a branch of the United Nations headquartered in Geneva. The ISO coordinates international standards for a wide variety of products and equipment. For example, the CD-ROM standard for tables of content and file directory entries, originally called the High Sierra Format, has been established as the ISO-9660 standard.

ISP An abbreviation for *Internet Service Provider,* a company that provides connections to the Internet. Larger ones are AOL, Prodigy, CompuServe and Microsoft Network, but there are hundreds of small, local ISPs. There are well over 200 in the Los Angeles area alone.

IVRU An abbreviation for *Interactive Voice Response Unit,* a system whereby the computer can play back digitized speech and accept requests from a touchtone telephone. These systems are now used by many companies to displace live human beings. It saves a lot of money for the companies because these systems never take a coffee break, go on vacations, or ask for a raise.

JPEG An acronym for the *Joint Photographic Experts Group* that has established an industry standard for photographic image compression.

.JPG The file extension for graphic image files stored with JPEG compression.

jumper A small, plastic-enclosed spring clip making an electrical connection between two adjacent square metal pins, usually in the form of a header. Jumpers are used to set device addresses and interrupt levels, and select other optional features of adapter cards. They are also found on motherboards.

karaoke A musical arrangement designed to accompany an added singing voice. Karaoke can be used to describe a consumer audio or audio-video component equipped with a microphone (and often with digital signal processing). The added singer's voice is combined with the accompaniment and heard through the same speakers.

LAN An acronym for *Local Area Network,* a network where several computers can be tied together. The area served may be a single building or several buildings, such as a campus.

luminance One of the characteristics defining a color in the Hue-Saturation-Luminance (HSL) system. Luminance is the collective intensity (lightness) of the color defined by hue and saturation. In television broadcasting, the signal containing the black and white image is referred to as the luminance signal.

MFLOPS An acronym for *Millions of Floating Point Instructions Per Second.*

MIDI An acronym for *Musical Instrument Digital Interface,* a means of communicating musical information among computers and microprocessor-based devices.

MIME An acronym for *Multipurpose Internet Mail Extensions,* a protocol for sending non-ASCII type data over the Internet. Such data may be sound, video and graphics.

MIPS An acronym for *Million of Instructions Per Second,* a measure of how fast a CPU operates.

MSRP An abbreviation for *Manufacturer's Suggested Resale Price,* usually much higher than the street price.

NAMM An acronym for the *National Association of Music Merchants.* NAMM is an industry association of music dealers and musical instrument manufacturers. NAMM hold a yearly exhibition where new MIDI devices and audio components are introduced.

nanosecond One billionth of a second, abbreviated ns. The speed of memory chips is measured in nanoseconds, usually ranging from about 30 to 100. Faster computer clock speeds require memory chips with lower nanosecond response times; 33 MHz computers, for instance, use 70 to 80 ns memory chips.

NBT An abbreviation for *The Next Big Thing,* what everybody is waiting breathlessly for. Time and again, NBT has been rumored and hinted at. When it arrives, it will be a real killer app or component.

NLQ An abbreviation for *Near Letter Quality.* Many printers, especially the dot matrix, can print fairly fast in a draft mode. In draft mode, there are usually spaces and jagged edges in the characters. For NLQ printing, more pins in the head are struck, so that the characters are better defined.

noninterlaced The preferred method of displaying computer images, usually on a multisynchronous video display unit, in which the image is created by displaying consecutive rather than alternate scanning lines.

OCR An abbreviation for *Optical Character Recognition,* a system used in scanners to recognize printed text and convert it into digital data.

oscillator A circuit or software that generates voltage signals.

PAL An acronym for *Phase-Alternative Line* system. PAL is the television transmission standard of Western Europe (except France). PAL displays 625 lines per frame at a rate of 25 frames per second.

palette A Windows data structure defining the colors of a bitmapped image in RGB format.

parallel interface A connection between devices that transfers one or more bytes of information simultaneously.

parameter A variable characteristic or value.

passive matrix LCD A system used on the less-expensive display panels for color laptops and portables. It uses a single transistor to activate rows and columns of pixels. It is much less expensive than active matrix, but the colors are not as bright. *See* active matrix LCD.

PCM An abbreviation for *Pulse Code Modulation,* a means of digitally encoding and decoding audio signals.

PCI An abbreviation for *Peripheral Component Interconnect,* a system that allows plug-in boards and devices to communicate with the CPU over a 32- or 64-bit high-speed bus.

.PCX The file extension created by ZSoft Corporation for storing images created by its PC Paintbrush application. PCX bitmapped files can be monochrome or color and are used by many other bitmapped image-creation (paint) and display applications.

Photo CD A trademark of the Eastman Kodak Company for its technology and CDs that provide copies of photographic color images in a format compatible with CD-I and CD-ROM XA drives. Photo CDs are produced from 35-mm film images by licensed photo-finishing facilities. These facilities have equipment that can write to the special Photo CD media.

pipeline In the Pentium, a pipeline is an arrangement of registers within the CPU. They are also called execution units. Each register performs part of a task, then passes the results to the next register. PCs such as the 486 computer have a single pipeline and can only process one instruction per clock cycle. The Pentium has two pipelines and can process two instructions per cycle.

POP An acronym for *Post Office Protocol,* the protocol used to send and retrieve Internet e-mail messages.

presentation A multimedia production consisting principally of still images or simple animation covering a single topic.

prosumer A contraction of *professional* and *consumer.* Prosumer describes video components, such as camcorders and VCRs, bridging the gap between consumer-grade products and industrial-quality devices.

QIC An acronym for *Quarter-Inch Cartridge,* magnetic tape used for tape backup.

RAM An acronym for *Random-Access Memory,* a computer's main memory in which data is temporarily stored, and which allows the user to enter and retrieve data at will.

RAID An acronym for *Redundant Array of Inexpensive Disks.* When the data is critical, a RAID system of two or more hard disks can be used to mirror each other so that the same data is recorded on each disk.

RBOC An abbreviation for *Regional Bell Operating Companies,* in other words, telephone companies.

Repetitive Strain Injury (RSI) Pain and numbness to areas of the hand, wrist, and arm. RSI is similar to Carpal Tunnel Syndrome, except that ordinarily, RSI may occur in any part of the body that is subjected to frequent motion or trauma. The injury usually occurs in tendons and in synovial sheaths that surrounds the nerves. This injury is sometimes called Repetitive Motion Injury, which is probably a better term.

ribbon cable A flat multiconductor cable having parallel individual conductors that are molded together. One side of the ribbon cable is marked with a printed line, usually blue or red. This line identifies the conductor corresponding to pin 1 of the attached connectors.

RIFF An acronym for the Windows *Resource Interchange File Format.* RIFF is used in conjunction with Multimedia Extensions. Depending upon their definition, these files may contain a MIDI sequence, sample dump, or system exclusive data, waveform audio files, or data to create graphic images. RIFF is the preferred file format for Windows multimedia files; however, few third-party applications currently create RIFF files, except in Wave format (.WAV files).

RTM What you might hear when you call a company for support, or ask someone for help: "Read The Manual."

RTDM Same as above, but a bit more imperative: Read The Damned Manual. Another version that can't be used in nice company is RTFM.

sample To digitally encode an analog signal.

sawtooth wave A waveform that contains every component of the natural harmonic series, also called a *ramp wave.*

scalability Scalable, multiprocessing operating systems allow a user to run the same application on single-processor and multiprocessor computers.

SCSI An acronym for *Small Computer System Interface*, pronounced *scuzzy;* an interface standard for connecting peripherals to a PC. The standard supports several different peripherals, such as hard drives, CD-ROMs, and scanners. As many as seven different devices can be connected to one SCSI card.

SDRAM An abbreviation for *Synchronous DRAM,* a type of DRAM that is synchronized with the CPU. It is much faster than most DRAM. It can only be used on motherboards that are designed for it.

SECAM The acronym for *Systeme Couleur avec Memoire.* SECAM is the French standard for television transmission (819 horizontal lines per frame displayed at 25 frames per second). SECAM is the standard for most of Eastern Europe, including the former USSR, and in African countries where French is the most common second language.

seek To locate a specific byte, sector, cluster, record, or chunk within a disk file.

serial interface A connection between devices that transfers information one bit after another.

signal-to-noise ratio (SNR) The ratio between an audio or video signal of a specific amplitude (level) and the underlying noise contributed to the signal by a component. The SNR is expressed in dB or dBr (relative), a large negative number being preferred.

sine wave A pure, simple waveform comprised of a single frequency with no overtones. It is a voltage signal that goes positive above zero to a certain height, then back to zero, then negative for a minus voltage, then back to zero. Alternating voltages are sine waves.

SKU An abbreviaton for *Stock-Keeping Unit.*

slave A device receiving signals from and controlled by a master device.

SOHO An acronym for *Small Office, Home Office.*

SMPTE A type of time code adopted by the Society of Motion Picture and Television Engineers, used to indicate location in time and synchronize playback.

SPEC92 Refers to the Systems Performance Evaluation Cooperative (SPEC), a group of organizations that got together in January of 1992 and developed a suite of benchmark programs to effectively measure the performance of computing systems in actual application environments.

SPECfp92 A benchmark that measures floating-point performance.

SPECint92 An effective benchmark to measure integer application performance.

square wave A pulse wave with a 50% duty cycle, consisting of odd harmonics only.

SRP An abbreviation for *Suggested Retail Price,* also called MSRP (Manufacturers Suggested Retail Price).

streaming The technique used to transfer information from a file structure, such as on a disk or CD drive, to the computer's memory. Streaming takes place in groups of bytes less than the entire file's length, usually processed in memory as a background activity.

stripe A synchronization signal recorded on one track of a multitrack tape recorder.

superscalar Refers to the fact the Pentium architecture has two parallel pipelines. It can process instructions in both pipelines simultaneously, or two instructions per clock cycle.

S-VHS A VHS-format videocassette recorder with S-video capability.

S-video An abbreviation for *Super-video.* S-video is a video signal with enhanced quality used for recording. S-video separates the chrominance signal from the luminance signals of composite video.

sync An abbreviation for *synchronization.*

TCP An abbreviation for *Transmission Control Protocol,* usually seen as *TCP/IP* (Transmission Control/Internet Protocol). It is used on LANs as well as on the Internet to guarantee reliable delivery by resending any lost packets or corrupted bits and bytes.

.TGA The file extension identifying files created in the format used by Truevision's TARGA series of graphic adapter cards.

.TIF An acronym for *Tagged Image Format.* TIF is a format for storing black and white, grayscale, and color bitmapped images developed by Aldus Corporation.

time code A method of identifying the time an event (such as a single motion picture or video frame) occurs in a format that can be understood by a computer.

time stamp The date and time data attributes applied to a disk file when it is created or edited. In MIDI files, a time stamp identifies the time MIDI events (such as Note On or Note Off) should occur, so the correct tempo is maintained.

triangle wave A waveform with a strong fundamental and weak overtones, comprised of odd-numbered harmonics only.

trigger A control signal that indicates the beginning of an event.

TrueType A trademark of Apple Computer, Inc., for its outline-based typeface design and display system that creates display and printer fonts in a manner similar to Adobe's PostScript. Microsoft Corporation has incorporated an improved version of TrueType technology in Windows

truncate In sampling, to remove recorded data before or after a sample.

TSR An abbreviation for *Terminate-and-Stay-Resident*, a term describing software that loads itself into RAM and stays there. It is available at any time, but it might use up a lot of the much-needed 640 Kb of RAM.

twip Window's smallest unit of graphic measurement. A twip is a twentieth of a point, or 1/1,440th of an inch.

typeface Print or display type of a single design. Typeface is often confused with the term *font*, which means a particular size of a typeface. A typeface may be a member of a typeface or type family including related designs with attributes such as bold, Roman (regular), italic, compressed, or extended.

UART An abbreviation for *Universal Asynchronous Receiver and Transmitter*, a chip that processes data through the serial port. For example, it takes eight bits to make a character. The parallel port can send a whole 8-bit character over eight lines at one time. To send data over the serial port, the chip takes the digital data and sends it through the port one bit at a time in a serial string. The early UARTs used an 8250 chip, which is rather slow. Newer devices use the 16550, which is much faster. Many of the less expensive multi-I/O boards still use the older 8250. To find out what you have, use the DOS MSD command.

URL An abbreviation for *Uniform Resource Locator*, the name of a site on the World Wide Web, For instance, http://www.pencomputing.com/dim. Ordinarily, the http:// can be omitted.

VESA An acronym for the *Video Electronic Standards Association*. VESA is a group of manufacturers and software developers who create standards for graphic and video display adapter cards.

VLB An abbreviation for *VESA Local Bus*, a system that allows plug-in boards or other devices to communicate with the CPU over a fast 32- or 64-bit bus.

Wave file A RIFF (Resource Interchange File Format) file containing PCM waveform audio data, usually with a .WAV extension. Microsoft and IBM have adopted .WAV files as their standard format for multimedia sound applications.

waveform audio A data-type standard of the Windows Multimedia Extensions. Waveform audio defines how digitally sampled sounds are stored in files and processed by Windows API functions.

wavetable A term describing the synthesis technique of simulating the sounds of musical instruments with short digitized recordings (PCM samples) of their sounds.

Whetstones Whetstones measures arithmetic operations. WinBench executes on top of Windows and gives WinMark measures.

wildcard A character that substitutes for and allows a match by any character or set of characters in its place, such as the ? and *.

WinBench A benchmark for use with Windows.

WinMark A benchmark for use with Windows.

WORM An acronym for *Write-Once Read-Many.* The WORM system uses a laser to write on a special optical disc. CD-WO (the write-once CD standard) is a special type of WORM format.

write-back cache A write-back system that only writes data back to the main memory that has been modified.

write-through cache A system where all data is immediately written back to memory.

WWW An abbreviation for *World Wide Web,* the portion of the Internet that is made up of thousands and thousands of sites and millions of home pages.

YC An encoding method used in S-Video. In YC, the luminance (Y) and chrominance (X) signals are separated. The chrominance signal incorporates both hue and saturation information.

ZIF An acronym for *Zero Insertion Force.* A 238-pin chip like the Pentium requires a large amount of force to insert and remove. It is a fragile device, and the pins can be easily damaged. A ZIF socket has a lever that opens the socket contacts so that the device can be dropped in. When the lever is pressed down, the socket contacts close around the pins.

zoom To magnify an image on a video display.

INDEX

A

Accelerated graphics port (AGP), 31
AMD K6 MMX, 67
Analog sine waves, 23
ASCII code, 24
Assembly steps, 329—353
ATX, 6, 40, 323

B

Backup, 171—189
  .BAK files, 173
  crash recovery, 177
    DriverSavers, 178
    OnTrack, 177
  delete protection, 174
  head crash, 176
  jumbled FAT, 174
  tape, 184
  types of backup, 183
    LapLink, 187
    RAID, 187
    recordable CD-ROM, 186
    removable disks, 185
    second hard disk, 187
    uninterruptible power supplies, 188
    Windows 95, 184
    Xtree, 184
  unerase software, 173
Bar codes, 430
Barebones system, 309

C

Case, 4
CD-ROM drives, 192
  access or seek time, 202
  CD-ROM Recorders (CD-R), 206
  data buffers, 202
  Digital Videodisc (DVD), 212
CD-ROM drives (*Cont.*):
  how CD-ROM works, 197
  installing CD-ROM drives, 213
  interface systems, 203
    IDE, 203
    SCSI, 203
  Kodak photo CD, 211
  laser color, 199
  multidisc systems, 204
  multidrive systems, 205
  rotational speed, 200
  transfer speed, 201
CMOS Battery, 52
COM serial ports, 55
Computers and devices for handicapped, 270—273
CPU, 64—89
  AMD, 67—71
  characteristics, 79
  Cyrix, 71—73
  frequency, 80
  IDT WinChip C6, 73—75
  memory bus, 81
  MMX, 66, 76
  Pentium II, 65—67
  sockets, 83
  voltage, 84
  ZIF, 85
Cyrix 6X86MX, 71

D

Desktop publishing, 435
Digital cameras, 440
DMA, 53

F

Fax, 11, 293, 294
Facsimile machines, 290—291
Floppy disks, 131
  clusters or allocation units, 135

Floppy disks (*Cont.*):
  cylinders, 135
  data compression, 131
  file allocation table (FAT), 136
  formatting, 138
  read aqccuracy, 137
  sectors, 135
  tracks per inch (TPI), 136
  tracks, 134
  virtual drive, 127
Floppy drives, 116—140
  1.44Mb, 116
  combination floppy, 127
  head actuator motor, 129
  Iomega zip, 118
  LS120, 118
  Sony HiFD, 122
Formatting:
  floppy disk, 138
  hard drive, 152, 348

G

Graphics tablets, 259

H

Hard disk:
  allocation units, 153
  clusters, 153
  cylinders, 155
  disk platters, 159
  file allocation table (FAT), 153
  head actuators or positioners, 155
  head spacing, 158
  installation and configuration, 162
  mean time between failures (MTBF), 161
  near field technology, 161
  physical sizes, 159
  speed of rotation and density, 156, 160
  speed or access time, 158
  timing, 157
  zone bit recording, 160
Hard drives, 142—169
  Avatar Shark 250, 147
  Fujitsu Dyna MO, 146
  IDE or ATA, 143
  Iomega 40Mb clik, 146
  Iomega Jaz, 146
  magneto-optical drives, 148
  Olympus MOS330E, 145
  parallel port hard drives, 147
  removable disk drives, 145
  SCSI, 143
  Syquest, 145
Home office, 424

I

IComp index, 88
IDT WinChip C6, 73
Internet, 356—372
  cable-TV Internet, 367
  distance learning, 367
    McGraw-Hill, 368
  e-mail, 364
  emoticons, 372
  free ISP, 359
  Internet magazines, 369
  modems and access numbers, 358
  voice and video, 357
  Web hosting, 371
  your own Web page, 370
IRQ, 54
ISA, 56
ISDN, 301

J

Joysticks, 259

K

Keyboards, 13, 248—255
  carpal tunnel syndrome, 249
  ergonomic keyboards, 251

Keyboards (*Cont.*):
keyboard bios, 51
Windows 95 keyboards, 249

M

Magazines and mail order, 466—480
Federal Trade Commission rules, 470
free magazines, 473
ten rules for ordering by mail, 468
Memory 11, 50, 91—113
cache, 108
DIMMs, 94
DRAM, 106
EDO, 95
fast page, 95
flash, 46—103
hit rate, 108
interleaved, 107
level 1 and level 2, 108
RAM, 96
refreshment and wait states, 106
ROM, 96
SDRAM, 95
SIMMs, 94
SRAM, 107
Write Back, 109
Write Through, 109
MMX, 76
Modem, 14, 276—294
56K modems, 278—280
baud rate, 278
bulletin boards, 287
cable modems, 301
fax/modem, 286
installing, 282
IRQ, 283
ITU, 280
plug-and-play, 284
protocols, 280
viruses, 288
Monitor adapter, 13, 60, 232—234
Monitors, 13, 217—246
3D Adapters, 221
Monitors (*Cont.*):
AGP adapters, 221
dithering, 235
dot pitch, 229
flat panel LCD, 219
glossary of monitor terms, 242
green monitors, 238
installation, 241
monitor basics, 227
monochrome versus color, 229
MPEG boards, 225
PCI bus adapters, 222
pixels, 230
radiation, 237
scan rate, 231
software for monitor testing, 238
true colors, 234
USB, 220
video accelerator boards, 222
video memory, 223
Moore's Law, 26
Motherboard, 2, 4, 27—62
ATX, 40
bus, 49
expansion slots, 48
NLX, 33
PC card bus, 57
PCI bus, 57
Pentium II, 38
specifications, 34
Mouse, 255—258
interfaces, 256
mouse-ball cleaning, 256
PS/2 mice, 257
trackballs, 258
wireless mice, 258

N

Networks, 432

O

OCR Software, 263

P

Power strip, 7
Power supply, 6, 40, 506
Pentium II motherboard, 315
Presentations, 436
Printers, 374—395
  color laser, 386
  dot matrix, 388
  green printers, 395
  inkjet, 375
  inkjet color, 375
  installing a printer or plotter, 392
  laser, 381
  memory, 382
  multifunction, 378
  paper, 385
  plotters, 387
  resolution, 384
  speed, 383
  wide-format, 380
Printer port LPT1, 60

R

Remote-control software, 297
ROM BIOS, 45

S

Scanners, 260—267
Serial Ports COM1 & COM2, 55
Single edge connector (SEC), 75
Soft power, 41
Software, 398—420
  CAD, 414
  competitive upgrade, 401
  databases, 406
  essential, 403
  live upgrade, 399
  miscellaneous, 415
  shareware, 402
  software catalogs, 402
  software training, 419
Software (*Cont.*):
  spreadsheets, 407
  suites, 409
  try before you buy, 402
  turbo tax, 413
  utilities, 410
  wordprocessors, 404
Sound, 444—462
  boards, 444
  catalogs, 461
  digital sampling, 450—453
  harmonics, 457
  installing a sound board, 453
  microphones, 446
  MIDI, 455—457
  music, 447
  music software, 461
  piano keyboards, 460
  speakers, 445
  synthesizers, 457
  trade shows, 462
  wave tables, 458
Square waves, 23
Surge protection, 8
System assembly 13, 328—353
System clock, 25

T

Tax programs, 427
Telecommuting, 296
Telephone directories, 300
Telephony, 298
  telephone conference, 299
Tools, 2, 13, 328
Touch screens and light pens, 258
Transistors, 20
Trouble shooting, 482—510
  beep error codes, 493
  cables, 490
  config.sys and autoexec.bat, 490
  common problems, 487
  computer basics, 482
  diagnostic and utility software, 496

Trouble shooting (*Cont.*):
- Check-It, 498
- MicroScope, 497
- Norton Utilities, 497
- electrostatic voltage, 484
- glitches, 504
- intermittent problems, 506
- instruments and tools, 485
- memory problems, 489
- POST cards, 495
- POST codes, 494
- power supply, 505
- serial ports, 507
- software problems, 508
- spares, 502

U

UART, 55
Uninterruptible power supply (UPS), 8, 188, 434
Upgrading, 12, 61, 310—315
- new hard disk, 305—307

USB, 59
Used computers, 308

V

Vacuum tubes, 21
Voice recognition, 276

About the Author

Aubrey Pilgrim has been twice listed by *MicroTimes* magazine as one of the most influential leaders in the computer industry, due in large part to his highly successful series of "Build Your Own. . .and Save a Bundle" books, which have sold more than 350,000 copies. *PC World* has dubbed him the "preeminent guru on the inner workings of computers" for his ability to present technical material in a no-nonsense, accessible fashion the average computer owner can understand. His other books include *Build Your Own Pentium Processor PC, Build Your Own 486/486DX™, Upgrade or Repair Your PC,* 5th Revision, *Build Your Own Multimedia PC, Build Your Own Pentium Pro Processor PC,* and *Build Your Own LAN.* You may contact Pilgrim on Prodigy at TJJC38A or on AOL at apilgrim@aol.com.